Public Speaking
An Audience-Centered Approach

Public Speaking
An Audience-Centered Approach
Tenth Edition

Steven A. Beebe
Texas State University

Susan J. Beebe
Texas State University

Portfolio Manager: Karon Bowers
Content Producer: Nicole Conforti
Content Developer: Ellen Keohane
Portfolio Manager Assistant: Dea Barbieri
Product Marketer: Christopher Brown
Field Marketer: Kelly Ross
Content Producer Manager: Melissa Feimer
Content Development Manager: Sharon Geary
Content Developer, Learning Tools: Amy Wetzel

Art/Designer: Blair Brown
Digital Producer: Amanda Smith
Full-Service Project Manager: Integra Software Services, Inc.
Compositor: Integra Software Services, Inc.
Printer/Binder: RRD/Menasha
Cover Printer: Phoenix Color
Cover Designer: Lumina Datamatics, Inc.
Cover Illustration: Greg Betza

Acknowledgments of third party content appear on pages 355–359, which constitutes an extension of this copyright page.

Library of Congress Cataloging-in-Publication Data

Beebe, Steven A., 1950- author. | Beebe, Susan J. author.
Public speaking: an audience-centered approach / Steven A. Beebe, Texas State
    University; Susan J. Beebe, Texas State University.
Tenth edition. | Hoboken: Pearson, 2017. | Includes
    bibliographical references and index.
LCCN 2016028583 | ISBN 9780134380919 (hardcover)
LCSH: Public speaking. | Oral communication.
LCC PN4129.15 .B43 2017 | DDC 808.5/1—dc23
LC record available at https://lccn.loc.gov/2016028583

1 17

Student Edition
ISBN-10:   0-13-438091-6
ISBN-13: 978-0-13-438091-9

Books a la Carte
ISBN-10:   0-13-440161-1
ISBN-13: 978-0-13-440161-4

Dedicated to our parents, Russell and Muriel Beebe and Herb and Jane Dye
And to our children, Mark, Amanda, and Matthew Beebe

Brief Contents

Contents

Preface

The tenth edition of *Public Speaking: An Audience-Centered Approach* is written to be the primary text in a course intended to help students become better public speakers. We are delighted that since the first edition of the book was published more than two decades ago, educators and students of public speaking have found our book a distinctively useful resource to enhance public-speaking skills. We've worked to make our latest edition a preeminent resource for helping students enhance their speaking skills by adding new features and retaining the most successful elements of previous editions.

New to the Tenth Edition

We've refined and updated this text to create a powerful and contemporary resource for helping speakers connect to their audience. We've added several new features and revised features that both instructors and students have praised. Like the previous edition, the tenth edition is also available in Revel, but this revision has enabled us to refine and improve our learning design and user experience, building on market feedback from current users and reviewers.

Revel™

Educational technology designed for the way today's students read, think, and learn

When students are engaged deeply, they learn more effectively and perform better in their courses. This simple fact inspired the creation of Revel: an immersive learning experience designed for the way today's students read, think, and learn. Built in collaboration with educators and students nationwide, Revel is the newest, fully digital way to deliver respected Pearson content.

Revel enlivens course content with media interactives and assessments—integrated directly within the authors' narrative—that provide opportunities for students to read about and practice course material in tandem. This immersive educational technology boosts student engagement, which leads to better understanding of concepts and improved performance throughout the course.

Learn more about Revel

http://www.pearsonhighered.com/revel/

SPECIAL FEATURES FOR PUBLIC SPEAKING STUDENTS   Revel is a dynamic learning experience that offers students a way to study the content and topics relevant to communication in a whole new way. Rather than simply offering opportunities to read about and study public speaking, Revel facilitates deep, engaging interactions with the concepts that matter most. For example, in Chapter 2, students are presented with the authors' hallmark audience-centered model as an interactive figure diagramming the various tasks involved in the speechmaking process. This figure is used throughout the text to emphasize the importance of being audience-centered. Throughout chapters in Revel students can interact with this figure to learn more about each stage of the process, and in the Chapter 13 Study Guide they can take a self-checking, drag-and-drop assessment to put the stages of the model in order. In addition, students are presented with video examples throughout the book on topics such as improving listening skills, audience analysis, primary sources, speech delivery, using presentation aids, informative speeches, outlines, intercultural listening, and the fear of public speaking. As part of our commitment to boosting students' communication confidence, our first discussion of improving your confidence in Chapter 1 features the Personal Report of Public Speaking Anxiety in Revel. Students can take this assessment right there in the context of our chapter, get their score, and continue reading about how to improve their own level of confidence. By providing opportunities to read about and practice public speaking in tandem, Revel engages students directly and immediately, which leads to a better understanding of course material. A wealth of student and instructor resources and interactive materials can be found within Revel. Some of our favorites include the following:

- **Audio Excerpts** Throughout the text, audio excerpts highlight effective speech examples. Students can listen to audio clips while they read, bringing examples to life in a way that a printed text cannot. These audio examples reinforce learning and add dimension to the printed text.

- **Videos and Video Self-Checks** Video clips appear throughout the narrative to boost mastery, and many videos are bundled with correlating self-checks, enabling students to test their knowledge.

- **Interactive Figures** Interactive figures help students understand hard-to-grasp concepts through interactive visualizations.

- **Integrated Writing Opportunities** To help students connect chapter content with personal meaning, each chapter offers two varieties of writing prompts: the Journal prompt, which elicits free-form, topic-specific responses addressing content at the module level, and the Shared Writing prompt, which encourages students to share and respond to each other's brief responses to high-interest topics in the chapter.

For more information about all the tools and resources in Revel and access to your own Revel account for *Public Speaking: An Audience-Centered Approach*, Tenth Edition go to www.pearsonhighered.com/revel.

DEVELOPING YOUR SPEECH STEP BY STEP

CONSIDER YOUR AUDIENCE

A Chinese proverb says that a journey of a thousand miles begins with a single step. Developing and delivering a speech may seem like a daunting journey. But if you take it one step at a time and keep your focus on your audience, you'll be rewarded with a well-crafted and well-delivered message.

To help you see how the audience-centered public speaking process unfolds step by step, we will explore how one student prepared and delivered a successful speech. Matthew, an undergraduate student at Texas State University, developed the informative presentation titled "Public-Speaking Anxiety," which is outlined in Chapter 8.[18] In the chapters ahead, we will walk you through the process Matthew followed to develop his speech.

Matthew thought about his audience even before selecting his topic. Realizing that his listeners would be student peers, he knew he had to find a topic of interest and relevance to them. And he knew he could discuss complex issues, using a fairly advanced vocabulary.

The *Developing Your Speech Step by Step* feature in the chapters ahead will provide a window through which you can watch Matthew at work on each step of the audience-centered public speaking process.

Remarks to the U.S. Congress[3]

by Pope Francis, September 24, 2015

I am most grateful for your invitation to address this joint session of Congress in "the land of the free and the home of the brave." I would like to think that the reason for this is that I, too, am a son of this great continent, from which we have all received so much and toward which we share a common responsibility.

Each son or daughter of a given country has a mission, a personal and social responsibility. Your own responsibility as members of Congress is to enable this country, by your legislative activity, to grow as a nation. You are the face of its people, their representatives. You are called to defend and preserve the dignity of your fellow citizens in the tireless and demanding pursuit of the common good, for this is the chief aim of all politics. A political society endures when it seeks, as a vocation, to satisfy common needs by stimulating the growth of all its members, especially those in situations of greater vulnerability or risk. Legislative activity is always based on care for the

---

New and Updated Features

In addition to the abundance of in-chapter interactive and media materials you'll find in Revel, we've refined and updated the text to create a powerful and contemporary resource for helping speakers connect to their audience.

NEW SPEECHES We've added new speech examples throughout the text. In addition, two speeches in our revised Appendix B are new, selected to provide readers with a variety of positive models of effective speeches.

NEW EXAMPLES AND ILLUSTRATIONS New examples and illustrations provide both classic and contemporary models to help students master the art of public speaking. As in previous editions, we draw on both student speeches and speeches delivered by well-known people.

NEW MATERIAL IN EVERY CHAPTER In addition to these new and expanded features, each chapter has been revised with new examples, illustrations, and references to the latest research conclusions. Here's a summary of the changes and revisions we've made:

Chapter 1: Speaking with Confidence

To capture student interest, the chapter now begins with a new example about the annual Technology, Education, and Design (TED) Conference. The section on the rich heritage of public speaking has been moved before coverage of the communication process. In addition, updated research reinforces advice on the importance of developing public speaking skills.

Chapter 2: Presenting Your First Speech

This chapter provides an overview of the audience-centered speaking process, jump-starting the speechmaking process for students who are assigned to present speeches early in the term. To better streamline the chapter and reduce repetitive topics, we've reduced the number of sections from nine to two. Additional coverage has been added on considering the culturally diverse backgrounds of your audience. New research on the importance of speech rehearsal has also been included.

Chapter 3: Speaking Freely and Ethically

To highlight the balance between the right to speak freely and the responsibility to speak ethically, the chapter begins with a new, real-world example on racial tension at the University of Missouri–Columbia. Coverage of free speech in the twenty-first century has been updated to include the Arab Spring and the terrorist attacks at the French humor magazine, *Charlie Hebdo*. We have also included new research on the consequences of plagiarism.

Chapter 4: Listening to Speeches

The chapter has been streamlined by removing topics already covered in other chapters. The discussion on prejudice has been updated. Research has been added on listening skills, including the influence of technology.

Chapter 5: Analyzing Your Audience

The discussion of sex, gender, and sexual orientation has been updated with new research and examples. This chapter introduces the first of the updated *Developing Your Speech Step by Step* boxes, which provide students with an extended example of how to implement audience-centered speechmaking concepts. The definition of race has also been revised.

Chapter 6: Developing Your Speech

This chapter includes a number of new figures, illustrating topics such as brainstorming, using Web directories, narrowing a broad topic, preparing a specific purpose statement, and wording the central idea. A new example on guidelines for selecting a topic has also been added. Discussions on using Web directories and writing a specific purpose have been streamlined and updated.

Chapter 7: Gathering and Using Supporting Material

Coverage of the Internet has been revised to provide more updated information on locating resources online. New figures have also been added to this chapter, including an illustration highlighting the limitations and advantages of *Wikipedia*. The section on interviewing has also been streamlined and revised.

Chapter 8: Organizing and Outlining Your Speech

This chapter now includes new examples of purpose statements, central ideas, and main ideas. In addition, new figures illustrate how to organize supporting material and how to use your preparation outline as a guide to analyzing and revising your speech. A new *Sample Preparation Outline* gives students a complete model of the best practices in organization and outlining.

Chapter 9: Introducing and Concluding Your Speech

New examples on humor, inspirational appeals, and references to the occasion have been added to the chapter. Coverage of illustrations and anecdotes has been updated and revised. Content throughout the chapter has been streamlined to reduce repetitive topics.

Chapter 10: Using Words Well: Speaker Language and Style

The chapter features three new tables: Table 10.1 provides explanations and examples of different types of figurative language; Table 10.2 offers four strategies for creating drama in speeches; and Table 10.3 summarizes ways to create cadence by using stylistic devices. A new figure illustrating three key guidelines for using memorable word structures effectively has also been added.

Chapter 11: Delivering Your Speech

Instead of seven sections, this chapter now has six. Selected content from former Section 11.4 (Audience Diversity and Delivery) has been distributed throughout the chapter where appropriate. Discussions on how to develop your message effectively and use gestures effectively have also been updated.

Chapter 12: Using Presentation Aids

This chapter has been reorganized so it now has a greater focus on computer-generated presentation aids. Additional content on visual rhetoric has been added. New Table 12.1 highlights the value of presentation aids, along with visual examples of each aid. The chapter also features updated figures, including examples of bar, pie, line and picture graphs.

Chapter 13: Speaking to Inform

Developing an Audience-Centered Informative Speech, the final section in this chapter, has been streamlined to reduce repetitive topics. Discussions on speeches about procedures and speeches about events have been revised.

Chapter 14: Understanding Principles of Persuasive Speaking

Additional content has been added about changing and/or reinforcing audience values. The discussion of fear appeal has also been updated.

Chapter 15: Using Persuasive Strategies

This chapter has been streamlined to eliminate repetitive topics. Discussions on how credibility evolves over time and improving your credibility have been updated and revised. We have also added suggestions for telling stories with an emotional message.

Chapter 16: Speaking for Special Occasions and Purposes

The chapter features a new discussion on mediated workplace presentations. New examples throughout the chapter demonstrate models of speeches for ceremonial occasions including acceptance speeches and commencement addresses. There is also a new table on formats for sharing group reports and recommendations with an audience. A new figure illustrating suggestions for enhancing teamwork has also been added to the chapter.

Successful Features Retained in This Edition

The goal of the tenth edition of *Public Speaking: An Audience-Centered Approach* remains the same as that of the previous nine editions: to be a practical and user-friendly guide to help speakers connect their hearts and minds with those of their listeners. While adding powerful new features and content to help students become skilled public speakers, we have also endeavored to keep what students and instructors liked best. Specifically, we retained five areas of focus that have proven successful in previous editions: our audience-centered approach; our focus on overcoming communication apprehension; our focus on ethics; our focus on diversity; and our focus on skill development. We also continue our partnership with instructors and students by offering a wide array of print and electronic supplements to support teaching and learning.

Our Audience-Centered Approach

The distinguishing focus of the book is our audience-centered approach. More than 2,300 years ago, Aristotle said, "For of the three elements in speechmaking—speaker, subject, and person addressed—it is the last one, the hearer, that determines the speaker's end and object." We think Aristotle was right. A good speech centers on the needs, values, and hopes of the audience, who should be foremost in the speaker's mind during every step of the speech development and delivery process. Thus, in a very real sense, the audience writes the speech. Effective and ethical public speaking does not simply tell listeners only what they want to hear—that would be a manipulative, speaker-centered approach. Rather, the audience-centered speaker is ethically responsive to audience interests without abandoning the speaker's end and object.

It is not unusual or distinctive for a public-speaking book to discuss audience analysis. What *is* unique about our audience-centered approach is that our discussion of audience analysis and adaptation is not confined to a single chapter; rather, we emphasize the importance of considering the audience throughout our entire discussion of the speech preparation and delivery process. From the overview early in the text of the public-speaking process until the final chapter, we illuminate the positive power of helping students relate to their audience by keeping their listeners foremost in mind.

Preparing and delivering a speech also involves a sequence of steps. Our audience-centered model integrates the step-by-step process of speech preparation and delivery with the ongoing process of considering the audience. Our audience-centered model of public speaking, shown here and introduced in Chapter 2, reappears throughout the text to remind students of the steps involved in speech preparation and delivery, while simultaneously emphasizing the importance of considering the audience. Viewing the model as a clock, the speaker begins the process at the 12 o'clock position with "Select and Narrow Topic" and moves around the model clockwise to "Deliver Speech." Each step of the speech preparation and delivery process touches the center portion of the model, labeled "Consider the Audience." Arrows connecting the center with each step of the process illustrate how the audience influences each of the steps involved in designing and presenting a speech. Arrows pointing in both directions around the central process of "Consider the Audience" represent how a speaker may sometimes revise a previous step because of further information or thought about the audience. A speaker may, for example, decide after having gathered supporting material for a speech that he or she needs to go back and revise the speech purpose. Visual learners will especially appreciate the illustration of the entire public-speaking process provided by the model. The colorful, easy-to-understand synopsis will also be appreciated by people who learn best by having an overview of the entire process before beginning the first step of speech preparation.

After introducing the model early in the book, we continue to emphasize the centrality of considering the audience by revisiting it at appropriate points throughout the book. A highlighted version of the model appears in several chapters as a visual reminder of the place the chapter's topic occupies in the audience-centered speechmaking process. Similarly, highlighted versions appear in *Developing Your Speech Step by Step* boxes. Another visual reminder comes in the form of a miniature version of the model, the icon shown here in the margin. *When you see this icon, it will remind you that the material presented has special significance for considering your audience.* In Revel, students can interact with this audience-centered model to learn more about each stage of the speechmaking process. At the

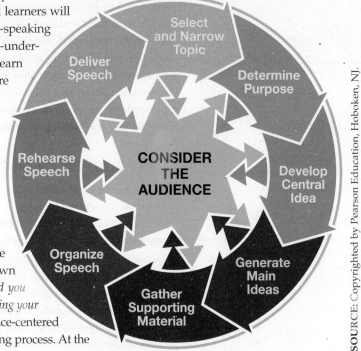

SOURCE: Copyrighted by Pearson Education, Hoboken, NJ.

end of Chapter 13, they can also test their knowledge using a drag-and-drop assessment to put the stages of the model in order.

Our Focus on Communication Apprehension

One of the biggest barriers that keeps a speaker, especially a novice public speaker, from connecting to his or her audience is apprehension. Fear of failure, forgetting, or fumbling words is a major distraction. In our text, we help students to overcome their apprehension of speaking to others by focusing on their listeners rather than on their fear. Our discussion of communication apprehension is covered in Chapter 1. We have continued to add the most contemporary research conclusions we can find to help students overcome the anxiety that many people experience when speaking publicly. To help students integrate confidence-boosting strategies through their study of public speaking, we offer students powerful pointers for managing anxiety in the *Confidently Connecting with Your Audience* features found in each chapter. For example, in Chapter 1 of the Revel course, students can complete the Personal Report of Public Speaking Anxiety and immediately get their score. In addition, as students read through the narrative in Revel, they will find videos, "Explore the Concept" activities, and assessment questions to engage their interest, enliven the content, and increase their confidence.

> **CONFIDENTLY CONNECTING WITH YOUR AUDIENCE**
>
> Begin with the End in Mind
>
> One of the habits cited by the late Stephen Covey in his influential book *The 7 Habits of Highly Successful People* is "Begin with the end in mind."[51] From the moment you begin thinking about preparing and presenting your speech, picture yourself being confident and successful. If you find your anxiety level rising at any point in the speech-preparation process, change your mental picture of yourself and imagine that you've completed your speech and the audience has given you a rousing round of applause. Begin imagining success rather than focusing on your fear. Using the principles, skills, and strategies we discuss in this text will help you develop the habit of speech success.

Our Focus on Ethics

Being audience-centered does not mean that a speaker tells an audience only what they want to hear; if you are not true to your own values, you will have become a manipulative, unethical communicator rather than an audience-centered one. Audience-centered speakers articulate truthful messages that give audience members free choice in responding to a message, while they also use effective means of ensuring message clarity and credibility.

From the first chapter onward, we link being an audience-centered speaker with being an ethical speaker. Our principles and strategies for being rhetorically skilled are anchored in ethical principles that assist speakers in articulating a message that connects with their audience. We not only devote an entire chapter (Chapter 3) to being an ethical speaker, but we also offer reminders, tips, and strategies for making ethical speaking and listening an integral part of human communication. As part of the *Study Guide* at the end of each chapter, students and instructors will find questions to spark discussion about and raise awareness of ethical issues in effective speechmaking. For example, in Revel, students can watch a short video on the ethics of decision and complete a video self-check to evaluate their knowledge on the topic.

Our Focus on Diversity

Just as the topic of audience analysis is covered in most public-speaking textbooks, so is diversity. Sometimes diversity is discussed in a separate section; sometimes it is presented in "diversity boxes" sprinkled throughout a book. We choose to address diversity not as an add-on to the main discussion but rather as an integral part of being an audience-centered speaker. To be audience-centered is to acknowledge the various ethnic and cultural backgrounds, attitudes, beliefs, values, and other differences present when people assemble to hear a speech. We suggest that inherent in the process of being audience-centered is a focus on the diverse nature of listeners in contemporary audiences. The topic of adapting to diverse audiences is therefore not a boxed afterthought but is integrated into every step of our audience-centered approach.

Our Focus on Skill Development

We are grateful for our ongoing collaboration with public-speaking teachers, many of whom have used our audience-centered approach for more than two decades. We have retained those skill development features of previous editions that both teachers and students have applauded. What instructors tell us most often is "You write like I teach" or "Your book echoes the same kind of advice and skill development suggestions that I give my students." We are gratified by the continued popularity of *Public Speaking: An Audience-Centered Approach*.

CLEAR AND INTERESTING WRITING STYLE   Readers have especially valued our polished prose, concise style, and engaging, lively voice. Students tell us that reading our book is like having a conversation with their instructor.

OUTSTANDING EXAMPLES   Students need to be not only *told* how to speak effectively, but also *shown* how to speak well. Our powerful and interesting examples, both classic and contemporary and drawn from both student speakers and famous orators, continue to resonate with student speakers.

BUILT-IN LEARNING RESOURCES   We've retained the following built-in pedagogical features of previous editions:

- *Learning Objectives* appear at the start of each chapter to provide students with strategies and key points for approaching the chapter. Objectives reappear at key points in the chapter to help students gauge their progress and monitor their learning.

- An updated *Study Guide* at the end of each chapter reviews the learning objectives and key terms, and guides students to think critically about chapter concepts and related ethical issues.

- *Recap* boxes and tables help students check their understanding and review for exams.

- An extended speech example appears in the *Developing Your Speech Step by Step* boxes, which appear throughout the book.

In the tenth edition, we have also added new tables and illustrations to help summarize content. In Revel, students can reinforce content from the text by completing "Explore the Concept" activities, watching videos, interacting with figures, listening to speech examples, and taking quizzes at the end of each section and chapter.

STUDY GUIDE: REVIEW, APPLY, AND ASSESS

The Power of Speech Delivery

11.1 Identify three reasons why delivery is important to a public speaker.

REVIEW: Nonverbal communication conveys the majority of the meaning of your speech and nearly all of your emotions to an audience. Nonverbal expectancy theory suggests that your credibility as a speaker depends on meeting your audience's expectations about nonverbal

ASSESS: How can you determine when you have rehearsed long enough so that you can extemporaneously deliver your key ideas to your listeners, but not so long that you are giving a memorized presentation?

Characteristics of Effective Delivery

11.3 Identify and illustrate the characteristics of effective delivery.

RECAP

GATHER SUPPORTING MATERIAL

Use your own knowledge and research to find supporting materials that accomplish the following:

- *Tell a Story.* Most audiences enjoy stories.
- *Appeal to the Senses.* Help the audience hear, see, touch, and experience what you describe.
- *Use Research Skills.* Find new, interesting material that the audience has not heard before.

Instructor and Student Resources

Public-speaking students rarely learn how to be articulate speakers only from reading a book. Students learn best in partnership with an experienced instructor who can guide them through the process of being an audience-centered speaker. And experienced instructors rely on support from textbook publishers. To support instructors and students who use *Public Speaking: An Audience-Centered Approach*, Pearson provides an array of supplementary materials for students and instructors. Key instructor resources include an Instructor's Manual (ISBN 0-13-440158-1), Test Bank (ISBN 0-13-440151-4), and PowerPoint™ Presentation Package (ISBN 0-13-440160-3). These supplements are available at www.pearsonhighered.com/irc (instructor login required). MyTest online test-generating software (ISBN 0-13-440153-0) is available at www.pearsonmytest.com (instructor login required). For a complete list of the instructor and student resources available with the text, please visit the Pearson Communication catalog, at www.pearsonhighered.com/communication.

of Pennsylvania; Jim Mancuso, Mesa Community College; Deborah F. Meltsner, Old Dominion University; Rebecca Mikesell, University of Scranton; Maxine Minson, Tulsa Junior College; Christine Mixan, University of Nebraska at Omaha; Barbara Monaghan, Berkeley College; Jay R. Moorman, Missouri Southern State University; Marjorie Keeshan Nadler, Miami University; Karen O'Donnell, Finger Lakes Community College; Rhonda Parker, University of San Francisco; Roxanne Parrott, University of Georgia; Richard L. Quianthy, Broward Community College; Carol L. Radetsky, Metropolitan State College; Renton Rathbun, Owens Community College; Mary Helen Richer, University of North Dakota; K. David Roach, Texas Tech University; Kellie W. Roberts, University of Florida; Rebecca Roberts, University of Wyoming; Val Safron, Washington University; Kristi Schaller, University of Hawaii at Manoa; Cara Schollenberger, Bucks County Community College; Shane Simon, Central Texas College; Cheri J. Simonds, Illinois State University; Glenn D. Smith, University of Central Arkansas; Valerie Smith, California State University, East Bay; David R. Sprague, Liberty University; Jessica Stowell, Tulsa Junior College; Edward J. Streb, Rowan College; Aileen Sundstrom, Henry Ford Community College; Susan L. Sutton, Cloud County Community College; Tasha Van Horn, Citrus College; Jim Vickrey, Troy State University; Denise Vrchota, Iowa State University; Beth M. Waggenspack, Virginia Polytechnic Institute and State University; David E. Walker, Middle Tennessee State University; Jamille Watkins-Barnes, Chicago State University; Lynn Wells, Saddleback College; Nancy R. Wern, Glenville State College; Charles N. Wise, El Paso Community College; Marcy Wong, Indian River State College; Argentina R. Wortham, Northeast Lakeview College; Merle Ziegler, Liberty University

Kosta Tovstiadi is a good friend and trusted researcher who assisted with research for this edition. We are grateful that Karon Bowers, Publisher, Communication, continued to be a strong source of support and encouragement to us as we worked on this edition, as she was on previous editions. Ellen Keohane, our skilled development editor, has done an exceptional job of offering excellent advice and creative suggestions to make this a better book. She helped lighten our workload with her attention to detail and many helpful suggestions.

We have enjoyed strong support and mentorship from a number of teachers, friends, and colleagues who have influenced our work over the years. Our colleagues at Texas State University continue to be supportive of our efforts. Tom Willett, retired professor from William Jewell College; Dan Curtis, emeritus professor at the University of Central Missouri; John Masterson, emeritus professor at Texas Lutheran University; and Thompson Biggers, professor at Mercer University, are longtime friends and exemplary teachers who continue to influence our work and our lives. Sue Hall, Department of Communication Studies senior administrative assistant at Texas State, again provided exceptional support and assistance to keep our work on schedule.

We view our work as authors of a textbook as primarily a teaching process. Both of us have been blessed with gifted teachers whose dedication and mentorship continue to inspire and encourage us. Mary Harper, former speech, English, and drama teacher at Steve's high school alma mater, Grain Valley High School, Grain Valley, Missouri; and Sue's speech teacher, the late Margaret Dent, who taught at Hannibal High School, Hannibal, Missouri, provided initial instruction in public speaking that remains with us today. We also value the life lessons and friendship we received from the late Erma Doty, another former teacher at Grain Valley High. We appreciate the patience and encouragement we received from Robert Brewer, our first debate coach at the University of Central Missouri, where we met each other more than forty-five years ago and where the ideas for this book were first discussed. We both served as student teachers under the unforgettable, energetic guidance of the late Louis Banker at Fort Osage High School, near Buckner, Missouri. Likewise, we have both benefited from the skilled instruction of Mary Jeanette Smythe, now retired from the University of Missouri–Columbia. We wish to express our appreciation to the late Loren Reid, emeritus professor from the University of Missouri–Columbia, one of the first people in the nation to earn a Ph.D. in speech, who lived to the age of 109; to us, he was the quintessential speech teacher.

Finally, we value the patience, encouragement, proud support, and love of our sons and daughter-in-law, Mark and Amanda Beebe and Matthew Beebe. They offer many inspiring lessons in overcoming life challenges and infusing life with joy and music. They continue to be our most important audience.

Steven A. Beebe

Susan J. Beebe

Speaking with Confidence

There are two kinds of speakers: those that are nervous and those that are liars.

—Mark Twain

Jean Jaures (1859-1914), *Speaking at the Tribune of the Chamber of Deputies*, 1903 (oil on canvas). *Photo:* The Bridgeman Art Library/Getty Images.

OBJECTIVES

After studying this chapter, you should be able to do the following:

1.1 Compare and contrast public speaking and conversation.

1.2 Explain why it is important to study public speaking.

1.3 Discuss in brief the history of public speaking.

1.4 Sketch and explain a model that illustrates the components and the process of communication.

1.5 Use several techniques to become a more confident speaker.

I t's a hot ticket. Even at $8,500, the annual four-day event always sells out. Some 3 million additional people watch and listen online every day.[1] But the performers are not, as you might guess, legendary singers or classic rock bands. They are, in fact, not performers at all. They are public speakers.

The live event is the annual Technology, Education, and Design (TED) Conference. And you are probably among the billions who have seen a TED video. Public speaking, whether presented to a live audience, via broadcast video, or online, remains a powerful and popular form of communication.

As you begin reading this text, chances are that you are also beginning a course in public speaking. You're in good company; nearly a half million college students take a public-speaking class each year.[2] If you haven't had much previous experience speaking in public, you're also in good company. Sixty-six percent of students beginning a public-speaking course reported having had little or no public-speaking experience.[3]

The good news is that this text will provide you with the knowledge and experience needed to become a competent public speaker—an active participant in what TED curator Chris Anderson calls "as important a task as humanity has."[4]

What Is Public Speaking?

1.1 Compare and contrast public speaking and conversation.

public speaking
The process of presenting a spoken message to an audience

Public speaking is the process of presenting a spoken message to an audience, small or large. You hear speeches almost every day. Each day when you attend class, an instructor lectures. When watching a newscast on TV or via the Internet, you get a "sound bite" of some politician delivering a speech. When you hear a comedian delivering a monologue on a late-night talk show or the Comedy Channel, you're hearing a speech designed to entertain you.

The skill of public speaking builds on your normal, everyday interactions with others. In fact, as you begin to study and practice public speaking, you will discover that it has much in common with conversation, a form of communication in which you engage in every day. Like conversation, public speaking requires you to focus and verbalize your thoughts.

When you have a conversation, you also have to make decisions "on your feet." If your friends look puzzled or interrupt with questions, you may need to explain your idea a second time. If they look bored, you insert a funny story or talk more animatedly. As a public speaker, you will learn to make similar adaptations based on your knowledge of your listeners, their expectations for your speech, and their reactions to what you are saying. In fact, because we believe that the ability to adapt to your audience is so vital, this text focuses on public speaking as an audience-centered activity.

Although there are some similarities, public speaking is not exactly like talking with a friend or an acquaintance. Let's take a look at some of the ways in which public speaking differs from conversation.

Public speakers take more time to prepare their remarks than conversationalists do. Public speaking is also more formal than conversation, with defined roles for speaker and audience. *Photo:* val lawless/Shutterstock.

- *Public speaking requires more preparation than conversation.* Although you may sometimes be asked to speak on the spur of the moment, you will usually know in advance whether you will be expected to give a talk on a specific occasion. A public speaker might spend hours or even days planning and practicing his or her speech.

- *Public speaking is more formal than conversation.* The slang or casual language we often use in conversation is usually not appropriate for most public speaking. Audiences expect speakers to use standard English grammar and vocabulary. A public speaker's delivery is also more formal than the way most people engage in ordinary conversation.

- *Public speaking involves more clearly defined roles for speaker and audience than conversation.* During a conversation, there is typically interaction between speaker and listener. But in public speaking, the roles of speaker and audience are more clearly defined and remain stable. A public speaker presents a more structured and less interactive message. Although in some cultures a call-and-response speaker–audience interaction occurs (such as saying "That's right" or "Amen" when responding to a preacher's sermon), in the majority of the United States, audience members rarely interrupt or talk back to speakers.

Why Study Public Speaking?

1.2 Explain why it is important to study public speaking.

Although you've heard countless speeches during your lifetime, you may still have questions about why it's important for *you* to study public speaking. Here are two reasons: By studying public speaking you will gain long-term advantages related to *empowerment* and *employment*.

Empowerment

You will undoubtedly be called on to speak in public at various times in your life: as a student participating in a seminar class; as a businessperson presenting to a potential client; as a concerned citizen addressing the city council's zoning board. In each of these situations, the ability to speak with competence and confidence will provide **empowerment**. To be empowered is to have the resources, information, and attitudes that allow you to take action to achieve a desired goal. Being a skilled public speaker will give you an edge that less skilled communicators lack—even those who may have superior ideas, education, or experience. It will position you for greater things by enhancing your overall communication skill.[5] Former presidential speechwriter James Humes, who labels public speaking "the language of leadership," says, "Every time you have to speak—whether it's in an auditorium, in a company conference room, or even at your own desk—you are auditioning for leadership."[6]

empowerment
Having resources, information, and attitudes that lead to action to achieve a desired goal

One of the empowering resources that you develop by studying public speaking is **critical thinking**. To think critically is to be able to listen and analyze information you hear so that you can judge its accuracy and relevance. While you are learning how to improve your speaking in this course, you are also learning the critical thinking skills to sort good ideas from bad ideas. Being a critical thinker and an effective communicator is a powerful and empowering combination.

critical thinking
Analyzing information to judge its accuracy and relevance

Yet, like most people, you may experience fear and anxiety about speaking in public. As you start your journey of becoming an effective public speaker, you may have questions about how to bolster your confidence and manage your apprehension. Before you finish this chapter, you'll have read about more than a dozen strategies to help you feel both more empowered and confident. Being both a confident and an empowered public speaker is within your grasp. And being an empowered speaker can open up leadership and career opportunities for you.

Employment

If you can speak well, you possess a skill that others value highly. In fact, industrialist Charles M. Schwab once said, "I'll pay more for a person's ability to speak and express himself than for any other quality he might possess."[7] Billionaire stock investor Warren Buffet agrees. In an interview with CNN reporter Christiane Amanpour, extolling the virtues of his public-speaking course, he said, "If you improve your communication skills I guarantee you that you will earn 50 percent more money over your lifetime."[8]

Whether you're currently employed in an entry-level position or aspire to the highest rung of the corporate leadership ladder, being able to communicate effectively with others is key to success in any line of work.[9] The skills you learn in a public-speaking course, such as how to ethically adapt information to listeners, organize your ideas, persuade others, and hold listeners' attention, are among the skills most sought after by any employer. In a nationwide survey, prospective employers of college graduates said they seek candidates with "public-speaking and presentation ability."[10] Other surveys of personnel managers, both in the United States and internationally, have confirmed that they consider communication skills *the top factor* in helping graduating college students obtain employment.[11] So by enhancing your speaking skill you are developing the number-one competency that employers seek.

The Rich Heritage of Public Speaking

1.3 Discuss in brief the history of public speaking.

By studying public speaking you are doing more than empowering yourself and enhancing your opportunities for employment. You are participating in a centuries-old tradition of developing your rhetorical skills that enhances your ability to both present ideas to others and analyze the speeches you hear. Long before many people could read, they listened to public speakers. **Rhetoric** is the strategic use of words and symbols to achieve a goal. Although rhetoric is often defined as the art of speaking or writing aimed at persuading others (changing or reinforcing attitudes, beliefs, values, or behavior), whether you're informing, persuading, or even entertaining listeners, you are using rhetoric because you are trying to achieve a goal.

rhetoric
The strategic use of words and symbols to achieve a goal

The Golden Age of Public Speaking

The fourth century B.C.E. is called the golden age of rhetoric in the Greek Republic because it was during this time that the philosopher Aristotle formulated guidelines for speakers that we still follow today. In later chapters in this text, you will be learning principles and practices of public speaking that were first summarized by Aristotle in his classic book *The Art of Rhetoric*, written in 333 B.C.E.

Roman orators continued the Greek rhetorical tradition by identifying five classical *canons*, or elements of preparing and presenting a speech:

- *Invention:* the creative process of developing your ideas
- *Arrangement:* how the speech is organized
- *Style:* your choice of words
- *Memory:* the extent to which you use notes or rely on your memory to share your ideas
- *Delivery:* the nonverbal expression of your message

These five classic elements of public speaking are embedded in the principles and practices that we present in this text.

The Roman orator Cicero was known not only for being an excellent public speaker but also for his writings on how to be an effective speaker. Marcus Fabius

Quintilianus, who was known as Quintilian and born in what is today Spain, also sought to teach others how to be effective speakers. As politicians and poets attracted large followings in ancient Rome, Cicero and Quintilian sought to define the qualities of the "true" orator. Quintilian famously wrote that the ideal orator should be "a good person speaking well." On a lighter note, it is said that Roman orators invented the necktie. Fearing laryngitis, they wore "chin cloths" to protect their throats.[12]

Centuries later, in medieval Europe, the clergy were the most polished public speakers in society. People gathered eagerly to hear Martin Luther expound his Articles of Faith. In the eighteenth century, British subjects in the colonies listened to the town criers and impassioned patriots of what would one day become the United States.

Nineteenth- and Twentieth-Century Age of Political Oratory

Vast nineteenth-century audiences heard speakers such as Henry Clay and Daniel Webster debate states' rights; they listened to Frederick Douglass, Angelina Grimke, and Sojourner Truth argue for the abolition of slavery and to Lucretia Mott plead for women's suffrage; they gathered for an evening's entertainment to hear Mark Twain as he traveled the lecture circuits of the frontier.

Yet students of nineteenth-century public speaking spent little time developing their own speeches. Instead, they practiced the art of **declamation**—the delivery of an already famous address. Favorite subjects for declamation included speeches by such Americans as Patrick Henry and William Jennings Bryan and by the British orator Edmund Burke. Collections of speeches, such as Bryan's own ten-volume set of *The World's Famous Orations*, published in 1906, were extremely popular.

declamation
The delivery of an already famous speech

Hand in hand with declamation went the study and practice of **elocution**, the expression of emotion through posture, movement, gesture, facial expression, and voice. From the mid-nineteenth century to the early twentieth century, elocution manuals—providing elaborate and specific prescriptions for effective delivery— were standard references not only in schools but also in nearly every middle-class home in the United States.[13]

elocution
The expression of emotion through posture, movement, gesture, facial expression, and voice

The Technological Age of Public Speaking

In the first half of the twentieth century, radio made it possible for people around the world to hear Franklin Delano Roosevelt decry December 7, 1941, as "a date which will live in infamy" following the attack on Pearl Harbor in Hawaii. In the last half of the century, television provided the medium through which audiences saw and heard the most stirring speeches:

- Martin Luther King Jr. proclaiming his dream of equality
- Ronald Reagan beseeching Mikhail Gorbachev to "tear down this wall"
- Holocaust survivor Elie Wiesel looking beyond the end of one millennium toward the next with "profound fear and extraordinary hope"

With the twenty-first century dawned a new era of speechmaking. It was to be an era that would draw

Civil rights leader and human rights activist Dr. Martin Luther King Jr. delivered one of the great speeches of history as the keynote of the August 1963 civil rights march on Washington, D.C. *Photo:* The LIFE Picture Collection/Getty.

on age-old public-speaking traditions. But it was also an era in which U.S. soldiers serving in Iraq and Afghanistan would watch their children's commencement addresses live via streaming video. And it was to be an era that would summon public speakers to meet some of the most difficult challenges in history—an era in which President Barack Obama would empathize with the grief felt by the community of Newtown, Connecticut, after twenty young children and six adults were shot to death at Sandy Hook Elementary School. He assured his listeners that "…you're not alone in your grief; that our world too has been torn apart; that all across this land of ours, we have wept with you, we've pulled our children tight."[14] Speakers of the future will continue to draw on a long and rich heritage, in addition to forging new frontiers in public speaking.

You may be more likely to hear a speech today presented as a pre-recorded TED Talk, YouTube video, or a podcast and delivered on your smartphone or other digital device than you are a live-and-in person presentation. In fact, you may be taking this course online and may present your speeches to your classmates and instructor as video recordings. Although the electronic context of the message influences both how the message may be prepared and received, the primary process of developing and presenting your speech is the same as it has been for centuries. Whether you are presenting your message in person or via video there are core processes of public speaking that will serve you well.

Another unchanging truth of public speaking is that the core of all you do in public speaking is a focus on your audience. Your audience will ultimately determine if your message has achieved your objective. For this reason, we suggest that you keep your audience foremost in your mind from the first moments of thinking about your speech topic to the time when you utter the concluding sentence of your speech.

The Communication Process

1.4 Sketch and explain a model that illustrates the components and the process of communication.

Even the earliest communication theorists recognized that communication is a process. The models they formulated were linear, suggesting a simple transfer of meaning from a sender to a receiver, as shown in Figure 1.1. More recently, theorists have created models that better demonstrate the complexity of the communication process. Let's explore what some of those models can teach us about what happens when we communicate.

Communication as Action

Although they were simplistic, the earliest linear models of communication as action identified most of the elements of the communication process. We will explain each element as it relates to public speaking.

source

The public speaker

encode

To translate ideas and images into verbal or nonverbal symbols

code

A verbal or nonverbal symbol for an idea or image

SOURCE   A public speaker is a **source** of information and ideas for an audience. The job of the source or speaker is to **encode**, or translate, the ideas and images in his or her mind into verbal or nonverbal symbols (a **code**) that an audience can recognize. The speaker may encode into words (for example, "The fabric should be 2 inches square") or into gestures (showing the size with his or her hands).

Figure 1.1 The earliest models viewed communication as the action of transferring meaning from source to receiver.

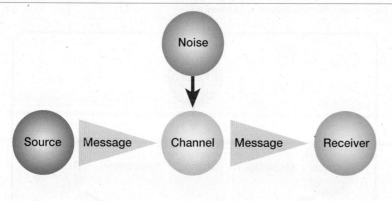

MESSAGE The **message** in public speaking is the speech itself—both what is said and how it is said. If a speaker has trouble finding words to convey his or her ideas or sends contradictory nonverbal symbols, listeners may not be able to **decode** the speaker's verbal and nonverbal symbols back into a message.

CHANNELS A message is usually transmitted from sender to receiver via two **channels**: *visual* and *auditory*. Audience members see the speaker and decode his or her nonverbal symbols—eye contact (or lack of it), facial expressions, posture, gestures, and dress. If the speaker uses any visual aids, such as graphs or models, these too are transmitted along the visual channel. The auditory channel is evident as the speaker speaks. Then the audience members hear words and recognize vocal cues such as inflection, rate, and voice quality.

RECEIVER The **receiver** of the message is the individual audience member, whose decoding of the message will depend on his or her own particular blend of past experiences, attitudes, beliefs, and values. As already emphasized, an effective public speaker should be receiver- or audience-centered.

NOISE Anything that interferes with the communication of a message is called *noise*. Noise may be physical and external. If your 8 A.M. public-speaking class is frequently interrupted by the roar of a lawn mower running back and forth under the window, it may be difficult to concentrate on what your instructor is saying. A noisy air conditioner, a crying baby, or incessant coughing is an example of **external noise** that may make it difficult for audience members to hear or concentrate on a speech.

Noise may also be internal. **Internal noise** may stem from either *physiological* or *psychological* causes and may directly affect either the source or the receiver. A bad cold (physiological noise) may cloud a speaker's memory or subdue his or her delivery. An audience member worrying about an upcoming exam (psychological noise) is unlikely to remember much of what the speaker says. Regardless of whether it is internal or external, physiological or psychological, or whether it originates in the sender or the receiver, noise interferes with the transmission of a message.

Communication as Interaction

Realizing that linear models were overly simplistic, later communication theorists designed models that depicted communication as a more complex process (see Figure 1.2). These models were circular, or interactive, and added two important new elements: feedback and context.

message
The content of a speech and the mode of its delivery

decode
To translate verbal or nonverbal symbols into ideas and images

channels
The visual and auditory means by which a message is transmitted from sender to receiver

receiver
A listener or an audience member

external noise
Physical sounds that interfere with communication

internal noise
Physiological or psychological interference with communication

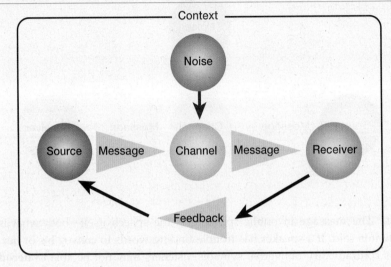

Figure 1.2 Interactive models of communication add the element of feedback to the previous action models. They also take into consideration the communication context.

SOURCE: Copyrighted by Pearson Education, Hoboken, NJ.

FEEDBACK   As we've noted, one way in which public speaking differs from casual conversation is that the public speaker does most or all of the talking. But public speaking is still interactive. Without an audience to hear and provide **feedback**, public speaking serves little purpose. Skillful public speakers are audience-centered. They depend on the nods, facial expressions, and murmurs of the audience to adjust their rate of speaking, volume, vocabulary, type and amount of supporting material, and other variables to communicate their message successfully.

feedback
Verbal and nonverbal responses provided by an audience to a speaker

CONTEXT   The **context** of a public-speaking experience is the environment or situation in which the speech occurs. It includes such elements as the time, the place, and the speaker's and audience's cultural traditions and expectations. To rephrase John Donne, no *speech* is an island. No speech occurs in a vacuum. Rather, each speech is a blend of circumstances that can never be replicated exactly.

context
The environment or situation in which a speech occurs

The person whose job it is to deliver an identical message to a number of different audiences at different times and in different places can attest to the uniqueness of each speaking context. If the room is hot, crowded, or poorly lit, these conditions affect both speaker and audience. The audience that hears a speaker at 10 A.M. is likely to be fresher and more receptive than a 4:30 P.M. audience. A speaker who fought rush-hour traffic for 90 minutes to arrive at his or her destination may find it difficult to muster much enthusiasm for delivering the speech.

Many of the skills that you will learn from this text relate not only to the preparation of effective speeches (messages) but also to the elements of feedback and context in the communication process. Our audience-centered approach focuses on "reading" your listeners' responses and adjusting to them as you speak.

Communication as Transaction

The most recent communication models do not label individual components. Instead, transactive models focus on communication as a simultaneous, transactive process. As Figure 1.3 suggests, we send and receive messages concurrently. In a two-person communication transaction, both individuals are sending and receiving *at the same time*. When you are listening, you are simultaneously expressing your thoughts and feelings nonverbally.

Figure 1.3 A transactive model of communication focuses on the simultaneous encoding and decoding that happens between source and receiver. Both source and receiver send and receive messages with ongoing feedback within a communication channel.

SOURCE: Copyrighted by Pearson Education, Hoboken, NJ.

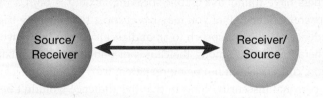

An effective public speaker should not only be focused on the message he or she is expressing but should also be tuned in to how the audience is responding to the message. A good public speaker shouldn't wait until the speech is over to gauge the effectiveness of a speech. Instead, because of the transactive nature of communication, a speaker should be scanning the audience during the speech for nonverbal clues to assess the audience's reaction, just as you do when having a conversation with someone.

Although communication models have been developed only recently, the elements of these models have long been recognized as the keys to successful public speaking. As you study public speaking, you will continue a tradition that goes back to the beginnings of Western civilization.

RECAP

THE COMMUNICATION PROCESS

Audience and speaker send messages simultaneously. Elements of the process include:

- Source: The originator of the message
- Message: The content of what is expressed both verbally and nonverbally
- Channel: The means by which a message is expressed from sender to receiver
- Receiver: The listener or audience member who sees and hears the message
- Feedback: Responses provided by an audience to a speaker
- Context: The situation and environment in which the speech occurs

Improving Your Confidence as a Speaker

1.5 Use several techniques to become a more confident speaker.

Actor and celebrated emcee George Jessel once wryly observed, "The human brain starts working the moment you are born and never stops...until you stand up to speak in public." Perhaps public speaking is a required class for you, but, because of the anxiety you feel when you deliver a speech, you've put it off for as long as possible.

The first bit of comfort we offer is this: It's *normal* to be nervous. In a classic survey seeking to identify people's phobias, public speaking ranked as the most anxiety-producing experience most people face. Forty-one percent of all respondents reported public speaking as their most significant fear: Fear of death ranked only sixth![15] Even comedian Jerry Seinfeld has said, "Given a choice, at a funeral most of us would rather be the one in the coffin than the one giving the eulogy." New research continues to confirm that most people are apprehensive about giving a speech.[16] Other studies have found that more than 80 percent of the population feels anxious when they speak to an audience.[17] Some people find public speaking quite frightening: Studies suggest that about 20 percent of all college students are highly apprehensive about speaking in front of others.[18]

Even if your anxiety is not overwhelming, you can benefit from learning some positive approaches that allow your nervousness to work *for you*.[19] First, we will help you understand why you become nervous. Then we will offer specific strategies to help you speak with greater comfort and less anxiety.

Understand Your Nervousness

What makes you feel nervous about speaking in public? Why do your hands sometimes shake, your knees quiver, your stomach flutter, and your voice seem to go up an octave? What is happening to you?[20]

Researchers have found that public-speaking anxiety is both a *trait* (a characteristic or general tendency that you may have) and a *state* (anxiety triggered by the specific incidence of giving a speech to an audience).[21] A study by two communication researchers found that among the causes of public-speaking anxiety were fear of humiliation, concern about not being prepared, worry about one's looks, pressure to perform, personal insecurity, concern that the audience wouldn't be interested in oneself or the speech, lack of experience, fear of making mistakes, and an overall fear of failure.[22] Another study found that men are likely to experience more anxiety than women when speaking to people from a culture different from their own.[23] There is also evidence that being a perfectionist may be linked to increased apprehension when speaking to others.[24] As you read the list of possible speaking-anxiety causes, you'll probably find a reason that resonates with you because most people feel some nervousness when they speak before others. You're not alone if you are apprehensive about giving a speech.[25] Understanding why you and many others may experience apprehension can give you insights into how to better address your anxiety.[26]

YOUR BIOLOGY AFFECTS YOUR PSYCHOLOGY   Increasingly, researchers are concluding that communication apprehension may have a genetic or biological basis: Some people may inherit a tendency to feel anxious about speaking in public.[27] You may wonder, "So if I have a biological tendency to feel nervous, is there anything I can do to help manage my fear?" The answer is *yes*. Even if you are predisposed to feeling nervous because of your genetic makeup, there are strategies you can use to help manage your apprehension.[28] Perhaps you've heard that the secret to serenity is to focus on the things you can change, rather than on the things you can't, and to have the wisdom to know the difference between what is changeable and what isn't. For increased serenity when speaking in public, we suggest you focus on behaviors that you can change, such as enhancing your speaking skills, rather than on your biologically based speaking apprehension, which is much more difficult to change. A better understanding of the biological reasons you feel apprehensive is a good starting point on the journey to speaking with greater confidence and serenity.[29]

YOUR PSYCHOLOGY ALSO AFFECTS YOUR BIOLOGY   Your view of the speaking assignment, your perception of your speaking skill, and your self-esteem interact to create anxiety.[30] You want to do well, but you're not sure that you can or will. Presented with this conflict, your brain signals your body to switch to its default fight-or-flight mode: You can either fight to respond to the challenge or flee to avoid the cause of the anxiety. Your body responds by summoning more energy to deal with the conflict you are facing. Your breathing rate increases, more adrenaline pumps through you, and more blood rushes through your veins.[31] To put it more technically, you are experiencing physiological changes because of your psychological state, which explains why you may have a more rapid heartbeat, shaking knees and hands, a quivering voice, and increased perspiration.[32] You may also experience butterflies in your stomach because of changes in your digestive system. As a result of your physical discomfort, you may make less eye contact with your audience, use more vocalized pauses ("Um," "Ah," "You know"), and speak too rapidly. Although you see your physical responses as hindrances, your brain and body are simply trying to help you with the task at hand. Sometimes they offer more "help" than needed, and their assistance is not useful.

YOUR APPREHENSION FOLLOWS A PREDICTABLE PATTERN   When are you most likely to feel nervous about giving a speech in your communication class? Research suggests there are typical times when people feel nervous. As shown in Figure 1.4, many people feel

Figure 1.4   Research reveals a pattern of nervousness common to many public speakers, who feel the most nervous right before their speech begins, with anxiety tapering off as the speech continues. Students may also feel a smaller peak of worry at the time their instructor assigns them to give a speech.

SOURCE: Copyrighted by Pearson Education, Hoboken, NJ.

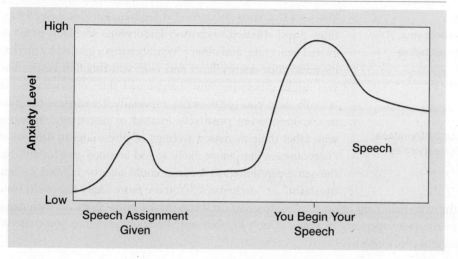

most nervous right before they give their speech. That's when the uncertainty about what will happen next is highest.[33] If you're like most people, you'll feel the second-highest level of anxiety when your instructor explains the speech assignment. You'll probably feel the *least* anxiety when you're preparing your speech.

One practical application of this research is that now you can understand when you'll need the most help managing your anxiety—right before you speak. It will also help to remember that as you begin to speak, anxiety begins to decrease—often dramatically. Another application of this research is realizing you'll feel less anxious about your speech when you're doing something positive to prepare for it. Don't put off working on your speech; if you start preparing well in advance, you'll not only have a better speech, but you'll also feel less anxious about presenting it.

What else can you do to understand and manage your fear and anxiety? Consider the following observations.

You Are Going to Feel More Nervous Than You Look   Realize that your audience cannot see evidence of everything you feel.

When she finished her speech, Carmen sank into her seat and muttered, "Ugh, was I shaky up there! Did *you* see how nervous I was?"

"Nervous? You were nervous?" asked Kosta, surprised. "You looked pretty calm to me."

Worrying that you are going to appear nervous to others may only *increase* your anxiety. Your body will exhibit more physical changes to deal with your self-induced state of anxiety. So even if you do feel nervous, remember that your listeners aren't able to see what you feel. The goal is to present an effective speech using the skills you are learning in this course.[34]

You Are Not Alone   President John F. Kennedy was noted for his superb public-speaking skills. When he spoke, he seemed perfectly at ease. Former British prime minister Winston Churchill was also hailed as one of the twentieth century's great orators. Amazingly, both Kennedy and Churchill were extremely fearful of speaking in public. The list of famous people who admit to feeling nervous before they speak may surprise you: singers Barbra Streisand, Andrea Bocelli, Mariah Carey, Adele, and Carly Simon; actors Julia Roberts and Jim Carrey; comedians Conan O'Brien and Jay Leno; weather forecaster Al Roker, and media magnet Oprah Winfrey have all reported

RECAP

UNDERSTAND YOUR NERVOUSNESS

Keep in mind:

- Nervousness is your brain trying to help you.
- Nervousness is predictable; it peaks right before you speak.
- You'll feel more nervous than you look.
- You are not alone.
- It's normal to be nervous.
- Your nervousness can improve your performance because of enhanced physiological responses.

feeling anxious and jittery before speaking in public.[35] *Almost everyone experiences some anxiety when speaking.* It is unrealistic to try to eliminate speech anxiety. Instead, your goal should be to manage your nervousness so that it does not create so much internal noise that it keeps you from speaking effectively.

YOU CAN USE YOUR ANXIETY Extra adrenaline, increased blood flow, pupil dilation, increased endorphins to block pain, elevated heart rate, and other physical changes caused by anxiety improve your energy level and help you function better than you might otherwise. Your heightened state of readiness can actually help you speak better, especially if you view the public-speaking event positively instead of negatively. Speakers who label their increased feelings of physiological arousal as "nervousness" are more likely to feel anxious and fearful, but the same physiological feelings could also be labeled as "enthusiasm" or "excitement." You are more likely to benefit from the extra help your brain is trying to give you if you think positively rather than negatively about speaking in public. Don't let your initial anxiety convince you that you cannot speak effectively.

How to Build Your Confidence

"Is there anything I can do to help manage my nervousness and anxiety when I give a speech?" you may wonder. Both contemporary research and centuries of experience from seasoned public speakers suggest some practical advice.[36] We summarize their suggestions in Table 1.1.

KNOW YOUR AUDIENCE Know to whom you will be speaking, and learn as much about your audience as you can. The more you can anticipate the kind of reaction

Table 1.1 How to Build Your Confidence

What to Do	How to Do It
Before You Speak	
Know your audience.	Learn as much as you can about the people who will be in your audience.
Don't procrastinate.	Start preparing your speech early. Give yourself plenty of time for rehearsal.
Select an appropriate topic.	Pick a topic that interests both you and your audience.
Prepare.	Well in advance of your speech, spend time developing your ideas, researching your message, and selecting interesting stories and information.
Be organized.	Prepare a well-structured talk, with clear major ideas, so that it is easier to remember.
Know your introduction and your conclusion.	Have your opening line well in mind, although it should not be memorized word for word.
Make practice real.	As you rehearse, recreate the speaking environment.
Breathe.	Whenever your apprehension or anxiety increases, take a slow, deep, relaxing, calming breath.
Channel your nervous energy.	Take a walk to relax before you speak or subtly squeeze your chair to release tension.
Visualize your success.	Picture yourself confidently presenting your message to your audience.
Give yourself a mental pep talk.	Remind yourself that you have prepared and worked hard to make your speech a success.
During Your Speech	
Focus on your message, not on your fear.	Stay focused on communicating your ideas to your listeners.
Look for positive support.	Seek out smiling, supportive listeners.
After You Speak	
Seek more speaking opportunities.	Actively look for places to share your ideas with other groups.
Focus on what you have accomplished, not on your fear.	Celebrate your speaking achievement after you complete your presentation.

your listeners will have to your speech, the more comfortable you will be in delivering your message.[37] As you are preparing your speech, periodically visualize your listeners' response to your message. Consider their needs, goals, and hopes as you prepare your message. Be audience-centered rather than speaker-centered. Don't keep telling yourself how nervous you are going to be.[38] An audience-centered speaker focuses on connecting to listeners rather than focusing on fear.

DON'T PROCRASTINATE One research study confirmed what you probably already know: Speakers who are more apprehensive about speaking put off working on their speeches, in contrast to speakers who are less anxious about public speaking.[39] The lack of thorough preparation often results in a poor speech performance, reinforcing the speaker's perception that public speaking is difficult. Realize that if you fear that you'll be nervous when speaking, you'll tend to put off working on your speech. Take charge and tackle the speech assignment early, giving yourself every chance to be successful. Don't let your fear freeze you into inaction. Prepare early.

SELECT AN APPROPRIATE TOPIC You will feel less nervous if you talk about something that is familiar to you or with which you have had some personal experience. Your comfort with the subject of your speech will be reflected in your delivery.

Judy Shepard, whose son Matthew Shepard was brutally murdered in 1998 for being gay, is a frequent conference speaker and ardent proponent of gay rights. Always apprehensive about giving a speech during her college years, she said, "Speech class was my worst nightmare."[40] But today, because of her fervent belief in her cause, she gives hundreds of speeches. "This is my survival; this is how I deal with losing Matt," she explained to students at South Lakes High School in Reston, Virginia.[41] Talking about something you are passionate about can boost your motivation and help you manage your fear.

PREPARE One formula applies to most speaking situations you are likely to experience: The better prepared you are, the less anxiety you will experience. Being prepared means that you have researched your topic and practiced your speech several times before you deliver it. One research study found clear evidence that rehearsing your speech reduces your apprehension.[42] Being prepared also means that you have developed a logically coherent outline rather than one that is disorganized and difficult to follow. Transitional phrases and summaries can help you present a well-structured, easy-to-understand message.

BE ORGANIZED One of the key skills you'll learn in this text is the value of developing a well-organized message. For most North American listeners, speeches should follow a logical outline pattern and have a clear beginning, middle, and end. Communication researcher Melanie Booth-Butterfield suggests that speakers can better manage their apprehension if they rely on the rules and structures of a speaking assignment, including following a clear outline pattern, when preparing and delivering a speech.[43] Her research showed that anxiety about a speech assignment decreased and confidence increased when speakers closely followed the directions and rules for developing a speech. So, to help manage your apprehension about speaking, listen carefully to what the specific assignment is, ask for additional information if you're unclear about the task, and develop a well-organized message.

KNOW YOUR INTRODUCTION AND YOUR CONCLUSION You are likely to feel the most anxious during the opening moments of your speech. Therefore, it is a good idea to have a clear plan for how you will start your speech. We aren't suggesting memorizing your introduction word for word, but you should have it well in mind. Being familiar with your introduction will help you feel more comfortable about the entire speech.

If you know how you will end your speech, you will have a safe harbor in case you lose your place. If you need to end your speech prematurely, a well-delivered conclusion can permit you to make a graceful exit.

MAKE PRACTICE REAL   When you practice your speech, pretend you are presenting the speech to the audience you will actually address. Stand up. Imagine what the room looks like, or consider rehearsing in the room where you will deliver your speech. What will you be wearing? Practice rising from your seat, walking to the front of the room, and beginning your speech. Practice your speech aloud, rather than just saying it to yourself. A realistic rehearsal will increase your confidence when your moment to speak arrives.

BREATHE   One symptom of nervousness is a change in your breathing and heart rate. Nervous speakers tend to take short, shallow breaths. To help break this anxiety-induced breathing pattern, consider taking a few slow, deep breaths before you rise to speak. No one will detect that you are taking deep breaths if you just slowly inhale and exhale before beginning your speech. Besides breathing deeply, try to relax your entire body. Deep breathing and visualizing yourself as successful will help you relax.

CHANNEL YOUR NERVOUS ENERGY   One common symptom of being nervous is shaky hands and wobbly knees. As we noted previously, what triggers this jiggling is the extra boost of adrenaline your body is giving you—and the resulting energy that has to go somewhere. Your muscles may move whether you intend them to or not. Take control by channeling that energy. One way to release tension is to take a leisurely walk before you arrive wherever you will be speaking. Taking a slow, relaxing walk can help calm you down and use up some of your excess energy. Once you are seated and waiting to speak, grab the edge of your chair (without calling attention to what you are doing) and gently squeeze it to release tension. No one needs to know you're doing this—just unobtrusively squeeze and relax, squeeze and relax. You can also purposely tense and then release the muscles in your legs and arms while you're seated. You don't need to look like you're going into convulsions; just imperceptibly tense and relax your muscles to burn energy. One more tip: You may want to keep both feet on the floor and gently wiggle your toes rather than sit with your legs crossed. Crossing your legs can sometimes cause one leg or foot to go to sleep. Keeping your feet on the floor and slightly moving your toes can ensure that your entire body will be wide awake and ready to go when it's your turn to speak.

As you wait to be introduced, focus on remaining calm. Then, when your name is called, walk to the front of the room in a calm and collected manner. Before presenting your opening, attention-catching sentence, take a moment to look for a friendly, supportive face. Think calm and act calm to feel calm.

Physical symptoms of nervousness are signs that your body is trying to help you meet the challenge of public speaking. Labeling your body's arousal as excitement can help build your confidence as you speak, as can the other tips described in this chapter. *Photo:* Image Source/Alamy Stock Photo.

VISUALIZE YOUR SUCCESS   Studies suggest that one of the best ways to control anxiety is to imagine a scene in which you exhibit skill and comfort as a public speaker.[44] As you imagine giving your speech, picture yourself walking confidently to the front and delivering your well-prepared opening remarks. Visualize yourself as a controlled, confident speaker. Imagine yourself calm and in command. Positive visualization is effective because it boosts your confidence by helping you see yourself as a more confident, accomplished speaker.[45]

Research has found that it's even helpful to look at a picture of someone confidently and calmly delivering a speech while visualizing yourself giving the speech; such positive visualization helps manage your apprehension.[46] You could even make a simple drawing of someone speaking confidently.[47] As you look at the picture or drawing, imagine that it's you confidently giving the speech. It's helpful if the image you're looking at is a person you can identify with—someone who looks like you or someone you believe is more like you than not.[48]

GIVE YOURSELF A MENTAL PEP TALK   You may think that people who talk to themselves are slightly loony. But silently giving yourself a pep talk can give you confidence and take your mind off your nervousness. There is some evidence that simply believing that a technique can reduce your apprehension may, in fact, help reduce your apprehension.[49] Giving yourself a positive message such as "I can do this" may be a productive way to manage your anxiety. Here's a sample mental pep talk you could deliver to yourself right before you speak: "I know this stuff better than anyone else. I've practiced it. My message is well organized. I know I can do it. I'll do a good job." Research provides evidence that people who entertain thoughts of worry and failure don't do themselves any favors.[50] When you feel yourself getting nervous, use positive messages to replace negative thoughts that may creep into your consciousness. Examples include the following:

Negative Thought	Positive Self-Talk
I'm going to forget what I'm supposed to say.	I've practiced this speech many times. I've got notes to prompt me. If I forget or lose my place, no one will know. I'm not following my outline.
So many people are looking at me.	I can do this! My listeners want me to do a good job. I'll seek out friendly faces when I feel nervous.
People think I'm dull and boring.	I've got some good examples. I can talk to people one-on-one, and people seem to like me.
I just can't go through with this.	I have talked to people all my life. I've given presentations in classes for years. I can get through this because I've rehearsed and I'm prepared.

CONFIDENTLY CONNECTING WITH YOUR AUDIENCE

Begin with the End in Mind

One of the habits cited by the late Stephen Covey in his influential book *The 7 Habits of Highly Successful People* is "Begin with the end in mind."[51] From the moment you begin thinking about preparing and presenting your speech, picture yourself being confident and successful. If you find your anxiety level rising at any point in the speech-preparation process, change your mental picture of yourself and imagine that you've completed your speech and the audience has given you a rousing round of applause. Begin imagining success rather than focusing on your fear. Using the principles, skills, and strategies we discuss in this text will help you develop the habit of speech success.

FOCUS ON YOUR MESSAGE, NOT ON YOUR FEAR   The more you think about being anxious about speaking, the more your level of anxiety will increase. Instead, think about what you are going to say. In the few minutes before you address your listeners, mentally review your major ideas, introduction, and conclusion. Focus on your ideas rather than on your fear.

LOOK FOR POSITIVE SUPPORT   Evidence suggests that if you think you see audience members looking critically at you or your message, you may feel more apprehensive and nervous when you speak.[52] Alternatively, when you are aware of positive audience support, you will feel more confident and less nervous. To reiterate our previous advice: It is important to be audience-centered. Although some audience members may not respond positively to you or your message, the overwhelming majority of listeners will be positive. Looking for supportive, reinforcing feedback and finding it can help you feel more confident as a speaker. One study found that speakers experienced less apprehension if they had a support group or a small "learning community" that provided positive feedback and reinforcement.[53] This research finding has implications for you as a speaker and listener. When you have a speaking assignment, work with others so they can provide support as you prepare and when you present your speech. When you're listening to speakers in class, help them by providing eye contact and offering additional positive nonverbal support, such as nodding in agreement and maintaining a positive but sincere facial expression. You can help your fellow students feel more comfortable as speakers, and they can do the same for you. One study found that nonnative speakers may feel anxious and nervous because English is not their native language; so providing positive and supportive feedback is especially important when you know a speaker is quite nervous.[54]

SEEK SPEAKING OPPORTUNITIES   The more experience you gain as a public speaker, the less nervous you will feel.[55] As you develop a track record of successfully delivering speeches, you will have more confidence.[56] This course in public speaking will give you opportunities to enhance both your confidence and your skill through frequent practice. Researchers have found that the most nervous speakers at the beginning of a public-speaking class experienced the greatest decreases in nervousness by the end of the class.[57] Another research study found that students who took a basic public-speaking course later reported having less apprehension and more satisfaction about speaking than students who had not taken such a course.[58] To add to the practice you will get in this class, consider joining organizations and clubs such as Toastmasters, an organization dedicated to improving public-speaking skills by providing a supportive group of people to help you polish your speaking and overcome your anxiety.

FOCUS ON WHAT YOU HAVE ACCOMPLISHED, NOT ON YOUR FEAR   When you conclude your speech, you may be tempted to fixate on your fear. You might amplify in your own mind the nervousness you felt and think everyone could see how nervous you looked. Resist that temptation. When you finish your speech, celebrate your accomplishment. Say to yourself, "I did it! I spoke and people listened." Don't replay your mental image of yourself as nervous and fearful. Instead, mentally replay your success in communicating with your listeners. There is evidence that as you continue to gain experience presenting speeches you will gain confidence and have a greater willingness to communicate. So when you finish your speech, congratulate yourself on having achieved your goal knowing that your success is likely to result in more success in the future.[59]

Because managing communication apprehension is such an important skill for most public speakers, we'll remind you of tips to help you enhance your confidence. Look for techniques of *confidently connecting with your audience* in the margins.

STUDY GUIDE: REVIEW, APPLY, AND ASSESS

What Is Public Speaking?

1.1 Compare and contrast public speaking and conversation.

REVIEW: Public speaking—presenting a message to an audience—builds on other communication skills. Public speaking is similar to conversation in that it requires focus, expression, and adapting to an audience. However, public speaking is more planned, more formal, and has more defined roles for speakers than conversation.

Key Term
public speaking

APPLY: What are similarities and differences between the conversations you have with others and public speaking?

ASSESS: Learning the new skills of public speaking can be challenging and take time. What are the benefits of putting in the effort to become an effective speaker?

Why Study Public Speaking?

1.2 Explain why it is important to study public speaking.

REVIEW: Because you are likely to be called on to speak in public at various times throughout your life, developing a skill in public speaking can empower you. It can also help you secure employment or advance your career.

Key Terms
empowerment   critical thinking

APPLY: How do you think this course in public speaking can help you with your career goals? With your personal life?

ASSESS: As you begin a course in public speaking, take stock of your general skill and experience as a speaker. Write a summary of your current perception of yourself as a speaker, including strengths and areas for development. At the end of the course, revise what you have written to assess how you have improved.

The Rich Heritage of Public Speaking

1.3 Discuss in brief the history of public speaking.

REVIEW: The study of public speaking goes back more than 2,000 years. As you develop your own public-speaking skills, your study will be guided by experience and knowledge gained over centuries of making and studying speeches. Today you are likely to hear speeches presented on TV, YouTube, or by other video means.

Key Terms
rhetoric   elocution
declamation

APPLY: What aspects of public speak have not changed during the past 2000 years and what aspects of speaking to an audience have changed with the advent of contemporary technology in comparison to the "Golden Age" of public speaking?

ASSESS: Identify a famous public speaker, perhaps someone in politics, community service, or a religious leader, who you believe is an excellent public speaker. What factors make this person an effective speaker? Which of those qualities would you like to develop to enhance your own speaking skill?

The Communication Process

1.4 Sketch and explain a model that illustrates the components and the process of communication.

REVIEW: Like other forms of communication, public speaking is a process. Different theorists have explained the communication process as (1) an action, by which a source transmits a message through a channel to a receiver; (2) an interaction, in which the receiver's feedback and the context of the communication add to the action; and (3) a transaction, in which source and receiver simultaneously send messages to build a shared meaning.

Key Terms
source   receiver
encode   external noise
code   internal noise
message   feedback
decode   context
channels

APPLY: Reflect on the most recent public-speaking situation in which you were an audience member. Identify the specific elements in the communication model presented earlier. If the speaker was effective, what elements of the model explain the effectiveness (for example, the message was interesting and there was little noise)? Or if the speaker was ineffective, which elements in the model explain why the speaker was ineffective?

ASSESS: Give an example of internal noise that is affecting you as you read this question. What could a public speaker do or say that would help you focus on the speaker instead of the internal noise that may distract you from his or her message?

Improving Your Confidence as a Speaker

1.5 Use several techniques to become a more confident speaker.

REVIEW: Some beginning public speakers feel nervous at even the thought of giving a speech. Don't be surprised if you feel more nervous than you look to others. Remember that almost every speaker experiences some nervousness and that some anxiety can be useful. Specific suggestions to help you manage your apprehension include being prepared and knowing your audience, imagining the speech environment when you rehearse, and using relaxation techniques such as visualization, deep breathing, and focusing thoughts away from your fears.

APPLY: Mike Roberts is preparing to address the university academic council in an effort to persuade its members to support the establishment of a Greek housing zone on campus. This is Mike's first major task as president of his fraternity, and he is understandably nervous about his responsibility. What advice would you give to help him manage his nervousness?

ASSESS: Take a quiz, available at www.jamescmccroskey .com/measures/prca24.htm, to assess your level of communication apprehension. At the end of your public-speaking class, reassess your level of communication apprehension to see if the course has had an effect on your overall level of communication apprehension.

Presenting Your First Speech

If all my talents and powers were to be taken from me by some inscrutable Providence, and I had my choice of keeping but one, I would unhesitatingly ask to be allowed to keep the Power of Speaking, for through it, I would quickly recover all the rest.

—Daniel Webster

Benjamin Robert Haydon (1832-33), *Meeting of the Birmingham Political Union* (oil on canvas). This meeting took place on Newhall Hill on May 16, 1832. *Photo:* Courtesy of the Birmingham Museum & Art Gallery. Lebrecht Music and Arts Photo Library/Alamy Stock Photo.

OBJECTIVES

After studying this chapter, you should be able to do the following:

2.1 Explain why it is important to be audience-centered during each step of the speechmaking process.

2.2 Describe and discuss the eight steps of the audience-centered speechmaking process.

Unless you have some prior experience in higher mathematics, you may not have the foggiest notion of what calculus is when you first take a class in that subject. But when you tell people that you are taking a public-speaking class, most have some idea of what a public speaker does. A public speaker talks while others listen. You hear speeches almost every day. Increasingly many of the speeches you hear are presented via electronic media. Online, whether in a YouTube video, a TED Talk, or even a video on Facebook, you are likely to encounter speeches. Yet even with the ubiquitous presence of social media, you undoubtedly experience many presentations live and in person, in your classes or where you work. Although you have heard countless speeches, you may still have questions about how a speaker prepares and presents a speech.

In Chapter 1, we discussed the importance of learning to speak publicly and described the components of effective communication. We also presented tips and strategies for becoming a confident speaker. In this chapter, we will preview the preparation and presentation skills that you will learn in this course. Undoubtedly, you will be given a speech assignment early in your public-speaking course. Although it would be ideal if you had time to read *Public Speaking: An Audience-Centered Approach* from cover to cover before tackling your first speech, doing so would be impractical. To help you begin, we present this chapter, a step-by-step overview designed to serve as the scaffolding on which to build your skill in public speaking.

Consider Your Audience

2.1 Explain why it is important to be audience-centered during each step of the speechmaking process.

You've been speaking to others since you were 2 years old. Talking to people has seemed such a natural part of your life that you may never have stopped to analyze the process. But as you think about preparing your first speech for class, you may wonder, "What do I do first?" Your assignment may be to introduce yourself or another student to the class. Or your first assignment may be a brief informative talk—to describe something to your audience. Regardless of the specific assignment, however, you need some idea of how to begin.

As we noted previously, you don't need to read this text in its entirety before giving your first speech. But it is useful to have an overview of the various steps and skills involved in giving a speech. To help you visualize this overview, Figure 2.1 diagrams the various tasks involved in the speechmaking process, emphasizing the audience as

Figure 2.1   The reminder to consider the audience is at the center of this model of the speechmaking process because your audience influences your work on each task involved in designing and presenting a speech. As we discuss each task in depth throughout the text, we also use a smaller image of this model to flag information and advice that remind you to consider your audience.

SOURCE: Copyrighted by Pearson Education, Hoboken, NJ.

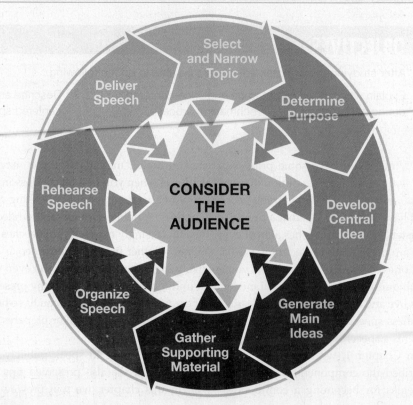

the central concern at every step of the process. We'll refer to this audience-centered model of public speaking throughout the text. *To emphasize the importance of being audience-centered, we have placed a smaller version of this model in the margins throughout the text to draw your attention to information that discusses the importance of always being mindful of your audience.* (See the icon in the margin.) When you see the icon, it means we're discussing the central theme of this text: **Always make choices in designing and delivering your speech with your audience in mind.**

We will preview our discussion of the speechmaking process with the central element: considering your audience. We will then discuss each step of the process, starting with selecting and narrowing a topic, and moving clockwise around the model, examining each interrelated step.

Why should the central focus of public speaking be the audience? Why is it not topic selection, outlining, or research? The simple truth is that your audience influences the topic you choose and every later step of the speechmaking process. Your selection of topic, purpose, and even major ideas should be based on a thorough understanding of your listeners. In a real sense, your audience "writes" the speech.[1] Think of this first step of speechmaking less as a "step"—something you do once and then move on to the next step—and more like the beginning of a continuous process. Whether pondering what to speak about or delivering your concluding remarks, we suggest that you never stop thinking about the reason you are speaking—to communicate with your audience.

Gather and Analyze Information about Your Audience

To be audience-centered, you should first identify and then analyze information about your listeners. For example, just by looking at your audience in your speech class, you will be able to determine such basic information as approximately how old they are and the percentage of men and women in your audience; you also know that they are all students in a public-speaking class. To determine less obvious information, you may need to ask them questions or design a short questionnaire.

As we've noted, audience analysis is not something you do only at the beginning of preparing your speech. It is an ongoing activity. The characteristics of your audience influence the choices you make about your speech at every step of the speech-preparation process. That's why, in the audience-centered speech model, arrows connect the center of the diagram with each stage of designing and delivering your speech. At any point during the preparation and delivery of your message, you may need to revise your thinking or your material if you learn new information about your audience. That is why the model has arrows pointing both ways across the boundary between the central element and each step in the process. Chapter 5 includes a comprehensive discussion of the principles and strategies involved in analyzing your audience.

When you speak to a live audience, you will be looking your listeners directly in the eye. So you'll have the benefit of seeing their immediate reactions, whether it be their rapt attention characterized by returned eye contact, a slight forward lean and no fidgeting, or unfocused stares signaling their inattentiveness. Speaking in person permits you to modify your message on the spot so that you can achieve your goal. However, when you use video technology to deliver your speech, you often can't see your listeners, especially if you record the speech for others to see and hear later, so it's more challenging to reactively modify your talk during your presentation. For video or online presentations where you can't see or hear your audience, you must, instead, do your best to *anticipate* how listeners may respond. Selecting examples and illustrations that you think will gain and maintain their attention, organizing your message for maximum clarity, and delivering your message with eye contact, appropriate vocal variation, and meaningful gestures can help you connect to your virtual audience.

Consider the Culturally Diverse Backgrounds of Your Audience

Different cultures have radically different expectations about public speaking. In Russia, for example, speakers have a "no frills" approach that emphasizes content over delivery. A presentation that seems perfectly sensible and acceptable to a U.S. businessperson who is accustomed to straightforward, problem-oriented logic may seem shockingly rude to a Chinese businessperson who expects more circuitous, less overtly purposeful rhetoric. When one of this text's authors taught public speaking for several semesters in the Bahamas he shocked students by suggesting that they should achieve a conversational, informal delivery style. Bahamian audiences, he quickly discovered, expect formal oratory from their speakers, very much as U.S. audiences in the nineteenth century preferred the grandiloquence of Stephen A. Douglas to the quieter, homespun style of Abraham Lincoln. As a result, your author had to embellish his own style when he taught the Bahamian class.

You need not give speeches in foreign countries to recognize the importance of adapting to different cultural expectations of individual audience members. People in the United States are highly diverse in terms of their culture, age, ethnicity, and religious tradition. Consider the various cultural backgrounds of your classmates. How many different cultural and ethnic traditions do they represent? Depending on who your audience members are and what topics they are interested in, you will want to adjust your delivery style and possibly your topic, pattern of organization, and the examples you select.

Being sensitive to your audience and adapting your message accordingly will serve you well not only when addressing listeners with cultural backgrounds different from your own, but also in all types of situations. If you learn to analyze your audience and adapt to their expectations, you can apply these skills in numerous settings: interviewing for a job via Skype, delivering a business presentation, or speaking to the city council—even while proposing marriage.

> **RECAP**
>
> ## CONSIDER YOUR AUDIENCE
>
> - Keep your audience in mind at every step of preparing your speech.
> - Gather and analyze as much information as you can.
> - Be sensitive to the cultural diversity of your audience.

The Audience-Centered Speechmaking Process

2.2 Describe and discuss the eight steps of the audience-centered speechmaking process.

Preparing a speech is a process of following eight steps, while keeping the interests, needs, and values of your audience in mind. After considering your audience, the steps of the audience-centered public speaking process are: Select and narrow your topic, determine your purpose, develop your central idea, generate main ideas, gather supporting material, organize your speech, rehearse your speech, and deliver your speech.

Select and Narrow Your Topic

While keeping your audience foremost in mind, your next task is to determine what you will talk about and to limit your topic to fit the constraints of your speaking assignment. Pay special attention to the guidelines your instructor gives you for your assignment.

If your first speech assignment is to introduce yourself to the class, your **speech topic** has been selected for you—*you* are the topic. It is not uncommon to be asked to speak on a specific subject. Often, though, you will not be given a topic. The task

speech topic
The key focus of the content of a speech

Packing Slip

Store: 630 HUSKY BOOKSTORE

Page: 2

Order Information
Web Number: 630000132840
SODA Number: 83458625-001
Customer Name: Aliana Pechan
Order Date: 09/14/2022 04:30 PM
Last Updated: 09/15/2022 08:35 AM
Patron ID: 14263843
Home Phone: (320) 632-4195
Customer Email: alipechan@gmail.com

Shipping Information
Shipping Method: Store Pick-Up

Shipping Address:
Aliana Pechan
201 8th Street South
Centennial Hall
Husky Bookstore
St. Cloud, MN 56301 - USA

Product/ Custom Info	SKU	Substitute? (Y/N)	Qty	Unit Price	Total Price
Public Speaking >CMST>211>01	<Used> 9780134380919	N	1	90.50	90.50 <Rent>
Rent Due Date: 12/15/22	Non Rtrn Fee: 189.48	Non Rtrn Proc Fee: 16.97			
CONVERT TO PURCHASE PRICE 79.19					
* APPLICABLE TAXES APPLY					

Shipping: .00

Financial Aid ****4095
20233P Terms and Conditions

CONSIDER
THE
AUDIENCE

our recent snowshoeing trip might
provide the basis for a good speech
opic. *Photo:* ARochau/Fotolia

RECAP

SELECT AND NARROW YOUR TOPIC

To pick a good topic, ask three questions:
- *Who is the audience?* Consider the audience members at every point in the speechmaking process.
- *What are my interests, talents, and experiences?* Narrow down your talk to fit time limits.
- *What is the occasion?* The setting for the presentation is important, too.

WHAT IS THE OCCASION? Besides your audience, you should consider the occasion for the speech when choosing a topic. A commencement address calls for a different topic, for example, than does a speech to a model railroad club. Another aspect of the occasion you'll want to consider is the physical setting of your speech. Will you be speaking to people seated in chairs arranged in a circle, will your listeners be sitting around a table watching you via a webcast or teleconference, or will you be standing in front of rows of people? The occasion and physical surroundings, including whether your speech is communicated via media, affect the degree of formality your audience expects in your choice of topics.

Determine Your Purpose

You might think that once you have selected your topic, you are ready to start the research process. Before you do that, however, you need to decide on both a general and a specific purpose.

general purpose
The overarching goal of a speech—to inform, persuade, or entertain

DETERMINE YOUR GENERAL PURPOSE Your **general purpose** is the overarching goal of your speech. There are three types of general purposes for speeches: to *inform*, to *persuade*, and to *entertain*.

- **Inform:** When you inform, you teach, define, illustrate, clarify, or elaborate on a topic. The primary objective of class lectures, seminars, and workshops is to inform. Chapter 13 will show you how to construct an effective speech with an informative purpose.
- **Persuade:** A speech to persuade seeks to change or reinforce listeners' attitudes, beliefs, values, or behavior. Ads on TV, the radio, and pop-up commercials on the Internet; sermons; political speeches; and sales presentations are examples of messages designed to persuade. To be a skilled persuader, you need to be sensitive to your audience's attitudes (likes and dislikes) toward you and your topic. Chapters 14 and 15 will discuss principles and strategies for preparing persuasive speeches.
- **Entertain:** To entertain listeners is the third general purpose of a speech. After-dinner speeches and comic monologues are mainly intended as entertainment. As Chapter 16 describes, often the key to an effective entertaining speech lies in your choice of stories, examples, and illustrations, as well as in your delivery. Appendix B includes examples of speeches designed to inform, persuade, and entertain.

specific purpose
A concise statement of the desired audience response, indicating what you want your listeners to remember, feel, or do when you finish speaking

DETERMINE YOUR SPECIFIC PURPOSE Your **specific purpose** is a concise statement indicating what you want your listeners to be able to do, remember, or feel when you finish your speech. A specific-purpose statement identifies the precise, measurable audience response you desire. Here again, we emphasize the importance of focusing on the audience as you develop your specific purpose. Perhaps you have had the experience of listening to a speaker and wondering, "What's the point? I know he's talking about education, but I'm not sure where he's going with this subject." You may have understood the speaker's general purpose, but the specific one wasn't clear. If you can't figure out what the specific purpose is, it is probably because the speaker does not know either.

Deciding on a specific purpose is not difficult once you have narrowed your topic: "At the end of my speech, the class will be able to identify three counseling facilities on campus and describe the best way to get help at each one." Notice that this purpose is phrased in terms of what you would like the audience to be able to *do* by the end of the speech. Your specific purpose should be a fine-tuned, audience-centered goal. For an informative speech, you may simply want your audience to restate an idea, define new words, or if the speech is about introducing yourself to the class, recall a dramatic or humorous incident in your life. In a persuasive speech, you may try to rouse your listeners to take a class, buy something, change a bad habit, or vote for someone. A persuasive speech can also reinforce a behavior as well as an attitude, belief, or value.

Once you have formulated your specific purpose, write it down and keep it before you as you read and gather ideas for your talk. Your specific purpose should guide your research and help you choose supporting materials that are related to your audience. As you continue to work on your speech, you may even decide to modify your purpose. But if you have an objective in mind at all times as you move through the preparation stage, you will stay on track.

Develop Your Central Idea

You should now be able to write the **central idea** of your speech. Whereas your statement of a specific purpose indicates what you want your audience to do when you have finished your speech, your central idea identifies the essence of your message. Think of it as a one-sentence summary of your speech. Here's an example:

TOPIC:	British TV shows that inspired American TV shows
GENERAL PURPOSE:	To inform
SPECIFIC PURPOSE:	At the end of my speech the audience will be able to identify three classic British TV shows that inspired American versions.
CENTRAL IDEA:	*The Office, Antiques Roadshow,* and *House of Cards* began as British TV programs that have become successful American TV shows.

Here's another way to think about how to develop your central idea sentence. Imagine that you have just finished presenting your speech and you get into an elevator. Someone on the elevator with you says, "Oh, I'm sorry I missed your speech. What did you say?" Between the second floor and the first, you have only 15 seconds to summarize your message. You might say, "I said there are two keys to parent and child communication: First, make time for communication, and second, listen effectively." That brief recap is your central idea sentence. To clarify, your purpose sentence is what you want the audience to be able to *do*; the central idea sentence is your speech in a nutshell—your speech in one sentence.

Generate the Main Ideas

In the words of columnist H. V. Prochnow, "A good many people can make a speech, but saying something is more difficult." Effective speakers are good thinkers; they say something. They know how to play with words and thoughts to develop their **main ideas**. The ancient Romans called this skill **invention**—the ability to develop or discover ideas that result in new insights or approaches to old problems. The Roman orator Cicero called this aspect of speaking the process of "finding out what [a speaker] should say."

RECAP
DETERMINE YOUR PURPOSE

Develop Your General Purpose

To inform	To share information by teaching, defining, illustrating, describing, or explaining
To persuade	To change or reinforce an attitude, belief, value, or behavior
To entertain	To amuse with humor, stories, or illustrations

Develop Your Specific Purpose

What do you want your audience to remember, do, or feel when you finish your speech?

General Purpose	Specific Purpose
To inform	At the end of my speech, the audience will be able to identify three counseling facilities on campus and describe the counseling services each facility offers to students.
To persuade	At the end of my speech, the audience will visit the counseling facilities on campus.
To entertain	At the end of my speech, the audience will be amused by the series of misunderstandings I created when I began making inquiries about career advisors on campus.

central idea
A one-sentence summary of the speech content

main ideas
The key points of a speech

invention
The development or discovery of ideas and insights

Once you have an appropriate topic, a specific purpose, and a well-worded central idea down on paper, the next task is to identify the major divisions of your speech or key points that you wish to develop. To determine how to subdivide your central idea into key points, ask these three questions:

1. **Does the central idea have logical divisions?** For example, if the central idea is "There are three ways to interpret the stock market page of your local newspaper or financial website," your speech can be organized into three parts. You will simply identify the three ways to interpret stock market information and use each as a major point.

2. **Can you think of several reasons why the central idea is true?** If, for example, your central idea is "New legislation is needed to ensure that U.S. citizens' privacy is protected," each major point of your speech could be a reason why you think new privacy laws are needed.

3. **Can you support the central idea with a series of steps?** Suppose your central idea is "Running for a campus office is easy to do." Your speech could be developed around a series of steps, telling your listeners what to do first, second, and third to get elected.

Your time limit, topic, and the information gleaned from your research will determine how many major ideas will be in your speech. A three- to five-minute speech might have only two major ideas. In a short speech, you may develop only one major idea with examples, illustrations, and other forms of support. Don't spend time trying to divide a topic that does not need to be divided. In Chapters 6 and 8, we will discuss how to generate major ideas and organize them.

Gather Supporting Material

With your main idea or ideas in mind, your next job is to gather material to support them—facts, examples, definitions, and quotations from others that illustrate, amplify,

If the central idea of your speech is, "You can conduct your own home energy audit," you might discuss energy audits of various rooms of a home or you might present a series of steps in conducting a home energy audit. *Photo:* auremar/Fotolia

clarify, provide evidence, or tell a story. Here, as always when preparing your speech, the importance of being an audience-centered speaker can't be overemphasized. There's an old saying that an ounce of illustration is worth a ton of talk. If a speech is boring, it is usually because the speaker has not chosen supporting material that is relevant or interesting to the audience. Don't just give people data; connect facts to their lives. As one sage quipped, "Data is not information any more than 50 tons of cement is a skyscraper."[3]

TELL A STORY   Don Hewitt, the founding and longtime producer of TV's popular and award-winning *60 Minutes*, was repeatedly asked by young journalists, "What's the secret of your success as a communicator?" Hewitt's answer: "Tell me a story." Everyone likes to hear a good story. As Hewitt noted, the Bible does more than describe the nature of good and evil; it masterfully tells stories about Job, Noah, David, and others.[4]

Tell stories based on your own experiences and provide vivid descriptions of things that are tangible so that your audience can visualize what you are talking about.

APPEAL TO THE SENSES   To be interesting, supporting material should be personal, concrete, and appeal to your listeners' senses. The more senses you trigger with words, the more interesting your talk will be. Descriptions such as "the rough, splintery surface of weather-beaten wood" or "the sweet, cool, refreshing flavor of cherry Jell-O" evoke sensory images. In addition, relating abstract statistics to something tangible can help communicate your ideas more clearly. For example, if you say Frito-Lay sells 2.6 billion pounds of snack food each year, your listeners will have a hazy idea that 2.6 billion pounds is a lot of corn and potato chips, but if you add that 2.6 billion pounds is triple the weight of the Empire State Building, you've made your point more memorably.[5] Or, rather than simply saying that 4,000 teens die each year in car accidents, say this: "If 12 fully loaded jumbo jets crashed every year, something would be done about it. Every year, more than 4,000 teens die in car crashes—the equivalent of 12 large plane crashes." Relating statistics to something listeners can visualize makes the point more effectively.[6] In Chapter 8 we will discuss the variety of supporting material available to you.

USE RESEARCH SKILLS TO FIND INTERESTING INFORMATION President Woodrow Wilson once admitted, "I use not only all the brains I have, but all that I can borrow." How does a public speaker find interesting and relevant supporting material? By developing good research skills. If you gave a short speech about a sport you had practiced for years or a recent trip you took, chances are you would not need to gather much additional information. But sooner or later, you will need to do some research on a topic to speak on it intelligently to an audience. By the time you have given several speeches in this course, you will have learned to use a number of resources: various electronic databases your library subscribes to, your library's computerized card catalog, an e-version of *Bartlett's Familiar Quotations*, and a wide assortment of Internet indexes such as Google Scholar.

In addition to becoming a skilled user of online information and resources from your library, you will also learn to be on the lookout as you read,

Good research skills are essential to the speechmaking process.
Photo: CREATAS/JUPITER IMAGES/Alamy Images

RECAP

GATHER SUPPORTING MATERIAL

Use your own knowledge and research to find supporting materials that accomplish the following:

- *Tell a Story.* Most audiences enjoy stories.
- *Appeal to the Senses.* Help the audience hear, see, touch, and experience what you describe.
- *Use Research Skills.* Find new, interesting material that the audience has not heard before.

disposition
The organization and arrangement of ideas and illustrations

watch TV or YouTube, receive tweets, and search the Internet for examples, illustrations, and quotations that could be used in a speech. Chapter 7 will more thoroughly explain how to use all these resources, with a special emphasis on Internet and electronic research tools.

Organize Your Speech

A wise person once said, "If effort is organized, accomplishment follows." A clearly and logically structured speech helps your audience remember what you say. A logical structure also helps you feel more in control of your speech, and greater control helps you feel more comfortable while delivering your message.

As we saw in Chapter 1, classical rhetoricians called the process of developing an orderly speech **disposition**. Speakers need to present ideas, information, examples, illustrations, stories, and statistics in an orderly sequence so that listeners can easily follow what they are saying.

Every well-prepared speech has three major divisions: the introduction, the body, and the conclusion. The introduction helps capture attention, serves as an overview of the speech, and provides your audience with reasons to listen to you. The body presents the main content of your speech. The conclusion summarizes your key ideas. You may have heard this advice on how to organize a speech: "Tell them what you're going to tell them (the introduction), tell them (the body of the speech), and tell them what you told them (the conclusion)."

As a student of public speaking, you will study and learn to apply variations of this basic pattern of organization (chronological, topical, cause–effect, problem–solution) that will help your audience understand your meaning. You will learn about previewing and summarizing—information that will help your audience remember your ideas. In the outline of a sample speech, notice how the introduction catches the listener's attention, the body of the speech identifies the main ideas, and the conclusion summarizes the key ideas.

It is important that you do not write a speech word for word as you would an essay for English class. Writing and then reading or memorizing you speech will sound mechanical and less appealing to your audience. After you have selected your topic and purpose, and generated your main ideas—start with the body of your speech. Because your introduction previews your speech and your conclusion summarizes it, most public-speaking teachers recommend that you prepare your introduction and conclusion *after* you have carefully organized the body of your talk. Indicate your major ideas by Roman numerals. Use capital letters for your supporting points. Use Arabic numerals if you need to subdivide your ideas further. Most communication teachers will tell you how many speaking notes you may use for your speech. Use brief notes—written cues on note cards—instead of a complete manuscript. Increasingly speakers are using handheld computer tablets such as iPads to display their speaking notes.

For your first speech, you may want to adapt the sample outline format shown on the next page.[7] Chapter 9 presents additional examples and suggestions for outlining your talk. Your instructor may want you to add more detailed information about your supporting material in outlines you submit in class. Follow the precise guidelines your instructor provides for outlining your speech.

In addition to developing a written outline to use as you speak, consider using presentation aids to add structure and clarity to your major ideas. Developing simple visual reinforcers of your key ideas can help your audience retain essential points.

SAMPLE OUTLINE

TOPIC
How to invest money

Your instructor may assign
a topic, or you may select it.

GENERAL PURPOSE
To inform

To inform, persuade, or
entertain. Your instructor
will probably specify your
general purpose.

SPECIFIC PURPOSE
At the end of my speech, the audience should be able to identify two principles that will help them better invest their money.

A clear statement indicating
what your audience should
be able to do after hearing
your speech

CENTRAL IDEA
Knowing the source of money, how to invest it, and how money grows can lead to increased income from wise investments.

A one-sentence summary
of your talk

INTRODUCTION
Imagine for a moment that it is the year 2065. You are sixty-five years old. You've just picked up your mail and opened an envelope that contains a check for $300,000! No, you didn't win the lottery. You smile as you realize your own modest investment strategy over the last forty years has paid off handsomely.

Today I'd like to answer three questions that can help you become a better money manager: First, where does money come from? Second, where do you invest it? And third, how does a little money grow into a lot of money?

Knowing the answers to these three questions can pay big dividends for you. With only modest investments and a well-disciplined attitude, you could easily have an annual income of $300,000 or more.

Attention-catching
opening line

Preview major ideas.

Tell your audience why they
should listen to you.

BODY
I. There are two sources of money.
    A. You already have some money.
    B. You will earn money in the future.
II. You can do three things with your money.
    A. You can spend it.
    B. You can lend it to others.
    C. You can invest it.
III. Two principles can help make you rich.
    A. The "magic" of compound interest can transform pennies into millions.
    B. Finding the best rate of return on your money can pay big dividends.

I. Major Idea
    A. Supporting idea
    B. Supporting idea
II. Major Idea
    A. Supporting idea
    B. Supporting idea
    C. Supporting idea
III. Major Idea
    A. Supporting idea
    B. Supporting idea

CONCLUSION
Today I've identified three key aspects of effective money management: (1) sources of money, (2) what you can do with money, and (3) money-management principles that can make you rich. Now, let's go "back to the future"! Remember the good feeling you had when you received your check for $300,000? Recall that feeling again when you are depositing your first paycheck. Remember this simple secret for accumulating wealth: Part of all you earn is yours to keep. It is within your power to "go for the gold."

Summarize main ideas
and restate central idea.

Figure 2.2 Presentation graphic for the first major idea in your speech.

SOURCES: Shannon Kingston. Copyrighted by Pearson Education, Hoboken, NJ. *Photo:* acekreations/Fotolia

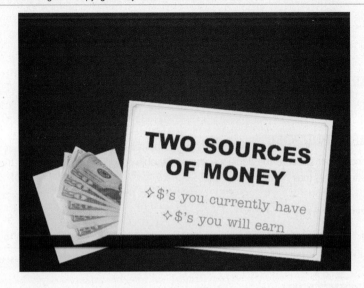

In Chapter 12 we offer tips for designing graphics using software such as PowerPoint, Keynote, or Prezi. For example, the second major idea explored in the outline could be reinforced with a visual such as the one in Figure 2.2.

For all the steps we have discussed so far, your success as a speaker will ultimately be determined by your audience. That is why throughout the text we refer you to the audience-centered speechmaking model presented in this chapter.

Once you are comfortable with the structure of your talk and you have developed your visual aids, you are ready to rehearse.

Rehearse Your Speech

Remember this joke? One man asks another, "How do you get to Carnegie Hall?" The answer: "Practice, practice, practice." The joke may be older than Carnegie Hall itself, but it is still good advice to all speakers, especially novice speakers. A speech is a performance. As with any stage performance, be it music, dance, or theater, you need to rehearse. Experienced carpenters know to "measure twice, saw once." Rehearsing your speech is a way to measure your message so that you get it right when you present it to your audience.

If you practice your speech as if you were actually delivering it, you will be a more effective speaker when you talk to the audience. And there is evidence that, like preparing early, spending time rehearsing your delivery will enhance the overall quality of your speech.[8]

The best way to practice is to rehearse your speech aloud, standing just as you will when you deliver it to your audience. As you rehearse, try to find a comfortable way to phrase your ideas, but don't try to memorize your talk. In fact, if you have rehearsed your speech so many times that you are using exactly the same words every time, you have rehearsed long enough. Rehearse just enough so that you can discuss your ideas and supporting material without leaving out major parts of your speech. It is all right to use notes, but most public-speaking instructors limit the number of notes you may use. Make sure you rehearse your speech using the same notes you plan to use when presenting it.

Practice making eye contact with your imaginary audience as often as you can. Also, be certain to speak loudly enough for all in the room to hear. If you are not sure what to do with your hands when you rehearse, just keep them at your side. Focus on your message rather than worrying about how to gesture. If you are delivering your speech via video (whether live or prerecorded), remember that the camera may make it appear to listeners that you are only a few feet away from them. For video, do not use overly animated gestures or facial expressions. A natural, conversational quality will be valued whether you are speaking in front of a camera or a live audience.

Besides rehearsing your physical delivery, you also will make decisions about the style of your speech. "Style," said novelist Jonathan Swift, "is proper words in proper places." The words you choose and your arrangement of those words make up the style of your speech. You can learn more about using words in Chapter 10. To be a good speaker, you must become familiar with the language your listeners are used to hearing and you must know how to select the right word or phrase to communicate an idea.

Deliver Your Speech

The time has come, and you're ready to present your speech to your audience. Delivery is the final step in the preparation process. Before you walk to the front of the room, look at your listeners to see if the audience assembled is what you were expecting. Are the people of the age, race, and gender that you had predicted? Or do you need to make last-minute changes in your message to adjust to a different mix of audience members?

When you are introduced, walk calmly and confidently to the front of the room. Then take a moment to establish eye contact with your audience, smile naturally, and deliver your attention-catching opening sentence. Concentrate on your message and your audience. Deliver your speech just as you rehearsed it using a conversational style before your imaginary audience: Maintain eye contact, speak loudly enough to be heard, and use some natural variation in pitch. Finally, remember the public-speaking advice of columnist Ann Landers: "Be sincere, be brief, and be seated."

Figure 2.3 summarizes this chapter's introduction to the audience-centered speaking process and refers you to other chapters for in-depth information about each step. For a model of many of the attributes of a well-crafted message that we have discussed, read the following speech by student Grace Hildenbrand.[9]

CONFIDENTLY CONNECTING WITH YOUR AUDIENCE

Use Your Communication Apprehension to Enhance Your Performance

Recall that most speakers' nervousness peaks right before giving a speech. You can use this anxiety to help you enhance your performance. How? Exercise the skill of reframing to get yourself to think positively rather than negatively about speaking in public. Remember that anxiety is your body's way of trying to give you more energy to help you improve your performance. Don't dwell on the symptoms of anxiety; reframe them as signals that your brain is increasing your mental powers. Knowing that some apprehension can enhance your mental alertness can help you deliver a well-presented speech.

So now that we've talked a little bit about the differences in the characters between the two versions and the differences in the royal ball scene, I'd like to discuss the way that Disney omitted some violence from their version of *Cinderella* compared to the Brothers Grimm version.

The Brothers Grimm version of *Cinderella* is much gorier than Disney's version. For example, when the prince is trying to figure out who Cinderella is and he's having various women try on the slipper, he comes to Cinderella's stepsisters and both of them have feet that are too big. The first stepsister actually cuts off her toe to make the shoe fit, and the second stepsister actually cuts off her heel to make the shoe fit. So it's a very bloody scene and it's actually kind of funny because even though they are bleeding, the prince doesn't seem to realize that neither one of the stepsisters is Cinderella. According to the *Greenwood Encyclopedia of Folktales and Fairytales*, the prince doesn't realize that neither of the stepsisters is Cinderella until the birds that serve the fairy godmother role tell him, "Hey, there's blood everywhere, neither one of these women is Cinderella!"

Another gory aspect of the Brothers Grimm version is that at Cinderella's wedding at the end of the story, as punishment for being wicked, the stepsisters actually get their eyes poked out by the birds and they are blinded. So with these changes, you can imagine that if Disney kept the fairy tale similar to the Brothers Grimm version, it likely would have changed the audience. You know, rather than having it geared toward children, it might be geared toward adults, and it definitely would have not become such a popular and important part of our childhood.

In conclusion, now you should have a better understanding of the differences between the Disney and Brothers Grimm versions of *Cinderella* and why Disney changed its version of *Cinderella*. Specifically these differences were that Disney added in and changed some of the characters; Disney also made changes to the royal ball scene and got rid of some of the violence from the Brothers Grimm version. So the next time that you're watching Disney's *Cinderella* or any other version of *Cinderella*, I'd like you to imagine that if there was blood dripping from the eyes and feet of the stepsisters how this would change your reaction to this classic fairy tale.

Here the speaker gives another oral citation, mentioning the source of her supporting material.

The speaker directly addresses the audience members to engage their attention and involve them in the speech.

In her conclusion, the speaker summarizes the main points of her speech.

The speaker closes with a vivid image and a suggestion for action. Both will help the audience remember the content of this speech.

STUDY GUIDE: REVIEW, APPLY, AND ASSESS

Consider your Audience

2.1 Explain why it is important to be audience-centered during each step of the speechmaking process.

REVIEW: Your audience influences your topic selection and every aspect of presenting a speech. The audience-centered model of public speaking introduced previously suggests that you should consider the audience each step of the way when preparing and presenting a speech.

Key Term
speech topic

APPLY: Jonathan has just received his first speech assignment in his public-speaking class. What key pieces of information should Jonathan keep in mind as he begins to prepare his speech?

ASSESS: What do you know about your public-speaking class as an audience, based only on observing them or hearing them introduce themselves to the class? How might you use this information to make your speech audience-centered?

The Audience-Centered Speechmaking Process

2.2 Describe and discuss the eight steps of the audience-centered speechmaking process.

REVIEW: Preparing a speech is a process of following eight steps, while keeping the interests, needs, and values of your audience in mind. After considering your audience, the steps of the audience-centered public speaking process are: Select and narrow your topic, determine your purpose, develop your central idea, generate main ideas, gather supporting material, organize your speech, rehearse your speech, and deliver your speech.

Key Terms

general purpose	main ideas
specific purpose	invention
central idea	disposition

APPLY: Barbara is planning to move to an independent living community for seniors and wants to tell other senior citizens the steps to follow when making a similar move. Write a possible specific purpose statement and then develop a central idea sentence for Barbara's speech.

ASSESS: After you deliver your first speech to your class, write a short self-analysis. Identify when you thought you were especially effective in connecting with your listeners. Also note times when you wondered if you were maintaining your classmates' interest. If you were to give the same speech to the same audience again, what would you do the same and what would you do differently?

Speaking Freely and Ethically

3

Je suis Charlie (I am Charlie)
—Solidarity slogan in support
of free speech following
the 2015 terrorist attacks
on French magazine
Charlie Hebdo

1873 South Carolina legislature, including
African-American delegates, passing an
appropriation bill. (Hand-colored halftone
of a 19th century illustration.) *Photo:* North
Wind Picture Archives—All rights reserved.

OBJECTIVES

After studying this chapter, you should be able to do the following:

3.1 Explain how free speech has been challenged and defended throughout history.

3.2 List and explain five criteria for ethical public speaking.

3.3 Explain the relationship between ethics and credibility.

---

free speech

The open exchange of information and ideas

When smoldering racial tension at the University of Missouri–Columbia reached a crisis point on November 9, 2015, members of a black student group gathered in a tent city on the Carnahan Quad to plan protests. The students were surrounded by supporters carrying signs saying "No Media" and attempting to block journalists from the scene, ostensibly to protect the students' right to free speech without interruption. Cell phone video of what happened next went viral. An assistant professor confronting a student reporter shouted, "Hey, who wants to help me get this reporter out of here? I need some muscle over here."[1]

Free speech, broadly defined as the open exchange of information and ideas, is protected by law in the United States and other countries. It is considered by many to be a universal human right. Certainly few would dispute that the student protestors in Missouri were exercising their right to free speech. But it could be claimed that their supporters were, too, along with the professor who called for "muscle" to remove the reporter—who in turn was exercising his own free speech rights. Free speech includes ideas and behaviors that we may consider offensive or unfair, as well as those we deem wise and just. However, the right to speak freely must be balanced by the responsibility to speak ethically.

Ethics—the beliefs, values, and moral principles by which we determine what is right or wrong—serve as criteria for many of the decisions we make in our personal and professional lives and for our judgments of others' behavior. The student who refuses to cheat on a test, the employee who will not call in sick to gain an extra day of vacation, and the property owner who does not claim more storm damage than she actually suffered have all made choices based on ethics.

We read and hear about ethical issues every day in the media. Cloning, stem-cell research, and drug testing have engendered heated ethical debates among medical professionals. Advertising by some attorneys has incensed those who believe that an overall increase in frivolous litigation is tarnishing the profession. And in the political arena, debates about reforms of social programs, fiscal responsibility, and the collection of personal data by the federal government all hinge on ethical issues.

Although you are undoubtedly familiar with many of these ethical issues, you may have given less thought to ethics in public speaking. The National Communication Association Credo for Communication Ethics emphasizes the fundamental nature and far-reaching impact of ethical communication:

> Ethical communication is fundamental to responsible thinking, decision making, and the development of relationships and communities within and across contexts, cultures, channels, and media. Moreover, ethical communication enhances human worth and dignity by fostering truthfulness, fairness, responsibility, personal integrity, and respect for self and others.[2]

ethics
The beliefs, values, and moral principles by which people determine what is right or wrong

Ethical considerations should guide you during every step of the public-speaking process. As you determine the goal of your speech, outline your arguments, and select your supporting material, think about the beliefs, values, and moral principles of your audience, as well as your own. Ethical public speaking is inherently audience-centered, always taking into account the needs and rights of the listeners.

In our discussion of speaking freely and ethically, we will turn first to free speech, offering a brief history of both its protection and its restriction. Then we will discuss the ethical practice of free speech, providing guidelines to help you balance your right to free speech with your responsibilities as an audience-centered speaker. Within this framework, we will define and discuss plagiarism, one of the most troublesome violations of public-speaking ethics. And, finally, we will discuss the relationship between ethics and speaker credibility.

Speaking Freely

3.1 Explain how free speech has been challenged and defended throughout history.

After a heckler interrupted Barack Obama for the third time during a presidential speech, Obama calmly reminded the woman that the right to free speech required not only that he listen to her but also that she listen to him. "You should let me finish my sentence," Obama admonished.[3] Even during a moment of confrontation—a moment in which one might question the heckler's *ethics*—Obama defended the right of both parties to *free speech*. A brief history of free speech is summarized in Table 3.1, and we discuss it in more detail next.

Table 3.1   A Brief History of Free Speech

1791	First Amendment to the U.S. Constitution guarantees that "Congress shall make no law…abridging the freedom of speech"
1798	Sedition Act is passed (expired in 1801)
1919	Supreme Court suggests that speech presenting a "clear and present danger" may be restricted
1920	American Civil Liberties Union is formed
1940	Congress declares it illegal to urge the violent overthrow of the federal government
1964	Supreme Court restricts definition of slander; Berkeley Free Speech Movement is born
1989	Supreme Court defends the burning of the U.S. flag as a speech act
1997	Supreme Court strikes down the Communications Decency Act of 1996, in defense of free speech on the Internet
1998	Oprah Winfrey successfully defends her right to speak freely on television
2001	September 11 terrorist attacks spark passage of the Patriot Act and new debate over the balance between national security and free speech
2006	State of Montana pardons those convicted under the Montana Sedition Act of 1918
2011	During the Arab Spring, advocates for political and social change protest openly in northern African countries not historically considered bastions of free speech
2013	Using the "Like" button on Facebook is defined by a federal court as a speech act protected by the U.S. Constitution
2015	*Je suis Charlie* ("I am Charlie") becomes the rallying cry of supporters of free speech rights, following terrorist attacks at the Paris offices of the satirical magazine *Charlie Hebdo*

SOURCE: Copyrighted by Pearson Education, Hoboken, NJ.

Free Speech and the U.S. Constitution

First Amendment

The amendment to the U.S. Constitution guaranteeing free speech; the first of the ten amendments to the U.S. Constitution known collectively as the Bill of Rights

In 1791, the **First Amendment** to the U.S. Constitution was written to guarantee that "Congress shall make no law…abridging the freedom of speech." In the more than 200 years since then, entities as varied as state legislatures, colleges and universities, the American Civil Liberties Union, and the federal courts have sought to define through both law and public policy the phrase "freedom of speech."

Only a few years after the ratification of the First Amendment, Congress passed the Sedition Act, providing punishment for those who spoke out against the government. When both Thomas Jefferson and James Madison declared this act unconstitutional, however, it was allowed to lapse.

Free Speech in the Twentieth Century

During World War I, the U.S. Supreme Court ruled that it was lawful to restrict speech that presented "a clear and present danger" to the nation. This decision led to the founding, in 1920, of the American Civil Liberties Union, the first organization formed to protect free speech. In 1940, Congress declared it illegal to urge the violent overthrow of the federal government. However, even as they heard the hate speech employed by Hitler and the Nazis, U.S. courts and lawmakers argued that only by *protecting* free speech could the United States protect the rights of minorities and the disenfranchised. For most of the last half of the twentieth century, the Supreme Court continued to protect rather than to limit free speech, upholding it as "the core aspect of democracy."[4]

In 1964, the Supreme Court narrowed the definition of slander, false speech that harms someone. The Court ruled that before a public official can recover damages for slander, he or she must prove that the slanderous statement was made with "actual malice."[5] Another 1964 boost for free speech occurred not in the courts but on a university campus. In December of that year, more than 1,000 students at the University of California in Berkeley took over three floors of Sproul Hall to protest the recent arrest of outspoken student activists. The Berkeley Free Speech Movement that arose from the incident permanently changed the political climate of U.S. college campuses. Today, more than 50 years later, college campuses

Since the 1700s, court rulings and laws have been shaping our interpretation of the First Amendment. The amendment protects free speech, including the rights of protest speakers to speak out about controversial issues. *Photo:* Yana Paskova/Getty Images.

continue to support freedom of speech. In December 2015, professors at the University of Wisconsin voiced their commitment by declaring that "the clash of ideas constitutes the heart and soul of what a university is."[6]

Free speech gained protection in the last two decades of the twentieth century, when the Supreme Court found "virtually all attempts to restrain speech in advance…unconstitutional," regardless of how hateful or disgusting the speech may seem to some.[7] In 1989, the Supreme Court defended the burning of the U.S. flag as a **speech act** protected by the First Amendment. In 1997, the Court struck down the highly controversial federal Communications Decency Act of 1996, which had imposed penalties for creating, transmitting, or receiving obscene material on the Internet. The Court ruled that "the interest in encouraging freedom of expression in a democratic society outweighs any theoretical but unproven benefit of censorship."[8]

Perhaps no twentieth-century test of free speech received more publicity than the sensational 1998 lawsuit brought by four Texas cattlemen against popular talk-show host Oprah Winfrey. In a show on "mad cow disease," Winfrey had declared that she would never eat another hamburger. Charging that her statement caused cattle prices to plummet, the cattlemen sued for damages; however, Winfrey's attorneys successfully argued that the case was an important test of free speech. Emerging from the courtroom after the verdict in her favor, Winfrey shouted, "My reaction is that free speech not only lives, it rocks!"[9]

speech act

A behavior, such as flag burning, that is viewed by law as nonverbal communication and is subject to the same protections and limitations as verbal speech

Free Speech in the Twenty-First Century

No sooner had the new century begun than the right to free speech in the United States experienced one of its most historically significant challenges. One month after the September 11, 2001, terrorist attacks, the pendulum again swung toward restriction of free speech with the passage of the Patriot Act, which broadened the investigative powers of government agencies. But even as Americans debated the restrictions imposed by the Patriot Act, they recognized and offered restitution for historical infringement on free speech. In May 2006, Montana Governor Brian Schweitzer formally pardoned seventy-eight late citizens of Montana who had been imprisoned

Figure 3.1 Ten Draft Principles for Global Free Speech

SOURCE: Published on Free Speech Debate (www.freespeechdebate.com). These principles were drafted as part of an Oxford University research project led by Timothy Garton Ash and published on Free Speech Debate www.freespeechdebate.com where they can also be debated online.

1 We – all human beings – must be free and able to express ourselves, and to seek, receive and impart information and ideas, regardless of frontiers.	**6** We neither make threats of violence nor accept violent intimidation.
2 We defend the internet and all other forms of communication against illegitimate encroachments by both public and private powers.	**7** We respect the believer but not necessarily the content of the belief.
3 We require and create open, diverse media so we can make well-informed decisions and participate fully in political life.	**8** We are all entitled to a private life but should accept such scrutiny as is in the public interest.
4 We speak openly and with civility about all kinds of human difference.	**9** We should be able to counter slurs on our reputations without stifling legitimate debate.
5 We allow no taboos in the discussion and dissemination of knowledge.	**10** We must be free to challenge all limits to freedom of expression and information justified on such grounds as national security, public order, morality and the protection of intellectual property.

or fined under the Montana Sedition Act of 1918, convictions that "violated basic American rights of speech…"[10]

The debate over the definition and protection of speech acts has continued into the twenty-first century. In 2013, a U.S. federal court ruled that using the "Like" button on Facebook is a free speech act protected by the constitution.[11]

Free speech has also become an increasingly global issue. During the 2011 Arab Spring, advocates for political and social change protested openly in northern African countries, which have not historically been considered strongholds of free speech.

Once played out primarily in public gatherings or on radio or television, free speech acts and movements in the twenty-first century have gained visibility via social media and the Web. After terrorists attacked the Paris offices of the satirical magazine *Charlie Hebdo* in January of 2015, demonstrators adopted the slogan "*Je suis Charlie*" ("I am Charlie") to show support for the publication's exercise of free speech. The hashtag #jesuischarlie and a free smartphone app allowed hundreds of thousands of others to demonstrate solidarity through social media. In addition, *FreeSpeechDebate.com*, an international, multilingual Web site for the discussion of free speech, offers and invites discussion and debate about ten draft principles for global free speech (Figure 3.1). There can be little doubt that in the months and years to come, both the United States and the world will continue to debate the "unprecedented chances for free expression" that the digital age offers.[12]

Speaking Ethically

3.2 List and explain five criteria for ethical public speaking.

ethical speech

Speech that is responsible, honest, and tolerant

As the boundaries of free speech expand, the importance of **ethical speech** increases. Speaking at a 2015 commencement ceremony in Pennsylvania, writer Ian McEwan told the graduates of Dickinson College,

> …you may reasonably conclude that free speech is not simple. It's never an absolute. We don't give space to proselytising paedophiles, to racists (and remember, race is not identical to religion), or to those who wish to incite violence against others.[13]

And Mathieu Davy, a French lawyer specializing in media rights, likewise asserted that freedom of expression is not exclusive of ethical boundaries:

> I have the right to criticize an idea, a concept, or a religion. I have the right to criticize the powers in my country. But I don't have the right to attack people and to incite hate.[14]

In the discussion that follows, we offer suggestions for observing these and other ethical guidelines. Although there is no definitive ethical creed for public speaking, teachers and practitioners generally agree that an ethical speaker is one who has a clear, responsible goal; uses sound evidence and reasoning; is sensitive to and tolerant of differences; acts honestly; and avoids plagiarism.

Have a Clear, Responsible Goal

The goal of a public speech should be clear to the audience. For example, if you are trying to convince the audience that your beliefs about gay marriage are more correct than those of others, you should say so at some point in your speech. If you keep your true agenda hidden, you violate your listeners' rights.

In addition to being clear, an ethical goal should be socially responsible. A socially responsible goal conveys respect and offers the listener choices, whereas an irresponsible, unethical goal is demeaning or psychologically coercive or oppressive. Adolf Hitler's speeches, which incited the German people to hatred and genocide, were demeaning and coercive.

If your overall objective is to inform or persuade, it is probably ethical; if your goal is to demean, coerce, or manipulate, it is unethical. But lawyers and ethicists do not always agree on this distinction. As we have pointed out, although Congress and the Supreme Court have at times limited speech that incites sedition, violence, and riot, they have also protected free speech rights "for both the ideas that people cherish and the thoughts they hate."[15]

In a recent study of the relationship between people's perceptions of free speech and hate speech, researchers Daniel Downs and Gloria Cowan found that participants who considered freedom of speech to be more important considered hate speech to be less harmful.[16] The investigators reason that "Free-speech defenders may recognize the harm of hate speech but believe that freedom of speech is more essential than is censoring speech content."

Use Sound Evidence and Reasoning

Ethical speakers use critical thinking skills such as analysis and evaluation to formulate arguments and draw conclusions. Unethical speakers substitute false claims and emotional manipulation for evidence and logical arguments.

In the early 1950s, Wisconsin senator Joseph McCarthy incited national panic by charging that Communists were infiltrating every avenue of American life. Never able to substantiate his claims, McCarthy nevertheless succeeded in his witch hunt by exaggerating and distorting the truth. One United Press reporter noted, "The man just talked in circles. Everything was by inference, allusion, never a concrete statement of fact. Most of it didn't make sense."[17] Although today we recognize the flimsiness of McCarthy's accusations, in his time he wielded incredible power. It may sometimes be tempting to resort to false claims to gain power over others, but it is always unethical to do so.

Like Hitler, Senator Joseph McCarthy knew how to manipulate emotions and fears to produce the results he wanted. McCarthy's false accusations of Communism cast suspicion over thousands of people, causing many of them to lose their jobs or their entire careers. *Photo:* National Archives and Records Administration.

Some speakers bypass sound evidence and reasoning to make their conclusions more provocative. One contemporary rhetoric scholar offers this example of such short-circuited reasoning:

Let's say two people are observing who speaks in college classrooms and they come up with

1. Women are not as good at public speaking as men.

2. In college classes on coed campuses where most professors are male, women tend to talk less in class, compared to men.[18]

The first conclusion, based on insufficient evidence, reinforces sexist stereotypes with an inflammatory overgeneralization. The second, more qualified conclusion is more ethical.

One last, but important, requirement for the ethical use of evidence and reasoning is to share with an audience all information that might help them reach a sound decision, including information that may be potentially damaging to your case. Even if you proceed to refute the opposing evidence and arguments, you have fulfilled your ethical responsibility by presenting the perspective of the other side. And you make your own arguments more convincing by anticipating and answering counterarguments and opposing evidence.

Be Sensitive to and Tolerant of Differences

The filmmaker who ate nothing but McDonald's meals for his Oscar-nominated movie *Super Size Me* apologized for a profanity-laced, politically incorrect speech at a suburban Philadelphia school.

Among other things, Morgan Spurlock joked about the intelligence of McDonald's employees and teachers smoking pot while he was speaking at Hatboro-Horsham High School....

Spurlock, 35, told *The Philadelphia Inquirer* in a telephone interview that he "didn't think of the audience" and could have chosen his words better.[19]

As noted in Chapter 2, being audience-centered requires that you become as aware as possible of others' feelings, needs, interests, and backgrounds. Spurlock violated this ethical principle in his remarks.

Sometimes called **accommodation**, sensitivity to differences does not mean that speakers must abandon their own convictions for those of their audience members. It does mean that speakers should demonstrate a willingness to listen to opposing viewpoints and learn about different beliefs and values. Such willingness not only communicates respect; it can also help a speaker select a topic, formulate a purpose, and design strategies to motivate an audience. And it has broader implications as well. DePaul University Communication Professor Kathy Fitzpatrick notes,

Our success in public diplomacy will turn on our ability to speak in ways that recognize and appreciate how [our audiences] will interpret our messages.[20]

accommodation

Sensitivity to the feelings, needs, interests, and backgrounds of other people

CONSIDER THE AUDIENCE

A speaker who is sensitive to differences also avoids language that might be interpreted as being biased or offensive. It may seem fairly simple and a matter of common sense to avoid overtly abusive language, but it is not always easy to avoid language that discriminates more subtly. In Chapter 10, we look at unintentionally offensive words and phrases that ethical speakers should avoid.

Be Honest

President Bill Clinton's finger-wagging declaration in January 1998 that "I did not have sexual relations with that woman—Miss Lewinsky" was a serious breach of ethics that came back to haunt him. Many Americans were willing to forgive the inappropriate relationship; fewer could forgive the dishonesty.

A seeming exception to the directive to avoid false information is the use of hypothetical illustrations—illustrations that never actually occurred but that might happen. Many speakers rely on such illustrations to clarify or enhance their speeches. As long as a speaker makes it clear to the audience that the illustration is indeed hypothetical—for example, prefacing the illustration with a phrase such as "Imagine that..."—such use is ethical.

Honesty also requires that speakers give credit for ideas and information that are not their own. The *Publication Manual of the American Psychological Association* states that "authors do not present the work of another as if it were their own work. This can extend to ideas as well as written words."[21] Presenting the words and ideas of others without crediting them is called *plagiarism*. This ethical violation is both serious enough and widespread enough to warrant a separate discussion in this chapter.

Don't Plagiarize

Although some cultures may view unacknowledged borrowing from sources as a sign of respect and humility and an attempt to be audience-centered, in the United States and most other Western cultures, using the words, sentence structures, or ideas of another person without crediting the source is a serious breach of ethics. Yet even people who would never think of stealing money or shoplifting may feel justified in **plagiarizing**—stealing words and/or ideas. One student commencement speaker who plagiarized a speech by the writer Barbara Kingsolver explained his action as resulting from the "expectation to produce something amazing."[22]

plagiarizing
Presenting someone else's words or ideas as though they were one's own

UNDERSTAND WHAT CONSTITUTES PLAGIARISM Even if you've never plagiarized anything as public as a commencement address, perhaps you can remember copying a grade-school report directly from an online or printed encyclopedia, or maybe you've even purchased or "borrowed" a paper to submit for an assignment in high school or college. These are obvious forms of plagiarism.

Less obvious forms include **patchwriting**—lacing a speech with compelling phrases you find in a source; failing to give credit to a source or to provide adequate

patchwriting
Failing to give credit for phrases taken from another source

CONFIDENTLY CONNECTING WITH YOUR AUDIENCE

Remember That You Will Look More Confident Than You May Feel

As you listen to other people presenting speeches, you will note that most speakers don't appear to be nervous. They are not dishonestly trying to hide their apprehension; most people simply do not outwardly appear as nervous as they may feel. When you deliver your presentation, you may experience some apprehension, but it is ethical to keep such feelings to yourself. And unless you tell your audience that you're nervous, it's unlikely that they will notice it.

information in a citation; or relying too heavily on the vocabulary or sentence structure of a source.[23] Your college or university may have an honor code that further defines plagiarism.

Suppose your source says, "Based on historical data, it's clear that large areas of the West Coast are overdue for a massive earthquake." You would be plagiarizing if you changed only a word or two to say, "Based on historical data, it's clear that many parts of the West Coast are overdue for a huge earthquake." A better paraphrase would be, "For much of the West Coast, historical trends show that 'the big one' should have already hit."

UNDERSTAND THAT PLAGIARISM MAY HAVE SIGNIFICANT CONSEQUENCES   According to one source, 75 to 98 percent of college students admit to having cheated at least once.[24] At least one Web site claims to provide "non-plagiarized" custom term papers—ironic, because using any such paper is exactly what constitutes plagiarism![25] And communication researcher Todd Holm reports that more than half of the students he surveyed acknowledged cheating in some way in a public-speaking class.[26]

Despite the near-epidemic occurrence of plagiarism, most colleges impose stiff penalties on students who plagiarize. Plagiarists almost always fail the assignment in question, frequently fail the course, and are sometimes put on academic probation or even expelled. And the risk of being caught is much greater than you might suspect. Many colleges subscribe to a Web-based plagiarism detection company such as Turnitin; other professors routinely use free detection sites such as Grammarly or even Google.

A few years ago, one of your authors heard an excellent student speech on the importance of detecting cancer early. The only problem was that she heard the same speech again in the following class period! On finding the "speech"—actually a *Reader's Digest* article that was several years old—both students were certain that they had discovered a surefire shortcut to an A. Instead, they failed the assignment, ruined their course grades, and lost your author's trust.

Other consequences of plagiarism may include the loss of a degree, the end of a promising career, or sometimes even civil or criminal prosecution resulting in fines or jail time.[27] In 2006, a graduate student in Connecticut was ordered by the state appeals court to pay more than $26,000 in damages for plagiarizing another student's paper.[28] In 2013, Montana Senator John Walsh was stripped of his master's degree after it became public that he had plagiarized his final paper for the U.S. Army War College in 2007.[29]

DO YOUR OWN WORK   The most flagrant cases of plagiarism result from not doing your own work. For example, while you idly surf the Internet for ideas for a speech assignment, you may discover a Web page that could easily be made into a speech. However tempting it may be to use this material, and however certain you are that no audience member could possibly have seen it, resist any urge to plagiarize. Not only is the risk of being detected great, but also you will be shortchanging yourself in the long run if you do not learn how to develop a speech step by step.

Another way speakers may attempt to shortcut the speech preparation process is to ask another person to edit their speech so extensively that it becomes more that other person's work than their own. This is another form of plagiarism and another way of cheating themselves out of the skills they need to develop.

ACKNOWLEDGE YOUR SOURCES   Our admonition to do your own work in no way suggests that you should not research your speeches and then share your findings with audience members. In fact, an ethical speaker is responsible for doing just that. Furthermore, some information is so widely known that you do not have to acknowledge a source for it. For example, you need not credit a source if you say that a person must be infected with the HIV virus to develop AIDS or that the Treaty of Versailles was signed in 1919. This information is widely available in a variety of reference sources. However, if you decide to use any of the following in your speech, you must give credit to the source:

- Direct quotations, even if they are only brief phrases
- Opinions, assertions, or others' ideas, even if you paraphrase rather than quote them verbatim
- Statistics
- Any nonoriginal visual materials, including graphs, tables, and pictures

To be able to acknowledge your sources, you must first practice careful and systematic note-taking. Indicate with quotation marks any phrases or sentences that you photocopy, copy by hand, or electronically cut and paste verbatim from a source. Be sure to record the author, title, publisher or Web site, publication date, and page numbers for all sources from which you take quotations, ideas, statistics, or visual materials. Additional suggestions for systematic note-taking are offered in Chapter 7. In addition to keeping careful records of your sources, you must also know how to cite sources for your audience, both orally and in writing.

Oral Citations   Perhaps you have heard a speaker say "Quote" while holding up both hands and curving his index and middle fingers to indicate quotation marks. This is an artificial and distracting way to cite a source; an **oral citation** can be integrated more smoothly into a speech.

oral citation
The spoken presentation of source information, including the author, title, and year of publication

For example, you might want to use the approach illustrated in the following sample oral citation. The publication date and author of a source are usually included in an oral citation. In this sample, the speaker also mentions the type of resource (Web page) and its title ("Bed Bugs"). Follow your instructor's preferences for the level of detail you should include in your oral citations. Note that when you include an oral citation in a speech, indicate the beginning and end of the quoted passage by pausing briefly. The sample preparation outline in Chapter 10 gives additional examples of oral citations.

Written Citations   You can also provide a **written citation** for a source. In fact, your public-speaking instructor may ask you to submit a bibliography with the outline or other written materials required for each speech. Instructors who require a bibliography will usually specify the format they want for the citations; if they do not, you can use a style guide published by the Modern Language Association (MLA) or the American Psychological Association (APA), both of which are available online as

written citation
The print presentation of source information including the author, title, and year of publication, usually formatted according to a conventional style guide

SAMPLE ORAL CITATION

On a 2013 Web page titled "Bed Bug FAQs," the Centers for Disease Control and Prevention outlines three problems caused by bed bug infestations: "property loss, expense, and inconvenience."

- Provide the date.
- Specify the type of resource.
- Give the title.
- Provide the author or source.

- Pause briefly to signal that you are about to begin quoting.
- Quote the source.
- Pause again to indicate that you are ending the quoted passage.

credibility

An audience's perception of a speaker as competent, knowledgeable, dynamic, and trustworthy

well as in print format. Here is an example of a written citation in MLA format for the source quoted in the sample oral citation:

"Bed Bug FAQs." *Centers for Disease Control and Prevention,* 10 Jan. 2013, www.cdc.gov/parasites/bedbugs/faqs.html. Accessed 8 Jan. 2016.

Notice that the citation provides two dates: the date the material was posted online and the date the researcher accessed it. If you are unable to find the date the material was posted—or any other element of information—proceed directly to the next item in the citation. Additional information about citing sources and preparing a bibliography can be found in Chapter 7.

Perhaps now you are thinking, "What about those 'gray areas,' those times when I am not certain whether the information or ideas I am presenting are common knowledge?" A good rule is this: When in doubt, document. You will never be guilty of plagiarism if you document something you didn't need to, but you could be committing plagiarism if you do not document something you should have.

Speaking Credibly

3.3   Explain the relationship between ethics and credibility.

Credibility is a speaker's believability. A credible speaker is one whom an audience perceives to be competent, knowledgeable, dynamic, and trustworthy. The last of those four factors—trustworthiness—is dependent in large part on the speaker's known consistent adherence to ethical principles.

You trust people whom you believe to be ethical. In fact, the Greek rhetorician Aristotle used the term *ethos*—the root word of *ethic* and *ethical*—to refer to a speaker's credibility. Quintilian, a Roman teacher of public speaking, believed that an effective public speaker should also be a person of good character, a "good person speaking well."

We examine credibility in more detail in Chapter 5, where we discuss analyzing your audience's attitudes toward you; in Chapter 10, where we talk about establishing credibility in your speech introduction; and in Chapter 15, where we cover the role of credibility in persuading an audience. For now, keep in mind that speaking ethically is one key to being perceived by your audience as a credible speaker.

STUDY GUIDE: REVIEW, APPLY, AND ASSESS

Speaking Freely

3.1 Explain how free speech has been challenged and defended throughout history.

REVIEW: Although the U.S. Congress and courts have occasionally limited the constitutional right to free speech, more often they have protected and broadened its application. Freedom of speech has also been upheld by such organizations as the American Civil Liberties Union and by colleges and universities. Social media are a new context for twenty-first-century challenges to free speech.

Key Terms

free speech	First Amendment
ethics	speech act

APPLY: Social media sites such as Facebook, Twitter, and Instagram continue to review and revise their policies regarding the protection of free speech. Given these sites' widely diverse audiences that include international users, commercial users, and political dissidents, how can social media best develop audience-centered policies regarding free speech?

ASSESS: Why do you think the U.S. Supreme Court has historically considered flag burning and pornography to be "free speech acts"?

Speaking Ethically

3.2 List and explain five criteria for ethical public speaking.

REVIEW: Speakers who exercise their right to free speech are responsible for tempering what they say by applying ethics. An ethical public speaker should have a clear, responsible goal, use sound evidence and reasoning, be sensitive to and tolerant of differences, be honest, and take appropriate steps to avoid plagiarism. Practice accommodation, or sensitivity to differences, by listening to opposing viewpoints and learning about different beliefs and values. Do not use language that might be interpreted as biased or offensive. Avoid plagiarizing by understanding what it is, doing your own work, and acknowledging—orally, in writing, or both—the sources for any quotations, ideas, statistics, or visual materials.

Key Terms

ethical speech	patchwriting
accommodation	oral citation
plagiarizing	written citation

APPLY: From at least the time of Franklin Delano Roosevelt, speechwriters have written many of the best speeches made by U.S. presidents. Is such use of speechwriters ethical? Is it ethical to give credit to the presidents for memorable lines when their speeches were written by professional speechwriters?

ASSESS: The following passage comes from the book *Abraham Lincoln, Public Speaker*, by Waldo W. Braden:

> The Second Inaugural Address, sometimes called Lincoln's Sermon on the Mount, was a concise, tightly constructed composition that did not waste words on ceremonial niceties or superficial sentiment. The shortest Presidential inaugural address up to that time, it was only 700 words long, compared to 3,700 words for the First, and required from 5 to 7 minutes to deliver.[30]

Which of the following statements should be credited to Braden if you were to use them in a speech?

- "Lincoln's second inaugural address is sometimes called Lincoln's Sermon on the Mount."
- "Because he was elected and sworn in for two terms as president, Abraham Lincoln prepared and delivered two inaugural addresses."
- "Lincoln's second inaugural address was 700 words and 5 to 7 minutes long."

Speaking Credibly

3.3 Explain the relationship between ethics and credibility.

REVIEW: Speaking ethically allows your audience to trust you. Being trustworthy is an important part of being credible, or believable.

Key Term

credibility

APPLY: An important requirement for the ethical use of evidence and reasoning is to share with an audience all of the information that might help them reach a sound decision, even if it is potentially damaging to your case. Would you consider a speaker who shares such information more or less credible than one who does not?

ASSESS: As you listen to classmates' speeches, try to identify specific ways in which they try to gain your trust. In what ways were they successful? In what ways were they not?

Listening to Speeches

Learn how to listen and you will prosper—even from those who talk badly.

—Plutarch

Sir Joshua Reynolds (1723–1792), *Self-Portrait as a Deaf Man*, 1775, Tate, London/Art Resource, N.Y.

OBJECTIVES

After studying this chapter, you should be able to do the following:

4.1 List and describe five barriers to effective listening.

4.2 Identify and implement strategies for becoming a better listener.

4.3 Identify and implement strategies for improving your critical listening skills and critical thinking skills.

4.4 Use criteria to effectively and appropriately evaluate speeches.

Several years ago a psychology professor who dedicated his life to teaching and worked hard to prepare interesting lectures, found his students sitting through his talks with glassy-eyed expressions.[1] To find out what was on his students' minds instead of psychology, he would, without warning, fire a blank from a gun and then ask his students to record their thoughts at the instant they heard the shot. Here is what he found:

20 percent were pursuing erotic thoughts or sexual fantasies.
20 percent were reminiscing about something (they weren't sure what they were thinking about).
20 percent were worrying about something or thinking about lunch.
8 percent were pursuing religious thoughts.

20 percent were reportedly listening.

12 percent were able to recall what the professor was talking about when the gun fired.

Like this professor, you would probably prefer that more than 12 percent of your audience could recall your messages. Understanding how people listen can help you improve your ability to connect with your audience. If you understand what holds listeners' attention, as well as how to navigate around the barriers to effective listening, you can make your messages stick like Velcro rather than slip from your listeners' minds like Teflon.

Considerable evidence also suggests that your own listening skills could be improved.[2] Within 24 hours after listening to a lecture or speech, you will most likely recall only about 50 percent of the message. Forty-eight hours later, you are above average if you remember more than 25 percent of the message. Learning about listening can help you increase your listening skills so you can gain more benefits from the speeches you hear.

Although listening can be a challenge, it is among the most valued skills to possess. Research confirms that good listening skills can improve the quality of both your life and career.[3] Chances are, the people who become your best friends are also good listeners. Several surveys suggest that listening is highly valued by employers.[4] If you are like most students, you spend more than 80 percent of your day involved in communication-related activities.[5] As shown in Figure 4.1, you listen a lot; research suggests you spend more than half of your communication time listening.[6] Your challenge is to stay on course and be a good listener.

Listening is a complex process of selecting, attending to, understanding, remembering, and responding to verbal and nonverbal messages. Being able to describe these listening components can help you retain more and become a better speaker and listener.

- **Selecting.** To **select** a sound, the first stage of listening, is to single out a message from several competing messages. As a public speaker, your job is to develop a presentation that motivates your listeners to focus on your message.

- **Attending.** The sequel to selecting is attending. To **attend** to a sound is to focus on it.[7] One of your key challenges as a public speaker is to capture and then hold your audience's attention.

- **Understanding.** Boiled down to its essence, communication is the process of *understanding*, or making sense of our experiences and sharing that sense with others.[8] We **understand** something when we create meaning out of what we experience. The challenge of being understood comes back to a focus on the audience.

- **Remembering.** The next stage in the listening process is *remembering*. To **remember** is to recall ideas and information. You hear more than one billion words each year, but how much information do you retain? It depends on how well you listen.

- **Responding.** The final stage in the listening process is to **respond**. When listeners respond, they react to what they have heard with their behavior. For example, it could be that you want them simply to remember and restate your key ideas. Or you may want them to vote for someone, buy something, or enroll in a course. That's why it's useful for public speakers to develop specific behavioral goals for their talks.

In this chapter we discuss how people listen, and we identify barriers and pitfalls that keep both speakers and audiences from listening effectively. Our goal is not only to help you remember what speakers say but also to be a more thoughtful, ethical, and critical listener to the messages you hear. We'll offer tips to improve your ability to analyze and evaluate speeches, including your own.

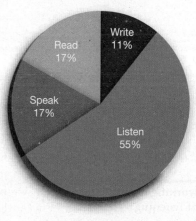

Figure 4.1 You listen a lot: A typical student spends about 11 percent of his or her communication time writing, 17 percent reading, 17 percent speaking, and at least 55 percent listening.

Copyrighted by Pearson Education, Hoboken, NJ.

listening
The process by which receivers select, attend to, understand, remember, and respond to senders' messages

select
To single out a message from several competing messages

attend
To focus on incoming information for further processing

understand
To assign meaning to the information to which you attend

remembering
Recalling ideas and information

responding
Reacting with a change in behavior to a speaker's message

Overcoming Barriers to Effective Listening

4.1 List and describe five barriers to effective listening.

Barriers are created when the listener doesn't select, attend, understand, remember, or respond to the message as planned by the speaker. The more you know about potential obstacles that keep your listeners from responding to your message the way you intend, the better able you will be to develop messages that hold their interest. We discuss those barriers next and how to deal with them.

Listener Fatigue

We spend a large part of each day listening. That's both good news and bad news. The good news is that because we listen a lot, we have the potential to become effective listeners. The bad news is that instead of getting better at it, we often tune out because we hear so much information that we get tired of listening and reduce our concentration on the message. Listening researchers have developed what they call the **working memory theory of listening**, which explains why we sometimes just don't listen well. The theory suggests that when a listener's capacity is reached (when our working memory is full), then it's harder to concentrate and remember what we hear.[9] Although this theory suggests that there's nothing you can do as either a speaker or a listener to manage this problem, listeners and speakers can actually use several strategies to overcome the limits of working memory.

WHAT YOU CAN DO AS A SPEAKER You can keep your audience from tuning out by making sure your speech has a balance between new information and supporting material such as stories and examples. A speech that is too dense—chock-full of facts, new definitions, and undeveloped ideas—can make listening a tiring, tedious process. On the other hand, people don't want to listen to a bare-bones outline of ideas; they need ideas that are fleshed out with illustrations. Pace the flow of new ideas and information. Communication expert Frank E. X. Dance recommends a 30:70 ratio: 30 percent of your speaking time should be spent presenting new ideas and information, and 70 percent of your time should be spent supporting your ideas with vivid examples and interesting stories.[10]

Another way to combat information overload as a speaker is to build redundancy into your message. If listeners miss the idea the first time you present it, perhaps they will catch it during your concluding summary. Repeating key ideas can be part of the 70 percent of your message that supports the new information you present.

WHAT YOU CAN DO AS A LISTENER If you find yourself tuning a speaker out because you're just tired of listening to someone talk, make a special effort to concentrate on the information you're hearing. The key to being a good listener is to recognize when you're not being a good listener and then to adjust how you are listening. Perk up your listening power by making sure that you are looking at the speaker, sitting up straight, and remaining focused on the message.

Personal Concerns

You are sitting in your African history class on a Friday afternoon. It's a beautiful day. You slump into your seat, open your notebook, and prepare to take notes on the lecture. As the professor talks about an upcoming assignment, you begin to think about how you are going to spend your Saturday. One thought leads to another as you mentally plan your weekend. Suddenly you hear your professor say, "For Monday's

working memory theory of listening
A theory that suggests that listeners find it difficult to concentrate and remember when their short-term working memories are full

test, you will be expected to know the principles I've just reviewed." What principles? What test? You were present in class, and you did *hear* the professor's lecture, but you're not sure what was said.

Your own thoughts are among the biggest competitors for your attention when you are a member of an audience. Most of us would rather listen to our own inner speech than to a public speaker's message. As the psychology professor with the gun found, sex, lunch, worries, and daydreams are distractions for the majority of listeners.

WHAT YOU CAN DO AS A SPEAKER To counteract the problem of listeners' focusing on their personal concerns instead of your message, consciously work to maintain your audience's attention by using occasional wake-up messages such as "Now listen carefully because this will affect your future grade (or family, or employment)." Delivering your message effectively by using good eye contact, speaking with appropriate volume and vocal variation, and using appropriate gestures for emphasis can also help keep listeners engaged.

WHAT YOU CAN DO AS A LISTENER To stay focused, it's important that you stop the mental conversation you're having with yourself about ideas unrelated to the speaker's message. Be aware of thoughts, worries, and daydreams that are competing for your attention. Then, once you are aware that you are off-task, return your attention to what the speaker is saying.

Outside Distractions

While sitting in class, you notice the person in front of you checking Facebook on her tablet computer. Two classmates behind you are discussing their favorite *Game of Thrones* episodes. You feel your phone vibrate in your pocket, which means someone just sent you a text. Looking out the window you see a varsity football hero struggling to break into his car to retrieve the keys he left in the ignition. As your history professor drones on about the Bay of Pigs invasion, you find it difficult to focus on his lecture. Most of us don't listen well when physical distractions compete with the speaker. And, with lives immersed in technology, the next distraction is only a text, phone call, or tweet away. Research has found that merely the visible presence of a smartphone can be a communication distraction and reduce our listening effectiveness.[11] We can't resist checking to see if someone wants to communicate with us.

WHAT YOU CAN DO AS A SPEAKER To minimize distractions, be aware of anything that might sidetrack your listeners' attention. For example, look at the way the chairs in the room are arranged. Do they allow listeners a clear view of you and any presentation aids you might use? Is there distracting or irrelevant information written on a chalkboard or whiteboard? Try to empathize with listeners by imagining what they will be looking at when you speak. Check out the room ahead of time, sit where your audience will be seated, and look for possible distractions. Then reduce or eliminate distractions (such as by closing windows or lowering shades to limit visual and auditory distractions or turning off blinking fluorescent lights, if you can). Also, tactfully discourage whispering in the audience.

WHAT YOU CAN DO AS A LISTENER When listening, you too can help manage the speaking and listening environment by being on the lookout for distractions or potential distractions. If you must, move

Personal concerns and distractions such as texts are challenges to effective listening for many students. You can, however, make yourself a better listener by learning to overcome these and other barriers. *Photo:* Monkey Business/Fotolia.

dialect, move closer so you can see the speaker's mouth. A good view can increase your level of attention and improve your understanding.

To increase your skill in accurately interpreting nonverbal messages, consider the following suggestions:

- *Consider nonverbal cues in context.* When interpreting an unspoken message, don't just focus on one nonverbal cue; consider the situation you and the speaker are in.

- *Look for clusters of cues.* Instead of focusing on just one bit of behavior, look for several nonverbal cues to increase the accuracy of your interpretation of a speaker's message.

- *Look for cues that communicate liking, power, and responsiveness.* A nonverbal cue (eye contact, facial expression, body orientation) can often express whether someone likes us. We note people's degree of power or influence over us by the way they dress, how much space they have around them, or whether they are relaxed or tense. People who perceive themselves as having more power than those around them are usually more relaxed. Or we can observe whether someone is interested or focused on us by his or her use of eye contact, head nods, facial expressions, and tone of voice.

ADAPT TO THE SPEAKER'S DELIVERY   Good listeners focus on a speaker's message, not on his or her delivery style. To be a good listener, you must adapt to the particular idiosyncrasies some speakers have. You may have to ignore or overlook a speaker's tendency to mumble, speak in a monotone, or fail to make eye contact. Perhaps more difficult still, you may even have to forgive a speaker's lack of clarity or coherence. Rather than mentally criticizing an unpolished speaker, you may need to be sympathetic and try harder to concentrate on the message. Good listeners focus on the message, not the messenger.

Poor speakers are not the only challenge to good listening. You also need to guard against glib, well-polished speakers. An attractive style of delivery does not necessarily mean that a speaker's message is credible. Don't let a smooth-talking salesperson convince you to buy something without carefully considering the content of his or her message.

> **RECAP**
>
> **LISTEN WITH YOUR EYES AS WELL AS YOUR EARS**
>
> Accurately interpret nonverbal messages:
> - Consider context.
> - Look for clusters.
> - Look for cues of liking.
> - Adapt your listening to the speaker's delivery.

Listen Mindfully

Mindful listeners are mentally focused on the listening task. Two listening researchers found that good listeners do the following:[15]

- Put their own thoughts aside
- Are present mentally as well as physically
- Make a conscious, mindful effort to listen
- Invest time in listening, patiently letting the speaker make his or her point
- Are open-minded

Bad listeners do just the opposite; they are distracted by their own thoughts, are mentally absent, are impatient, and are less open to what they hear. To be a mindful listener is to be aware of what you are doing when listening to others. How do you do that? Here are specific strategies to help you be a mindful listener.

BE AWARE OF WHETHER YOU ARE LISTENING   Listening boils down to this: You are either on-task or off-task. If you are not either selecting or attending to a message, then you are not mentally engaged with what you are hearing. What's vital, yet simple, is that you be *aware* of whether you are on- or off-task when listening to someone. Unmindful listeners are not conscious of whether they are paying attention or daydreaming. As you listen, occasionally take a moment to think about your own thoughts. Pretend you are in that class when the professor fires the gun. At the moment, are you thinking about the message, or have you allowed your thoughts to stray off-task?

If you become aware that you're not listening, research has found that you can increase your motivation to stay on-task by reminding yourself why listening is important.[16] Periodically engage in "self-talk" to tell yourself why the message you're hearing can be helpful or useful to you.

Monitor Your Emotional Reaction to a Message Heightened emotions can affect your ability to understand a message. If you become angry at a word or phrase a speaker uses, your listening comprehension decreases. Depending on their cultural backgrounds, religious convictions, and political views, listeners may become emotionally aroused by certain words. For most listeners, words that connote negative opinions about their ethnic origin, nationality, or religious views can trigger strong emotions. Cursing and obscene language are red flags for other listeners.

How can you keep your emotions in check when you hear something that sets you off? First, recognize when your emotional state is affecting your rational thought. Second, use self-talk to calm yourself down. Say to yourself, "I'm not going to let this anger get in the way of listening and understanding." Finally, focus for a moment on your breathing to calm down.

Good listeners are mentally fully present and invest effort in listening rather than allowing themselves to be distracted. *Photo:* Kzenon/Fotolia.

Be a Selfish Listener Although it may sound crass, being a selfish listener can help you maintain your powers of concentration. If you find your attention waning, ask yourself questions such as "What's in it for me?" and "How can I use information from this talk?" Granted, you will find more useful information in some presentations than in others—but be alert to the possibility in all speeches. Find ways to benefit from the information you are receiving, and try to connect it with your own experiences and needs.

Listen Skillfully

Besides being aware of nonverbal messages and being mindful listeners, good listeners exercise several skills that help them stay focused and remember what they've heard. They identify their listening goal, listen for major ideas, practice good listening methods, adapt their listening style as necessary, and are active listeners.

Listen for Major Ideas In a classic study, both good and poor listeners were asked what their listening strategies were.[17] The poor listeners indicated that they listened for facts, such as names and dates. The good listeners reported that they listened for major ideas and principles. Facts are useful only when you can connect them to a principle or concept. In speeches, facts as well as examples are used primarily to support major ideas. As you listen, try to mentally summarize the major ideas that the specific facts support.

If you heard President Barack Obama deliver his Second Inaugural Address in Washington, D.C., on the sunny morning of January 22, 2013, you heard him introduce his key idea about two minutes into his speech by repeating these three words: "We the people...." A good listener would recognize that these words reveal a core idea of the speech—that it takes a collaborative effort to do good things.

How can you tell what the major ideas in a speech are? A speaker who is well organized or familiar with good speaking techniques will offer a preview of the major ideas early in the speech. If no preview is provided, listen for the speaker

---

RECAP

LISTEN MINDFULLY

- Be aware of whether you are listening or not.
- Monitor and control your emotional reactions.
- Be a selfish listener.

to enumerate major points: "My first point is that the history of Jackson County is evident in its various styles of architecture." Transitional phrases and a speaker's internal summaries are other clues that can help you identify the major points. If your speaker provides few overt indicators, you may have to discover them on your own. In that event, mentally summarize the ideas that are most useful to you. Be a selfish listener: Treat a disorganized speech as a river with gold in its sands, and take your mental mining pan and search for the nuggets of meaning.

PRACTICE LISTENING   Because you spend at least 55 percent of your day listening, you may wonder why we suggest that you practice listening. The reason is that listening skills do not develop automatically. You learn to swim by getting proper instruction; you're unlikely to develop good aquatic skills just by jumping in the water and flailing around. Similarly, you will learn to listen more effectively by practicing the methods we recommend. Researchers believe that poor listeners avoid challenges. For example, they listen to and watch TV situation comedies rather than documentaries or other informative programs. Your listening skill develops as you mindfully listen to speeches, music, and programs with demanding content.

UNDERSTAND YOUR LISTENING STYLE   New research suggests that not everyone listens to information in the same way. There are at least four different **listening styles**—preferred ways of making sense out of spoken messages. Listening researchers have discovered that many listeners have one of the following listening styles: relational, analytical, critical, or task-oriented.[18] Understanding your listening style can help you become a better and more flexible listener.[19] About 40 percent of listeners have one primary listening style; another 40 percent use more than one style; and about 20 percent don't have a listening style preference. As you read the descriptions of the four listening styles, see if you can determine which of these segments of the listening population you belong to.[20] There is evidence that you adapt your style to fit your listening goal.[21] The best listeners are flexible listeners who can adapt their style to fit the occasion and the person speaking.[22]

Relational-Oriented Listeners   If you are comfortable listening to people express feelings and emotions, most likely you are a **relational-oriented listener**. This type of listener is highly empathic and attempts to seek common ground with the person he or she is listening to. Relational-oriented listeners are also easily moved by poignant illustrations and anecdotes. They enjoy hearing stories about people and personal relationships. When speaking with others in interpersonal and group situations, they are generally less apprehensive than other types of listeners.[23]

Task-Oriented Listeners   Task-oriented listeners want to know what to do with the information they hear. They listen for the verbs—the action words that indicate what task should be completed after listening to the information. The **task-oriented listener** wants people to get to the point and listens for actions that need to be taken. To a task-oriented listener, a long story or a lengthy personal example without some direction is less satisfying than a call for action. Task-oriented listeners also seem to be more skeptical than people with other listening styles. They prefer to be given evidence to support the recommendations for action.

Analytical Listeners   Analytical listeners prefer to listen to complex information laced with facts and details. They often withhold judgment before reaching a specific conclusion. You're an **analytical listener** if you reject messages because they don't have adequate evidence to support their conclusions. In addition, analytical listeners don't like rambling stories that don't seem to have a point; they want to know what the key facts are rather than listen to a long narrative. Analytical listeners make good judges or lawyers because they enjoy listening to debates and hearing arguments for and against ideas.[24]

Critical Listeners   You're a **critical listener** if you spend time evaluating the messages you hear. Critical listeners are comfortable listening to detailed, complex information

listening styles
Preferred ways of making sense out of spoken messages

relational-oriented listener
Someone who is comfortable listening to others express feelings and emotions

task-oriented listener
Someone who prefers information that is well organized, brief, and precise

analytical listener
Someone who prefers messages that are supported with facts and details

yet can focus on contradictions and inconsistencies in the information presented. Critical listeners are also likely to catch errors in the overall reasoning and evidence that are used to reach a conclusion.

critical listener
Someone who prefers to evaluate messages

Knowing your listening style can help you better adapt to a speaker whose style is different from your own. The best listeners adapt their style to fit the situation and the listening goal.[25]

BECOME AN ACTIVE LISTENER   An active listener is one who remains alert and mentally re-sorts, rephrases, and repeats key information while listening to a speech. Because you can listen to words much faster than a speaker can say them, it's natural for your mind to wander. But you can use the extra time to focus on interpreting what the speaker says.

1. **Re-sort.**   Use your listening time to re-sort disorganized or disjointed ideas.[26] If a speaker is rambling, seek ways to rearrange his or her ideas into a new, more logical pattern. For example, re-sort ideas into a chronological pattern: What happened first, second, and so on? If the speaker hasn't used a logical framework, see if you can find a structure to help you reorganize the information. When a speaker isn't organized, you'll benefit if you can turn a jumbled mass of information into a structure that makes sense to you.

2. **Rephrase.**   Mentally summarize the key points or information you want to remember. Listen for the main ideas and then paraphrase them in your own words. You are more likely to remember your mental paraphrase of the information than the exact words of the speaker. If you can, try to summarize what the speaker says into a phrase that could fit on a bumper sticker. Listening for "information handles" in the form of previews, transitions, signposts, and summary statements can also help you remain actively involved as a listener.

3. **Repeat.**   Finally, do more than just rephrase the information as you listen to it. Periodically *repeat* key points you want to remember. Go back to essential ideas and restate them to yourself every five minutes or so. If you follow these steps for active listening, you will find yourself feeling stimulated and engaged instead of tired and bored as you listen to even the dullest of speakers.

RECAP

LISTENING STYLES

Relational-oriented listening	Listeners prefer to attend to feelings and emotions and to search for common areas of interest when listening to others.
Task-oriented listening	Listeners are focused on accomplishing something; they like efficient, clear, and brief messages. They listen for verbs to determine what action needs to be taken.
Analytical listening	Listeners prefer to withhold judgment, listen to all sides of an issue, and wait until they hear the facts before reaching a conclusion.
Critical listening	Listeners are likely to listen for the facts and evidence to support key ideas and an underlying logic; they also listen for errors, inconsistencies, and discrepancies.

RECAP

ACTIVE LISTENING

Steps	Definition	Example
Re-sort	Reorganize jumbled or disorganized information.	What the speaker said: "There are several key dates to remember in America's history: 1776, 1492, 1861." You re-sort: 1492, 1776, 1861
Rephrase	Paraphrase to simplify the speaker's ideas rather than trying to remember his or her exact words.	What the speaker said: "If we don't stop the destructive overspending of the defense budget, our nation will very quickly find itself much deeper in debt and unable to meet the many needs of its citizens." You rephrase: "We should spend less on defense, or we will have more problems."
Repeat	Periodically, mentally restate the key ideas you want to remember.	Repeat key points to yourself every five minutes or so as you listen to the speech.

Listen Ethically

An effective listener does more than just gain an accurate understanding of a speaker's message; effective listeners are also ethical listeners. When participating in a communication event, an ethical listener honestly communicates his or her expectations, provides helpful feedback, and expresses sensitivity to and tolerance for differences when listening to others. In the fourth century B.C.E., Aristotle warned, "Let men be on their guard against those who flatter and mislead the multitude." And contemporary rhetorician Harold Barrett has said that the audience is the "necessary source of correction" for the behavior of a speaker.[27] The following guidelines for ethical listening incorporate what Barrett calls "attributes of the good audience."

COMMUNICATE YOUR EXPECTATIONS AND FEEDBACK   As an audience member, you have the right—even the responsibility—to enter a communication situation with expectations about the message and how the speaker will deliver it. Know what information and ideas you want to get out of the communication transaction. Expect a coherent, organized, and competently delivered presentation. Communicate your objectives and react to the speaker's message and delivery with appropriate nonverbal and verbal feedback. There is evidence that by being a supportive listener (by maintaining eye contact with the speaker, nodding in agreement, and being attentive) you help the speaker feel more comfortable and less nervous.[28] We are not suggesting, however, that you fake your support for a speaker. If you show, with an honest quizzical look, that you do not understand a speaker's point, you can help an attentive, audience-centered speaker recognize that he or she needs to rephrase the message for better listener comprehension.

BE SENSITIVE TO AND TOLERANT OF DIFFERENCES   As an ethical listener, remember that your preferred approach to speaking and listening may differ from the speaker's. But your preference doesn't make the speaker's approach a wrong one. For example, suppose you attended a high school baccalaureate ceremony where the speaker was a dynamic African American minister who used a duet-style, call-and-response type of speaking, in which the audience periodically responds verbally. If you were to disregard the minister's delivery for being too flamboyant, you might miss out on a powerful message. Different cultures have different styles of speaking.

To summarize, be an attentive and courteous listener. Consider cultural norms and audience expectations as part of the context within which you listen to and evaluate a speaker. Making an effort to understand the needs, goals, and interests of both the speaker and other audience members can help you judge how to react appropriately and ethically. Table 4.1 summarizes the better listening skills we have discussed.

> **RECAP**
>
> **LISTEN ETHICALLY**
>
> - Communicate your expectations and feedback.
> - Be sensitive to and tolerant of cultural and individual differences.

Improving Critical Listening and Thinking Skills

4.3 Identify and implement strategies for improving your critical listening skills and critical thinking skills.

critical listening

Evaluating the quality of information, ideas, and arguments presented by a speaker

Critical listening is the process of listening to evaluate the quality, appropriateness, value, or importance of the information you hear. When listening critically, you sort good information from inaccurate information or pinpoint unethical communication strategies. Related to being a critical listener is being a critical thinker.

critical thinking

Making judgments about the conclusions presented in what you see, hear, and read

Critical thinking is the process of making judgments about the conclusions presented in what you see, hear, and read. The goal of a critical listener and thinker is to evaluate information to make an informed choice. Whether you are listening to a political candidate seeking your vote, a radio announcer extolling the virtues of a

Table 4.1 How to Enhance Your Listening Skills

	The Good Listener ...	The Poor Listener ...
Listen with Your Eyes as Well as Your Ears	• Looks for nonverbal cues to enhance understanding • Adapts to the speaker's delivery	• Focuses only on the words • Is easily distracted by the delivery of the speech
Listen Mindfully	• Is aware of whether or not he or she is listening • Controls emotions • Mentally asks himself or herself, "What's in it for me?"	• Is not aware of whether he or she is on-task or off-task • Erupts emotionally when listening • Does not attempt to relate to the information personally
Listen Skillfully	• Identifies the listening goal • Listens for major ideas • Seeks opportunities to practice listening skills • Understands and adapts his or her listening style to the speaker • Listens actively by re-sorting, rephrasing, and repeating what is heard	• Does not have a listening goal in mind • Listens for isolated facts • Avoids listening to difficult information • Is not aware of how to capitalize on his or her listening style • Listens passively, making no effort to engage with the information heard
Listen Ethically	• Clearly communicates listening expectations • Is sensitive to and tolerant of differences	• Makes no effort to respond appropriately to a speaker's message • Expects others to have the same beliefs, values, and cultural expectations he or she has

Copyrighted by Pearson Education, Hoboken, NJ.

new herbal weight-loss pill, or someone asking you to invest in a new technology company, your goal as a critical listener and thinker is to assess the quality of the information and the validity of the conclusions presented.

Being a critical listener does not mean you're only focused on identifying what's wrong in a speech; we're not suggesting that you listen to a speaker just to pounce on the message and the messenger at the speech's conclusion. Instead, listen to identify what the speaker does effectively as well as what conclusions don't hold up. The educator John Dewey penned a lasting description of criticism:

> Criticism...is not fault-finding. It is not pointing out evils to be reformed. It is judgment engaged in discriminating among values. It is talking through as to what is better and worse...with some consciousness of why the worse is worse.[29]

How does a critical listener do all of this? Consider the following skills.

Separate Facts from Inferences

The ability to separate facts from inferences is a basic critical thinking and listening skill. **Facts** are information that has been proven to be true by direct observation. For example, it has been directly observed that water boils at 212 degrees Fahrenheit and that the direction of the magnetic north pole can be found by consulting a compass. An **inference** is a conclusion based on partial information or an evaluation that has not been directly observed. You infer that your favorite sports team will win the championship or that it will rain tomorrow. You can also infer that if more Republicans than Democrats are elected to Congress, the next president might be a Republican. But you can only know this for a *fact* after the presidential election. Facts are in the realm of certainty; inferences are in the realm of probability and opinion—where most arguments advanced by public speakers reside. A critical listener knows that when a politician running for office claims, "It's a fact that my opponent is not qualified to be elected," this statement is *not* a fact but an inference.

facts

Information that has been proven to be true by direct observation

inference

A conclusion based on partial information or an evaluation that has not been directly observed

Critical listeners must pay close attention and keep an open mind to separate facts from inferences and to evaluate the quality of evidence, logic, reasoning, and the use of rhetorical strategies. *Photo:* Rob/Fotolia.

evidence

The facts, examples, opinions, and statistics that a speaker uses to support a conclusion

Evaluate the Quality of Evidence

Evidence consists of the facts, examples, opinions, and statistics that a speaker uses to support a conclusion. Researchers have documented that the key element in swaying a jury is the quality and quantity of the evidence presented to support a case.[30] Without credible supporting evidence, it would not be wise to agree with a speaker's conclusion.

What should you listen for when trying to decide whether evidence is credible? First, determine whether a stated fact is actually a fact. Has it been verified based on direct observation? If a speaker uses an example, is it representative or atypical? Are enough examples provided to reach a reasonable conclusion? Another form of evidence is an opinion. Simply stated, an opinion is a quoted comment from someone. The best opinions come from reliable, expert, credible sources. Another kind of evidence often used, especially with skeptical listeners, is statistics. A statistic is a number that summarizes a collection of examples. Many of the same questions that should be asked about other forms of evidence should also be asked about statistics: Are the statistics reliable, unbiased, recent, representative, and valid?

Here we've introduced you to the importance of *listening for* good evidence. Because evidence is an important element of public speaking we'll provide more information about how to *use* evidence when we discuss gathering supporting material in Chapter 7 and using evidence to persuade in Chapter 15. We will also discuss how evidence can be used to develop reasonable and logical conclusions.

You might reasonably suspect that a primary goal of a public-speaking class would be to enhance your speaking skill, and you'd be right. But in addition to becoming a better speaker, a study of communication principles and skills should help you to become a better *consumer* of messages. Becoming a critical listener and thinker is an important benefit of learning how messages are constructed. Researchers have found that a student who has completed any communication course—debate, argumentation, or public speaking—is likely to show improved critical thinking ability. This introduction to critical listening and thinking skills is reinforced throughout the rest of the text by discussions on how to become an audience-centered public speaker.

> ### RECAP
>
> ## IMPROVING LISTENING AND CRITICAL THINKING SKILLS
>
> **Separate facts from inferences**
> - Are the facts really facts—something that has been proven to occur or exist?
> - Is the conclusion an inference—something that is based on partial or unobserved evidence?
>
> **Evaluate evidence**
> - Facts: Are the facts from credible sources?
> - Examples: Are there enough examples to prove the point?
> - Opinions: Are the opinions from knowledgeable experts?
> - Statistics: Is the source of the statistic reliable and unbiased?
> - Is there enough evidence to support the conclusion?

Analyzing and Evaluating Speeches

4.4 Use criteria to effectively and appropriately evaluate speeches

Your critical thinking and listening skills will help you evaluate not only the speeches of others but your own speeches as well. When you evaluate something, you judge its worth and appropriateness. When making a judgment about the value of something, it's important to use relevant criteria. **Rhetorical criticism** is the process of using a method or standards to evaluate the effectiveness and appropriateness of messages.

rhetorical criticism

The process of using a method or standards to evaluate the effectiveness and appropriateness of messages

To better understand the concept of rhetorical criticism, it's important to understand the meaning of the words *rhetoric* and *criticism*. The term *rhetoric* is both classical and contemporary.[31] The ancient Greek scholar Aristotle defined rhetoric as the faculty of discovering in any given case the available means of persuasion.[32] A more contemporary rhetorical scholar, Kenneth Burke, said that rhetoric is a "symbolic means of inducing cooperation."[33] In summary, **rhetoric** is the process of using symbols to create meaning to achieve a goal. As a public speaker, you are a rhetorician in that you're

rhetoric

The use of symbols to create meaning to achieve a goal

using **symbols**—words, images, nonverbal cues—to create meaning in the minds of your listeners to achieve a goal (to inform, to persuade, to entertain). To be a rhetorical critic is to evaluate the effectiveness and appropriateness of the message and the delivery of a presentation as well as to *illuminate* or make better sense of the message.[34]

Rhetorician Robert Rowland offers a simple but comprehensive framework for analyzing and evaluating rhetorical messages: Be conscious of the goal of the message, its organization, the speaker's role, the overall tone of the message, the intended audience, and the techniques the speaker uses to achieve the goal.[35] Whether it's a speaker in your public-speaking class, the president delivering a State of the Union address, a member of the clergy delivering a sermon, or a parent addressing the school board, each speaker uses rhetorical strategies to achieve a goal. The more clearly you can identify and analyze the speaker's methods, the more effectively you can assess whether the message and the messenger are worthy of your support—and you become a more discerning rhetorical critic.[36]

Giving Feedback to Others

As you enhance your ability to effectively listen to messages and identify rhetorical strategies, you may be asked to evaluate other people's speeches and provide feedback. The speech evaluation questions in Figure 4.2 can serve you well as you evaluate others' messages. Your instructor may also provide you with a speech evaluation form to help you focus on the essential elements of public speechmaking.

When you're invited to critique your classmates, your feedback will be more effective if you keep the following general principles in mind. Because the word *criticism* means "to judge or discuss," to criticize a speech is to discuss the speech—identifying both its strengths and those aspects that could be improved. Effective criticism stems from developing a genuine interest in the speaker, not from seeking to find fault.

1. **Be Descriptive.** In a neutral way, describe what you saw the speaker doing. Act as a mirror for the speaker to help him or her identify gestures and other non-verbal signals of which he or she may not be aware. (If you and the speaker are watching a videotape of the speech together, you can point out these behaviors.) Avoid providing only a list of your likes and dislikes; describe what you observe.

   Effective: Stan, I noticed that about 50 percent of the time you maintained
                       direct eye contact with your listeners.
   Less Effective: Your eye contact was lousy.

2. **Be Specific.** When you describe what you see a speaker doing, be precise enough so the speaker has a clear image of your perceptions. Saying that a speaker had "poor delivery" doesn't give him or her much information—it's only a general evaluative comment. Be as specific and thoughtful as you can.

   Effective: Dawn, the use of color in your PowerPoint slides helped to
                       keep my attention.
   Less Effective: I liked your visuals.

3. **Be Positive.** Begin and end your feedback with positive comments. Beginning with a negative comment immediately puts the speaker on the defensive and can create so much internal noise that he or she stops listening. Starting and ending with positive comments engenders less defensiveness. Some teachers call this approach the feedback sandwich. First, tell the speaker something he or she did well. Then share a suggestion or two that may help the speaker improve the presentation. End your evaluation with another positive comment or restate what you liked best about the presentation.

symbols
Words, images, and behaviors that create meaning

Figure 4.2 Audience-Centered Speaking Evaluation Questions

Audience Orientation
☐ Did the speaker make a specific effort to adapt to the audience?

Select and Narrow Topic
☐ Was the topic appropriate for the audience, the occasion, and the speaker?
☐ Was the speech narrowed to fit the time limits?

Determine Purpose
☐ Was the general purpose (to inform, to persuade, to entertain) clear?
☐ Was the specific purpose appropriate for the audience?

Develop Central Idea
☐ Was the central idea clear enough to be summarized in one sentence?

Generate Main Ideas
☐ Were the main ideas clearly identified in the introduction of the speech, developed in the body of the speech, and summarized in the conclusion of the speech?

Gather Supporting Material
☐ Did the speaker use varied and interesting supporting material?
☐ Did the speaker use effective and appropriate evidence to support conclusions?
☐ Did the speaker use credible supporting material?

Organize Speech
☐ Did the speech have a clear introduction that caught your attention, provided a preview of the speech, and established the speaker's credibility?
☐ Did the speaker organize the body of the speech in a logical way?
☐ Did the speaker use transitions, summaries, and signposts to clarify the organization?
☐ Did the speaker appropriately summarize the major ideas and provide closure to the speech during the conclusion?

Rehearse the Speech
☐ Did the speech sound as though it was well rehearsed?
☐ Did the speaker seem familiar with the speech content?

Deliver Speech
☐ Did the speaker make appropriate eye contact with the audience?
☐ Did the speaker use appropriate volume and vocal variation?
☐ Did the speaker use gestures and posture appropriately?
☐ Did the speaker use presentation aids that were easy to see and of high quality?
☐ Did the speaker handle presentation aids effectively?

Effective: Gabe, your opening statistic was effective in catching my attention. You also maintained direct eye contact when you delivered it. Your overall organizational pattern would have been clearer to me if you had used more signposts and transition statements. Or perhaps you could use a visual aid to summarize the main points in the body of your speech. You did a good job of summarizing your three points in your conclusion. I also liked the way you ended your speech by making a reference to your opening statistics.

Less Effective: I got lost in the body of your speech. I couldn't figure out what your major ideas were. I also didn't know when you made the transition between the introduction and the body of your speech. Your intro and conclusion were good, but the organization of the speech was weak.

4. **Be Constructive.**   Give the speaker suggestions or alternatives for improvement. It's not especially helpful to rattle off a list of things you don't like without offering some ideas for improvement. As a student of public speaking, your comments should reflect your growing skill and sophistication in the speechmaking process.

Effective: Jerry, your speech had several good statistics and examples that suggest you spent a lot of time researching your topic. I think you could add credibility to your message if you shared your sources with the listener. Your vocal quality was effective, and you had considerable variation in your pitch and tone, but at times the speech rate was a little fast for me. A slower rate would help me catch some of the details in your message.

Less Effective: You spoke too fast. I had no idea whom you were quoting.

5. **Be Sensitive.**   "Own" your feedback by using I-statements rather than you-statements. An *I-statement* is a way of phrasing your feedback so that it is clear that your comments reflect your personal point of view. "I found my attention drifting during the body of your speech" is an example of an I-statement. A *you-statement* is a less sensitive way of describing someone's behavior by implying that the other person did something wrong. "You didn't summarize well in your conclusion" is an example of a you-statement. A better way to make the same point is to say, "I wasn't sure I understood the key ideas you mentioned in your conclusion." Here's another example:

Effective: Mark, I found myself so distracted by your gestures that I had trouble focusing on the well-organized message.

Less Effective: Your gestures were distracting and awkward.

6. **Be Realistic.**   Provide usable information. Offer feedback about aspects of the presentation that the speaker can improve rather than about those things he or she cannot control. Maybe you have heard this advice: "Never try to teach a pig to sing. It wastes your time. It doesn't sound pretty. And it annoys the pig." Saying "You're too short to be seen over the lectern," "Your lisp doesn't lend itself to public speaking," or "You looked nervous" is not constructive. Comments of this kind will only annoy or frustrate the speaker because they refer to things the speaker can't do much to change. Concentrate on behaviors over which the speaker has some control.

Effective: Taka, your closing quote was effective in summarizing your key ideas, but it didn't end your speech on an uplifting note. Another quote from Khalil Gibran that I'll share with you after class would also summarize your key points and provide a positive affirmation of your message. You may want to try it if you give this speech again.

Less Effective: Your voice isn't well suited to public speaking.

As you provide feedback, whether in your public-speaking class or to a friend who asks you for a reaction to his or her speech, remember that the goal is to offer descriptive and specific feedback that will help a speaker build confidence and skill.

formal survey of your listeners. In addition to demographics, a survey allows you to gather information about what audience members like or dislike, believe to be true or false, or think is good or bad about the topic or issues you will discuss. To gather information formally requires that you develop a carefully written survey or questionnaire.

How do you develop a formal survey? There are four steps:

- First, think about what you want to know.
- Second, develop questions to learn more about your listeners.
- Third, if possible, test your survey on a few people to see if your questions are clear.
- Finally, distribute your survey and summarize the results.

IDENTIFY WHAT YOU WANT TO LEARN ABOUT YOUR AUDIENCE Let your topic and the speaking occasion help you determine the kinds of questions you should pose. You may want to confirm some of your hunches about demographic information or you may want to assess how much the audience knows about your topic, as well as their attitudes toward your ideas.

DEVELOP CLEAR QUESTIONS Once you have an idea of what you would like to know, ask your potential audience straightforward questions about such demographic information as age, sex, occupation, and their membership in professional organizations. Figure 5.2 shows a sample questionnaire.

To gather useful information about audience members' attitudes, beliefs, and values, you can ask two types of questions. **Open-ended questions** allow for unrestricted answers without limiting responses to specific choices or alternatives. Essay questions, for example, are open-ended. Use open-ended questions when you want detailed feedback from your audience. **Closed-ended questions** offer alternatives from which to choose. Multiple-choice, true/false, and agree/disagree questions are examples of closed-ended questions.

open-ended questions

Questions that allow for unrestricted answers by not limiting answers to choices or alternatives

closed-ended questions

Questions that offer alternatives from which to choose, such as true/false, agree/disagree, or multiple-choice questions

Figure 5.2 You can use a questionnaire like this to gather demographic information about the people in your audience.

SOURCE: Copyrighted by Pearson Education, Hoboken, NJ.

Demographic Audience-Analysis Questionnaire

1. Name (optional): _____

2. Sex: Male ☐ Female ☐

3. Occupation: _____

4. Religious affiliation: _____

5. Marital status: Married ☐ Single ☐ Divorced ☐

6. Years of schooling beyond high school: _____

7. Major in college: _____

8. Annual income: _____

9. Age: _____

10. Ethnic background: _____

11. Hometown and state: _____

12. Political affiliation: Republican ☐ Democrat ☐ Other ☐ None ☐

13. Membership in professional or fraternal organizations: _____

Figure 5.3 Samples of open-ended and closed-ended questions.

Open-Ended Questions

1. What are your feelings about having high-school health clinics dispense birth-control pills?
2. What are your reactions to the current rate of teenage pregnancy?
3. What would you do if you discovered your daughter was receiving birth-control pills from her high-school health clinic?

Closed-Ended Questions

1. Are you in favor of school-based health clinics dispensing birth-control pills to high-school students?
   Yes ☐ No ☐

2. Birth-control pills should be given to high-school students who ask for them in school-based health clinics. (Circle the statement that best describes your feeling.)

   Agree strongly   Agree   Undecided   Disagree   Disagree strongly

3. Check the statement that most closely reflects your feelings about school-based health clinics and birth-control pills.
   - ☐ Students should receive birth-control pills in school-based health clinics whenever they want them, without their parents' knowledge.
   - ☐ Students should receive birth-control pills in school-based health clinics whenever they want them, as long as they have their parents' permission.
   - ☐ I am not certain whether students should receive birth-control pills in school-based health clinics.
   - ☐ Students should not receive birth-control pills in school-based health clinics.

4. Rank the following statements from most desirable (1) to least desirable (5).
   - ___ Birth-control pills should be available to all high-school students in school-based health clinics, whenever students want them, and even if their parents are not aware that their daughters are taking the pills.
   - ___ Birth-control pills should be available to all high-school students in school-based health clinics, but only if their parents have given their permission.
   - ___ Birth-control pills should be available to high-school students without their parents' knowledge, but not in school-based health clinics.
   - ___ Birth-control pills should be available to high-school students, but not in school-based health clinics, and only with their parents' permission.
   - ___ Birth-control pills should not be available to high-school students.

TEST THE CLARITY OF YOUR QUESTIONS After you develop the questions, test them out on a small group of people to make sure they are clear and encourage meaningful answers. Suppose you plan to address an audience about in-school health clinics that dispense birth-control pills to high-school students. The sample open-ended and closed-ended questions in Figure 5.3 might yield useful audience information on this subject.

DISTRIBUTE THE SURVEY Instead of, or in addition to, a paper-and-pencil survey, you have the option of distributing your survey electronically. You could use e-mail, send text messages, or invite people to click on a Web site or a Facebook page that you've designed to identify audience-member demographics and assess their attitudes and opinions. Several companies, such as Polldaddy or SurveyMonkey, offer free online survey capabilities.

RECAP

GATHERING INFORMATION TO ADAPT YOUR MESSAGE TO YOUR AUDIENCE

Gather demographic information informally.
- Observe your audience and ask questions before you speak.

Formally survey demographics and attitudes:
- Closed-ended questions
- Open-ended questions

Ethically adapt your message:
- Topic
- Objectives
- Content
- Delivery

Analyzing Information about Your Audience

5.2 Explain how to analyze information about your audience.

audience analysis

The process of examining information about those who are expected to listen to a speech

Audience analysis is the process of examining information about the listeners who will hear your speech. That analysis helps you adapt your message so your listeners will respond as you wish. Whether you realize it or not, you analyze audiences every day as you speak to others or join in group conversations. For example, most of us do not deliberately make offensive comments to family members or friends. Rather, we quickly analyze our audience and then adapt our messages to them. Public speaking involves the same sort of process.

Precisely what do you look for when analyzing the information you have gathered about your audience? Ask yourself the following questions:

1. How are audience members similar to one another?
2. How are audience members different from one another?
3. Based on audience members' similarities and differences, how can I establish common ground with them?

Identify Similarities

Knowing what several members of your audience have in common can help you craft a message that resonates with them. For example, if your audience members are approximately the same age, you will have some basis for selecting examples and illustrations that your listeners will understand.

When looking for similarities, consider the following questions: What ethnic and cultural characteristics do audience members have in common? Are they all from the same geographic region? Do they (or did they) attend the same college or university? Do they have similar levels of education? Answering these and other questions will help you develop your own ideas and better relate your message to your listeners.

Identify Differences

Besides noting similarities, you should note differences among your audience members. It is unlikely that audience members for the speeches you give in class will have similar backgrounds. The range of cultural backgrounds, ethnicities, and religious traditions among students at most colleges and universities is rapidly expanding. You can also note the range of differences in age and gender, as well as the varying perspectives about your topic.

Identify Common Ground

common ground

Similarities between a speaker and audience members in attitudes, values, beliefs, or behaviors

When you know what your audience members have in common as well as how they differ, then you can seek to establish a common ground. To establish **common ground** with your audience is to identify ways in which you and your listeners are alike.

Sometimes you may find that the only common ground is that both you and your listeners believe the issue you are addressing is a serious problem; you may have different views about the best solution. If, for example, you were addressing a group of people who were mostly against increasing taxes to pay teachers higher salaries, but you were in favor of a tax increase, you could establish common ground by noting that both you and your listeners value education and want high-quality teachers in classrooms.

When you meet someone for the first time, you may spend time identifying people whom you both know or places you've both visited; in this way you begin

What are some possible areas of common ground this speaker might find with his audience? *Photo:* Jamie Wilson/Shutterstock.

relationship
An ongoing connection you have with another person

to establish a relationship. A **relationship** is an ongoing connection you have with another person. A public speaker seeks to establish a relationship with audience members by identifying common ground with them. Use the information from your audience analysis to establish a relationship with your listeners; build bridges between you and your audience.

Adapting to Your Audience

5.3 Identify and use strategies for adapting to your audience.

Audience adaptation is the process of ethically using information you've gathered when analyzing your audience to help your listeners clearly understand your message and to achieve your speaking objective. To adapt is to modify your message to enhance its clarity and to increase the likelihood that you will ethically achieve your goal. When adapting to your listeners, the goal is not merely to appease them but also to ensure that your listeners remain listeners. You don't want audience members to prematurely dismiss your ideas before they understand them. By learning about your audience and adapting to them, you can help your listeners maintain their attention and become more receptive to your ideas.

Here's an example of how analyzing and adapting to others works: Imagine you live in an apartment complex that doesn't allow pets without the landlord's approval. You see an adorable cocker spaniel puppy that you'd like to buy. In fact, you've already named him Martin. Before you bring Martin home, however, you need your landlord's approval as well as your roommate's blessing.

When trying to convince your landlord you say, "I've always paid the rent on time and never caused a problem. I will also pay an extra $300 security deposit if I can have a dog in my apartment." Your message to your roommate is, "No worries about you getting stuck with taking care of Martin if I go out of town. My friend Chris, who also lives in our apartment complex, has agreed to step in for me whenever I'm out of town." You had the same goal for each audience—approval for having a dog in your apartment—but you customized your message, tailoring your appeal to each listener based on his or her interests and concerns. You adapted to your audience.

RECAP

ANALYZING INFORMATION ABOUT YOUR AUDIENCE

Look for:

- Similarities among listeners
- Differences among listeners
- Common ground with listeners

audience adaptation
The process of ethically using information about an audience in order to adapt one's message so that it is clear and achieves the speaking objective

Table 5.1 Audience-Centered Adaptation

Consider Your Audience
- To whom am I speaking?
- What topic would be most suitable for my audience?

Consider Your Speech Goal
- What is my general objective (to inform, persuade, or entertain)?
- What is my specific objective (precisely what do I want the audience to do)?

Consider Your Speech Content
- What kind of information should I share with my audience?
- How should I present the information to them?
- How can I gain and hold their attention?
- What kind of examples would work best?
- What method of organizing information will be most effective?

Consider Your Delivery
- What language differences and expectations do audience members have?
- What style of delivery will my audience members expect?

SOURCE: Copyrighted by Pearson Education, Hoboken, NJ.

When you speak in public, you should follow the same process. The principle is simple yet powerful: An effective public speaker is audience-centered. The key questions in Table 5.1 can help you formulate an effective approach to your audience.

Being audience-centered does not mean you should tell your listeners only what they want to hear or that you should fabricate information simply to please your audience or achieve your communication goal. You also don't want to tell listeners things you know are not true. If you adapt to your audience by abandoning your own values and sense of truth, then you will become an unethical speaker rather than an audience-centered one. It was President Truman who pondered, "I wonder how far Moses would have gone if he'd taken a poll in Egypt?"[1] The audience-centered speaker ethically adapts his or her topic, purpose, central idea, main ideas, supporting material, organization, and even delivery so as to encourage the audience to listen to his or her ideas. The goal is to make the audience come away from the speaking situation, if not persuaded, then at least feeling thoughtful rather than offended or hostile.

Analyzing Your Audience before You Speak

5.4 Develop methods of analyzing your audience before you speak by seeking demographic, psychological, and situational information about your audience and the speaking occasion.

Learning about your audience members' backgrounds and attitudes can help you select a topic, define a purpose, develop an outline, and carry out virtually all other speech-related activities. You can gather and analyze three primary types of information:

1. Demographic
2. Psychological
3. Situational

Demographic Audience Analysis

As we noted previously, *demographics* are statistics about such audience characteristics as age, gender, sexual orientation, race and culture, group membership, and socioeconomic status. Some demographic audience characteristics can be inferred through observation (such as age), but not all are as easily determined (such as sexual orientation, cultural background, and group membership). If you are presenting your speech online or via video where you can't see your listeners, it's especially important to do some pre-speech analysis to make sure your inferences about the demographic characteristics of your audience are accurate. Now let's consider how examining demographic information, or **demographic audience analysis**, can help you better understand and adapt to your audience.

AGE Although you must use caution in generalizing from only one factor, information about the age of audience members can suggest the kinds of examples, humor, illustrations, and other types of supporting material to use in your speech. Many students in your public-speaking class will probably be in their late teens or early twenties; some may be older. The younger students may know the latest hip-hop performers or musicians, for example, but the older ones may not be familiar with Wiz Khalifa, Lil Wayne, A$AP Rocky, or Nicki Minaj. If you are going to give a talk on music, you will have to explain who the performers are and describe or demonstrate their style if you want all the members of your class to understand what you are talking about.

For centuries, adults have lamented that younger generations don't seem to share the same values as older generations. More than two thousand years ago, the ancient Greek philosopher Socrates is reported to have complained, "The children now love luxury; they show disrespect for elders and love chatter in place of exercise.... They contradict their parents, chatter before company, gobble up dainties at the table, cross their legs, and tyrannize over their teachers."[2] Table 5.2 summarizes the values and generational characteristics of five generations—matures, baby boomers, generation X, millennials, and generation Z.[3]

demographic audience analysis
Examining demographic information about an audience so as to develop a clear and effective message

Table 5.2 Summary of Generational Characteristics

Generation Name	Birth Years	Typical Values and Characteristics
Matures	1925–1942	• Duty • Sacrifice • A sense of what is right • Work hard • Work fast
Baby Boomers	1943–1960	• Personal fulfillment and optimism • Crusading causes • Buy now/pay later • Everybody's rights • Work efficiently
Generation X	1961–1981	• Live with uncertainty • Balance is important • Enjoy today • Every job is a contract • Save to prepare for uncertainty
Millennials	1982–2002	• Close to parents • Feel "special" • Goal-oriented • Team-oriented • Focus on achievement
Generation Z	2003-	• Diversity is important • It's a challenge to achieve the "American Dream" • They will likely have multiple jobs • Technology and social media are integral to their lives • Multitasking is normal

SOURCE: Copyrighted by Pearson Education, Hoboken, NJ.

What do these generational differences have to do with public speaking? Aristotle noted that a good speaker knows how to adapt to audiences of different age levels. Your credibility as a speaker—how positively you are perceived by your audience—depends on your sensitivity to the values and assumptions of your listeners. Of course, the broad generalizations we've summarized here don't apply across the board, but it's wise to consider how generational differences may affect how your message is interpreted.

GENDER   Josh began his speech by thanking his predominantly female audience for taking time from their busy schedules to attend his presentation on managing personal finances. Not a bad way to begin a talk. He continued, however, by noting their job of raising children, keeping their homes clean, and feeding their families was among the most important of jobs. Josh thought he was paying his audience a compliment. He did not consider that most women today work outside the home as well as in it. Many of his listeners were insulted. Many of his listeners stopped listening.

gender
The culturally constructed and psychologically based perception of one's self as feminine or masculine

A key question to ask when considering your audience is "What are the gender roles and gender identifications of my audience?" **Gender** is the culturally constructed and psychologically based perception of one's self as feminine or masculine. One's gender-role identity, which falls somewhere on the continuum from masculine to feminine, is learned or socially reinforced by others as well as by one's own personality and life experiences; genetics also plays a part in shaping gender-role identity.

Try to ensure that your remarks reflect sensitivity to the diversity in your listeners' points of view and gender identities. No matter what the mix, you don't want to make judgments based on gender stereotypes, as Josh did.

sex
A person's biological status as male or female, as reflected in his or her anatomy and reproductive system

Just knowing the sex of your audience members—the number of males and females—doesn't tell you the whole story about your listeners. A person's **sex** is determined by biology, as reflected in his or her anatomy and reproductive system; someone is born either male or female. Drawing conclusions about members of your audience based only on their biological sex profile could lead you to adapt to your listeners inappropriately. For example, many of the men in Josh's audience were the ones who took a prime role in caring for their children.

Also be cautious about assuming that men and women will respond differently to your message. Early social science research found some evidence that females were more susceptible to persuasive efforts than were males.[4] For many years, communication teachers and texts presented this conclusion to students. More contemporary research, however, suggests there is no major difference between men and women in their susceptibility to persuasive messages.[5]

And finally, avoid sexist language or remarks. A sexist perspective stereotypes or prejudges how someone will react based on his or her biological sex or gender orientation. Remember, it's your audience, not you, who determines whether a comment is sexist or not. Think carefully about the implications of words and phrases you take for granted. For example, many people still use the words *ladies* and *matrons* without thinking about their connotations in U.S. culture. Take time to educate yourself about what words, phrases, or perspectives are likely to offend or create psychological noise for your listeners.

SEXUAL ORIENTATIONS   An audience-centered speaker is sensitive to issues and attitudes not only about gender but also about sexual orientation and gender identification in contemporary society. Sexual and gender orientations are not easily sorted into exclusive either-or categories.

The audience-centered speaker's goal is to enhance understanding rather than create noise that may distract an audience from listening. Sometimes our unintentional use or misuse of language can offend others. For example, gays and lesbians typically prefer to be referred to as "gay" or "lesbian" rather than "homosexual." Stories, illustrations, and humor whose point or punch line rely on ridiculing a person because of his or her sexual

CONFIDENTLY CONNECTING WITH YOUR AUDIENCE

Learn as Much as You Can about Your Audience

By learning about your audience's interests, attitudes, and beliefs as well as their demographic details, you'll be better able to customize a message for your listeners. The more you tailor your message directly to your audience, the more you'll be able to confidently connect with them. Because you have customized your message, they will want to hear it, and you'll be speaking directly to their interests and needs. Also, by focusing on your audience instead of on your nervousness about speaking, you will enhance your confidence. Because you're not dwelling on your own anxieties, you'll be focused on communicating your audience-centered message.

or gender orientation as lesbian, gay, bisexual, transgender/transsexual, questioning, intersex, or asexual (LGBTQIA) may lower perceptions of your credibility among the LGBTQIA members of your audience as well as those who disdain bias. Further, it is not appropriate to single out separate categories of people who are assumed to hold political, ideological, or religious views consistently different from those of straight people. Monitor your language choice and use of illustrations so you don't alienate members of your audience.[6] Be sensitive and audience-centered as you interact with those whose sexual orientation is different from your own.

CULTURE, ETHNICITY, AND RACE   **Culture** is a learned system of knowledge, behavior, attitudes, beliefs, values, and norms shared by a group of people. **Ethnicity** is that portion of a person's cultural background that includes such factors as nationality, religion, language, and ancestral heritage, which are shared by a group of people who have a common geographic origin. **Race** is a term that has evolved to include a group of people with a common cultural history, nationality, or geographical location, as well as genetically transmitted physical attributes.[7] One geneticist has concluded that there is much more genetic variation *within* any given racial category than *between* one race and another.[8] The cultural, ethnic, or racial background of your audience influences the way they perceive your message. An effective speaker adapts to differences in culture, race, and ethnicity.[9]

As you approach any public-speaking situation, avoid an ethnocentric mind-set. **Ethnocentrism** is the assumption that your own cultural approaches are superior to those of other cultures. The audience-centered speaker is sensitive to cultural differences and avoids saying anything that would disparage the cultural background of the audience.

You need not have international students in your class to have a culturally diverse audience. Different ethnic and cultural traditions thrive among people who have lived in the United States all their lives. Students from a Polish family in Chicago, a German family in Texas, or a Haitian family in Brooklyn may all be native U.S. citizens and all have cultural traditions different from your own. Effective public speakers learn as much as possible about the cultural values and knowledge of their audience so that they can understand the best way to deliver their message.

Researchers classify or describe cultural value differences along several lines.[10] We summarize six categories of differences in Table 5.3 and discuss them here. Understanding these value classifications may provide clues to help you adapt your message when you speak before diverse audiences.

- **Individualistic and collectivistic cultures.**   Some cultures place a greater value on individual achievement; others place more value on group or collective achievement. Among the countries that tend to value individual accomplishment are Australia, Great Britain, the United States, Canada, Belgium, and Denmark.

culture

A learned system of knowledge, behavior, attitudes, beliefs, values, and norms shared by a group of people

ethnicity

The portion of a person's cultural background that includes such factors as nationality, religion, language, and ancestral heritage, which are shared by a group of people who also share a common geographic origin

race

A group of people with a common cultural history, nationality, or geographical location, as well as genetically transmitted physical attributes

ethnocentrism

The assumption that one's own cultural perspectives and methods are superior to those of other cultures

Table 5.3 Describing and Adapting to Cultural Differences

Cultural Value	Cultural Characteristic	How to Adapt to Cultural Characteristics
Individualistic Culture	Individual achievement is emphasized more than group achievement.	• Stress the importance of individual rewards and recognition. • Identify how audience members will benefit from your ideas or proposal.
Collectivistic Culture	Group or team achievement is emphasized more than individual achievement.	• Stress the importance of community values. • Help audience members save face and be perceived in a positive way.
High-Context Culture	The context of a message—including nonverbal cues, tone of voice, posture, and facial expression—is often valued more than the words.	• Don't boast about your specific accomplishments. • Use a more subtle, less dramatic delivery style.
Low-Context Culture	The words in a message are valued more than the surrounding context.	• Be sure to make your ideas and recommendations explicit. • Although delivery cues are important, listeners will expect your message to be clear.
Tolerance for Uncertainty	People can accept ambiguity and are not bothered when they do not know all the details.	• It is not so important to develop a specific solution to a problem you may present in your speech. • The purpose of the speech need not be clearly explicated.
Need for Certainty	People want specifics and dislike ambiguity.	• Provide an explicit overview of what you will present in your speech. • Create a logical and clear organizational pattern for your speech.
High-Power Culture	Status and power differences are emphasized; roles and chains of command are clearly defined.	• Remember that listeners perceive people in leadership positions as powerful and credible. • Develop messages that acknowledge differences in status among people.
Low-Power Culture	Status and power differences receive less emphasis; people strive for equality rather than exalting those in positions of leadership.	• Discuss shared approaches to governance and leadership. • Develop solutions that involve others in reaching consensus.
Long-Term Time Orientation	Time is abundant, and accomplishing goals may take considerable time.	• Appeal to listeners' persistence, patience, and delayed gratification. • Emphasize how ideas and suggestions will benefit future generations.
Short-Term Time Orientation	Time is an important resource.	• Identify how the ideas and proposals you discuss will have an immediate impact on listeners. • Note how actions will have a direct impact on achieving results.
High-Indulgence Culture	The pursuit of happiness is important.	• Motivate listeners by highlighting opportunities for leisure and fun. • Appeal to people's enjoyment of the pleasures life has to offer.
Low-Indulgence Culture	Hard work is valued and expected.	• Emphasize the importance of making an effort to get ahead. • Remember that listeners tend to control their impulses and desires.

SOURCE: Copyrighted by Pearson Education, Hoboken, NJ.

By contrast, Japan, Thailand, Colombia, Taiwan, and Venezuela are among countries that have more collectivistic cultures.

How to adapt to listeners from individualistic and collectivistic cultures. Audience members from individualistic cultures, such as the majority of people in the United States, value and respond positively to appeals that encourage personal accomplishment and recognize individual achievement. People from individualistic cultures are expected to speak up to champion individual rights.

Audience members from collectivistic cultures, such as many people who were raised in an Asian culture, may be more likely to value group or team recognition. They may not like to be singled out for individual accomplishments. Community is an important value for those from collectivistic cultures. And they value making sure others are perceived in a positive way; it's important for them and others to be seen as valued people. When speaking to a predominantly collectivistic audience, you might want to emphasize areas of consensus or community agreement on issues, use examples of community involvement, or ethically highlight the importance of shared effort and achievement in your proposals or appeals.

● **High-context and low-context cultures.** The terms *high-context* and *low-context cultures* refer to the importance of unspoken or nonverbal messages. In high-context cultures, people place considerable importance on contextual factors such as tone of voice, gestures, facial expression, movement, and other nonverbal aspects of communication. People from low-context traditions place greater emphasis on the words themselves; the surrounding context has a relatively low impact on the meaning of the message. The Arab culture is a high-context culture, as are the cultures of Japan, Asia, and southern Europe. Low-context cultures, which place a higher value on words, include those of Switzerland, Germany, the United States, and Australia.

How to adapt to listeners from high-context and low-context cultures. Listeners from low-context cultures will need and expect more detailed and explicit information from you as a speaker. Subtle and indirect messages are less likely to be effective.

People from high-context cultures will pay particular attention to your delivery and to the communication environment when they try to interpret your meaning. They will be less impressed by a speaker who boasts about his or her accomplishments; such an audience will expect and value more indirect ways of establishing credibility. A listener from a high-context culture will also expect a less dramatic and dynamic style of delivery.

● **Tolerance of uncertainty and need for certainty.** Some cultures are more comfortable with ambiguity and uncertainty than others. In contrast, cultures in which people need to have details nailed down tend to develop very specific regulations and rules. People from cultures with a greater tolerance of uncertainty are more comfortable with vagueness and are not upset when all the details aren't spelled out. Cultures with a high need for certainty include those of Russia, Japan, France, and Costa Rica. Cultures that have a higher tolerance for uncertainty include those of Great Britain and Indonesia. The United States is about in the middle of the scale for tolerance of uncertainty.[11]

How to adapt to listeners from cultures that tolerate or avoid uncertainty. If you are speaking to an audience of people who have a high need for certainty, make sure you provide concrete details when you present your message; they will also want and expect to know what action steps they can take. People who value certainty will respond well if you provide a clear and explicit preview of your message in your introduction; they also seem to prefer a clear, logical, and linear step-by-step organizational pattern.

People from cultures that are more comfortable with uncertainty do not necessarily need to have the explicit purpose of the message spelled out for them. In addition, they are generally less likely to need specific prescriptions to solve problems, compared to listeners who want to avoid uncertainty. Telling a story in which the main point is implied rather than explicitly identified may be an effective approach when communicating with listeners who have a high tolerance for uncertainty.

● **High-power and low-power cultures.** Power is the ability to influence or control others. Some cultures prefer clearly defined lines of authority and responsibility; these are said to be high-power cultures. People in low-power cultures are more comfortable with blurred lines of authority and less formal titles. Austria, Israel, Denmark, Norway, Switzerland, and Great Britain typically have an equitable approach to power distribution. Cultures with high power dimensions include those of the Philippines, Mexico, Venezuela, India, Brazil, and France. The United States is slightly lower (40 points out of 100) on this scale, meaning there is some expectation for shared authority.[12]

How to adapt to listeners from high-power and low-power cultures. People from high-power cultures are more likely to perceive people in leadership roles—including speakers—as credible. They will also be more comfortable with proposals or solutions that identify or acknowledge differences in social class.

Those from low-power cultures often favor more shared approaches to leadership and governance. When speaking to people from low-power cultures, you may want to emphasize democratic collaborative approaches to solving problems or areas of consensus on an issue.

- **Long-term and short-term time orientation.**   Some cultures take the view that it may take a long time to accomplish certain goals. People from Asian cultures, for example, and from some South American cultures such as that of Brazil often value patience, persistence, and deferred gratification more than people from cultures with a short-term orientation to time. People with a short-term time orientation, which is often a characteristic of industrialized Western cultures such as those of Canada and the United States, are attuned to time and time management. Short-term cultures also value quick responses to problems.

    How to adapt to listeners from cultures with long-term and short-term time orientations. When speaking to people who take a long-term orientation to time, you should stress how issues and problems affect not only the present but also the future, especially future generations. It's not that people with a long-term orientation don't value efficiency and effectiveness; they simply accept that things don't always happen quickly.

    People with a short-term orientation to time will want to learn about immediate action steps that can solve a problem. They are also results-oriented and expect that individual or group effort should result in a specific positive outcome. When possible, provide statistics or other evidence that documents results.

- **High-indulgent and low-indulgent cultures.**   Some cultures place a high priority in indulging in activities to pursue happiness. The more indulgent a culture, the less focused they are on controlling their desires and impulses. High-indulgent cultures actively seek and expect freedom. They also tend to place a high value on leisure activities and sports. Other cultures are less indulgent; they are more restrained and do not expect to have all of their needs met to be happy. The United States scores high on indulgence compared to many other cultures.[13]

    How to adapt to listeners from cultures with high-indulgent and low-indulgent orientations. High-indulgent cultures, such as the United States, will value and appreciate appeals to "life, liberty and the pursuit of happiness." Motivating factors for highly indulgent cultures include having the time and opportunity for sports, leisure activities, and fun. Those from lower indulgent cultures, such as Russia, China, and much of Eastern Europe, tend to be less motivated by these kinds of opportunities. Instead, appealing to hard work and accomplishment are more likely to be strong, positive motivators.

GROUP MEMBERSHIP   It's said we are all members of a gang—it's just that some gangs are more socially acceptable than others. We are social creatures; we congregate in groups to gain an identity, to help accomplish projects we support, and to have fun. So it's reasonable to assume that many of your listeners belong to groups, clubs, or organizations. One way to gather information about a specific group you plan to speak to is to see if the group or organization has a Web site, Facebook page, or other social media presence. Knowing something about the history, purpose, values, and accomplishments of a group can help you customize your message.

- **Religious groups.**   When touching on religious beliefs or an audience's values, use great care in what you say and how you say it. Remind yourself that some members of your audience will undoubtedly not share your beliefs, and that few beliefs are held as intensely as religious ones. If you do not wish to offend your listeners, plan and deliver your speech with much thought and sensitivity.

- **Political groups.**   Are members of your audience active in politics? Knowing whether your listeners are active in such groups as Young Republicans, Young

Democrats, or Young Libertarians can help you address political topics. Members of environmental groups may also hold strong ecological opinions on issues and political candidates.

- **Work groups.** Most professions give rise to professional organizations or associations to which people can belong. If you are speaking to an audience of professionals, it's important to be aware of the professional organizations they may belong to (there may be several) and to know, for example, whether those organizations have taken formal stands that may influence audience members' views on certain issues. Work groups may also have abbreviations or acronyms that may be useful to know. Your communication instructor, for example, may be a member of the National Communication Association (NCA) and may also belong to a specific division of the NCA, such as the IDD (Instructional Development Division).

- **Social groups.** Some groups exist just so that people can get together and enjoy a common activity. Book clubs, film clubs, cycling clubs, cooking groups, dancing groups, and bowling teams exist to bring people with similar ideas of fun together to enjoy an activity. Knowing whether members of your audience belong to such groups may help you adapt your topic to them or, if you are involved in similar groups, to establish common ground with them.

- **Service groups.** Many people are actively involved in groups that emphasize community service as their primary mission. If you are speaking to a service group such as the Lions Club or the Kiwanis Club, you can reasonably assume that your listeners value community service and will be interested in learning how to make their community a better place.

SOCIOECONOMIC STATUS **Socioeconomic status** is a person's perceived importance and influence based on such factors as income, occupation, and education level. In Europe, Asia, the Middle East, and other parts of the world, centuries-old traditions of acknowledging status differences still exist today. Status differences in the United States and Canada are often subtler. A general estimate of your audience members' incomes, occupations, and education levels can be helpful as you develop a message that connects with listeners.

socioeconomic status

A person's perceived importance and influence based on income, occupation, and education level

- **Income.** Having some general idea of the income level of your listeners can be of great value to you as a speaker. For example, if you know that most audience members are struggling to meet weekly expenses, it will be unwise to talk about how to see the cultural riches of Europe by traveling first class. But talking about how to get paid to travel to Europe by serving as a courier may hold considerable interest.

- **Occupation.** Knowing what people do for a living can give you useful information about how to adapt your message to them. Speaking to teachers, you will want to use different examples and illustrations than if you were speaking to lawyers, ministers, or automobile assembly-line workers. Many college-age students may hold jobs but not with the kinds of employers they aspire to after graduation. Knowing their future career plans can help you adjust your topic and supporting material to your listeners' professional goals.

- **Education.** About 30 percent of American adults obtain a college degree. Slightly more than 10 percent of the population earns graduate degrees.[14] The educational background of your listeners is yet another component of socioeconomic status that can help you plan your message. For example, you have a good idea that your classmates in your college-level public-speaking class value education because they are striving, often at great sacrifice, to advance their education. Knowing the educational background of your audience can help you make decisions about your choice of vocabulary, language style, and use of examples and illustrations.

ADAPTING TO DIVERSE LISTENERS We live in an increasingly diverse society. The U.S. Census predicts that in about three decades, the United States will become a

If a graduation speaker focuses on the target audience of graduating students, how can the speaker address the interests of graduates' families and friends too? *Photo:* Mat Hayward/Fotolia.

"majority-minority" nation, with no single ethnic group making up a majority of the population.[15] This swell of immigrants translates to increased diversity in all aspects of society, including in most audiences you'll face—whether in business, at school board meetings, or in your college classes.

Audience diversity, however, involves factors beyond ethnic and cultural differences. Central to our point about considering your audience is examining the full spectrum of audience diversity, not just cultural differences. Each topic we've reviewed when discussing demographic and psychological aspects of an audience contributes to overall audience diversity. Diversity simply means differences. Audience members are diverse. The question and challenge for a public speaker is, "How do I ethically adapt to listeners with such different backgrounds and experiences?" We offer several general strategies. You could decide to focus on a target audience, consciously use a variety of methods of adapting to listeners, seek common ground, or consider using powerful visual images to present your key points.

target audience

A specific segment of an audience that you most want to influence

● **Focus on a target audience.** A **target audience** is a specific segment of your audience that you most want to address or influence. When consciously focusing on a target audience, the challenge is not to lose or alienate the rest of your listeners—to keep the entire audience in mind while simultaneously making a specific attempt to hit your target segment. For example, Sasha was trying to convince his listeners to invest in the stock market instead of relying only on Social Security. He wisely decided to focus on the younger listeners; those approaching retirement age have already made their major investment decisions. Although he focused on the younger members of his audience, however, Sasha didn't forget the mature listeners. He suggested that older listeners encourage their children or grandchildren to consider his proposal. He focused on a target audience, but he didn't ignore others.

● **Use diverse strategies for a diverse audience.** Another approach you can adopt, either separately or in combination with a target audience focus, is to use a variety of strategies to reflect the diversity of your audience. If you've made an effort to gather information about your audience, you should know the various constituencies that will likely be present for your talk. Consider using several methods to reach the different listeners in your audience. For example, review the following strategies:

  ● Use a variety of supporting materials, including illustrations, examples, statistics, and opinions. Learn more about supporting materials in Chapter 7.

- Remember the power of stories. People from most cultures appreciate a good story. And some people, such as those from Asian and Middle Eastern cultures, prefer hearing stories and parables used to make a point or support an argument rather than facts and statistics.

- If you're uncertain about cultural preferences, use a balance of both logical support (statistics, facts, specific examples) and emotional support (stories and illustrations).

- Consider showing the audience a brief outline to provide an overview of your key ideas, using PowerPoint™ or Prezi™. If there is a language barrier between you and your audience, being able to read portions of your speech as they hear you speaking may improve audience members' comprehension. If an interpreter is translating your message, an outline can also help ensure that your interpreter will communicate your message accurately.

- **Identify common values.** People have long debated whether there are universal human values. Several scholars have made strong arguments that common human values do exist. Communication researcher David Kale suggests that all people can identify with the individual struggle to enhance one's own dignity and worth, although different cultures express that struggle in different ways.[16] A second common value is the search for a world at peace. Underlying that quest is a fundamental desire for equilibrium, balance, and stability. Although there may always be a small but corrosive minority of people whose actions do not support the universal value of peace, the prevailing human values in most cultures ultimately do. Intercultural communication scholars Larry Samovar and Richard Porter suggest other commonalities that people from all cultures share. They propose that all humans seek physical pleasure as well as emotional and psychological pleasure and confirmation, and seek to avoid personal harm.[17] These similarities offer some basis for developing common messages with universal meaning.

  Identifying common cultural issues and similarities can help you establish common ground with your audience, a goal we introduced in this chapter. If you are speaking about an issue on which you and your audience have widely different views, identifying a larger common value that is relevant to your topic (such as the importance of peace, prosperity, or family) can help you find a foothold so that your listeners will at least listen to your ideas.

- **Rely on visual materials that transcend language differences.** Pictures and other images can communicate universal messages—especially emotional ones. Although there is no universal language, most listeners, regardless of culture and language, can comprehend visible expressions of pain, joy, sorrow, and happiness. An image of a mother holding the frail, malnourished body of her dying child communicates the ravages of famine without elaborate verbal explanations. The more varied your listeners' cultural experiences, the more effective it can be to use visual materials to illustrate your ideas.

> **RECAP**
>
> **ADAPTING TO DIVERSE LISTENERS**
>
> - Focus on a target audience without losing or alienating the rest of your listeners.
> - Use diverse supporting materials that reflect a balance of logical and emotional support.
> - Tell stories.
> - Use visual aids, including both images and an outline of your key points.
> - Appeal to such common values as peace, prosperity, and family.

Psychological Audience Analysis

Demographic information lets you make useful inferences about your audience and predict likely responses. A **psychological audience analysis** explores an audience's attitudes toward a topic, purpose, and speaker while probing the underlying beliefs and values that might affect these attitudes. Learning whether members of your audience agree or disagree with your purpose may provide specific clues to help you anticipate their reactions to your message.

psychological audience analysis

Examining the attitudes, beliefs, values, and other psychological information about an audience in order to develop a clear and effective message

If you establish your credibility before you begin to discuss your topic, your listeners will be more likely to believe what you say and to think that you are knowledgeable, interesting, and dynamic. Make a connection between you, your topic, and your audience: Tell your listeners why you are interested in the topic, describe your personal experience with the subject matter, or explain why you are passionate about your message.[19] We will provide additional strategies for enhancing your credibility in Chapters 9 and 15.

Situational Audience Analysis

situational audience analysis
Examination of the time and place of a speech, the audience size, and the speaking occasion in order to develop a clear and effective message

So far we have concentrated on the people who will be your listeners, as the primary focus of being an audience-centered speaker. You should also consider your speaking situation. **Situational audience analysis** includes an examination of the time and place of your speech, the size of your audience, and the speaking occasion. Although these elements are not technically characteristics of the *audience*, they can have a major effect on how listeners respond to you.

TIME   You may have no control over when you will be speaking, but when designing and delivering a talk, a skilled public speaker considers the time of day as well as audience expectations about the speech length. If you are speaking to a group of exhausted parents during a midweek evening meeting of the band-boosters club, you can bet they will appreciate a direct, to-the-point presentation more than a long oration. If you are on a program with other speakers, speaking first or last on the program carries a slight edge because people tend to remember what comes first or last. Speaking early in the morning when people may not be quite awake, after lunch when they may feel a bit drowsy, or late in the afternoon when they are tired may mean you'll have to strive consciously for a more energetic delivery to keep your listeners' attention.

Be mindful of your time limits. If your audience expects you to speak for 20 minutes, it is usually better to end either right at 20 minutes or a little earlier; most North Americans don't appreciate being kept overtime for a speech. In your public-speaking class you will be given time limits, and you may wonder whether such strict time-limit expectations occur outside public-speaking class. The answer is a most definite yes. Whether it's a business presentation or a speech to the city council or school board, time limits are often strictly enforced.

SIZE OF AUDIENCE   The size of your audience directly affects speaking style and audience expectations about delivery. As a general rule, the larger the audience, the more likely they are to expect a more formal style. With an audience of ten or fewer, you can punctuate a conversational style by taking questions. If you and your listeners are so few that you can fit around a table, they may expect you to stay seated for your presentation. Many business "speeches" are given around a conference table.

A group of 20 to 30 people—the size of most public-speaking classes—will expect more formality than an audience of a dozen or fewer. Your speaking style can still be conversational, but your speech should be appropriately structured and well organized; your delivery may include more expansive gestures than you would display during a one-on-one chat with a friend or colleague. If you are speaking to a much larger group in a lecture hall, you may also want to use more expansive gestures as well as a microphone to amplify your voice.

LOCATION   In your speech class, you have the advantage of knowing what the room looks like, but in a new speaking situation, you may not have that advantage. If at all possible, visit the place where you will speak to examine the physical setting and find out, for example, how far the audience will be from the lectern. Physical conditions such as room temperature and lighting can affect your performance, the audience response, and the overall success of the speech.

How can a speaker analyze and adapt to a videoconference speaking situation? *Photo:* Blend Images/John Fedele/Vetta/Getty Images.

Occasion Another important way to gain clues about your listeners is to consider the reason why they are here. What occasion brings this audience together? The mind-set of people gathered for a funeral will obviously be different from that of people who've asked you to say a few words after a banquet. Knowing the occasion helps you predict both the demographic characteristics of the audience and their state of mind.

If you're presenting a speech at an annual or monthly meeting, you have the advantage of being able to ask those who've attended previous presentations what kind of audience typically gathers for the occasion. Your best source of information may be either the person who invited you to speak or someone who has attended similar events. Knowing when you will speak on the program or whether a meal will be served before or after you talk will help you gauge audience expectations.

Advance preparation will help you avoid last-minute surprises about the speaking environment and the physical arrangements for your speech. Table 5.5 provides a list of essential questions you should ask when preparing for a speaking assignment, as well as several suggestions for adapting to your speaking situation. A well-prepared speaker adapts his or her message not only to the audience but also to the speaking environment.

RECAP

ELEMENTS OF AUDIENCE ANALYSIS

Demographic Characteristics
- Age
- Gender
- Sexual orientation
- Cultural, ethnic, or racial background
- Group membership
- Socioeconomic status

Psychological Characteristics
- Attitudes: Likes and dislikes
- Beliefs: What is perceived to be true or false
- Values: What is perceived to be good or bad

Situational Characteristics
- Time
- Audience size
- Location
- Occasion

Adapting to Your Audience as You Speak

5.5 Identify methods of assessing and adapting to your audience's reactions while your speech is in progress.

So far, we have focused on discovering as much as possible about an audience before the speaking event. Pre-speech analyses help with each step of the public-speaking process: selecting a topic, formulating a specific purpose, gathering supporting material, identifying major ideas, organizing the speech, and planning its delivery. Each of these components depends on your understanding your audience. But audience

SELECT AND NARROW YOUR TOPIC

CONSIDER
THE
AUDIENCE

After Matthew reads Chapter 2, listens to his instructor's discussion of public-speaking anxiety, and hears his classmates talk about how nervous they feel about their upcoming informative speech assignment, it dawns on him that public-speaking anxiety might make a good speech topic. His classmates would find the topic relevant and important, and he could contribute to their understanding of, and strategies for managing, public speaking anxiety. The topic also seems appropriate for his three- to five-minute time limit.

Determine Your Purpose

6.2 Write an audience-centered specific-purpose statement for a speech.

Now that you have selected and narrowed your topic, you need to decide on a purpose (the next step in Figure 6.1). If you do not know what you want your speech to achieve, chances are your audience won't either. Ask yourself "What is really important for the audience to hear?" and "How do I want the audience to respond?" Clarifying your objectives at this stage will ensure a more interesting speech and a more successful outcome.

General Purpose

general purpose

The broad reason for a speech: to inform, to persuade, or to entertain an audience

The **general purpose** of any speech is to inform, persuade, or entertain. The speeches you give in class will generally be either informative or persuasive. It is important that you fully understand what constitutes each type of speech so you do not confuse them and fail to fulfill an assignment. Although Chapters 13 through 16 discuss the three general purposes at length, we summarize them here so that you can understand the basic principles of each.

SPEAKING TO INFORM   An informative speaker is a teacher. Informative speakers give listeners information. They define, describe, or explain a thing, person, place, concept, process, or function. In this excerpt from an informative speech on anorexia nervosa, the student describes the disorder and its magnitude for her audience:

> Anorexia nervosa is an eating disorder that affects 1 out of every 200 American women. It is a self-induced starvation that can waste its victims to the point that they resemble victims of Nazi concentration camps.
>
> Who gets anorexia nervosa? Ninety-five percent of its victims are females between the ages of twelve and eighteen. Men are only rarely afflicted with the disease.

Most lectures you hear in college are informative, as is a university president's annual "state of the university" speech or a museum tour guide's talk. Such speakers are all trying to increase the knowledge of their listeners. Although they may use an occasional bit of humor in their presentations, their main objective is not to entertain. And although they may provoke an audience's interest in the topic, their main objective is not to persuade. Chapter 13 provides specific suggestions for preparing an informative speech.

SPEAKING TO PERSUADE   Persuasive speakers may offer information, but they use this information to try to change or reinforce an audience's convictions and often to urge some sort of action. For example, Nick told a compelling personal story to help persuade his audience to support regulation of the supplement industry:

> I myself fell victim to the claims the supplement industry was making. In an attempt to "get fit quick," I became heavily reliant on diet pills and other supplements. It took losing all of my savings, coughing up blood, and losing half of my hair … to get my attention.[5]

The representative from Mothers Against Drunk Driving (MADD) who spoke at your high-school assembly urged you not to drink and drive and to help others realize the inherent dangers of the practice. Appearing on television during the last election, the candidates for president of the United States asked for your vote. All these speakers gave you information, but they used that information to try to get you to believe or do something. Chapters 14 and 15 focus on persuasive speaking.

SPEAKING TO ENTERTAIN The entertaining speaker tries to get the members of an audience to relax, smile, perhaps laugh, and generally enjoy themselves. Storyteller Garrison Keillor spins tales of the town and residents of Lake Wobegon, Minnesota, to amuse his listeners. Comedian Louis C.K. delivers comic patter to make his audience laugh. As we describe in Chapter 16, most after-dinner speakers talk to entertain banquet guests. Like persuasive speakers, entertaining speakers may inform their listeners, but providing knowledge is not their main goal. Rather, their objective is to produce at least a smile and at best a belly laugh.

Early on, you need to decide which of the three general purposes your speech will have. The way you organize, support, and deliver your speech depends, in part, on your general purpose.

RECAP

GENERAL PURPOSES FOR SPEECHES

To inform	To share information with listeners by defining, describing, or explaining a thing, person, place, concept, process, or function
To persuade	To change or reinforce a listener's attitude, belief, value, or behavior
To entertain	To help listeners have a good time by getting them to relax, smile, and laugh

Specific Purpose

Now that you have a topic and you know generally whether your speech should inform, persuade, or entertain, it is time you decided on its specific purpose. A **specific purpose** is a concise audience-centered statement of what your listeners should be able to do by the time you finish your speech. Table 6.2 provides sample specific purpose statements for an informative speech, a persuasive speech, and a speech to entertain.

FORMULATING THE SPECIFIC PURPOSE Note that all of the specific-purpose statements in Table 6.2 begin with the same nine words: "At the end of my speech, the audience will… ." The next word should be a verb that names an observable, measurable action that the audience should perform or be able to perform by the end of the speech. Use verbs such as *list, explain, describe,* or *write.* Do not use words such as *know, understand,* or *believe.* You can discover what your listeners know, understand, or believe only by having them show their increased capability in some measurable way.

specific purpose
A statement of what listeners should be able to do by the end of the speech

Table 6.2 Specific Purpose Statements

General Purpose	Specific Purpose
To inform	At the end of my speech, the audience will be able to use the principles of feng shui to select wall colors.
To persuade	At the end of my speech, the audience will join the campaign for stable Internet access for all Americans.[6]
To entertain	At the end of my speech, the audience will laugh and applaud.

The specific purpose of a speaker whose general purpose is to entertain is often simply to help the audience laugh and smile about the topic of the speech. The late entertainer Mississippi Slim (Walter Horn) also hoped these students would be able to recall and use information about the blues musical tradition. *Photo:* Delta Democrat Times/Bill Johnson/AP Images.

Note too that a specific purpose statement should not express what the *speaker* will do. To say, "In my speech, I will talk about the benefits of studying classical dance" emphasizes your performance as a speaker. Instead, say "At the end of my speech, the audience will be able to list three ways in which studying classical dance can benefit them." This statement places the audience members and their behavior at the center of your concern. This latter statement provides a tangible goal that can guide your preparation and by which you can measure the success of your speech.

The guidelines and examples in Figure 6.5 will help you prepare your specific purpose statement.

USING THE SPECIFIC PURPOSE Everything you do while preparing and delivering the speech should contribute to your specific purpose. For example, the specific purpose can help you assess the supporting material you gather for your speech. You may find that an interesting statistic, although related to your topic, does not help achieve your specific purpose. In that case, you should not use it. Instead, find material that directly advances your purpose.

As soon as you have decided on it, write the specific purpose on a 3-by-5-inch note card. That way you can refer to it as often as necessary while developing your speech.

CONSIDER THE AUDIENCE

RECAP

SPECIFIC PURPOSES FOR SPEECHES

Your specific purpose should …
- Use words that refer to observable or measurable behavior.
- Be limited to a single idea.
- Reflect the needs, interests, expectations, and level of knowledge of your audience.

Figure 6.5 Guidelines for a Specific Purpose

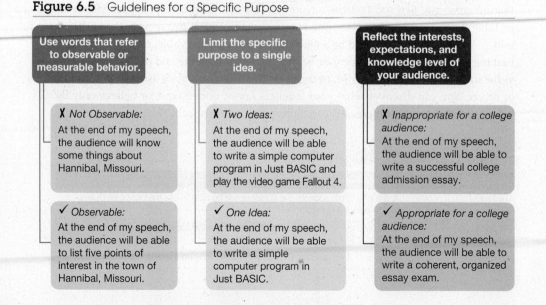

Use words that refer to observable or measurable behavior.	Limit the specific purpose to a single idea.	Reflect the interests, expectations, and knowledge level of your audience.
X *Not Observable:* At the end of my speech, the audience will know some things about Hannibal, Missouri.	**X** *Two Ideas:* At the end of my speech, the audience will be able to write a simple computer program in Just BASIC and play the video game Fallout 4.	**X** *Inappropriate for a college audience:* At the end of my speech, the audience will be able to write a successful college admission essay.
✓ *Observable:* At the end of my speech, the audience will be able to list five points of interest in the town of Hannibal, Missouri.	✓ *One Idea:* At the end of my speech, the audience will be able to write a simple computer program in Just BASIC.	✓ *Appropriate for a college audience:* At the end of my speech, the audience will be able to write a coherent, organized essay exam.

DEVELOPING YOUR SPEECH STEP BY STEP

DETERMINE YOUR PURPOSE

Because Matthew's assignment is an informative speech, he knows that his general purpose is to inform. He will define public-speaking anxiety, explain its causes, and explore strategies for managing it.

Matthew also knows that his specific purpose must begin with the phrase, "At the end of my speech, the audience will...." So he jots down,

> At the end of my speech, the audience will understand public-speaking anxiety and how to manage it.

As Matthew thinks further about his draft specific purpose, he sees problems with it. How can he determine whether or not his audience "will understand" something? He edits his purpose statement to read,

> At the end of my speech, the audience will take steps to manage public-speaking anxiety.

This version is more observable, but "take steps to manage" seems more appropriate for a persuasive speech than an informative one. He wants his audience to demonstrate their understanding of public-speaking anxiety and how to manage it. Maybe a better informative purpose statement would be:

> At the end of my speech, the audience will be able to explain the physiology of public-speaking anxiety and strategies for managing it.

Matthew is pleased with this third version. It reflects an informative general purpose and specifies an observable behavioral objective. He is ready to move on to the next step of the process.

Develop Your Central Idea

6.3 State a single audience-centered central idea with direct, specific language in a complete declarative sentence.

Having stated the specific purpose of your speech, you are ready to develop your **central idea**, the first step highlighted in Figure 6.6. The central idea (sometimes called the *thesis*) states in one sentence what the speech is *about*. You can use your purpose statement to help you as you write your central idea. However, as Table 6.3 summarizes, a central idea differs from a purpose statement in both focus and application. A purpose statement focuses on audience behavior; the central

central idea
A one-sentence statement of what a speech is *about*

Table 6.3 Purpose Statement Versus Central Idea

The Purpose Statement	The Central Idea
Indicates what the audience should know or be able to do by the end of the speech	Summarizes the speech in one sentence
Guides the speaker's choices throughout the preparation of the speech, but is not stated in the speech	Guides the speaker's choices throughout the preparation of the speech, and is stated in the speech
	The Central Idea Should...
	Be a complete declarative sentence
	Use direct, specific language
	Be a single idea
	Be an audience-centered idea

Figure 6.6   State your central idea as a one-sentence summary of your speech, and then generate main ideas by looking for natural divisions, reasons, or steps to support your central idea.

SOURCE: Copyrighted by Pearson Education, Hoboken, NJ.

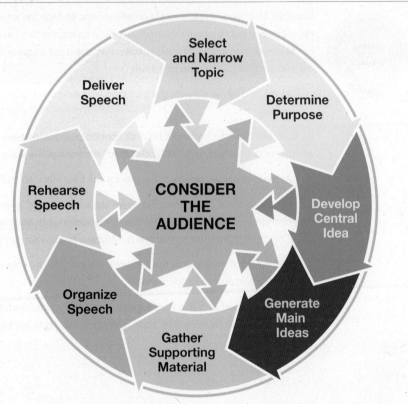

idea focuses on the content of the speech. A purpose statement guides your decisions and choices as you prepare your speech; the central idea becomes part of your final speech.

Professional speech coach Judith Humphrey explains the importance of a central idea:

> Ask yourself before writing a speech… "What's my point?" Be able to state that message in a single clear sentence. Everything else you say will support that single argument.[7]

The following guidelines can help you put your central idea into words.

A Complete Declarative Sentence

declarative sentence
A grammatically complete sentence, rather than a clause, phrase, or question

The central idea should be a complete **declarative sentence**—not a phrase or clause, and not a question, but a grammatically complete sentence. Figure 6.7 illustrates this guideline.

In Figure 6.7, the phrase "car maintenance" is a topic, not a central idea. It does not tell you anything about car maintenance. The question "Is regular car maintenance important?" is more complete but does not reveal whether the speaker is going to support an affirmative or negative answer. By the time you have finalized the wording of your central idea, you should be ready to summarize your stand on your topic in a complete declarative sentence.

Figure 6.7 The central idea should be a complete declarative sentence.

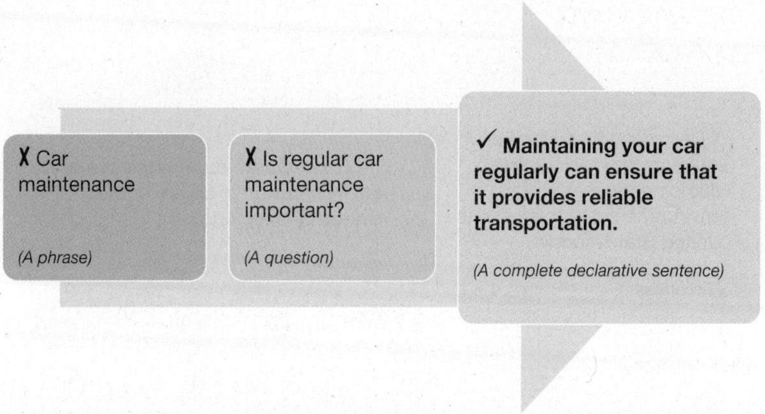

✗ Car maintenance

(A phrase)

✗ Is regular car maintenance important?

(A question)

✓ **Maintaining your car regularly can ensure that it provides reliable transportation.**

(A complete declarative sentence)

Direct, Specific Language

The central idea should be stated in direct, specific language rather than qualifiers and vague generalities. Figure 6.8 illustrates how the language of a central idea can be revised from qualified to direct, and from vague to specific.

Figure 6.8 The central idea should be worded in direct and specific language.

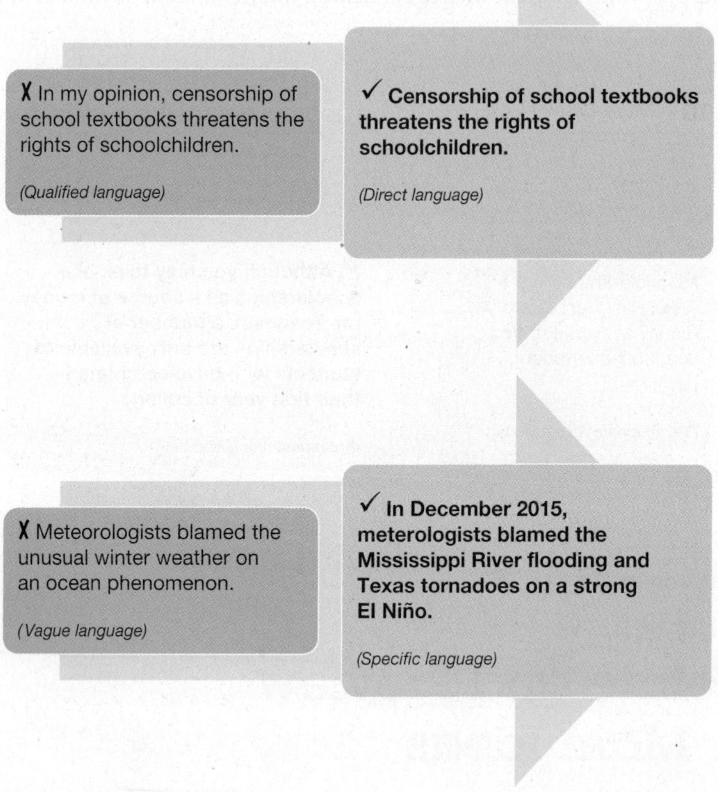

✗ In my opinion, censorship of school textbooks threatens the rights of schoolchildren.

(Qualified language)

✓ **Censorship of school textbooks threatens the rights of schoolchildren.**

(Direct language)

✗ Meteorologists blamed the unusual winter weather on an ocean phenomenon.

(Vague language)

✓ **In December 2015, meteorologists blamed the Mississippi River flooding and Texas tornadoes on a strong El Niño.**

(Specific language)

A Single Idea

The central idea should be a single idea. Figure 6.9 illustrates this guideline.

Having more than one central idea, like more than one idea in a purpose statement, only leads to confusion and a lack of coherence in a speech.

Figure 6.9 The central idea should be a single idea.

X Deforestation by lumber interests and toxic-waste dumping are major environmental problems in the United States today.

(Two ideas)

✓ Toxic-waste dumping is a major environmental problem in the United States today.

(One idea)

An Audience-Centered Idea

The central idea should reflect consideration of the audience. You considered your audience when selecting and narrowing your topic and when composing your purpose statement. In the same way, you should take into account your audience's needs, interests, expectations, and knowledge when stating your central idea. If you do not consider your listeners, you run the risk of losing their attention before you even begin developing the speech. For example, only one of the central ideas in Figure 6.10 would be appropriate for an audience consisting mainly of college juniors and seniors.

Figure 6.10 The central idea should be appropriate for the audience.

X Scholarships from a variety of sources are readily available to first-year college students.

(Inappropriate for audience)

✓ Although you may think of scholarships as a source of money for freshmen, a number of scholarships are only available to students who have completed their first year of college.

(Appropriate for audience)

Generate and Preview Your Main Ideas

6.4 Apply three ways of generating main ideas from a central idea.

Next to selecting a topic, probably the most common stumbling block in developing speeches is coming up with a speech plan. Trying to decide how to subdivide your central idea into two, three, or four **main ideas**—detailed points of focus that help you develop your central idea—can make you chew your pencil, scratch your head, and end up as you began, with a blank sheet of paper. The task will be much easier if you use the following strategy.

main ideas
Detailed points of focus for developing your central idea

DEVELOP YOUR CENTRAL IDEA

From reading this chapter, Matthew knows his central idea should be a complete declarative statement reflecting a single audience-centered idea. He knows, too, that sometimes you can extract your central idea from your specific-purpose statement. He writes,

> Both cognitive and physical public-speaking anxiety can be managed with specific strategies.

Generating Your Main Ideas

Write the central idea at the top of a clean sheet of paper or computer screen. Then ask these three questions:

- Does the central idea have *logical divisions*? (They may be indicated by such phrases as "three types" or "four means.")
- Can you think of several *reasons* the central idea is true?
- Can you support your central idea with a series of *steps* or a chronological progression?

You should be able to answer yes to one or more of these questions. With your answer in mind, write down the divisions, reasons, or steps you thought of. Let's see this technique at work with some sample central idea statements.

FINDING LOGICAL DIVISIONS Suppose your central idea is "A liberal arts education benefits the student in two ways." You now consider the first of the three questions listed previously. Does the central idea have logical divisions? The phrase "two ways" indicates that it does. So you can logically divide your speech into the two ways the student benefits:

1. Appreciation of culture
2. Concern for humankind

A brief brainstorming session at this point could help you come up with more specific examples of ways a liberal arts education might benefit students.

At this stage, you needn't worry about Roman numerals, parallel form, or even the order in which the main ideas are listed. We will discuss these and the other features of outlining in Chapter 8. Your goal now is simply to generate ideas. Moreover, just because you write them down, don't think that the ideas you come up with now are engraved in stone. They can—and probably will—change. After all, this is a *preliminary* plan. It may undergo many revisions before you actually deliver your speech.

ESTABLISHING REASONS Suppose your central idea is "Upholstered-furniture fires are a life-threatening hazard."[8] Asking yourself whether this idea has logical divisions is no help at all. There are no key phrases indicating logical divisions—no "ways," "means," "types," or "methods" appear in the wording. The second question, however, is more productive: Having done some initial reading on the topic, you can think of *reasons* this central idea is true. Asking yourself "Why?" after the statement yields three answers:

A student can use logical divisions to divide the contents of her closet into three main categories: bedding, clothing, and towels. You might also be able to use logical divisions to divide your central idea into main ideas. *Photo:* Kekyalyaynen/Shutterstock.

1. Standards to reduce fires caused by smoldering cigarettes have lulled furniture makers into a false sense of security.

2. Government officials refuse to force the furniture industry to reexamine its standards.

3. Consumers are largely ignorant of the risks.

Notice that these main ideas are expressed in complete sentences, whereas the ones in the preceding example were in phrases. At this stage, it doesn't matter. What does matter is getting your ideas down on paper; you can rewrite and reorganize them later.

TRACING SPECIFIC STEPS "NASA's space shuttle program resulted in both great achievement and tragic failure." You stare glumly at the central idea you so carefully formulated yesterday. Now what? You know a lot about the subject; your aerospace science professor has covered it thoroughly this semester. But how can you organize all the information you have? Again, you turn to the three-question method.

Does the main idea have logical divisions? You scan the sentence hopefully, but you can find no key phrases suggesting logical divisions.

Can you think of several reasons why the central idea is true? You read the central idea again and ask "Why?" Answering that question may indeed produce a plan for a speech, one in which you would talk about the reasons for the achievements and failures. But your purpose statement reads, "At the end of my speech, the audience will be able to trace the history of the space shuttle." Giving reasons for the space shuttle program's achievements and failures would not directly contribute to your purpose. So you turn to the third question.

Can you support your central idea with a series of steps? By answering this third question, you can generate main ideas for a speech about almost any historical topic

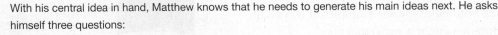

DEVELOPING YOUR SPEECH STEP BY STEP

GENERATE YOUR MAIN IDEAS

With his central idea in hand, Matthew knows that he needs to generate his main ideas next. He asks himself three questions:

- Does my central idea have *logical divisions*?
- Can I establish several *reasons* my central idea is true?
- Can I support my central idea by tracing specific *steps*?

Matthew can't think of *reasons* his central idea is true. He could possibly support it by tracing specific *steps* his listeners can take to manage public-speaking anxiety. But he also wants his audience members to be able to explain both the cognitive and physical components of public-speaking anxiety. Maybe his central idea has *natural divisions*:

1. Cognitive anxiety
2. Physical anxiety

Matthew now has two possible main ideas—a good start. But he looks back at his specific-purpose statement and remembers that he also wants his listeners to be able to manage public-speaking anxiety. So he adds a third main idea:

3. Strategies for managing public speaking-anxiety

Now Matthew has three main ideas that both support his central idea and fulfill his specific purpose.

or any topic requiring a chronological progression (for example, topics for how-to speeches). You therefore decide that your main ideas will be a chronology of important space shuttle flights:[9]

1. April 1981: Test flight of the space shuttle.
2. January 1986: Shuttle *Challenger* explodes on launch.
3. April 1990: Hubble space telescope deployed.
4. May–June 1999: Shuttle *Discovery* docks with the International Space Station.
5. February 2003: Shuttle *Columbia* disintegrates on re-entry.
6. July 2011: Shuttle *Atlantis* makes the program's final flight.

You know that you can add to, eliminate, or reorganize these ideas later. But now you have a place to start.

Notice that for this last example, you consulted your purpose statement as you generated your main ideas. If these main ideas do not help achieve your purpose, you need to rethink your speech. You may change either your purpose or your main ideas; but whichever you do, you need to synchronize them. Remember, it is much easier to make changes at this point than after you have done your research and produced a detailed outline.

Previewing Your Main Ideas

Once you have generated your main ideas, you can produce a **blueprint** for your speech by adding a preview of those main ideas to your central idea. Preview the ideas in the same order you plan to discuss them in the speech. (In Chapter 8, we discuss how to organize your speech.)

blueprint
The central idea of a speech plus a preview of the main ideas

Some speakers, like Nicole, integrate their central idea and preview into one blueprint sentence:

> Obsolete computers are straining landfills because they contain hazardous materials and take a distinctively long time to decay.[10]

In this example, Nicole started with her central idea: "Obsolete computers are straining landfills." Asking herself "Why?" yielded two reasons, which became her two main points: "They contain hazardous materials" and "They take a distinctively long time to decay." Combining these reasons with her central idea produced a blueprint.

Other speakers, like Patrick in his speech on problems associated with mining oil by hydraulic fracturing, state their blueprint in several sentences:

> In order to understand the fundamental threat fracturing poses, we must first understand the dangers at each step of the process. Second, we need to expose the corrupt legal maneuvering which protects it. And, finally, we must champion the simple solution that will save American lives.[11]

Patrick also started with a central idea: Fracturing poses a fundamental threat. Like Nicole, he generated reasons for his central idea, which in this case were "dangers at each step of the process" and "corrupt legal maneuvering which protects it." At this early point in the speech, he decided simply to mention that there is a "simple solution that will save American lives." Thinking that a single sentence might become unwieldy, Patrick decided to use three shorter sentences for his blueprint.

MEANWHILE, BACK AT THE COMPUTER...

It's been a while since we abandoned Ed Garcia, the procrastinating student in the opening paragraphs of this chapter who was struggling to write a speech on college football. If he gets down to work and follows the steps we have discussed, he should still be able to plan a successful informative speech.

Ed has already chosen his topic. His audience is likely to be interested in his subject. Because Ed is a varsity defensive tackle, the audience will probably expect him to talk about college football. And he himself is passionately interested in and knowledgeable about the subject. It meets all the requirements of a successful topic.

But "college football" is too broad a subject for a three- to five-minute talk. Ed needs to narrow his topic to a manageable size. He goes online to the DMOZ Web directory and clicks on the category Sports, then in rapid succession, clicks on Football, American Colleges and Universities, News and Media, and *CBS Sports.com*. There, a recent story on traumatic brain injury catches his eye. Hmmmm.... Ed himself once suffered a concussion and has a personal interest in this aspect of football. Ed doesn't need to go further. He has his topic: "traumatic brain injuries in college football."

Now that he has narrowed the topic, Ed needs a purpose statement. He decides that his audience may know something about concussions, but they probably do not know about the potential long-term consequences of such injuries. He types, "The audience will be able to list and explain three possible long-term consequences of traumatic brain injuries suffered by college football players."

A few minutes later, Ed derives his central idea from his purpose: "Former college football players may experience at least three long-term consequences of traumatic brain injuries suffered during their days as players."

Generating main ideas is also fairly easy now. Because his central idea mentions three consequences, he can plan his speech around those three ideas (logical divisions). Under the central idea, Ed lists

1. Loss of cognitive function
2. Impaired sensation
3. Emotional changes

Now Ed has a plan and is well on his way to developing a successful three- to five-minute informative speech.

STUDY GUIDE: REVIEW, APPLY, AND ASSESS

Select and Narrow Your Topic

6.1 Select and narrow a speech topic that is appropriate to the audience, the occasion, the time limits, and yourself.

REVIEW: As a speaker, you may be asked to address a specific topic or given only broad guidelines, such as a time limit and an idea of the occasion. Being aware of several boundaries can help you select an appropriate speech topic. Keep in mind the interests, expectations, and knowledge levels of the audience. Choose an important topic. Consider the special demands of the occasion. Be sure to take into account your own interests, abilities, and experiences. If you are still undecided, brainstorming strategies, such as consulting the media or scanning Web directories for potential topics, may give you topic ideas. After choosing a broad topic area, narrow the topic so it fits within the time limits that have been set.

Key Terms
brainstorming
clustering

APPLY:

1. Some speakers prepare a stock speech and deliver it to a variety of audiences and on a variety of occasions. Is this practice ethical? Explain your answer.

2. A candidate for the state legislature visits your public-speaking class and talks for thirty minutes on the topic "Why the state should increase public transportation funding." Analyze the candidate's choice of topic according to the guidelines presented in this chapter.

ASSESS: Review Table 6.1. For each of the audiences listed in the left-hand column, generate at least one additional audience-centered topic.

Determine Your Purpose

6.2 Write an audience-centered specific-purpose statement for a speech.

REVIEW: After choosing a topic, first decide on your general purpose and then your specific purpose. Your general purpose for speaking will be to inform, to persuade, or to entertain your listeners. Your specific purpose should state what your audience will *do* at the end of the speech. Specifying target behaviors in your specific-purpose statement provides a yardstick for you to measure the relevance of your ideas and supporting materials.

Key Terms
general purpose
specific purpose

APPLY: In Chapter 3, we define ethical speech as speech that offers the listener choices. Do specific-purpose statements preclude listeners' right to choose?

ASSESS:

1. Consider the following specific-purpose statements. Analyze each according to the criteria presented in this chapter. Rewrite the statements to correct any problems.

   - At the end of my speech, the audience will know more about the Mexican Free-Tailed Bat.
   - I will explain some differences in nonverbal communication between Asian and Western cultures.
   - At the end of my speech, the audience will be able to list some reasons for xeriscaping one's yard.
   - To describe the reasons I enjoy spelunking as a hobby.

2. As you develop your specific purpose for your next speech, explain how you will be able to observe or measure your audience's response.

Develop Your Central Idea

6.3 State a single audience-centered central idea with direct, specific language in a complete declarative sentence.

REVIEW: Specific-purpose statements indicate what speakers hope to accomplish; they tell what the speaker wants the *audience* to be able to do. Your central idea, in contrast, summarizes what *you*, the speaker, will say. The central idea should be a single idea, stated in a complete declarative sentence. Be direct and specific without using qualifiers.

Key Terms
central idea
declarative sentence

APPLY: Below are the topic, general purpose, and specific purpose Marylin has chosen for her persuasive speech.

- Topic: America's crumbling roads and bridges
- General Purpose: To persuade
- Specific Purpose: At the end of my speech, the audience will be able to list and explain three reasons America should invest in its roads and bridges.

Write an appropriate central idea for Marylin's speech.

Generate and Preview Your Main Ideas

6.4 Apply three ways of generating main ideas from a central idea.

REVIEW: After formulating your central idea, use it to generate main ideas. Determine whether the central idea (1) has logical divisions, (2) can be supported by several reasons, or (3) can be traced through a series of steps. These divisions, reasons, or steps become the blueprint, or plan, of your speech. You will preview them in your introduction and summarize them in your conclusion.

Key Terms
main ideas
blueprint

APPLY: You have already written a central idea for Marylin's persuasive speech on America's crumbling roads and bridges. Now use your central idea to generate main ideas for this speech. Be prepared to explain *how* you derived the main ideas from the central idea.

ASSESS: Check the main ideas you drafted for the previous "apply" question against Marylin's specific-purpose statement. If any main idea does not contribute to what she wants the audience to do at the end of her speech, make appropriate revisions to either the specific purpose or the main idea(s).

Gathering and Using Supporting Material

*Learn, compare, collect the facts!
... always have the courage to
say to yourself—I am ignorant.*
    —Ivan Petrovich Pavlov

George Adamson, (1913–2005). *Modern Young Writer Gets Inspiration from Multimedia Muses.* Gouache on card, Private Collection/Bridgeman Images.

OBJECTIVES

After studying this chapter, you should be able to do the following:

7.1 List five potential sources of supporting material for a speech.

7.2 Explain five strategies for a methodical research process.

7.3 List and describe six types of supporting material.

7.4 List six criteria for determining the best supporting material to use in a speech.

A pple pie is your specialty. Your family and friends relish your flaky crust, spicy filling, and crunchy crumb topping. Fortunately, not only do you have a never-fail recipe and technique, but you also know where to go for the best ingredients. Fette's Orchard has the tangiest pie apples in town. For your crust, you use only Premier shortening, which you buy at Meyer's Specialty Market. Your crumb topping requires both stone-ground whole-wheat flour and fresh creamery butter, available on Tuesdays at the farmer's market on the courthouse square.

Just as making your apple pie requires that you know where to find specific ingredients, creating a successful speech requires knowledge of sources, research strategies, and types of supporting material that speechmakers typically use. This chapter covers the speech-development step highlighted in Figure 7.1: Gather Supporting Material.

Figure 7.1 Finding, identifying, and effectively using supporting material are activities essential to the speech-preparation process.

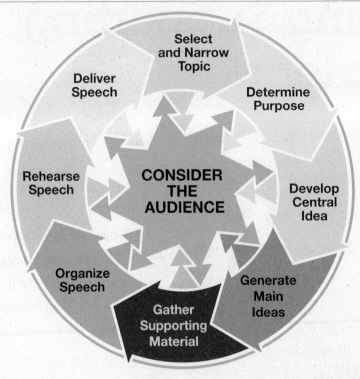

Sources of Supporting Material

7.1 List five potential sources of supporting material for a speech.

Supporting material for your speech can come from a variety of sources, including personal knowledge and experience, the Internet, online databases, traditional library holdings, and interviews.

Personal Knowledge and Experience

Because you will probably give speeches on topics you are particularly interested in, you may find that *you* are your own best source. You may be able to provide an effective illustration, explanation, definition, or other type of supporting material from your own knowledge and experience. As an audience-centered speaker, you should realize, too, that personal knowledge often has the additional advantage of heightening your credibility in the minds of your listeners. They will accord you more respect as an authority when they realize that you have firsthand knowledge of a topic.

The Internet

When facing a research task, most people turn first to the Internet. Understanding how to locate and evaluate Internet resources can help make your search for supporting material more productive.

LOCATING INTERNET RESOURCES   If you feel overwhelmed by the number of hits generated from your Google search, you can use various strategies to narrow your results. For example, try enclosing your search phrase in quotation marks or parenthesis so that your search yields only those sites on which the exact phrase appears. Another

Figure 7.2 Nine Types of Web Sites

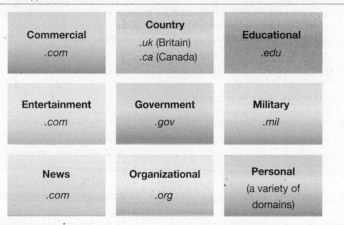

option is to use a more specialized **vertical search engine**. For example, Google Scholar indexes academic sources, and Indeed indexes job sites.

Exploring Internet Resources   As you begin to explore the search results you've generated, you will discover a wide variety of sites—from Web pages that try to sell you something, to the official sites of government agencies and news organizations. One clue to the type of site you have found is the **domain**, indicated by the last three letters of the site's URL (for example, *.com* or *.org*).

Although sites can be classified in a number of different ways, most fall into one of the nine types listed in Figure 7.2.[1]

Evaluating Internet Resources   Although the Web was founded on the principle of free speech, the lack of legal, financial, or editorial restriction on what is published online presents both a logistical and an ethical challenge to researchers.

As you begin to explore the sites you discover, you will need to evaluate them according to a consistent standard. The six criteria in Table 7.1 can serve as such a standard.[2] The first four criteria can act as guidelines for evaluating any resource, regardless of whether it is a Web site, a print document, or even information you obtain in an interview.

No discussion of evaluating Internet resources would be complete without mentioning *Wikipedia*, the resource that often appears as the first hit from a Web search. As *Wikipedia*'s own site project page notes, the

vertical search engine
A Web site that indexes World Wide Web information in a specific field

domain
Category in which a Web site is located on the Internet, indicated by the last three letters of the site's URL

RECAP

FINDING SUPPORTING MATERIAL ON THE WEB

1. Use a directory or search engine to find relevant Internet sites.
2. Evaluate sites according to these six criteria: accountability, accuracy, objectivity, timeliness, usability, and diversity.

Figure 7.3 Limitations and Advantages of *Wikipedia*

SOURCE: "About Wikipedia," Site project page, https://en.wikipedia.org/wiki/Wikipedia:About

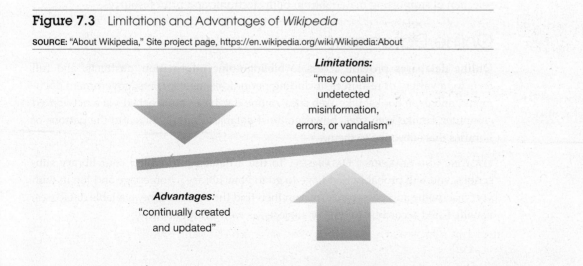

Limitations:
"may contain undetected misinformation, errors, or vandalism"

Advantages:
"continually created and updated"

Table 7.1   Six Criteria for Evaluating Internet Resources

Criterion	Applying the Criterion	Drawing Conclusions
Accountability: Who is responsible for the site?	• The individual or organization responsible for the site may be clear from the title of the site and/or its URL. • See whether the site is signed. • Follow links or search the author's name to determine his or her expertise and authority. • If the site is unsigned, search for a sponsoring organization. Follow links, search the organization's name, or consider the domain to determine reputability.	• If you cannot identify or verify an author or sponsor, be wary of the site.
Accuracy: Is the information correct?	• Consider whether the author or sponsor is a credible authority. • Assess the care with which the site has been written. • Conduct additional research into the information on the site.	• If the author or sponsor is a credible authority, the information is more likely to be accurate. • A site should be relatively free of writing errors. • You may be able to verify or refute the information by consulting another resource.
Objectivity: Is the site free of bias?	• Consider the interests, philosophical or political biases, and the source of financial support for the author or sponsor of the site. • Does the site include advertisements that might influence its content?	• The more objective the author and sponsor of the site are, the more credible their information may be.
Timeliness: Is the site current?	• Look at the bottom of the site for a statement indicating when the site was created and when it was last updated. • If you cannot find a date on the site, click on Page Info (for example, from the Tools menu at the top of the browser screen in Firefox) to find a "Last Modified" date. • Enter the title of the site in a search engine. The resulting information should include a date.	• In general, when you are concerned with factual data, the more recent it is, the better.
Usability: Do the layout and design of the site facilitate its use?	• Does the site load fairly quickly? • Is a fee required to gain access to any of the information on the site?	• Balance graphics and any fees against practical efficiency.
Diversity: Is the site inclusive?	• Do language and graphics reflect and respect differences in gender, ethnicity, race, and sexual preference? • Do interactive forums invite divergent perspectives? • Is the site friendly to people with disabilities (e.g., does it offer a large-print or video option)?	• A site should be free of bias, representative of diverse perspectives, and accessible by people with disabilities.

SOURCE: Copyrighted by Pearson Education, Hoboken, NJ.

resource has both advantages and disadvantages, which are summarized in Figure 7.3. *Wikipedia* can be useful for general information about current events and new technology that may not find its way into print resources for years. But users need to keep in mind that because anyone, regardless of expertise, can add to or change the content of a Wikipedia entry, the site's reliability and appropriateness for academic use are limited.

Later in this chapter we provide additional criteria to help you make your final selection of supporting material from both electronic and print resources.

Online Databases

online databases

Subscription-based electronic resources that may offer access to abstracts or the full texts of entries, as well as bibliographic data

Online databases provide access to bibliographic information, abstracts, and full texts for a variety of resources, including periodicals, newspapers, government documents, and even books. Like Web sites, online databases are reached via a networked computer. Unlike Web sites, however, most databases are restricted to the patrons of libraries that subscribe to them.

LOCATING AND SEARCHING DATABASES   To use a database to which your library subscribes, you will probably first have to go to your library's homepage and log in with your username and password. You can then find the names of the available databases, usually listed according to type or subjects, as well as alphabetically.

Searching a database is relatively simple. Each database opens with a search box where you can type relevant information such as keywords and date ranges. Most also allow other types of advanced searches.

In some cases, you may be able to search more than one database at a time by using providers that offer access to multiple databases. ProQuest, for example, provides single source access to databases of alternative newspapers, criminal justice periodicals, doctoral dissertations, and education journals as well as its popular *ABI/INFORM Global* database of business and finance publications.

EXPLORING DATABASE RESOURCES   Many online databases that began as computerized indexes now provide access to full texts of the resources themselves. Your library may subscribe to several or all of the following popular full-text databases:

- **Academic Search Complete.**   This database offers many full-text articles from 1887 to the present, covering a wide variety of subjects.
- **JSTOR.**   This is a multi-subject, full-text database of journal articles from the first volume to the present.
- **LexisNexis Academic.**   Focusing on business and law, this database provides many full-text articles from newspapers, magazines, journals, newsletters, and wire services. Dates of coverage vary.
- **Newspaper Source.**   This database offers many full-text articles from more than 40 U.S. and international newspapers; television and radio news transcripts from CBS News, CNN, CNN International, FOX News, NPR, and others; and selected full-text articles from more than 330 regional (U.S.) newspapers.

Traditional Library Holdings

Despite the rapid development of Internet and database resources, the more traditional holdings of libraries, both paper and electronic, remain rich sources of supporting material.

LOCATING TRADITIONAL LIBRARY HOLDINGS   Spend some time becoming familiar with your library's services and layout so that you know how to access and locate books and reference materials. Many encyclopedias, dictionaries, directories, atlases, almanacs, yearbooks, books of quotations, and biographical dictionaries are now available online. But if you are not able to find a specific reference resource online, you may be able to locate a print version through your library's online holdings catalog. As shown in the example in Figure 7.4, the catalog supplies each book's *call number*, which you will need to find the title.

Figure 7.4   An online catalog entry for a book. The same entry will appear on the screen regardless of whether the work is accessed using its title, author, or subject area.

SOURCE: Courtesy of Albert B. Alkek Library, Texas State University.

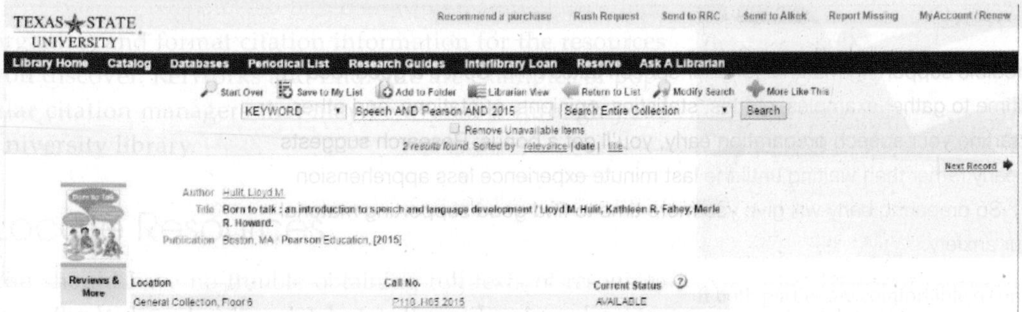

accurately or fairly. As you evaluate sources, try to find out how the statistics were gathered. Of course, finding out about the statistical methodology may be more difficult than discovering the source of the statistic, but if you can find it, the information will help you to analyze its value.

INTERPRETING STATISTICS ACCURATELY   People are often swayed by statistics that sound good but have in fact been wrongly calculated or misinterpreted. For example, a speaker might say that the number of children killed by guns in the United States has doubled every year since 1950. But Joel Best, author of *Damned Lies and Statistics: Untangling Numbers from the Media, Politicians, and Activists*, points out that actually doing the math quickly demonstrates how wildly inaccurate this statistic is. If one child was killed in 1950, two in 1951, four in 1952, and so on, the annual number by now would far exceed the entire population of not just the United States, but also of the entire Earth.[19]

Both as a user of statistics in your own speeches and as a consumer of statistics in articles, books, and speeches, be constantly alert to what the statistics actually mean.

MAKING STATISTICS UNDERSTANDABLE AND MEMORABLE   You can make your statistics easier to understand and more memorable in several ways:

1. First, you can *dramatize* a statistic by strategically choosing the perspective from which you present it. Authors of a popular book about statistics offer this example of how dramatizing a statistic attracted the attention of the press:

    > Researchers found that a genetic variant…present in 10 percent of the population *protected* them against high blood pressure. Although published in a top scientific journal, the story received negligible press coverage until a knowing press officer rewrote the press release to say that a genetic variant…had been discovered which *increased* the risk of high blood pressure in 90 percent of people.[20]

2. Second, you can *compact* a statistic, or express it in units that are more meaningful or more easily understandable to your audience. The president and CEO of the nonprofit Heifer International, compacted a statistic to drive home the appalling poverty of a family:

    > Virginia Carrillo, a coffee farmer in Guatemala … and her husband have eight children, and their annual household income from all activities is $3,285. At 90 cents per person per day, this family clearly lives in extreme poverty.[21]

3. You might also make your statistics more memorable by *exploding* them. Exploded statistics are created by adding or multiplying related numbers—for example, cost per unit times number of units. Because it is larger, the exploded statistic seems more significant than the original figures from which it was derived. The CEO of AARP used the "exploding" strategy to emphasize the impact of lowering the growth rate of health care costs by just 1.5 percentage points per year:

    > [L]owering the growth rate of health care costs by 1.5 percentage points per year will increase the real income of middle-class families by $2,600 in 2020; $10,000 in 2030; and $24,300 by 2040. That's real relief for real people.[22]

4. Finally, you can *compare* your statistic with another that heightens its impact. To communicate to her audience the brightness of a recently discovered supernova, a speaker might say,

    > It is more than twice as luminous as any supernova observed to date, including the previous record-holders.

At its peak intensity, is believed to be 20 times more luminous than the entire Milky Way. Some estimates put it at 50 times brighter.

And try this statistic on for size: It is 570 billion times brighter at its peak than our sun.[23]

Opinions

Three types of **opinions** may be used as supporting material in speeches: the testimony of an expert authority, the testimony of an ordinary (lay) person with firsthand or eyewitness experience, and a quotation from a literary work.

EXPERT TESTIMONY Having already offered statistics on the number of cigars Americans smoke annually, Dena emphasized the danger to both smokers and recipients of secondhand smoke by providing **expert testimony** from a National Cancer Institute adviser:

> James Repace, an adviser to the National Cancer Institute, states, "If you have to breathe secondhand smoke, cigar smoke is a lot worse than cigarette smoke."[24]

In Chapter 3, we discuss the importance of citing your sources orally. In the course of doing so, you can provide additional information about the qualifications of those sources, as illustrated in the previous example.

The testimony of a recognized authority can add a great deal of weight to your arguments. Or if your topic requires that you make predictions—statements that can be supported in only a marginal way by statistics or examples—the statements of expert authorities may prove to be your most convincing support.

LAY TESTIMONY You are watching the nightly news. Newscasters reporting on the forest fires that continue to rage in Colorado explain how these fires started. They provide statistics on how many thousands of acres have burned and how many hundreds of homes have been destroyed. They describe the intense heat and smoke at the scene of one of the fires, and they ask an expert—a veteran firefighter—to predict the likelihood that the fires will be brought under control soon. But the most poignant moment of this story is an interview with a woman who has just returned to her home and has found it in smoldering ashes. She is a layperson—not a firefighter or an expert on forest fires, but someone who has experienced the tragedy firsthand.

Like an illustration, **lay testimony** can stir an audience's emotions. And, although neither as authoritative nor as unbiased as expert testimony, lay testimony is often more memorable.

LITERARY QUOTATION Another way to make a point memorable is to include a **literary quotation** in your speech. Speaking on changes essential to the survival of the automotive industry, Chrysler Corporation CEO Sergio Marchionne drew on the words of philosopher Friedrich Nietzsche:

> The philosopher Friedrich Nietzsche once said that "what really arouses indignation against suffering is not suffering as such but the senselessness of suffering... ." And a crisis that does not result in enduring changes, in fundamental changes, will have been very senseless indeed.[25]

Note that the Nietzsche quotation is short. Brief, pointed quotations usually have greater audience impact than longer, more rambling ones.

---

opinions
Statements expressing an individual's attitudes, beliefs, or values

expert testimony
An opinion offered by someone who is an authority on a subject

lay testimony
An opinion or description offered by a nonexpert who has firsthand experience

literary quotation
An opinion or description by a writer who speaks in a memorable and often poetic way

---

RECAP

TYPES OF SUPPORTING MATERIAL

Illustrations	Relevant stories
Explanations	Statements that clarify how something is done or why it exists in its present form or existed in a past form
Descriptions	Word pictures
Definitions	Concise explanations of a word or concept
Analogies	Comparisons between two things
Statistics	Numbers that summarize data or examples
Opinions	Testimony or quotations from someone else

Figure 7.11 Using Opinions Effectively

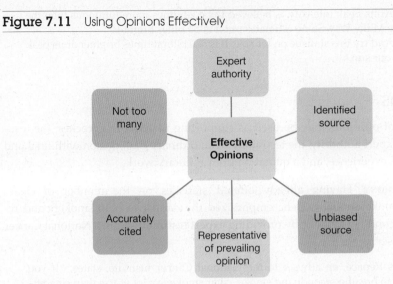

Literary quotations have the additional advantage of being easily accessible. You'll find any number of quotation dictionaries on the Web and in the reference sections of most libraries. Arranged alphabetically by subject, these compilations are easy to use.

Figure 7.11 provides six suggestions for using opinions effectively in your speeches.

The Best Supporting Material

7.4 List six criteria for determining the best supporting material to use in a speech.

In this chapter, we discussed six criteria for evaluating Web sites: accountability, accuracy, objectivity, timeliness, usability, and diversity. We also presented guidelines for using each of the six types of supporting material effectively. However, even after you have applied these criteria and guidelines, you may still have more supporting material than you can possibly use for a short speech. How do you decide what to use and what to eliminate? The criteria presented in Figure 7.12 and discussed here can help you make that final cut.

- **Magnitude.**   Bigger is better. The larger the numbers, the more convincing your statistics. The more experts who support your point of view, the more your expert testimony will command your audience's attention.

- **Relevance.**   The best supporting material is whatever is the most relevant to your listeners, or the closest to home. If you can demonstrate how an incident could affect audience members themselves, that illustration will have far greater impact than a more remote one.

- **Concreteness.**   If you need to discuss abstract ideas, explain them using concrete examples and specific statistics.

- **Variety.**   A mix of illustrations, opinions, definitions, and statistics is much more interesting and convincing than the exclusive use of any one type of supporting material.

- **Humor.**   Audiences usually appreciate a touch of humor in an example or opinion. However, humor is not appropriate if your audience is unlikely to understand it or if your speech is on a somber or serious topic.

Figure 7.12 Criteria for the Best Supporting Material

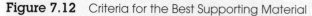

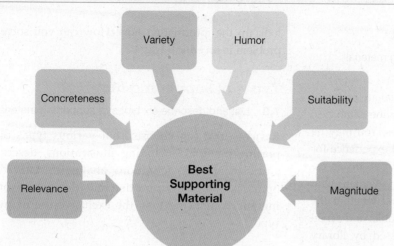

● **Suitability.** Your final decision about whether to use a certain piece of supporting material will depend on its suitability to you, your speech, the occasion, and—as we continue to stress throughout the text—your audience. For example, you would probably use more statistics in a speech to a group of scientists than in an after-luncheon talk to the local Rotary Club.

STUDY GUIDE: REVIEW, APPLY, AND ASSESS

Sources of Supporting Material

7.1 List five potential sources of supporting material for a speech.

REVIEW: Five sources of supporting material are personal knowledge and experience, the Internet, online databases, traditional library holdings, and interviews. You may be able to draw on your own knowledge and experience for some supporting material. Internet resources are accessible through Web searches, but you must evaluate who is accountable for the sources you find and whether the sources are accurate, objective, current, usable, and sensitive to diversity. Online databases, accessed by library subscription via a networked computer, provide access to bibliographic information, abstracts, and full texts for a variety of resources, including periodicals, newspapers, government documents, and even books. Traditional library holdings include books and other types of reference resources. When conducting an interview, take written notes or record the interview.

Key Terms

vertical search engine	online databases
domain	stacks

APPLY:

1. Electronic and print indexes and databases sometimes include abstracts of books and articles rather than full texts. If you have read only the abstract of a source, is it ethical to include that source in your preliminary bibliography?

2. Explain how you might use each of the five key sources of supporting material to help you develop an informative speech on how to choose a new computer.

Research Strategies

7.2 Explain five strategies for a methodical research process.

REVIEW: A methodical research process includes the following strategies: Develop a preliminary bibliography, locate resources, assess the usefulness of resources, take notes, and identify possible presentation aids.

Key Terms

preliminary bibliography	citation manager

APPLY: You neglected to record complete bibliographic information for one of your best information sources, a journal article you found on a database. You discover your omission as you are reviewing your outline just before you deliver your speech, and you have no way to

look up the information now. How can you solve your problem in an ethical way?

Types of Supporting Material

7.3 List and describe six types of supporting material.

REVIEW: You can choose from various types of supporting material, including illustrations, descriptions and explanations, definitions, analogies, statistics, and opinions. A mix of supporting material is more interesting and convincing than the exclusive use of any one type.

Key Terms

illustration	operational definition
brief illustration	analogy
extended illustration	literal analogy
personal illustration	figurative analogy
hypothetical illustration	statistics
description	opinions
explanation	expert testimony
definition	lay testimony
definition by classification	literary quotation

APPLY: Is it ever ethical to invent supporting material if you have been unable to find what you need for your speech? Explain your answer.

ASSESS: Review the guidelines for each type of supporting material. Which of these guidelines for the *effective* use of supporting material might also be considered a guideline for the *ethical* use of supporting material? Explain your choice(s).

The Best Supporting Material

7.4 List six criteria for determining the best supporting material to use in a speech.

REVIEW: Once you have gathered a variety of supporting material, look at your speech from your audience's perspective and decide where an explanation might help listeners understand a point, where statistics might convince them of the significance of a problem, and where an illustration might stir their emotions. Six criteria—magnitude, proximity, concreteness, variety, humor, and suitability—can help you choose the most effective support for your speech.

ASSESS: The best supporting material is whatever is the most relevant to your listeners or "closest to home." Applying this criterion to the supporting material you gather for your next speech, determine which item or items are likely to be most effective.

Organizing and Outlining Your Speech

Organized thought is the basis of organized action.

—Alfred North Whitehead

Anne Desmet (b. 1964), *Tower of Babble*, 2000. Wooden type, wood engraving and collage on paper. Private Collection/ Bridgeman Images.

OBJECTIVES

After studying this chapter, you should be able to do the following:

8.1 List and describe five patterns for organizing the main ideas of a speech.

8.2 Explain how to organize supporting material.

8.3 Use verbal and nonverbal signposts to organize a speech for the ears of others.

8.4 Develop a preparation outline and speaking notes for a speech.

Maria went into the lecture hall feeling exhilarated. After all, Dr. Anderson was a Nobel laureate in literature. He would be teaching and lecturing on campus for at least a year. What an opportunity! Maria took a seat in the middle of the fourth row, where she had a clear view of the podium. She opened the notebook she had bought just for this lecture series, took out one of the three pens she had brought with her, and waited impatiently for Dr. Anderson's appearance. She didn't have to wait long. Dr. Anderson was greeted by thunderous applause when he walked onto the stage. Maria was aware of an almost electric sense of expectation among the audience members. Pen poised, she awaited his first words.

Five minutes later, Maria still had her pen poised. He had gotten off to a slow start. Ten minutes later, she laid her pen down and decided to concentrate just on listening. Twenty minutes later, she still had no idea what point Dr. Anderson was trying

to make. And by the time the lecture was over, Maria was practically asleep. Disappointed, she gathered her pens and her notebook (which now contained one page of lazy doodles) and decided she would skip the remaining lectures in the series.

Dr. Anderson was not a dynamic speaker. But his motivated audience of young would-be authors and admirers might have forgiven that shortcoming. What they were unable to do was to unravel his seemingly pointless rambling—to get some sense of direction or some pattern of ideas from his talk. Dr. Anderson had simply failed to organize his thoughts.

This scenario actually happened. Dr. Anderson (not his real name) disappointed many who had looked forward to his lectures. His inability to organize his ideas made him an ineffectual speaker. You, too, may have had an experience with a teacher who possessed expertise in his or her field but could not organize his or her thoughts well enough to lecture effectively. No matter how knowledgeable speakers may be, they must organize their ideas in logical patterns to ensure that their audience can follow, understand, and remember what is said. Our model of audience-centered communication, shown in Figure 8.1, emphasizes that speeches are organized *for* audiences. Decisions about organization should be based in large part on an analysis of the audience.

In the first seven chapters of this book, you learned how to plan and research a speech based on audience needs, interests, and expectations. The planning and research process has taken you through five stages of speech preparation:

- Selecting and narrowing a topic
- Determining your purpose
- Developing your central idea
- Generating main ideas
- Gathering supporting material

Figure 8.1 Organize your speech to help your audience remember your key ideas and to give your speech clarity and structure.

SOURCE: Copyrighted by Pearson Education, Hoboken, NJ.

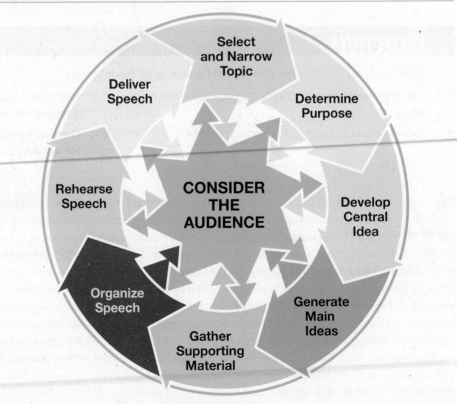

CONFIDENTLY CONNECTING WITH YOUR AUDIENCE

Organize Your Message

Taking the time to plan a well-organized message can boost your confidence. A jumble of ideas and information without a logical structure is more difficult to remember and present than a well-organized speech. Researchers have discovered that the *less* organized you are, the *more* apprehensive you may feel.[1] A logically organized speech can help you feel more confident about the content you're presenting.

As the arrows in the model in Figure 8.1 suggest, you may have moved *recursively* through these first five stages, returning at times to previous stages to make changes and revisions based on your consideration of the audience. Now, with the results of your audience-centered planning and research in hand, it is time to move to the next stage in the audience-centered public-speaking process:

- Organizing your speech

In this chapter, we will discuss the patterns of organization commonly used to arrange the main ideas of a speech. Then we will explain how to organize supporting material. We will talk about previews, transitions, and summaries. And, finally, we will discuss and illustrate two types of speech outlines: the preparation outline and speaking notes. Chapter 9 discusses introductions and conclusions, the final component of the organizational stage of the preparation process.

Organizing Your Main Ideas

8.1 List and describe five patterns for organizing the main ideas of a speech.

In Chapter 6, we discussed how to generate a preliminary plan for your speech by determining whether your central idea has logical divisions, could be supported by several reasons, or could be explained by identifying specific steps. These divisions, reasons, or steps become the main ideas of the body of your speech and the basis for the organization task highlighted in Figure 8.1.

Now you are ready to decide which of your main ideas to discuss first, second, and so on. As summarized in Table 8.1, you can choose from among five organizational patterns: (1) topical, (2) chronological, (3) spatial, (4) causal, and (5) problem-solution. Or you can combine several of these patterns. One additional variation of the problem-solution pattern is the motivated sequence. Because it is used almost exclusively in persuasive speeches, the motivated sequence is discussed in Chapter 15.

Table 8.1 Organizing Your Main Points

Pattern	Description
Topical	Organization according to primacy, recency, or complexity
Chronological	Organization by time or sequence
Spatial	Organization based on location or direction
Cause and effect	Organization that focuses on a situation and its causes or a situation and its effects
Problem-solution	Organization that focuses on a problem and then its solutions or on a solution and then the problems it would solve

SOURCE: Copyrighted by Pearson Education, Hoboken, NJ.

Organizing Ideas Topically

If your central idea has natural divisions, you can often organize your speech topically. Speeches on such diverse topics as factors to consider when selecting a mountain bike, types of infertility treatments, and the various classes of ham-radio licenses could all reflect **topical organization**.

Natural divisions are often essentially equal in importance. It may not matter which point you discuss first, second, or third. You can simply arrange your main ideas as a matter of personal preference. At other times, you may want to organize your main points based on one of three principles: primacy, recency, or complexity.

topical organization
Arrangement of the natural divisions in a central idea according to recency, primacy, complexity, or the speaker's discretion

primacy
Arrangement of ideas from the most to the least important

PRIMACY   The principle of **primacy** suggests that you discuss your most important or convincing point *first* in your speech. The beginning of your speech can be the most important position if your listeners are either unfamiliar with your topic or hostile toward your central idea.

When your listeners are uninformed, your first point must introduce them to the topic and define unfamiliar terms integral to its discussion. What you say early in your speech will affect your listeners' understanding of the rest of your speech. If your listeners are likely to be hostile toward your central idea, putting your most important or convincing point first will lessen the possibility that you might lose or alienate them before you reach the end of your speech. In addition, your strongest idea may so influence your listeners' attitudes that they will be more receptive to your central idea.

Recognizing the controversial nature of stem-cell research, the speaker in the following example arranges the three main ideas of the speech according to primacy, advancing the most persuasive argument first.

PURPOSE STATEMENT:	At the end of my speech, the audience will be able to explain the applications of stem-cell research.[2]
CENTRAL IDEA:	Stem-cell research has three important applications.
MAIN IDEAS:	I. At the most fundamental level, understanding stem cells can help us learn more about the process of human development.
	II. Stem-cell research can streamline the way we develop and test drugs.
	III. Stem-cell research can generate cells and tissue that could be used for "cell therapies."

recency
Arrangement of ideas from the least to the most important

RECENCY   According to the principle of **recency**, the point discussed *last* is the one audiences will remember best. If your audience is at least somewhat knowledgeable about and generally favorable toward your topic and central idea, you should probably organize your main points according to recency.

For example, in her speech on the responsibilities of a resident assistant (RA), Brooke wants to emphasize one responsibility her student audience might not have previously considered: role modeling. With the recency principle in mind, Brooke places that responsibility last in her speech outline:

PURPOSE STATEMENT:	At the end of my speech, the audience will be able to list and explain a resident assistant's responsibilities.
CENTRAL IDEA:	The responsibilities of a resident assistant fall into three categories.
MAIN IDEAS:	I. Community development
	II. Staff membership
	III. Role modeling[3]

COMPLEXITY One other set of circumstances may dictate a particular order of the main ideas in your speech. If your main ideas range from simple to complicated, it makes sense to arrange them in order of **complexity**, progressing from the simple to the more complex. If, for example, you were to explain to your audience how to compile a family health profile and history, you might begin with the most easily accessible source and proceed to the more involved.

complexity
Arrangement of ideas from the simple to the more complex

PURPOSE STATEMENT:	At the end of my speech, the audience will be able to compile a family health profile and history.
CENTRAL IDEA:	Compiling a family health profile and history can be accomplished with the help of three sources.
MAIN IDEAS:	I. Elderly relatives
	II. Old hospital records and death certificates
	III. National health registries[4]

Teachers, from those in the early elementary grades on up, use order of complexity to organize their courses and lessons. The kindergartner traces circles before learning to print a lowercase *a*. The young piano student practices scales and arpeggios before playing Beethoven sonatas. The college freshman practices writing short essays before undertaking a major research paper. You have learned most of your skills in order of complexity.

> **RECAP**
>
> **PRIMACY, RECENCY, AND COMPLEXITY**
>
> - Primacy—most important point first
> - Recency—most important point last
> - Complexity—simplest point first, most complex point last

Ordering Ideas Chronologically

If you decide that your central idea could be explained best by a number of steps, you will probably organize those steps chronologically. **Chronological organization** is organization by time or sequence; that is, your steps are ordered according to when each step occurred or should occur. Historical speeches and how-to speeches are the two kinds of speeches usually organized chronologically.

chronological organization
Organization by time or sequence

Examples of topics for historical speeches might include the history of the women's movement in the United States, the sequence of events that led to the 1974 resignation of President Richard Nixon, or the development of the modern Olympic Games. You can choose to organize your main points either from earliest to most recent (forward in time) or from recent events back into history (backward in time). The progression you choose depends on your personal preference and on whether you want to emphasize the beginning or the end of the sequence. As we observed, according to the principle of recency, audiences tend to remember best what they hear last.

In the following outline for a speech discussing the development of YouTube, the speaker wants to emphasize the inauspicious origins of the popular video site. Thus, she organizes the speech backward in time:

PURPOSE STATEMENT:	At the end of my speech, the audience will be able to describe YouTube's rapid rise from its humble beginnings.
CENTRAL IDEA:	Within a decade, YouTube had far exceeded its humble beginnings.
MAIN IDEAS:	I. 2015: More than 10,000 videos have been produced in YouTube Spaces.
	II. 2010: YouTube exceeds 2 billion views per day.
	III. 2005: YouTube is founded in a garage in Menlo Park, California.[5]

Like causes and effects, problems and solutions can be discussed in either order. When speaking to an audience that is already fairly aware of a problem but uncertain how to solve it, you will probably discuss the problem first and then the solution(s). Speechwriter Cynthia Starks explains how Robert Kennedy utilized problem-solution organization to comfort and inspire a crowd in Indianapolis on April 4, 1968, immediately following the assassination of Martin Luther King Jr.:

> With sensitivity and compassion, [Kennedy] told them of King's death (the devastating "problem"). He praised King's dedication to "love and to justice between fellow human beings," adding that, "he died in the cause of that effort."
>
> Then he offered a solution—to put aside violence and to embrace love and understanding toward each other.[10]

Starks concludes by offering evidence of the effectiveness of Kennedy's problem-solution speech:

> Many American cities burned after King's death, but there was no fire in Indianapolis, which heard the words of Robert Kennedy.

If your audience knows about an action or program that has been implemented but does not know the reasons for its implementation, you might select instead a solution-problem pattern of organization. In the following example, the speaker knows that her listeners are already aware of a new business-school partnership program in their community but believes that they may be unclear about why it has been established:

PURPOSE STATEMENT:	At the end of my speech, the audience will be able to explain how business-school partnership programs can help solve two of the major problems facing our public schools today.
CENTRAL IDEA:	Business-school partnership programs can help alleviate at least two of the problems faced by public schools today.
MAIN IDEAS:	I. (*Solution*): In a business-school partnership, local businesses provide volunteers, financial support, and in-kind contributions to public schools.
	II. (*Problem*): Many public schools can no longer afford fine arts and special programs.
	III. (*Problem*): Many public schools have no resources to fund enrichment materials and opportunities.

motivated sequence

A five-step adaptation of the problem-solution pattern; used to organize persuasive speeches

A specific adaptation of the problem-solution pattern is the **motivated sequence**, a five-step plan for organizing persuasive speeches. The motivated sequence is discussed in Chapter 15.

Acknowledging Cultural Differences in Organization

Although the five patterns discussed so far in this chapter represent ways speakers in the United States are expected to organize and process information, they are not necessarily typical of all cultures.[11] In fact, each culture teaches its members patterns of thought and organization that are considered appropriate for various occasions and audiences.

In general, U.S. speakers tend to be more linear and direct than speakers from Semitic, Asian, Romance, or Russian cultures. Semitic speakers may support their main points by pursuing tangents that could seem "off topic" to many U.S. speakers. Asian

Figure 8.2 Organizational patterns of speaking will vary by culture.

SOURCE: Lieberman, *Public Speaking in the Multicultural Environment*, "Organizational patterns by culture" © 1997. Reproduced by permission of Pearson Education, Inc.

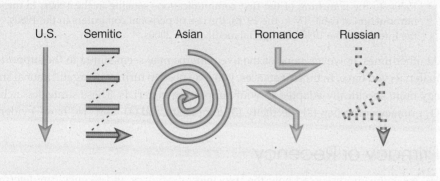

speakers may only allude to a main point through a circuitous route of illustration and parable. And speakers from Romance and Russian cultures tend to begin with a basic principle and then move to facts and illustrations that they only gradually connect to a main point. The models in Figure 8.2 illustrate these culturally diverse patterns of organization.

Of course, these are broad generalizations. But as an audience-centered speaker, you might acknowledge or even adapt elements of your organizational strategy when presenting to listeners from a culture other than your own. And as a listener who recognizes the existence of cultural differences, you can better appreciate and understand that a speaker from another culture may not be disorganized but simply using organizational strategies different from those presented in this chapter.

Organizing Your Supporting Material

8.2 Explain how to organize supporting material.

Once you have organized your main ideas, you are ready to organize the supporting material for each idea. You may realize that in support of your second main idea you have an illustration, two statistics, and an opinion. In what order should you present these items?

You can sometimes use one of the five standard organizational patterns to arrange your supporting material. Illustrations, for instance, may be organized chronologically.

DEVELOPING YOUR SPEECH STEP BY STEP

ORGANIZE YOUR SPEECH

As he begins to organize his speech on public-speaking anxiety, Matthew sees that his three main ideas represent two *problems*—in this case, cognitive and physical anxiety—and a *solution* in the form of strategies for managing speaker anxiety. It is evident to Matthew that a problem-solution organizational strategy will be ideal for his speech.

But should Matthew discuss cognitive anxiety or physical anxiety first? He reasons that because the cognitive processes *cause* the physical symptoms, he can logically apply a cause-effect order.

In the following example, the speaker uses a chronological sequence when presenting several brief illustrations of cutting-edge technology:

> [M]iracle has followed upon miracle—from a television in every home in the 1950s, to the launching of the first communications satellite in the 1960s, to the introduction of cable TV in the 1970s, the rise of personal computers in the 1980s, the Internet in the 1990s, and social media in the 2000s.[12]

At other times, however, none of the five patterns may seem suited to the supporting materials you have. In those instances, you may need to turn to an organizational strategy more specifically adapted to your supporting materials. These strategies include (1) primacy or recency, (2) specificity, (3) complexity, and (4) "soft" to "hard" evidence.

Primacy or Recency

We have already discussed how the principles of primacy and recency can determine whether you put a main idea at the beginning or the end of your speech. These patterns are used so frequently to arrange supporting materials that we mention them again here.

Suppose that you have several brief illustrations to support a main point. All are relevant and significant, but one is especially gripping. American Cancer Society CEO John Seffrin showed visual images while sharing the following brief illustrations of international tobacco advertising:

> The effort to build brand loyalty begins early. Here is an example of that in Africa—a young man wearing a hat with a cigarette brand logo....
>
> Look at this innocent baby wearing a giant Marlboro logo on his shirt....
>
> Notice how this ad links smoking to American values that are attractive to third-world kids—wealth, sophistication, and urbanity. It also shows African Americans living the American Dream. If you're a poor kid in Africa, this image can be very powerful.
>
> And finally, this one from Bucharest, Romania, which is my favorite. When the Berlin Wall came down, no one rushed into Eastern Europe faster than the tobacco industry. Here you can see the Camel logo etched in the street lights. In my opinion, this is one of the most disturbing examples of the public sector partnering with private industry to the detriment of its citizens.[13]

You can increase the impact of hard evidence by accompanying your presentation of statistics with a visual aid, such as a graph. *Photo:* Monty Rakusen/Cultura/Getty Images.

It is evident that Seffrin applied the principle of recency to his examples because he identifies the final one as "my favorite" and "one of the most disturbing." The principle of primacy or recency can also be applied to groups of statistics, opinions, or any combination of supporting material.

Specificity

Sometimes your supporting material will range from specific examples to more general overviews of a situation. You may either offer your specific information first and end with your general statement, or make the general statement first and support it with specific evidence.

Another application of specificity might be to compact or explode statistics, as discussed in Chapter 7. Compacting moves statistics from general to specific. Exploding moves them in the other direction, from specific to general. In her speech on alternatives to imprisonment, Anastasia uses both tactics. She begins with a broad statistic and makes it more specific by compacting it. Then she moves back toward a general statement by exploding a related statistic:

> [T]here are more than 2.4 million U.S. residents who serve time in prison. That means that one in every 142 residents is in prison right now, or approximately 2.3 percent of the total population. While this number may seem reasonable, when you think about how many people went through prison at some point of their lives, that number rises to 25 percent of the total population.[14]

Complexity

We have discussed organizing main ideas by moving from the simple to the more complex. The same method of organization may also determine how you order your supporting material. In many situations, it makes sense to start with the materials that are easy to understand and work up to the more complex ones. In her speech on solar radiation, Nichole's supporting materials include explanations of two effects of solar storms. She presents the simpler explanation first—of electrical blackouts and disruptions in radio broadcasts—and then goes on to the more complex explanation of cosmic radiation:

> The sun produces storms on its surface in eleven-year cycles. During solar maximum, these storms will make their presence known to the land-bound public through electrical blackouts and disruptions in radio broadcasts. These storms cause the sun to throw off electrically charged ions that, combined with charged particles, enter the Earth's atmosphere from outer space. This is known collectively as cosmic radiation.[15]

soft evidence

Supporting material based mainly on opinion or inference; includes hypothetical illustrations, descriptions, explanations, definitions, and analogies

hard evidence

Factual examples and statistics

From Soft to Hard Evidence

Supporting material can also be arranged along a continuum from "soft" to "hard." **Soft evidence** rests on opinion or inference. Hypothetical illustrations, descriptions, explanations, definitions, analogies, and opinions are usually considered soft. **Hard evidence** includes factual examples and statistics.

Soft-to-hard organization of supporting material relies chiefly on the principle of recency—that the last statement is remembered best. Note how Thomas moves from a definition (soft evidence) to a statistic and then a personal illustration (both hard evidence) in his speech on disability discrimination in the workplace, as illustrated in Figure 8.3.[16]

RECAP

INTEGRATING YOUR SUPPORTING MATERIAL

Strategy	Description
Primacy	Most important material first
Recency	Most important material last
Specificity	From specific information to general overview or from general overview to specific information
Complexity	From simple to more complex material
Soft to hard	From opinion or hypothetical illustration to fact or statistic

Figure 8.3 Organizing supporting material from soft to hard.

**Definition
(soft evidence):**

The Americans with Disabilities Act classifies a disabled person as a person who has a physical or mental impairment that substantially limits one or more major life activities; a person who has a history or record of such impairment; and a person who is perceived by others as having such an impairment.

Statistic (hard evidence):
Ten percent of the world's population is disabled.

**Personal illustration
(hard evidence):**
My hand was webbed together when I was born, the disorder known as *syndactyly*. I had it surgically repaired at a few months old, but as you see, it has not grown as much.

Organizing Your Presentation for the Ears of Others: Signposting

8.3 Use verbal and nonverbal signposts to organize a speech for the ears of others.

You have a logically ordered, fairly complete plan for your speech. But if you delivered the speech at this point, your audience might become frustrated or confused as they tried to discern your organizational plan. So your next task is to develop **signposts**—organizational cues for your audience's ears. Signposts include previews, transitions, and summaries.

Previews

In Chapter 10, we discuss the differences between writing and speaking styles. One significant difference is that public speaking is more repetitive. Audience-centered speakers need to remember that the members of their audience, unlike readers, cannot go back to review a missed point. A **preview** "tells them what you're going to tell them," building audience anticipation for an important idea. Like transitions, previews also provide coherence.

INITIAL PREVIEWS   An **initial preview** is a statement of what the main ideas of the speech will be. As discussed in Chapter 6, it is usually presented in conjunction with the central idea at or near the end of the introduction, as a *blueprint* for the speech.

Speaking on problems with the U.S. patent system, Robert offered the following blueprint at the end of his introduction:

> While patents are a good idea in principle, in practice they have turned into a disaster. First, I'll take you on a tour of our broken patent system. Then I'll walk you through the havoc it wreaks on us, our economy, and our future. Finally, we'll explore hope in potential solutions....[17]

In this blueprint, Robert clearly previews his main ideas and introduces them in the order in which he will discuss them in the body of the speech.

signposts
Cues about the relationships between a speaker's ideas

preview
A statement of what is to come

initial preview
A statement in the introduction of a speech about what the main ideas of the speech will be

INTERNAL PREVIEWS   In addition to using previews near the beginning of their speeches, speakers use them at various points throughout the speech. An **internal preview** introduces and outlines ideas that will be developed as the speech progresses. Sometimes speakers couch internal previews in the form of questions they plan to answer. Note how the following question from a speech on hotel security provides an internal preview:

> [T]he question remains, what can we do, as potential travelers and potential victims, to protect ourselves?[18]

Just as anticipating an idea helps audience members remember it, mentally answering a question helps them plant the answer firmly in their minds.

Transitions

A **transition** is a verbal or nonverbal signal that a speaker has finished discussing one idea and is moving to another.

VERBAL TRANSITIONS   A speaker can sometimes make a **verbal transition** simply by repeating a key word from a previous statement or by using a synonym or a pronoun that refers to a prior key word or idea. This type of transition is often used to make one sentence flow smoothly into the next. (The previous sentence itself is an example: "This type of transition" refers to the sentence that precedes it.)

Other verbal transitions are words or phrases that show relationships between ideas. Note the italicized transitional phrases in the following examples:

- *In addition to* transitions, previews and summaries are also considered to be signposts.
- *Not only* does plastic packaging use up our scarce resources, it contaminates them *as well*.
- *In other words*, as women's roles have changed, they have *also* contributed to this effect.
- *In summary*, Fanny Brice was the best-known star of Ziegfeld's Follies.
- *Therefore*, I recommend that you sign the grievance petition.

Simple enumeration (*first, second, third*) can also point up relationships between ideas and provide transitions.

One type of transitional signpost that can occasionally backfire and do more harm than good is one that signals the end of a speech. *Finally* and *in conclusion* give the audience implicit permission to stop listening, and they often do. Better strategies for moving into a conclusion include repeating a key word or phrase, using a synonym or pronoun that refers to a previous idea, offering a final summary, or referring to the introduction of the speech. We discuss the final summary later in this chapter. Both of the last two strategies are also covered in Chapter 9.

As summarized in Table 8.2, repetition of key words or ideas, transitional words or phrases, and enumeration all provide verbal transitions from one idea to the next.

internal preview
A statement in the body of a speech that introduces and outlines ideas that will be developed as the speech progresses

transition
A verbal or nonverbal signal indicating that a speaker has finished discussing one idea and is moving to another

verbal transition
A word or phrase that indicates the relationship between two ideas

Table 8.2   Verbal Transitions

Strategy	Example
Repeating a key word, or using a synonym or pronoun that refers to a key word.	"*These problems* cannot be allowed to continue."
Using a transitional word or phrase	"*In addition* to the facts that I've mentioned, we need to consider one more problem."
Enumerating	"*Second*, there has been a rapid increase in the number of accidents reported."

SOURCE: Copyrighted by Pearson Education, Hoboken, NJ.

Your nonverbal transition signals, as well as your verbal signposts, can help your audience follow the organization of your speech. One effective technique is to pause before moving to a new point, as this speaker is doing. *Photo:* Blend Images/Alamy Stock Photo.

You may need to experiment with several alternatives before you find the smooth transition you seek in a given instance. If none of these alternatives seems to work well, consider a nonverbal transition.

nonverbal transition

A facial expression, vocal cue, or physical movement indicating that a speaker is moving from one idea to the next

NONVERBAL TRANSITIONS   A **nonverbal transition** can occur in several ways, sometimes alone and sometimes in combination with a verbal transition. A change in facial expression, a pause, an altered vocal pitch or speaking rate, or a movement all may indicate a transition.

For example, a speaker talking about the value of cardiopulmonary resuscitation began his speech with a powerful anecdote about a man suffering a heart attack at a party. No one knew how to help, and the man died. The speaker then looked up from his notes and paused, while maintaining eye contact with his audience. His next words were "The real tragedy of Bill Jorgen's death was that it should not have happened." His pause, as well as the words that followed, indicated a transition into the body of the speech.

Like this speaker, most good speakers use a combination of verbal and nonverbal transitions to move from one point to another through their speeches. You will learn more about nonverbal communication in Chapter 11.

Summaries

summary

A recap of what has been said

Like a preview, a **summary**, or recap of what has been said, provides additional exposure to a speaker's ideas and can help ensure that audience members will grasp and remember them. Most speakers use two types of summaries: the final summary and the internal summary.

final summary

A restatement of the main ideas of a speech, occurring near the end of the speech

FINAL SUMMARIES   A **final summary** restates the main ideas of a speech and gives an audience their *last* exposure to those ideas. It occurs just before the end of a speech, often doing double duty as a transition between the body and the conclusion.

Here is an example of a final summary from a speech on the U.S. Customs Service:

Today, we have focused on the failing U.S. Customs Service. We have asked several important questions, such as "Why is Customs having such a hard time doing its job?" and "What can we do to remedy this situation?" When the cause of a serious problem is unknown, the continuation of the dilemma is understandable.

However, the cause for the failure of the U.S. Customs Service is known: a lack of personnel. Given that fact and our understanding that Customs is vital to America's interests, it would be foolish not to rectify this situation.[19]

This final summary leaves no doubt as to the important points of the speech. We discuss the use of final summaries in more detail in Chapter 9.

INTERNAL SUMMARIES   As the term suggests, an **internal summary** occurs within the body of a speech; it restates the ideas that have been developed up to that point. Susan uses the following internal summary in her speech on the teacher shortage:

> So let's review for just a moment. One, we are endeavoring to implement educational reforms; but two, we are in the first years of a dramatic increase in enrollment; and three, fewer quality students are opting for education; while four, many good teachers want out of teaching; plus five, large numbers will soon be retiring.[20]

internal summary

A restatement in the body of a speech of the ideas that have been developed so far

Internal summaries are often used in combination with internal previews to form transitions between major points and ideas. Each of the following examples makes clear what has just been discussed in the speech as well as what will be discussed next:

> Many are unaware of their own inadequate levels and uninformed about the importance of Vitamin D in their lives. And yet Vitamin D deficiency is a problem that can be so easily solved! The solutions are twofold and can be implemented on a universal and individual level.[21]

> So now [that] we are aware of the severity of the disease and unique reasons for college students to be concerned, we will look at some steps we need to take to combat bacterial meningitis.[22]

> It seems as though everyone is saying that something should be done about NutraSweet. It should be retested. Well, now that it is here on the market, what can we do to see that it does get investigated further?[23]

> **RECAP**
> ## TYPES OF SIGNPOSTS
> Initial previews
> Internal previews
> Verbal transitions
> Nonverbal transitions
> Final summaries
> Internal summaries

Outlining Your Speech

8.4   Develop a preparation outline and speaking notes for a speech.

Although few speeches are written in paragraph form, most speakers develop a **preparation outline**, a fairly detailed outline of the central idea, main ideas, and supporting material. Depending on your instructor's specific requirements, it may also include your specific purpose (discussed in Chapter 6), your introduction and conclusion (discussed in Chapter 9), and your references (discussed in Chapter 3). One CEO notes,

> Unless you sit down and write out your thoughts and put them in a cogent order, you can't deliver a cogent speech. Maybe some people have mastered that art. But I have seen too many people give speeches that they really haven't thought out.[24]

preparation outline

A detailed outline of a speech that includes the central idea, main ideas, and supporting material; and that may also include the specific purpose, introduction, conclusion, and references

From your detailed preparation outline, you will eventually develop **speaking notes**, a shorter outline that you will use when you deliver your speech. Let's look at the specific characteristics of both types of outlines.

speaking notes

A brief outline used when a speech is delivered

Developing Your Preparation Outline

To begin your preparation outline, you might turn again to the strategy of clustering, a visual mapping strategy discussed in Chapter 6 as an aid to generating speech topics. At this stage of the preparation process, you can use geometric shapes and arrows to indicate the logical relationships among main ideas, subpoints, and supporting material, as shown in Figure 8.4.

Figure 8.4 This map shows the relationships among each of a speaker's three main ideas and their subpoints. Main ideas are enclosed by rectangles; subpoints, by ovals. Supporting material could be indicated by another shape and connected to the appropriate subpoints.

SOURCE: Copyrighted by Pearson Education, Hoboken, NJ.

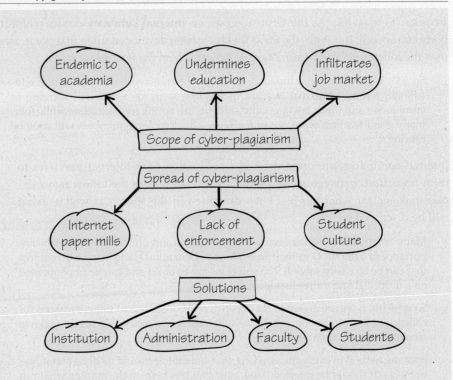

Nationwide Insurance speechwriter Charles Parnell describes another technique for beginning an outline:

> I often start by jotting down a few ideas on the [computer] screen, then move them around as necessary to build some sort of coherent pattern. I then fill in the details as they occur to me.
>
> What that means is that you can really start anywhere and eventually come up with an entire speech, just as you can start with any piece of a puzzle and eventually put it together.[25]

You may have experimented in the past with outlining tools embedded in word-processing programs, dedicated outlining software, or outlining apps for tablets or smartphones. Some people find such tools helpful. Others find that outlining technology restricts their creativity, can be inflexible when they want to revise and edit a draft outline, and may not follow the conventions for formal outlining summarized in Figure 8.5. If you wish to use outlining technology, practice with it well in advance of depending on it for a speech assignment with a due date and specific requirements for outline content and format.

Regardless of how you begin your outline, your goal is to produce a plan that helps you judge the unity and coherence of your speech: to see how well the parts fit together and how smoothly the speech flows. The following suggestions will help you complete your preparation outline. However, keep in mind that different instructors may have different expectations for what an outline must include and how it is formatted. Be sure to understand and follow your own instructor's guidelines.

WRITE YOUR PREPARATION OUTLINE IN COMPLETE SENTENCES Unless you write complete sentences, you will have trouble judging the coherence of the speech. Moreover,

Figure 8.5 Use this summary as a reminder of the rules of proper outlining when you write your preparation outline.

SOURCE: Copyrighted by Pearson Education, Hoboken, NJ.

CORRECT OUTLINE FORM

Rule	Example
1. Use standard outline numbers and letters.	I. 　A. 　　1. 　　　a. 　　　　(1) 　　　　　(a)
2. Use at least two subpoints, if any, for each main idea.	I. 　A. 　B.
3. Properly indent main ideas, subpoints, and supporting material.	I. First main idea 　A. First subpoint of I 　　1. First subpoint of A 　　2. Second subpoint of A 　B. Second subpoint of I II. Second main idea

complete sentences will help during your early rehearsals. If you write cryptic phrases, you may not remember what they mean.

USE STANDARD OUTLINE FORM   Although you did not have to use standard outline form when you began to sketch out your ideas, you need to do so now. **Standard outline form** lets you see at a glance the exact relationships among various main ideas, subpoints, and supporting material in your speech. It is an important tool for evaluating your speech, as well as a requirement in many public-speaking courses. An instructor who requires speech outlines will generally expect standard outline form. To produce a correct outline, follow the instructions given here and summarized in Figure 8.5.

USE STANDARD OUTLINE NUMBERING   Logical and fairly easy to learn, outline numbering follows this sequence:

> I. First main idea
>   A. First subpoint of I
>   B. Second subpoint of I
>   1. First subpoint of B
>   2. Second subpoint of B
>   a. First subpoint of 2
>   b. Second subpoint of 2
>   II. Second main idea

Although it is unlikely that you will subdivide beyond the level of lowercase letters (a, b, etc.) in most speech outlines, next would come numbers in parentheses followed by lowercase letters in parentheses.

USE AT LEAST TWO SUBDIVISIONS, IF ANY, FOR EACH POINT   Logic dictates that you cannot divide anything into one part. If, for example, you have only one piece of supporting material, incorporate it into the subpoint or main idea that it supports. If you have

standard outline form
Numbered and lettered headings and subheadings arranged hierarchically to indicate the relationships among parts of a speech

BODY OUTLINE

I. When you first hear that you will have to present a speech, your brain responds by cognitively processing the information.

    A. The fear of embarrassment or being judged poorly, while not causing us any physical harm, is scary enough for the brain to trigger an arousal response.

    B. We begin to think about negative "what if" outcomes: "What if they think I'm boring?" "What if they don't laugh at my jokes?"

    C. "What if" thoughts can work as a self-fulfilling prophecy and can be detrimental to our performance.

II. When your brain perceives something to be dangerous, your body responds.

    A. Your body goes into "fight or flight" mode.

    B. Your body responds by activating the sympathetic nervous system, a bundle of nerves that directly stimulate the organs.

        1. Your heart beats faster.

        2. Your breathing speeds up.

        3. You feel "butterflies" in your stomach.

    C. Your perception of danger also stimulates your adrenal medulla, which is responsible for releasing adrenaline.

    Signpost. So what can I do to reduce my feelings of anxiety? Chapter 1 of our course text, *Public Speaking: An Audience-Centered Approach*, offers practical advice based on both research and experience.

III. There are many ways to decrease your public-speaking anxiety.

    A. The most widely accepted way to manage public-speaking anxiety is with cognitive-behavioral therapy.

        1. Recognize when you are experiencing anxiety.

        2. Counter negative thoughts by imagining yourself presenting an amazing speech.

        3. Manage the physiological response by deep breathing and relaxation techniques.

    B. The best way to reduce your public-speaking anxiety is to seek out opportunities to speak publicly.

CONCLUSION

I hope what I have shared today will help you in your upcoming speeches. We have looked at how your brain processes fear and anxiety and how your body responds to help you perform better in stressful situations. I have also provided you with several techniques to reduce your anxiety, but really the best way to handle your anxiety is through persistent practice in public speaking. In the following class periods I ask you to apply what you have learned today. Gandhi once said "Your thoughts become your words, your words become your actions." Take what you have learned here today and turn your weakness into a strength.

REFERENCES

Beebe S., & Beebe, S. (2018). *Public speaking: An audience-centered approach* (10th ed.). Boston, MA: Pearson.

Behnke, R., and Beatty, M. (1981). A cognitive-physiological model of speech anxiety. *Communication Monographs, 48* (2), 158–163.

Comer R., (2015). *Abnormal psychology* (9th ed.). New York, NY: Macmillan.

Dwyer, K., and Davidson, M. (2012). Is public speaking really more feared than death?" *Communication Research Reports, 29* (2), 99–107.

The first main idea of the speech, cognitive anxiety, is indicated by the Roman numeral I. The three explanations of how cognitive anxiety works are indicated by A, B, and C.

A signpost between main ideas II and III poses a rhetorical question as a transition. Matthew also cites this textbook, used in his class, as a source of strategies for decreasing public-speaking anxiety.

In his conclusion, Matthew first reminds his audience how they can apply the information he has provided, then summarizes his main ideas. He quotes Gandhi as part of his closing inspirational appeal. Chapter 9 offers additional strategies for concluding your speech.

Following his instructor's requirements, Matthew includes in his preparation outline a list of his references, formatted in APA style.

Developing Your Speaking Notes

As you rehearse your speech, you will find that you need your preparation outline less and less. Both the structure and the content of your speech will become set in your mind. At this point, you are ready to prepare a shorter outline to serve as your speaking notes.

Your speaking notes should not be so detailed that you will be tempted to read them word for word to your audience. Instead, this shorter outline should provide clearly formatted details sufficient to ensure that you can make your presentation as you have planned in your preparation outline. NASA blamed the loss of the space shuttle *Columbia* in part on the fact that an outline on possible wing damage was "so crammed with nested bullet points and irregular short forms that it was nearly impossible to untangle."[27]

Figure 8.7 illustrates speaking notes for Matthew's presentation on public-speaking anxiety. Here are a few specific suggestions for developing your own speaking notes.

Figure 8.7   Your speaking notes can include delivery cues and reminders. Be sure to differentiate your cues from the content of your speech. One good way is to write or display speaking cues in a different color or font.

SOURCE: Copyrighted by Pearson Education, Hoboken, NJ.

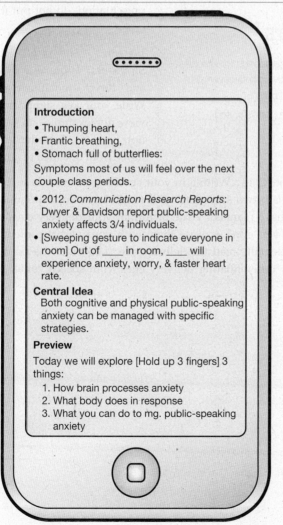

CHOOSE YOUR TECHNOLOGY   Speaking notes can be either high tech or low tech. You may decide to display your outline on a smartphone or tablet—perhaps using one of several apps available for speaking notes—or you may opt to use old-fashioned note cards. Even if you plan to use an electronic option, you may want to have a backup outline on note cards in case of technical difficulty. Note cards don't rustle like paper does and are small enough to hold in one hand. Write on one side only, and number your note cards in case they get out of order just before or during your speech. Regardless of the technology you select, make sure your letters and words are large enough to be read easily.

USE STANDARD OUTLINE FORM   Standard outline form will help you find your exact place when you glance down at your speaking notes. You will know, for example, that your second main idea is indicated by "II." In addition, lay out your outline so your introduction, each main idea, and your conclusion are distinct.

INCLUDE YOUR INTRODUCTION AND CONCLUSION IN ABBREVIATED FORM   Even if your instructor does not require you to include your introduction and conclusion on your preparation outline, include abbreviated versions of them in your speaking notes. You might even feel more comfortable delivering the presentation if you have your first and last sentences written out in front of you.

INCLUDE YOUR CENTRAL IDEA, BUT NOT YOUR PURPOSE STATEMENT   Be sure to include your central idea. But as you will not actually say your purpose statement during your presentation, do not put it in your speaking notes.

INCLUDE SUPPORTING MATERIAL AND SIGNPOSTS   Write out in full any statistics and direct quotations and their sources. Write your key signposts—your initial preview, for example—to ensure that you will not have to flounder awkwardly as you move from one idea to another.

INCLUDE DELIVERY CUES   Writing in your speaking note cards such cues as "Louder," "Pause," or "Walk two steps left" will remind you to communicate the nonverbal messages you have planned. Write or format your delivery cues in a different color or font so that you don't confuse them with your verbal content. President Gerald Ford once accidentally read the delivery cue "Look into the right camera" during a speech. Clearly differentiating delivery cues from speech content will help prevent such mistakes.

RECAP

TWO TYPES OF SPEECH OUTLINES

Preparation Outline	Allows speaker to examine the speech for completeness, unity, coherence, and overall effectiveness. May serve as a first rehearsal outline.
Speaking Notes	Include supporting material, signposts, and delivery cues.

STUDY GUIDE: REVIEW, APPLY, AND ASSESS

Organizing Your Main Ideas

8.1 List and describe five patterns for organizing the main ideas of a speech.

REVIEW: Organizing the main ideas of your speech in a logical way will help audience members follow, understand, and remember these ideas. For North American audiences, the five most common patterns of organization include topical, chronological, spatial, cause and effect, and problem-solution. These patterns are sometimes combined. Other organizational patterns may be favored in different cultures. The principles of primacy, recency, and complexity can also help you decide which main idea to discuss first, next, and last.

Key Terms

topical organization
primacy
recency
complexity
chronological
  organization

spatial organization
cause-and-effect
  organization
problem-solution
  organization
motivated sequence

APPLY: Identify the organizational pattern most likely applied to the main ideas for each of the following speeches. If the pattern is topical, do you think the speaker also considered primacy, recency, or complexity? If so, identify which one.

1. PURPOSE STATEMENT: At the end of my speech, the audience will be able to explain three theories about what happened to the dinosaurs.

   CENTRAL IDEA: There are at least three distinct theories about what happened to the dinosaurs.

   MAIN IDEAS:
   I. A large asteroid hit Earth.
   II. A gradual climate shift occurred.
   III. The level of oxygen in the atmosphere gradually changed.

2. PURPOSE STATEMENT: At the end of my speech, the audience will be able to describe the layout and features of the new university multipurpose sports center.

   CENTRAL IDEA: The new university multipurpose sports center will serve the activity needs of the students.

   MAIN IDEAS:
   I. The south wing will house an Olympic-size pool.
   II. The center of the building will be a large coliseum.
   III. The north wing will include handball and indoor tennis facilities, as well as rooms for weight lifting and aerobic workouts.

ASSESS: If your topic is controversial and you know or suspect that your audience will be skeptical of or hostile to your ideas, where should you place your most important or convincing idea for maximum effectiveness? Explain your answer.

Organizing Your Supporting Material

8.2 Explain how to organize supporting material.

REVIEW: With your main ideas organized, your next task is to organize your supporting material for each main idea. You can organize supporting material according to one of the five common patterns, or according to such strategies as primacy, recency, specificity, complexity, or soft-to-hard evidence.

Key Terms

soft evidence   hard evidence

APPLY:

1. The principles of primacy and recency are referred to several times in this chapter. If a statistic offers overwhelming evidence of the severity of a given problem, is it ethical for a speaker to save that statistic for last, or should the speaker immediately reveal to the audience how severe the problem is? In other words, is there an ethical distinction between primacy and recency? Discuss your answer.

2. Take notes while listening to either a live or recorded speech. Then organize your notes in standard outline form to reflect the speaker's organization of both main ideas and support material. Try to determine the speaker's organizational strategy, the reasons for it, and its effectiveness.

Organizing Your Presentation for the Ears of Others: Signposting

8.3 Use verbal and nonverbal signposts to organize a speech for the ears of others.

REVIEW: Various types of signposts can help you communicate your organization to your audience. Signposts include verbal and nonverbal transitions, previews, and summaries.

Key Terms

signposts	verbal transition
preview	nonverbal transition
initial preview	summary
internal preview	final summary
transition	internal summary

ASSESS: Identify and explain three strategies for helping your audience remember the main ideas of your speech.

Outlining Your Speech

8.4 Develop a preparation outline and speaking notes for a speech.

REVIEW: A preparation outline includes your carefully organized main ideas, subpoints, and supporting material; it may also include your specific purpose, introduction, blueprint, internal previews and summaries, transitions, and conclusion. Write each of these elements in complete sentences and standard outline form. Use the preparation outline to begin rehearsing your speech and to help you revise it, if necessary. After you have rehearsed several times from your preparation outline, you are ready to prepare speaking notes. Although less detailed than a preparation outline, speaking notes usually include supporting material, signposts, and delivery cues.

Key Terms

preparation outline	standard outline form
speaking notes	

APPLY:

1. Can a speaker legitimately claim that a speech is extemporaneous if he or she has constructed a detailed preparation outline? Explain your answer.

2. Geoff plans to deliver his speech using hastily scrawled notes on a sheet of paper torn from his notebook. What advice would you offer him for preparing better speaking notes?

Introducing and Concluding Your Speech

The average man thinks about what he has said; the above average man about what he is going to say.

—Anonymous

Alfred Sisley (1839–899), *The Rotating Road, View on the Seine. Photo:* Active Museum/ Alamy Stock Photo.

OBJECTIVES

After studying this chapter, you should be able to do the following:

9.1 Explain the functions of a speech introduction.

9.2 List and discuss methods for introducing a speech.

9.3 Explain the functions of a speech conclusion.

9.4 List and discuss methods for concluding a speech.

Like all teachers, public-speaking instructors have pet peeves when it comes to their students' work. Of the pet peeves identified by public-speaking teachers in one study, more than 25 percent relate to introductions and conclusions. They include the following:

- Beginning a speech with "OK, ah…"
- Apologizing or making excuses at the beginning of the speech for not being prepared
- Beginning a speech with "Hello, my speech is on…"
- Saying "In conclusion"
- Ending a speech with "Thank you"
- Ending a speech with "Are there any questions?"[1]

Not every public-speaking instructor considers all of the preceding items to be pet peeves or even tactics to be avoided. But the fact that they appear on this list suggests that you will probably want to consider alternatives. After all, your introduction and conclusion provide your listeners with important first and final impressions of both you and your speech.

CONFIDENTLY CONNECTING WITH YOUR AUDIENCE

Be Familiar with Your Introduction and Conclusion

You may feel the most nervous just as you begin your speech. But if you have a well-prepared and well-rehearsed introduction, you'll be able to start with confidence. Rehearse your opening sentences enough times that you can present them while maintaining direct eye contact with your listeners. Being familiar with your conclusion can give you a safe harbor to head for as you end your message. A thoughtfully planned and well-rehearsed introduction and conclusion can help you start and end your speech with poise and assurance.

Organizing the body of your speech should precede the crafting of both the introduction and the conclusion. In Chapter 8, we discussed strategies for organizing the body of your speech; using previews, transitions, and summaries to signpost your speech for your audience; and developing a presentation outline and speaking notes. In this chapter we will complete our discussion of speech organization by discussing introductions and conclusions.

Purposes of Introductions

9.1 Explain the functions of a speech introduction.

A speech introduction may engage you, or it may suggest that a speaker is ill-prepared and his or her message is not worth your time. In a ten-minute speech, the introduction will probably last no more than a minute and a half. To say that the introduction needs to be well planned is an understatement, considering how important and yet how brief this portion of any speech is.

As a speaker, your task is to ensure that your introduction convinces your audience to listen to you. As summarized and illustrated in Table 9.1, a good introduction must perform five important functions:

- Get the audience's attention.
- Give the audience a reason to listen.
- Introduce the subject.
- Establish your credibility.
- Preview your main ideas.

Let's examine each of these five functions in detail.

Table 9.1 Purposes of Your Introduction

Purpose	Method
Get the audience's attention.	Use an illustration, a startling fact or statistic, a quotation, humor, a question, a reference to a historical or recent event, a personal reference, a reference to the occasion, or a reference to a preceding speech.
Give the audience a reason to listen.	Tell your listeners how the topic directly affects them.
Introduce the subject.	Present your central idea to your audience.
Establish your credibility.	Offer your credentials. Tell your listeners about your commitment to your topic.
Preview your main ideas.	Tell your audience what you are going to tell them.

SOURCE: Copyrighted by Pearson Education, Hoboken, NJ.

Get the Audience's Attention

A key purpose of the introduction is to gain favorable attention for your speech. Because listeners form their first impressions of a speech quickly, the introduction must capture their attention and cast the speech in a favorable light or the rest of the speech may be wasted on them. The speaker who walks to the podium and drones, "Today I am going to talk to you about…" has probably lost most of the audience with those first few boring words. Specific ways to gain the attention of audiences will be discussed later in this chapter.

We emphasize *favorable* attention for a good reason. It is possible to gain an audience's attention with words or presentation aids that alienate or disgust them so that they become irritated instead of interested in what you have to say. For example, one student began his speech on the importance of donating blood by appearing to savagely slash his wrists in front of his stunned audience. As blood spurted, audience members screamed, and one fainted. The blood was real blood, but it wasn't his. The speaker worked at a blood bank, and he was using the bank's blood. He had placed a device under each arm that allowed him to pump out the blood as if it flowed from his wrists. He certainly captured his audience's attention! But they never heard his message. The shock and disgust of seeing such a display made that impossible; he did not gain favorable attention.

The moral of this tale: By all means, be creative with your speech introductions. But also use common sense in deciding how best to gain the favorable attention of your audience. Alienating them is even worse than boring them.

Give the Audience a Reason to Listen

Even after you have captured your listeners' attention, you have to give them some reason to want to listen to the rest of your speech. An unmotivated listener quickly tunes out. You can help establish listening motivation by showing the members of your audience how the topic affects them directly.

In Chapter 7 we presented six criteria for determining the effectiveness of your supporting material. One of those criteria is *proximity*, the degree to which the information affects your listeners directly. Just as proximity is important to supporting materials, it is also important to speech introductions. "This concerns me" is a powerful reason to listen. Notice how Lauren involved her listeners firsthand with abhorrent labor conditions in Florida tomato fields:

> [If] you've eaten a tomato from a fast-food restaurant, grocery store, or food services business in the last year, you've eaten a tomato picked by the hand of a slave. [She shows two tomatoes to audience.] Can you tell which one? Now I know I'm taking a chance here offering tomatoes to an audience at the beginning of a speech. But the difference between these two is the difference between a fair market and slavery.[2]

It does not matter so much *how* or *when* you demonstrate proximity. But it is essential that, like Lauren, you *do* at some point establish that your topic is of vital personal concern to your listeners.

Introduce the Subject

The most obvious purpose of an introduction is to introduce the subject of a speech. Within a few seconds after you begin your speech, the audience should have a pretty good idea of what you are going to talk about. Do not get so carried away with jokes or illustrations that you forget this basic purpose. Few things will frustrate your audience more than having to wait until halfway through your speech to figure out what you are talking about! The best way to ensure that your introduction does indeed introduce the subject of your speech is to include a statement of your central idea in the introduction.

Establish Your Credibility

Nineteenth-century abolitionist Frederick Douglass was renowned as a great orator. According to biographer Charles W. Chesnutt, Douglass's audiences recognized him as

> a man whose...past history gave him the highest right to describe and denounce the iniquities of slavery and contend for the rights of a race.[3]

In other words, audiences considered Douglass to be a credible speaker on issues of slavery and racial justice.

As you begin your speech, you should be mindful of your listeners' attitudes toward you. Ask yourself, "Why should they listen to me? What is my background with respect to the topic? Am I personally committed to the issues I am going to speak about?" If you can establish your credibility early in a speech, it will help motivate your audience to listen.

One way to build credibility in the introduction is to be well prepared and to appear confident. Thorough research and good organization help give the audience confidence that you know what you are talking about. Speaking fluently while maintaining eye contact does much to convey a sense of confidence. If you seem to have confidence in yourself, your audience will have confidence in you.

A second way to establish credibility is to tell the audience about your personal experience with your topic. Instead of thinking you boastful, most audience members will listen to you with respect. Twitter CEO Dick Costolo opened a University of Michigan commencement speech by photographing the graduates, then telling them as he tweeted the photo,

> I'm a professional, so this will only take a second.[4]

Credibility is discussed in more detail in Chapter 15.

Preview Your Main Ideas

A final purpose of the introduction is to preview the main ideas of your speech. As discussed in Chapter 8, an initial preview statement usually comes near the end of the introduction, included in or immediately following a statement of the central idea. This preview statement allows your listeners to anticipate the main ideas of your speech, which in turn helps ensure that they will remember those ideas after the speech.

Dick Costolo, president of Twitter, effectively reinforced his credibility by tweeting a photo of the graduates during the introduction to his address at the University of Michigan.
Photo: Todd McInturf/*The Detroit News*/AP Images.

As we also noted in Chapter 8, an initial preview statement is an organizational strategy called a *signpost*. Just as signs posted along a highway tell you what is coming up, a signpost in your speech tells the listeners what to expect by enumerating the ideas or points you plan to present. If, for example, you were giving a speech about racial profiling, you might say,

> To end these crimes against color, we must first paint an accurate picture of the problem, then explore the causes, and finally establish solutions that will erase the practice of racial profiling.[5]

Identifying your main ideas helps organize the message and enhances listeners' learning.

The introduction to your speech, then, should capture your audience's attention, give the audience a reason to listen, introduce the subject, establish your credibility, and preview your main ideas. All this—and brevity too—may seem impossible to achieve. But it isn't!

Effective Introductions

9.2 List and discuss methods for introducing a speech.

With a little practice, you will be able to write satisfactory central ideas and preview statements. It may be more difficult to gain your audience's attention and give them a reason to listen to you. Fortunately, there are several effective methods for developing speech introductions. Not every method is appropriate for every speech, but among these alternatives, you should be able to discover at least one type of introduction to fit your speech topic and purpose, whatever they might be.

We will discuss ten ways of introducing a speech:

- Illustrations or anecdotes
- Startling facts or statistics
- Quotations
- Humor
- Questions
- References to historical events
- References to recent events
- Personal references
- References to the occasion
- References to preceding speeches

Illustrations or Anecdotes

Not surprisingly, because it is the most inherently interesting type of supporting material, an illustration or **anecdote** can provide the basis for an effective speech introduction. In fact, if you have an especially compelling illustration that you had planned to use in the body of the speech, you might do well to use it in your introduction instead. A relevant and interesting anecdote will introduce your subject and almost invariably gain an audience's attention. Student speaker Jacob opened his speech on child migrant workers with this extended illustration:

anecdote
An illustration or story

> Santos Polendo's workday harvesting onions begins at six a.m. and ends twelve hours later. Exhausted, he falls into bed for a short sleep before his work begins again. This arduous schedule continues seven days a week without a break. Santos remembers that once, when he began working in the onion fields, he slashed his foot with a hoe, but because he couldn't afford a trip to the doctor, he clumsily wrapped his own foot as best he could and returned to the sweltering fields for the rest of his shift. Santos was six years old.[6]

Jacob's story effectively captured the attention of his audience and introduced the subject of his speech.

An opening illustration may also be conveyed by a short (less than a minute for most classroom speeches), engaging video clip. If you decide to open your speech with a video clip, be sure that video projection technology is available in the room where you are speaking. Plan and practice transitioning from the video to the speech itself. And on the day of the speech, arrive early enough to load and cue your video before you speak. You can find additional guidelines for using video presentation aids in Chapter 12.

Startling Facts or Statistics

A second method of introducing a speech is to use a startling fact or statistic. Grabbing an audience's attention with the extent of a situation or problem invariably catches listeners' attention, motivates them to listen further, and helps them remember afterward what you had to say. Will's audience of prospective law students must have been startled to attention by the statistics in his introduction:

> Ninety-eight percent of the 2012 graduates of the Thomas Jefferson School of Law in San Diego, California, graduated with an average of $168,800 in student debt.[7]

Quotations

Using an appropriate quotation to introduce a speech is a common practice. Often another writer or speaker has expressed an opinion on your topic that is more authoritative, comprehensive, or memorable than what you can say. Terrika opened her speech on the importance of community with a quotation from poet Johari Kungufu:

> Sisters, Men
> What are we doin?
> What about the babies, our children?
> When we was real we never had orphans or children in joints.
> Come spirits
> drive out the nonsense from our minds and the crap from our dreams
> make us remember what we need, that children are the next life.
> bring us back to the real
> bring us back to the real

> "The Real." Johari Kungufu, in her poem, specifically alludes to a time in African history when children were not confused about who they were.[8]

A different kind of quotation, this one from an expert, was chosen by another speaker to introduce the topic of the disappearance of childhood in America:

> "As a distinctive childhood culture wastes away, we watch with fascination and dismay." This insight of Neil Postman, author of *Disappearance of Childhood*, raised a poignant point. Childhood in America is vanishing.[9]

Because the expert was not widely recognized, the speaker included a brief statement of his qualifications. This authority "said it in a nutshell"—he expressed in concise language the central idea of the speech.

Although a quote can effectively introduce a speech, do not fall into the lazy habit of turning to a collection of quotations every time you need an introduction. There are so many other interesting, and sometimes better, ways to introduce a speech. Quotes should be used only if they are extremely interesting, compelling, or very much to the point.

Like the methods of organization discussed in Chapter 8, the methods of introduction are not mutually exclusive. Often, two or three are effectively combined in a single introduction. For example, Thad combined a quotation and an illustration for this effective introduction to a speech on the funeral industry:

> "Dying is a very dull, dreary affair. And my advice to you is to have nothing whatsoever to do with it." These lingering words by British playwright Somerset Maugham were meant to draw a laugh. Yet the ironic truth to the statement has come to epitomize the grief of many, including Jan Berman of Martha's Vineyard. In a recent interview with National Public Radio, we learn that Ms. Berman desired to have a home funeral for her mother. She possessed a burial permit and was legally within her rights. But when a local funeral director found out, he lied to her, telling her that what she was doing was illegal.[10]

Humor

Humor, handled well, can be a wonderful attention-getter. It can help relax your audience and win their goodwill for the rest of the speech. Michael Ward of Oxford University in England opened his recent commencement speech at Hillsdale College in Michigan with this humorous greeting:

> I bring cordial greetings from your erstwhile colonial overlords. I bear warmest felicitations from Her Majesty The Queen, Professor Stephen Hawking, James Bond, Sherlock Holmes, and the entire cast of Downton Abbey.[11]

Humor need not always be the slapstick comedy of the Three Stooges. It does not even have to be a joke. It may take subtler forms, such as irony or incredulity. When General Douglas MacArthur, an honor graduate of the U.S. Military Academy at West Point, returned to his alma mater in 1962, he delivered his now-famous address "Farewell to the Cadets." He opened that speech with this humorous illustration:

> As I was leaving the hotel this morning, a doorman asked me, "Where are you bound for, General?" And when I replied, "West Point," he remarked, "Beautiful place. Have you ever been there before?"[12]

MacArthur's brief illustration caught the audience's attention and made them laugh—in short, it was an effective way to open the speech.

If your audience is linguistically diverse or composed primarily of listeners whose first language is not English, you may want to choose an introduction strategy other

Humor can be an effective way to catch your audience's attention in your introduction. Remember, however, to use humor appropriate to the occasion and the audience. *Photo:* Digital Vision/Photodisc/Getty Images.

than humor. Because much humor is created by verbal plays on words, people who do not speak English as their native language may not perceive the humor in an anecdote or quip that you intended to be funny.

Just as certain audiences may preclude your use of a humorous introduction, so may certain subjects—for example, Sudden Infant Death Syndrome and rape. Used with discretion, however, humor can provide a lively, interesting, and appropriate introduction for many speeches. Using humor effectively is discussed in more detail in Chapter 16.

Questions

Remember the pet peeves listed at the beginning of this chapter? Another pet peeve for some is beginning a speech with a question ("How many of you...?"). The problem is not so much the strategy itself but the lack of mindfulness in the "How many of you?" phrasing.

rhetorical question
A question intended to provoke thought rather than elicit an answer

A thoughtful **rhetorical question**, on the other hand, can prompt your listeners' mental participation in your introduction, getting their attention and giving them a reason to listen. President and CEO of Coca-Cola, Muhtar Kent, began a speech to investors and financial analysts by asking,

Are we ready for tomorrow, today?[13]

And Richard opened his speech on teenage suicide with this simple question:

Have you ever been alone in the dark?[14]

Although it does not happen frequently, an audience member may blurt out a vocal response to a question intended to be rhetorical. If you plan to open a speech with a rhetorical question, be aware of this possibility, and plan appropriate reactions. If the topic is light, responding with a Jimmy Fallon–style quip may win over the audience and turn the interruption into an asset. If the topic is more serious or the interruption is inappropriate or contrary to what you expected, you might reply with something like "Perhaps most of the rest of you were thinking...," or you might answer the question yourself.

Questions are commonly combined with another method of introduction. For example, University of Akron president Luis Proenza opened a speech on new strategies for success in higher education with a question followed by a startling statistic:

What if the airplane had advanced as far and as fast as the computer? Today's jumbo jet would carry one hundred thousand passengers, and it would fly them to the moon and back for $12.50 at 23,400 miles per hour.[15]

Either by themselves or in tandem with another method of introduction, questions can provide effective openings for speeches. Like quotations, however, questions can also be crutches for speakers who have not taken the time to explore other options. Unless you can think of a truly engaging question, work to develop one of the other introduction strategies.

References to Historical Events

What American is not familiar with the opening line of President Abraham Lincoln's classic Gettysburg Address: "Four score and seven years ago, our fathers brought forth on this continent a new nation, conceived in liberty, and dedicated to the proposition that all men are created equal"? Lincoln's famous opening sentence refers to the historical context of his speech. You, too, may find a way to begin a speech by making a reference to a historic event.

Every day is the anniversary of something. Perhaps you could begin a speech by drawing a relationship between a historic event that happened on this day and your speech objective. Executive speechwriter Cynthia Starks illustrated this strategy in a speech delivered on February 16:

> On this date—Feb. 16, 1923—archeologist Howard Carter entered the burial chamber of King Tutankhamen. There he found a solid gold coffin, Tut's intact mummy, and priceless treasures.
>
> On Feb. 16, 1959, Fidel Castro took over the Cuban government 45 days after overthrowing Fulgencio Batista.
>
> And America's first 9-1-1 emergency phone system went live in Haleyville, Alabama, on Feb. 16, 1968.
>
> Today, I won't be revealing priceless treasures. I promise not to overthrow anyone, or generate any 9-1-1 calls. But I do hope to reveal a few speechwriting secrets, provide a little revolutionary thinking and a sense of urgency about the speeches you ought to be giving.[16]

How do you discover anniversaries of historic events? You could consult "This Day in History" online or download it as an app for your tablet or smartphone.

References to Recent Events

If your topic is timely, a reference to a recent event can be a good way to begin your speech. An opening taken from a recent news story can take the form of an illustration, a startling statistic, or even a quotation, gaining the additional advantages discussed under each of those methods of introduction. Moreover, referring to a recent event increases your credibility by showing that you are knowledgeable about current affairs.

"Recent" does not necessarily mean a story that broke just last week or even last month. An event that occurred within the past year or so can be considered recent. Even a particularly significant event that is slightly older can qualify. The key, says one speaker,

> is to avoid being your grandfather. No more stories about walking up hill both ways to school with a musket on your back and seventeen Redcoats chasing you. Be in the now, and connect with your audience.[17]

Personal References

A reference to yourself can take several forms. You might express appreciation or pleasure at having been asked to speak, as did this speaker:

> I am delighted to participate in this engaging meeting at my graduate alma mater.[18]

Or you might share a personal experience, as did this speaker:

> Like some of you in the audience, I've held many jobs before finding my true calling, from washing cars to waiting tables and taking care of animals....[19]

Although personal references take a variety of forms, what they do best, in all circumstances, is to establish a bond between you and your audience.

References to the Occasion

References to the occasion are often made at weddings, birthday parties, dedication ceremonies, and other such events. For example, Jeffrey Immelt, Chair and CEO of General Electric, opened a recent commencement speech this way:

> [A]fter hitting up Yik Yak this morning...I realized my biggest mistake may have been just showing up today. You guys really know how to count down the last 40 days of college.[20]

The reference to the occasion can also be combined with other methods of introduction, such as an illustration or a rhetorical question.

References to Preceding Speeches

If your speech is one of several being presented on the same occasion, such as in a speech class, at a symposium, or as part of a lecture series, you will usually not know until shortly before your own speech what other speakers will say. Few experiences will make your stomach sink faster than hearing a speaker just ahead of you speak on your topic. Worse still, that speaker may even use some of the same supporting materials you had planned to use.

When this situation occurs, you must decide on the spot whether referring to one of those previous speeches will be better than using the introduction you originally prepared. Your introduction then becomes a transition from that earlier speech to yours. Here is an example of an introduction delivered by a fast-thinking student speaker under such circumstances:

> When Juli talked to us about her experiences as a lifeguard, she stressed that the job was not as glamorous as many of us imagine. Today I want to tell you about another job that appears to be more glamorous than it is—a job that I have held for two years. I am a bartender at the Rathskeller.[21]

As you plan your introduction, remember that any combination of the methods previously discussed is possible. With a little practice, you will become confident at choosing from several good possibilities as you prepare your introduction.

Purposes of Conclusions

9.3 Explain the functions of a speech conclusion.

Whereas your introduction creates an important first impression, your conclusion leaves an equally important final impression. Long after you finish speaking, your audience is likely to remember the effect, if not the content, of your closing remarks.

Unfortunately, many speakers pay less attention to their conclusions than to any other part of their speeches. They believe that if they can get through the first 90 percent of their speech, they can think of some way to conclude it. Perhaps you have had the experience of listening to a speaker who failed to plan a conclusion. Awkward final seconds of stumbling for words may be followed by hesitant applause from an audience that is not even sure the speech is over. It is hardly the best way to leave people who came to listen to you.

An effective conclusion will serve two purposes: It will summarize the speech and provide closure.

Summarize the Speech

A conclusion is a speaker's last chance to review his or her central and main ideas for the audience.

REEMPHASIZE THE CENTRAL IDEA IN A MEMORABLE WAY The conclusions of many famous speeches rephrase the central idea in a memorable way. When on July 4, 1939, New York Yankees legend Lou Gehrig addressed his fans in an emotional farewell to a baseball career cut short by a diagnosis of amyotrophic lateral sclerosis (ALS), he concluded with the memorable line,

> I may have had a tough break, but I have an awful lot to live for.[22]

Speechwriting instructor and former speechwriter Robert Lehrman identifies a more recent memorable conclusion, that of Barack Obama's 2008 presidential victory speech:

> [T]hat long closing story about Ann Nixon Cooper, the 106-year-old woman whose life encapsulated the history of the 20th century ("a man touched down on the moon...she touched her finger to a screen and cast her vote...").[23]

Lehrman notes, "When I teach that speech, students stop texting and start crying."

But memorable endings are not the exclusive property of famous speakers. With practice, most people can prepare similarly effective conclusions. Chapter 10 offers ideas for using language to make your statements more memorable.

The end of your speech is your last chance to impress the central idea on your audience. Do it in such a way that they cannot help but remember it.

RESTATE THE MAIN IDEAS In addition to reemphasizing the central idea of the speech, the conclusion is also likely to restate the main ideas. Note how John effectively summarized the main ideas of his speech on emissions tampering, casting the summary as an expression of his fears about the problem and the actions that could ease those fears:

> I'm frightened. Frightened that nothing I could say would encourage the 25 percent of emissions-tampering Americans to change their ways and correct the factors that cause their autos to pollute disproportionately. Frightened that the American public will not respond to a crucial issue unless the harms are both immediate and observable. Frightened that the EPA will once again prove very sympathetic to industry. Three simple steps will alleviate my fear: inspection, reduction in lead content, and, most importantly, awareness.[24]

Most speakers summarize their main ideas in the first part of the conclusion or as part of the transition between the body of the speech and its conclusion.

Provide Closure

Probably the most obvious purpose of a conclusion is to bring **closure**—to cue the audience that the speech is coming to an end by making it "sound finished."

closure
The quality of a conclusion that makes a speech "sound finished"

USE VERBAL OR NONVERBAL CUES TO SIGNAL THE END OF THE SPEECH You can attain closure both verbally and nonverbally. Verbal techniques include using such transitional words and phrases as "finally," "for my last point," and perhaps even "in conclusion."

You may remember that "in conclusion" appears on that list of instructors' pet peeves at the beginning of this chapter. Like opening your speech by asking a rhetorical question, signaling your closing by saying "in conclusion" is not inherently wrong. It is a pet peeve of some instructors because of the carelessness with which student speakers often use it. Such a cue gives listeners unspoken permission to tune out. (Notice what students do when their professor signals the end of class: Books and notebooks slam shut, pens are stowed away, and the class generally stops listening.) For this reason, if you use a concluding transition, it needs to be followed quickly by the final statement of the speech.

You can also signal closure with nonverbal cues. You may want to pause between the body of your speech and its conclusion, slow your speaking rate, move out from behind a podium to make a final impassioned plea to your audience, or signal with falling vocal inflection that you are making your final statement.

MOTIVATE THE AUDIENCE TO RESPOND Another way to provide closure to your speech is to motivate your audience to respond in some way. If your speech is informative, you may want your audience to take some sort of appropriate action—write a letter,

RECAP

PURPOSES OF YOUR SPEECH CONCLUSION

- Summarize the speech.
- Reemphasize the central idea in a memorable way.
- Restate the main ideas.
- Provide closure.
- Give verbal or nonverbal signals at the end of the speech.
- Motivate the audience to respond.

buy a product, make a telephone call, or get involved in a cause. In fact, an *action* step is essential to the persuasive organizational strategy called the motivated sequence, which we discuss in Chapter 15.

At the close of her speech on rape law reform, Tiffany offered to help her listeners take action:

> …inform yourself and get involved. To make this easier, I created individualized state call-to-action sheets.
> They include your senator's contact information, statistics, and the specific laws that need reform. You can also download my app *Demand Change*.[25]

Tiffany drew on the principle of proximity, discussed previously in this chapter, to motivate her audience. When audience members feel they are or could be personally involved or affected, they are more likely to respond to your message.

Effective Conclusions

9.4   List and discuss methods for concluding a speech.

Effective conclusions may employ illustrations, quotations, personal references, or any of the other methods of introduction we have discussed. In addition, there are at least two other distinct ways of concluding a speech: with references to the introduction and with inspirational appeals or challenges.

Methods Also Used for Introductions

Any of the methods of introduction previously discussed can also help you conclude your speech. Quotations, for example, are frequently used in conclusions, as in this commencement address by U2 lead singer Bono:

> Remember what John Adams said about Ben Franklin: "He does not hesitate at our boldest measures but rather seems to think us too irresolute."
> Well, this is the time for bold measures. This is the country, and you are the generation.[26]

References to the Introduction

In our discussion of closure, we mentioned referring to the introduction as a way to end a speech. Finishing a story, answering a rhetorical question, or reminding the audience of the startling fact or statistic you presented in the introduction are excellent ways to provide closure. Like bookends, a related introduction and conclusion provide unified support for the ideas in between.

In this chapter, you read the extended illustration Jacob used to open his speech on child migrant workers. He concluded the speech by referring to that introduction:

> Santos…—and all other migrant child workers—deserve to be protected.[27]

Jacob's conclusion alludes to his introduction to make his speech memorable, to motivate his audience to respond, and to provide closure.

Inspirational Appeals or Challenges

Another way to end your speech is to issue an inspirational appeal or to challenge to your listeners, rousing them to an emotional pitch at the conclusion of the speech. The conclusion becomes the climax. Speechwriter and communication consultant James W. Robinson explains why such conclusions can work well:

> It's almost as if, for a few brief moments [audience members] escape from the stressful demands of our high-pressure world and welcome your gifts: insightful vision, persuasive rhetoric, a touch of philosophy, a little emotion, and yes, even a hint of corniness.[28]

One famous example of a concluding inspiration appeal comes from Martin Luther King Jr.'s "Dream" speech, which can be read in its entirety in Appendix B. That King's conclusion was both inspiring and memorable has been affirmed by the growing fame of his closing passage.

More recently, Kailash Satyarthi, Indian child rights activist and co-recipient of the 2014 Nobel Peace Prize, ended his Nobel acceptance speech with these stirring words:

> I call for a march from exploitation to education, from poverty to shared prosperity, a march from slavery to liberty, and a march from violence to peace.
> Let us march from darkness to light. Let us march from mortality to divinity. Let us march![29]

Both King's and Satyarthi's conclusions reemphasized their central ideas in a memorable way, provided closure to their speeches, and inspired their listeners.

Child rights activist Kailash Satyarthi accepts the Nobel Prize in Oslo, Norway, on December 10, 2014. *Photo:* Nigel Waldron/ Getty Images.

RECAP

TECHNIQUES FOR EFFECTIVE CONCLUSIONS

- Use any of the techniques for an effective introduction.
- Refer to the introduction of your speech.
- Issue an inspirational appeal or a challenge.

presentation aid

Any image, object, or sound that reinforces your point visually or aurally so that your audience can better understand it

visual rhetoric

The use of images as an integrated element in the total communication effort a speaker makes to achieve a speaking goal

help you avoid being a PowerPoint "executioner" and ensure that your presentation aids add life to your speech rather than kill your message.

A **presentation aid** is any image, object, or sound that reinforces your point visually or aurally so that your audience can better understand it. Charts, photographs, posters, drawings, graphs, PowerPoint slides, movies, and videos are the types of presentation aids that we will discuss.

Contemporary communicators understand the power of visual rhetoric in informing and persuading others. **Visual rhetoric** is the use of images as an integrated element in the total communication effort a speaker makes to achieve his or her speaking goal.[1] The predominance of visual images—on our phones, tablets, computers, and TVs—attests to how central images are in the communication of information to modern audiences.[2] In fact, it has been estimated that more than 80 percent of all information comes to us through sight.[3] For many people, seeing is believing. Whether on Facebook, Instagram, YouTube, or even via text, today's audience members often expect visual support.

Almost any speech can benefit from presentation aids. As shown in Table 12.1, presentation aids can help you gain attention, enhance understanding and memory, organize ideas, and illustrate a sequence of events or procedures.[4] A speech for which you are expected to use presentation aids is not as different from other types of speeches as you might at first think. Your general objective is still to inform, persuade, or entertain. The key difference is that you will use supporting material that can be seen and sometimes heard.

Types of Presentation Aids

12.1 Describe six types of presentation aids and identify tips for using them effectively.

The first question many students ask when they learn they are required to use presentation aids is "What type of presentation aid should I use?" There are six types of presentation aids: images, text, video, audio, objects, and people.

Images

The most common presentation aids are such two-dimensional images as drawings, photographs, maps, graphs, and charts. To illustration your message, most likely you will incorporate these images into PowerPoint or another type of presentation software. Even if you don't use a computer to display images *during* your speech, you may use one to prepare "hard copy" images, such as a large poster or chart. As we discuss incorporating images in your speech, we'll offer general suggestions both for using them in the old-fashioned way (such as holding up a large graph or object) and for incorporating them into presentation software. Later in the chapter we'll also offer suggestions for using computer-generated graphics.

DRAWINGS   Drawings are popular, often-used presentation aids because they are easy and inexpensive to make. They can also be tailored to your specific needs. To illustrate the functions of the human brain, for example, one student traced an outline of the brain and added labels to indicate the location of specific brain functions. Another student wanted to show the different sizes and shapes of the tree leaves in the area, so she drew enlarged pictures of the leaves, using appropriate shades of green.

You don't have to be a master artist to develop effective drawings. As a rule, large and simple line drawings are more effective than detailed images. If you have absolutely no artistic skill, you can probably find a friend or relative to help you prepare a useful drawing. Alternatively, you could also use software to generate simple line drawings.

Table 12.1   The Value of Presentation Aids

Function	Example	
Gain and maintain attention	Begin a speech with a photo of a malnourished child to illustrate the problem of poverty.	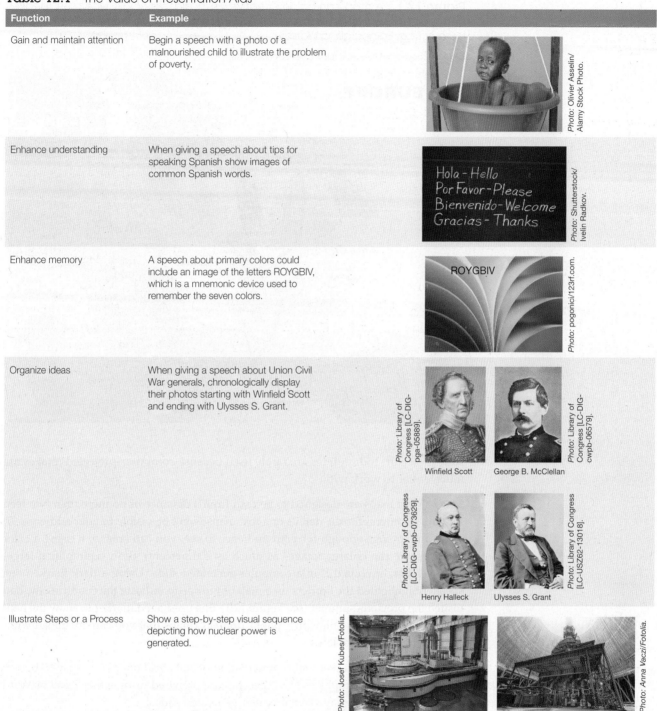
Enhance understanding	When giving a speech about tips for speaking Spanish show images of common Spanish words.	
Enhance memory	A speech about primary colors could include an image of the letters ROYGBIV, which is a mnemonic device used to remember the seven colors.	
Organize ideas	When giving a speech about Union Civil War generals, chronologically display their photos starting with Winfield Scott and ending with Ulysses S. Grant.	
Illustrate Steps or a Process	Show a step-by-step visual sequence depicting how nuclear power is generated.	

PHOTOGRAPHS   Photographs can be used to show objects or places that cannot be illustrated with drawings or that an audience cannot view directly. The problem with printed photos or photos on a smartphone, however, is that they are usually too small to be seen clearly from a distance. If your listeners occupy only two or three rows, it might be possible to hold a photograph close enough for them to see a key feature. But keep in mind that passing a photograph among your listeners is not a good idea; it creates competition for your audience's attention. So if you need to use a photograph, enlarge it or scan and electronically project it.

Thirty years ago, in the era BP (Before PowerPoint), public speakers who wanted to illustrate a talk with photos used 36-millimeter slides projected with a

Figure 12.1   A map can be an effective visual aid, especially when the speaker personalizes it by highlighting relevant information—such as the route followed in a journey from Edinburgh to Warsaw.

slide projector. Today slides are rarely used because computer-projected images are much easier to work with.

MAPS   Most maps are designed to be read from a distance of no more than two feet. As with photographs, the details on most maps won't be visible to your audience. To make a map large enough for your audience to see, you can enlarge it using a color copier (some can enlarge images as much as 200 percent), draw a simplified large-scale version, or embed it in a computer-generated slide. Using a dark marker, one speaker highlighted the borders on a map of Europe to indicate the countries she had visited the previous summer (see Figure 12.1). She used a red marker to show the path of her journey. Search online for "public domain" maps that you can download without violating copyright laws.

graph
A pictorial representation of statistical data

GRAPHS   A **graph** is a pictorial representation of statistical data in an easy to-understand format. Most graphs used in speeches are prepared using either Excel or Word software and then displayed as computer-generated slides.

Why use a graph? Seeing relationships among numbers is better than just hearing statistics. Statistics are abstract summaries of many examples. Most listeners find that graphs help make statistical data more concrete and easier to understand. Yet research also suggests that in addition to presenting information in a graph, it's important to talk about the information presented.[5] Graphs are particularly effective for showing overall trends and relationships among data. By watching news programs, hearing reports, and seeing presentations, you have undoubtedly seen the four most common types of graphs: bar graphs, pie graphs, line graphs, and picture graphs. Most speakers today use computer-generated graphs rather than drawing them freehand, but occasionally you may want to sketch a simple graph on a chalkboard, whiteboard, or flip chart during your talk.

bar graph
A graph in which bars of various lengths represent information

● **Bar Graphs.**   A **bar graph** consists of flat areas—bars—of various lengths to represent information. The bar graph in Figure 12.2 clearly shows the growth

Figure 12.2 Bar graphs can help make statistical information clearly and immediately visible to your audience.

SOURCE: Statista, Number of smartphone users (past and projected) in the United States from 2010 to 2019 (in millions), www.statista.com/statistics/201182/forecast-of-smartphone-users-in-the-us.

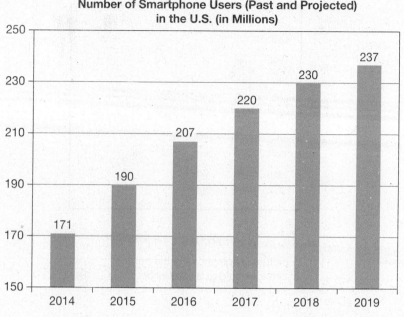

rates of wireless subscribers. It would be more difficult to illustrate your point with words and numbers alone. A graph helps your listeners quickly see comparisons.

- **Pie Graphs.** A **pie graph** shows the individual shares of a whole. The pie graph in Figure 12.3 shows the top Internet search providers. Pie graphs are especially useful in helping your listeners see how quickly data are distributed in a given category or area.
- **Line Graphs.** A **line graph** shows relationships between two or more variables. Like bar graphs, line graphs organize statistical data to show overall trends (Figure 12.4). A line graph can cover a greater span of time or numbers than a bar graph without looking cluttered or confusing. As with other types of presentation aids, a simple line graph communicates better than a cluttered one.

pie graph
A circular graph divided into wedges that show each part's percentage of the whole

line graph
A graph that uses lines or curves to show relationships between two or more variables

Figure 12.3 A pie graph visually shows the percentage of a whole that belongs to each part of it.

SOURCE: Data from Netmarketshare www. netmarketshare.com/search-engine-marketshare.aspx?qprid=4&qpcustomd=0

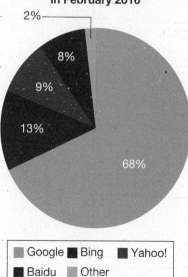

Figure 12.4 Line graphs show relationships between two or more variables.

SOURCE: U.S. Bureau of Labor Statistics 2016 http://data.bls.gov/pdq/SurveyOutputServlet?request_action=wh&graph_name=LN_cpsbref3

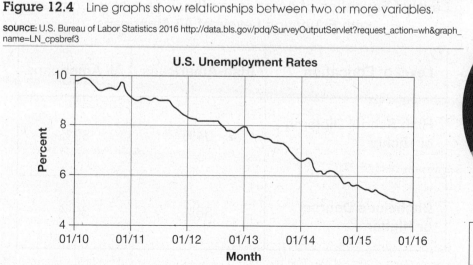

Figure 12.5 Adding visual symbols, such as those in this picture graph, can help your audience maintain interest and understand complex information.

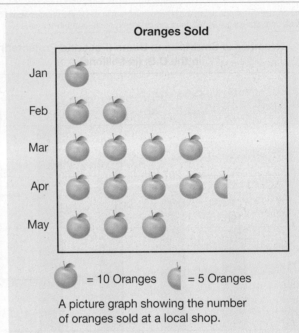

Oranges Sold

= 10 Oranges   = 5 Oranges

A picture graph showing the number of oranges sold at a local shop.

picture graph

A graph that uses images or pictures to symbolize data

- **Picture Graphs.** In place of either a line or a bar, you can use pictures or symbols to supplement the data you are summarizing (Figure 12.5). A **picture graph** looks somewhat less formal and less intimidating than other kinds of graphs. One of the advantages of picture graphs is that they use few words or labels, which makes them easier for your audience to read. There are online sources that can help you create your own picture graphs.

chart

A display that summarizes information by using words, numbers, or images

CHARTS A **chart** summarizes and presents a great deal of information in a small amount of space (Figure 12.6). Charts have several advantages: They are easy to use, re-use, and enlarge. They can also be displayed in a variety of ways, such as on a flipchart,

Figure 12.6 Charts summarize and present information in a small amount of space.

SOURCE: Data from U.S. Census Bureau, "Facts for Features: Irish-American Heritage Month and St. Patrick's Day," www.census.gov/newsroom/facts-for-features/2016/cb16-ff04.html 20 January 2016.

Level of Education of Americans of Irish Ancestry, Compared with Education Levels of All Americans

Level of Education	Irish-Americans	All Americans
High School Diploma or Higher	94%	89%
Bachelor's Degree or Higher	36%	30%

poster, or computer-generated slide. As with all other presentation aids, charts must be simple and easy to read. Do not try to put too much information on one chart.

The key to developing effective charts is to prepare the lettering of the words and phrases you use very carefully. If a chart contains too much information, audience members may feel it is too complicated to understand, and ignore it. If your chart looks cramped or crowded, divide the information into several charts and display each as needed. Use simple words or phrases, and eliminate unnecessary words. Avoid creating a hand-lettered chart as it may appear unprofessional.

Text

In addition to images, many speakers use text, which could be just a word or two, or a brief outline of the key points. The key to using text as a presentation aid is to not overdo it. You want your listeners focused on you rather than reading lengthy bullet points. Many PowerPoint presentations suffer because the speaker has used too many words to accompany the spoken message. To use text effectively, consider these principles:

- Use no more than seven lines of text on any single visual, especially on a computer-generated visual.
- Use *brief* bullet points to designate individual items or thoughts.
- Use parallel structure in bulleted lists (for example, begin each bulleted phrase with the same word, as we do in this list).
- Use the heading of each slide to summarize the essential point of the visual so listeners can follow the key point you are making.[6]

If you're using a computer, you'll be able to choose from dozens of typefaces and **fonts**. But make an informed choice rather than selecting a typeface just because it strikes your fancy. Graphic designers divide typefaces into four types: serif, sans serif, script, and decorative. You'll see each of these illustrated in Figure 12.7. Serif fonts, like the one you are reading now, are easier to read for longer passages because the

fonts
Particular styles of typefaces

Figure 12.7   Typefaces grouped by font type.

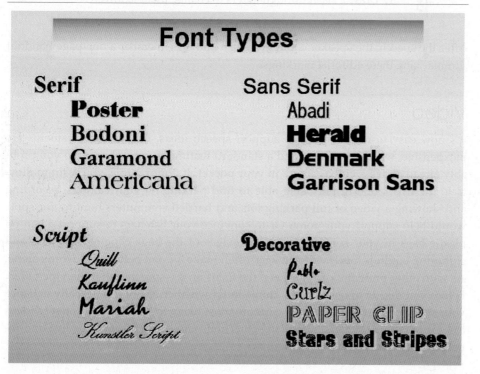

little lines at the tops and bottoms of the letters (called *serifs*) help guide the eye from one letter to the next. Sans serif fonts (*sans* means "without") do not have the extra lines. Script fonts are designed to look like handwriting; although interesting and dramatic, script fonts should be used sparingly because they are harder to read. And you should use decorative fonts only when you want to communicate a special tone or mood. Regardless of which font style or typeface you use, don't use more than one or two typefaces on a single visual; if you do use two, designers suggest they should be from different font categories.

Here's an outline for an informative speech that uses a simple display of text and images (which could be presented on a chart or as a computer-generated graphic) to clearly communicate the ideas the speaker wishes to convey.[7]

TOPIC:	Standard editorial symbols
GENERAL PURPOSE:	To inform
SPECIFIC PURPOSE:	At the end of my speech, the audience should be able to use and interpret five standard symbols for editorial changes in hardcopy written material.

I. The following seven editorial symbols are commonly used to change written text.

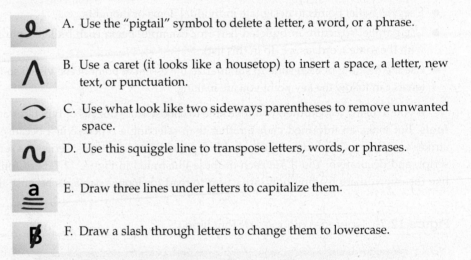

   A. Use the "pigtail" symbol to delete a letter, a word, or a phrase.

   B. Use a caret (it looks like a housetop) to insert a space, a letter, new text, or punctuation.

   C. Use what look like two sideways parentheses to remove unwanted space.

   D. Use this squiggle line to transpose letters, words, or phrases.

   E. Draw three lines under letters to capitalize them.

   F. Draw a slash through letters to change them to lowercase.

After the speech, the speaker could give each audience member a one-page handout summarizing these editorial markings.

Video

It's now easy to record video to support speech ideas. Digital video cameras are inexpensive, widely available, and a standard feature of smartphones, so you probably already have a video camera in your pocket. If, for example, you want to illustrate the frustration of not being able to find parking on your campus, recording and showing a video of full parking lots and harried commuters hunting for spots would help support your point. Or to convince your listeners to support a ban on plastic bags in your community, show images of the bags clinging to fences and cluttering landfills. Such video images often make a point better than words alone. As with other presentation aids, keep the focus on the speech rather than the video. Before you decide to use a video, think about whether or not it will really enhance your speech. Short, well-selected clips are most likely to be effective. Longer videos can exceed your listeners' attention spans and may detract from your live-and-in-person presentation.

Showing a *short* clip from a movie or TV show may help you make your point or provide an attention-catching opening or a memorable closing to your talk. If you are using clips from movies or TV to support your talk, you'll likely find the video footage you need on YouTube, other Internet sources, such as Hulu, or commercially prerecorded digital video disks (DVDs).

It can be helpful to incorporate video files (if you can obtain them) into your own computer-generated slides. Building the video into a slide can give you more control over precisely what clip you are showing as well as the visual context and timing when you play it. You could, for example, show printed lyrics next to footage of a musician performing.

You can use a variety of devices and technologies to store your videos and play them back during your speech:

- **DVD player.** You may wish to play part of a prerecorded movie or TV show from a DVD. But with the widespread availability of video streaming on the Internet, it is unwise to assume there will be a DVD player available for your use. Check to make sure you have access to a DVD player for your speech.

- **Computers and other electronic devices.** You can store your own videos or clips from other sources on your smartphone, tablet computer, or your iPod or other MP3 player. Unless the audience is very small, all of these options, as well as a DVD player, will require you to connect your device to a monitor or a projection system. A 32-inch screen is generally visible to an audience of 25 or 30 people. For a larger audience, you will need either several TVs or monitors or a large-projection TV system. Make sure monitors are available and compatible with your device, or bring your own.

- **The Internet.** If the room where you are delivering your speech has Wi-Fi or direct Internet access, you could skip storing your video and instead stream it directly from YouTube or another Internet source. You could also retrieve your video or audio material from the "cloud"—computer storage in a remote location. Having a backup of your material on a cloud or flash drive can enhance security and ensure that your material will be there when you need it.

When using any of these technologies, you'll want to practice using your video and make sure all the equipment you need is available. Unless you're using a wireless system, for example, you might need a cable to connect your storage device to a monitor. Before giving your speech, do a technical run-through, ensuring that your video image will be ready when you want it.

Audio

Audio can be used to complement visual displays. As with video, you can either create your own audio content or use prerecorded sources. You also have a number of options for storage and playback. You might play a few measures of Bach's *Toccata and Fugue in D Minor* from your iPod—or even live, on a portable electronic keyboard—to illustrate a point.

Used sparingly, sound can effectively establish a mood or support your points. While showing PowerPoint slides of her recent Caribbean vacation, one student used a recording of soft steel drum music as an introductory background for her talk. But it's not a good idea to have a competing soundtrack during your entire speech. Besides music you could also use recordings of spoken messages. One student played brief excerpts of taped interviews with frustrated students who had difficulty figuring out the most recent changes in how to apply for financial aid. As with video, be sure to rehearse with and master any technology involved with audio aids, and don't let your soundtrack overwhelm or distract from your own words.

Objects and Models

Listeners like looking at real, tangible items. They can be touched, smelled, heard, and even tasted, as well as seen. Objects are real, and audiences like the real thing. Using an object or, if the object is too big or illegal to bring to your speech, using a model, can enhance audience interest.

OBJECTS   You have played the trombone since you were in fifth grade, so you decide to give an informative speech about the history and function of this instrument. Your trombone is the obvious presentation aid that you would show to your audience as you describe how it works. You might even play a few measures to demonstrate its sound and your talent. Or perhaps you are an art major and you have just finished a watercolor painting. Why not bring your picture to class to illustrate your talk about watercolor techniques?

When you use an object to illustrate an idea, make sure that you can handle the object with ease. If an object is too large, it can be unwieldy and difficult to show to your audience. Tiny objects can only be seen close up. It will be impossible for your listeners to see the detail on your antique thimble, the intricate needlework on your cross-stitch sampler, or the attention to detail in your miniature log cabin. Other objects can be dangerous to handle. One speaker, who attempted a demonstration of how to string an archery bow, made his audience extremely uncomfortable when his almost-strung bow flew over their heads. He certainly got their attention, but he lost his credibility.

model
A small object that represents a larger object

MODELS   If it is not possible to bring along the object you would like to show your audience, consider showing them a **model** of it. You cannot bring a World War II fighter plane to class, so buy or build a scale model instead. To illustrate her lecture about human anatomy, one student brought a plastic model of a skeleton; an actual human skeleton is illegal to possess in most states as well as difficult to carry to class. Make sure, however, that any model you use is large enough to be seen by all members of your audience. When Brad brought his collection of miniature hand-carved guitars to illustrate his talk on rock music, his tiny visuals didn't add to the message; they detracted from it.

Three-dimensional models can help you to explain an object, process, or procedure to your audience in situations where it is impractical or impossible to use the actual object. *Photo:* Cultura Limited/SuperStock.

People

At least since Ronald Reagan, U.S. presidents have used people as visual aids during their State of the Union addresses, relating a poignant story and then asking the protagonist of the story, seated in the balcony, to stand and be recognized. One speechwriter noted that presidents have learned to use this strategy to especially good effect, finding it "a way of coming down from the stage, as it were, and mingling with the crowd."[8]

In classroom speeches, too, people can serve as presentation aids. Amelia, a choreographer for the Ballet Folklorico Mexicano, wanted to illustrate an intricate Latin folk dance, so she arranged to have one of the troupe's dancers attend her speech to demonstrate the dance.

Using people to illustrate your message can be tricky, however. It is usually unwise to ask for spur-of-the-moment help from volunteers while you are delivering your speech. Instead, choose a trusted friend or colleague before your presentation so that you can fully inform him or her about what needs to be done. Rehearse your speech using your living presentation aid.

Also, it is distracting to have your support person stand beside you doing nothing. If you don't need the person to demonstrate something during your opening remarks, wait and introduce the person to your audience when needed.

Finally, do not allow your assistants to run away with the show. For example, don't let your dance student perform the *pas de bourré* longer than necessary to illustrate your technique. Nor should you permit your models to prance about provocatively while displaying your dress designs. And don't allow your buddy to throw you when you demonstrate the wrestling hold that made you the district wrestling champ. Remember, your presentation aids are always subordinate to your speech. You must remain in control.

You can also serve as your own presentation aid to demonstrate or illustrate major points. If you are talking about tennis, you might use your racquet to illustrate your superb backhand or to show the proper way to hold it. If you are a nurse or an emergency department technician giving a talk about medical procedures, by all means wear your uniform to establish your credibility.

Using Computer-Generated Presentation Aids

12.2 Describe how computers may be used to generate high-quality presentation aids.

Richard had worked hard on his presentation to the finance committee. He had prepared an impressive-looking hand-drawn poster, distributed a handout of his key conclusions, and rehearsed his speech so that he had a well-polished delivery. But as he sat down after concluding his speech, certain he had dazzled his listeners, a colleague poked him and asked, "Why didn't you use PowerPoint or Prezi slides?" Computer-generated images can add professional polish to your presentation. For your classroom speeches, however, check with your instructor to determine his or her recommendations and policies about using computer-generated graphics.

Because most students learn to use presentation software in school, you will no doubt be familiar with the basic elements of developing a computer-generated image. And because you've undoubtedly seen many computer-generated presentations, you also know that you can incorporate video clips as well as digital photos on a slide. But, as with any presentation aid, the images or clips you use must help develop your central idea; otherwise, they will distract your audience from it.

Basic Principles of Using Computer-Generated Presentation Aids

Most audiences, especially those in the corporate world, expect a speaker to use computer-generated presentation aids.[9] The most popular presentation software, PowerPoint, helps you create and present images, photos, words, charts, and graphs. PowerPoint can also incorporate video and sound.

Prezi is another increasingly popular presentation software program that is cloud-based—the information is accessed on demand via the Internet rather than on your own computer. Prezi has many features similar to PowerPoint, but it also has features that let you zoom in and out to help you focus your audience's attention. But just because Prezi permits you to zoom in and out on images and text, be careful not to overdo it. The goal is to make your listeners remember your message, not make them dizzy. Prezi also has a feature that allows you to look at all of your slides at once. So rather than predetermining the precise order of your slides, you can more readily adapt your presentation to your audience during your speech.

Keynote, another popular presentation software, was developed for Apple™ computers and devices, although it can be exported to PowerPoint or a PDF for use on PCs. Like other graphics programs, it permits users to easily maintain consistency in fonts and colors. Some people especially like its sleek, contemporary appearance.

Tips for Using Computer-Generated Presentation Aids

One of the biggest problems with using computer-generated images is that a speaker may be tempted to shovel large amounts of information at listeners without regard for their attention span. Resist that temptation.[10] Research supports our now-familiar admonition that the audience should be foremost in your mind as you develop visual images to support your verbal message.[11] To remain audience-centered when using computer-generated presentation aids consider the following suggestions.

KEEP SIGHTS AND SOUNDS SIMPLE In most aspects of communication, simple is better.[12] Even though you *can* use fancy fonts and add as many images as you like to your visual, we have a suggestion for you: Don't. Keep in mind what we've stressed throughout this chapter: Presentation aids *support* your message; they are not your message.[13] Or, as CEO John W. Roe wisely expressed, "Visual aids should be made to steer, not to row."[14]

Most presentation software lets you add sound effects to highlight your message. But the sound of a racecar zooming across a computer screen or a typewriter clacking as letters pop up in place can detract from your speech. Cute sounds will lose their novelty after the first slide or two and can become irritating. We suggest that *you* be the soundtrack, not your computer.

CONTROL COMPUTER IMAGES When using computer-generated slides, there may be times when you want to speak to your audience and not refer to a slide or image. During these times, use a blank slide or use the projector's remote control to temporarily project no image.

REPEAT VISUAL ELEMENTS TO UNIFY YOUR PRESENTATION Use a common visual element, such as a bullet or other symbol, at the beginning of each word or phrase on a list. Use common color schemes and spacing to give your visuals coherence. Also avoid mixing different fonts. You'll get a professional, polished look if you use the same visual style for each of your images.

The most significant advantage of computer-generated graphics is the ease with which they allow you to display attractive visual images. Both color and black-and-white images are available as **clip art**. Clip art consists of pictures and other images that are either in printed or electronic form. Clip art (as shown in Figure 12.8) can give your visuals and graphics a professional touch even if you did not excel in art class. But when using clip art, try to avoid images that your listeners may have seen before; look for fresh, contemporary visuals.

MAKE INFORMED DECISIONS ABOUT USING COLOR Color communicates. Red and orange are warm colors that often evoke feelings of excitement and interest (which is why most fast-food restaurant chains use red, yellow, and orange in their color schemes; they want to make you hungry and catch your attention). Cooler colors such as green and blue have a more calming effect on viewers. Warm colors tend to come forward and jump out at the viewer, whereas cooler colors recede into the background. What are the implications of the power of color to communicate? Consider using warm colors for positive messages (for example, "Profits are up") and cooler colors for more negative messages ("We're losing money").

Designers caution against using certain color combinations. For example, if some audience members are color-blind, they won't be able to distinguish between red and green. And you don't want to get carried away with using too much color. To unify your presentation, use the same background color on all visuals and no more than two colors for words. A light background with darker-colored words can have a pleasing effect and is easy to see.

CONSIDER THE AUDIENCE

clip art
Images or pictures stored in a computer file or in printed form that can be used in a presentation aid

Figure 12.8 Copyright-free clip art is readily available on many Web sites. It can give a professional look to your visuals and memorably reinforce your verbal messages.

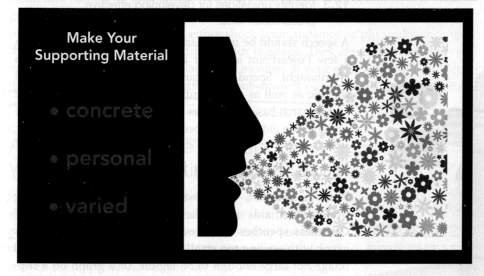

The key advantage of using computer-generated graphics is that virtually anyone can use them to craft professional-looking images. In addition to learning the mechanics of the software program, keep the tips summarized in Table 12.2 in mind when using computer-generated images.[15]

Table 12.2 Develop Effective Computer-Generated Visuals

Make text simple	• Use no more than seven lines of text on a single slide • Use bullets • Use parallel structure when writing text
Make visuals unified	• Use a common visual image on each slide • Use a common font • Use a similar background or style for each slide
Choose fonts carefully	• Use serif fonts to increase ease of reading • Use script and sans serif fonts sparingly • Use decorative fonts only for dramatic impact
Choose colors carefully	• Use red and orange to communicate warmth • Use green and blue to communicate calm coolness • Be cautious about using red and green together • Use a light background with darker text to catch attention

CONFIDENTLY CONNECTING WITH YOUR AUDIENCE

Practice with Your Presentation Aids to Boost Your Confidence

One source of communication apprehension is uncertainty. By rehearsing with your presentation aids, you reduce uncertainty about your presentation. Whether you are using PowerPoint slides or some other technology, be sure you have practiced using the equipment you will use when you present your message. By reducing the chance for errors and technical miscues, you will also be increasing your confidence in your ability to use your presentation aids without a hitch.

pedagogy

The art and science of teaching children

andragogy

The art and science of teaching adults

Use Principles and Techniques of Adult Learning

Most public-speaking audiences you face will consist of adults. Perhaps you've heard of **pedagogy**? The word *pedagogy* is based on the Greek words *paid*, which means "child," and *agogus*, which means "guide." Thus, pedagogy is the art and science of teaching children. In contrast, adult learning is called **andragogy**.[5] *Andr* is the Greek word that means "adult." So andragogy is the art and science of teaching adults. Researchers and scholars have found andragogical approaches are best for adults. (If you're a college student older than 18, you are an adult learner.) What are andragogical, or adult-learning, principles? Here are the most important ones.[6]

- **Provide information that is applicable to audience members' needs and interests.** Most people who work in business have an in basket on their desk to receive letters and memos that must be read and work that must be done. Each of us also has a kind of mental in basket, an agenda for what we want or need to accomplish. If you present adult listeners with information that they can immediately apply to their "in basket," they are more likely to focus on and understand your message.

- **Actively involve listeners in the learning process.** Rather than have your listeners sit passively as you speak, ask questions for them to think about or, in some cases, to respond to on the spot.

- **Connect listeners' life experiences with new information.** Adult listeners are more likely to understand your message when you help them connect new information with their past experiences. If you know the kinds of experiences your listeners have had, then you can refer to those experiences as you present your ideas.

- **Make new information relevant to listeners' needs and their busy lives.** Most adults are busy—probably, if pressed, most will say they are too busy for their own good. People working, going to school, raising families, and being involved in their communities need to be shown how the ideas you share are relevant to them.

- **Help listeners solve their problems.** Most people have problems and are looking for solutions to them. People will be more likely to pay attention to information that helps them better understand and solve their problems.

Which of the andragogical principles presented in this chapter is this instructional speaker following? *Photo:* WavebreakMediaMicro/Fotolia.

Clarify Unfamiliar Ideas or Complex Processes

If you want to tell your listeners about a complex process, you will need more than definitions to explain what you mean. Research suggests you can demystify a complex process if you first provide a simple overview of the process with an analogy, a vivid description, or a word picture.[7]

USE ANALOGIES   If a speaker said, "The Milky Way galaxy is big," you'd have a vague idea that the cluster of stars and space material making up the Milky Way is large. But if the speaker said, "If the Milky Way galaxy were as big as the continent of North America, our solar system would fit inside a coffee cup," you'd have a better idea of just how big the Milky Way is and, by comparison, how small our solar system is.[8] As we discussed in Chapter 7, an analogy is a comparison of two things. It's an especially useful technique for describing complex processes because it can help someone understand something difficult to grasp (the size of the Milky Way) by comparing it to something already understood (the size of a coffee cup).[9]

By helping your listeners compare something new to something they already know or can visualize, you can make your message clearer. Here's an example of this idea based on what professor of business Chip Heath and communication consultant Dan Heath call the principle of "using what's there—using the information you have (what's there) and relating it to something more familiar."[10] Try this short exercise. Take 15 seconds to memorize the letters below; then close the book and write the letters exactly as they appear here.

J FKFB INAT OUP SNA SAI RS

Most people, say these experts, remember about half of the letters. Now, look below to see the same letters organized differently. The letters haven't changed, but we have regrouped them into acronyms that may make more sense to you. We are more likely to make sense out of something we already have a mental category for. An analogy works in the same way.

JFK FBI NATO UPS NASA IRS

USE A VIVID, DESCRIPTIVE WORD PICTURE   When you *describe,* you provide more detail than when you just define something. One way to describe a situation or event is with a word picture. A **word picture** is a lively description that helps your listeners form a mental image by appealing to their senses of sight, taste, smell, sound, and touch.

To create an effective word picture, begin by forming your own clear mental image of the person, place, object, or process before you try to describe it. See it with your "mind's eye."

- What would a listener see if he or she were looking at it?
- What would listeners hear?
- If they could touch the object or participate in the process, how would it feel to them?
- If your listeners could smell or taste it, what would that be like?

word picture
A vivid description that appeals to the senses

To describe these sensations, choose the most specific and vivid words possible. Onomatopoeic words—words that resemble the sounds they name, such as *buzz, snort, hum, crackle,* or *hiss*—are powerful. So are similes and other comparisons. "The rock was rough as sandpaper" and "the pebble was as smooth as a baby's skin" appeal to both the visual and the tactile senses.

Be sure to describe the emotions a listener might feel if he or she were to experience the situation you relate. Ultimately, your goal is to use just the right words to evoke an emotional response from the listener. If you experienced the situation, describe your own emotions. Use specific adjectives rather than general terms such as *happy* or *sad.*

One speaker, talking about receiving her first speech assignment, described her reaction with these words:

> My heart stopped. Panic began to rise up inside. Me?...For the next five days I lived in dreaded anticipation of the forthcoming event.[11]

Note how effectively her choice of such words and phrases as "my heart stopped," "panic," and "dreaded anticipation" describe her terror at the prospect of making a speech—much more so than if she had said simply, "I was scared." The more vividly and accurately you can describe emotion, the more intimately involved in your description the audience will become.

As you develop your speech and supporting materials, consider how you can appeal to a variety of learning styles at the same time. Because you'll be giving a speech, your auditory learners will like that. Visual learners like and expect an informative talk to be illustrated with PowerPoint™ images. They will appreciate seeing pictures or having statistics summarized using bar or line graphs or pie charts. Visual print learners will like handouts, which you could distribute after your talk. Kinesthetic learners will appreciate movement, even small actions such as raising their hands in response to questions.

Strategies to Maintain Audience Interest

13.3 Effectively and appropriately use four strategies to maintain audience interest.

No matter how carefully you craft definitions, how skillfully you deliver descriptions, or how you visually reinforce presentation aids, if your listeners aren't paying attention, you won't achieve your goal of informing them. Strategies for gaining and holding interest are vital in achieving your speaking goal.

When discussing how to develop attention-catching introductions in Chapter 9, we itemized specific techniques for gaining your listeners' attention. The following strategies build on those techniques.

Motivate Your Audience to Listen to You

Most audiences will probably not be waiting breathlessly for you to talk to them. You will need to motivate them to listen to you.

Some situations have built-in motivations for listeners. A teacher can say, "There will be a test covering my lecture tomorrow. It will count toward 50 percent of your semester grade." Such methods may not make the teacher popular, but they will certainly motivate the class to listen. Similarly, a boss might say, "Your ability to use these sales principles will determine whether you keep your job." Your boss's statement will probably motivate you to learn the company's sales principles. However, because you will rarely have the power to motivate your listeners with such strong-arm tactics, you will need to find more creative ways to get your audience to listen to you.

Never assume your listeners will be interested in what you have to say. Pique their interest with a rhetorical question. Tell them a story. Explain how the information you present will be of value to them. As the British writer G. K. Chesterton once said, "There is no such thing as an uninteresting topic; there are only uninterested people."[12]

Tell a Story

Good stories with interesting characters and riveting plots have fascinated listeners for millennia; the words "once upon a time" are usually sure-fire attention-getters. A good story is inherently interesting. Stories are also a way of connecting your message to people from a variety of cultural backgrounds.[13]

One author suggests that, of all the stories ever told since the beginning of time, in all cultures, there are only seven basic plots: overcoming the monster, rags to riches, the quest, voyage and return, comedy, tragedy, and rebirth. Think of a favorite story and see if it fits into one of these categories. Another theory boils the history of stories down even further. It suggests that there is really only one basic plot: All stories are about overcoming obstacles to find "home." This view does not suggest that all characters literally find their way home; rather, all stories are about striving to find a place, literal or metaphorical, that represents "home" in some way.[14]

Humorous stories are one way to get and hold listeners' attention. When listeners are interested in your speech, they are more likely to learn the information you want to share with them. What other strategies could the speaker use to keep this audience interested? *Photo:* Fotolia/dglimages.

In addition to the plot, the characteristics of a well-told tale are simple yet powerful. Here we elaborate on some of the ideas about storytelling we introduced in Chapter 7. A good story includes conflict, incorporates action, creates suspense, and may also include humor.

- **A good story includes conflict.**   Stories that pit one side against another foster attention, as do descriptions of opposing ideas and forces in government, religion, or personal relationships. The Greeks learned long ago that the essential ingredient for a good play, be it comedy or tragedy, is conflict. Conflict is often the obstacle that keeps the people in a story from finding "home."

- **A good story incorporates action.**   An audience is more likely to listen to an action-packed message than to one that listlessly lingers on an idea. Good stories have a beginning that sets the stage, a heart that moves to a conclusion, and then an ending that ties up all the loose ends. The key to interest is a plot that moves along.

- **A good story creates suspense.**   TV dramas and soap operas long ago proved that the way to ensure high ratings is to tell a story with the outcome in doubt. Keeping people on the edge of their seats because they don't know what will happen next is another element in good storytelling.

- **A good story may incorporate humor.**   A fisherman went into a sporting-goods store. The salesperson offered the man a wonderful lure for trout: It had beautiful colors, eight hooks, and looked just like a rare Buckner bug. Finally, the fisherman asked the salesperson, "Do fish really like this thing?" "I don't know," admitted the salesperson, "I don't sell to fish."

We could have simply said, "It's important to be audience-centered." But using a bit of humor makes the point while holding the listener's attention.

Not all stories have to be funny. Stories may be sad or dramatic. But adding humor when appropriate usually helps maintain interest and attention.

Present Information That Relates to Your Listeners

Throughout this book we have encouraged you to develop an audience-centered approach to public speaking. Being an audience-centered informative speaker means being aware of information that your audience can use. If, for example, you are going

Figure 13.1   You can follow the steps of the audience-centered model of public speaking to craft a successful informative speech.

SOURCE: Copyrighted by Pearson Education, Hoboken, NJ.

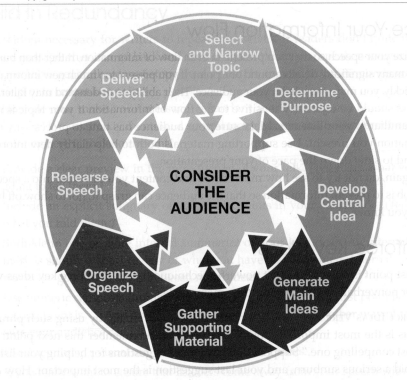

you may still wonder how to go about preparing an informative speech. Our advice: Use the audience-centered speaking model, shown in Figure 13.1, to guide you step-by-step through the process. We conclude this chapter with a reminder to consider your audience.

As with any type of speech, an informative talk requires that you consider three general questions of audience analysis: To whom are you speaking? What are their interests, attitudes, beliefs, and values? What do they expect from you? When your general purpose is to inform, you should focus on specific aspects of these three general questions. Part of considering who your audience is will include figuring out, as best you can, their preferred learning styles. Determining listeners' interests, attitudes, beliefs, and values can help you balance your use of strategies to enhance understanding and recall with your need to maintain their interest. You won't need to work as hard to maintain the interest of an audience who is already highly interested in your topic, for example. Careful consideration of the audience's expectations can also help you maintain their interest, perhaps by surprising them with something they do not expect.

Once your topic and purpose are clearly established, continue to consider your audience when developing your central idea and generating your main ideas. Interesting and appropriate supporting material will make your message clear, engaging, and memorable. Most informative speeches are primarily organized using topical, chronological, or complexity strategies. As with any speech, rehearsing your speech several times will help you deliver a message that your audience will listen to and perceive as credible.

RECAP

AUDIENCE-CENTERED INFORMATIVE SPEAKING

- Select topic: Consider who your listeners are, as well as their interests and needs.
- Formulate central and main ideas: Make them clear and simple.
- Gather supporting material: Decide what will help the audience maintain interest and learn.
- Organize: Consider topical, chronological, or complexity as the primary organizational strategy for an informative speech.
- Rehearse: Deliver a polished message that your audience will listen to and perceive as credible.

STUDY GUIDE: REVIEW, APPLY, AND ASSESS

Informative Speech Topics

13.1 Describe five different types of informative speech topics.

REVIEW: To inform is to teach someone something you know. Informative speeches have three goals—to enhance understanding, to maintain interest, and to be remembered. There are several different types of informative speeches. Speeches about objects discuss tangible things. Speeches about procedures explain a process or describe how something works. Speeches about people can be about either the famous or the little known. Speeches about events describe major occurrences or personal experiences. Speeches about ideas discuss often-abstract principles, concepts, or theories.

Key Term
speech to inform

APPLY: You are a chemistry major considering whether you should give an informative speech to your public-speaking class about how pipe bombs are made. Is this an appropriate topic for your audience?

ASSESS: Hillary Webster, MD, will be addressing other physicians at a medical convention to discuss the weight-loss technique she has recently used successfully with her patients. What advice would you give to help her present an effective talk?

Strategies to Enhance Audience Understanding

13.2 Effectively and appropriately use three strategies to enhance audience understanding.

REVIEW: To enhance your listeners' understanding of a message: (1) define ideas clearly, (2) use principles and techniques of adult learning, and (3) clarify unfamiliar ideas or complex processes.

Key Terms
pedagogy   word picture
andragogy

APPLY:

1. To give a 5-minute speech about nuclear energy, you must greatly simplify what is a very complex process. How can you avoid misrepresenting your topic? Should you let your audience know that you are oversimplifying the process?

2. You have been asked to speak to a kindergarten class about your chosen profession. Identify approaches to this task that would help make your message clear, interesting, and memorable to your audience.

ASSESS: Imagine you are going to teach a group of adult learners how to prepare an informative speech. How could you incorporate principles of adult learning as presented in this chapter to ensure that you addressed their needs?

Strategies to Maintain Audience Interest

13.3 Effectively and appropriately use four strategies to maintain audience interest.

REVIEW: To gain and maintain interest in your informative talk, follow three important principles. First, motivate your audience to listen to you. Second, tell a story; a well-told story almost always keeps listeners focused on you and your message. Third, present information that relates to your listeners' interests; in essence, be audience-centered. Finally, use the unexpected to surprise your audience.

APPLY: Before giving a speech to your class in which you share a story that includes personal information about one of your friends, should you ask permission from your friend?

Strategies to Enhance Audience Recall

13.4 Effectively and appropriately use four strategies to enhance audience recall of information presented in an informative speech.

REVIEW: Help your listeners remember what you tell them by being redundant. Keep your main ideas short and simple. Pacing the flow of your information helps listeners recall your ideas. Reinforcing important points verbally and nonverbally can also help your audience members remember them.

ASSESS: What strategies does your public-speaking teacher use in class to enhance listener recall?

Developing an Audience-Centered Informative Speech

13.5 Develop an audience-centered informative speech.

REVIEW: You can apply principles of informative speaking to adapt the audience-centered model of speaking. The needs of your audience and topic will help you organize your speech and gather supporting materials. Use interesting and appropriate supporting material. Most informative speeches are primarily organized using topical, chronological, or complexity strategies. Rehearse your speech.

APPLY: Brendan is planning on sharing his experiences with his fraternity brothers about his recent study abroad trip to Oxford, England. As he prepares and presents his message, what specific aspects of Brendan's audience should he keep in mind?

ASSESS: Redundancy can be especially helpful when you and the audience have language differences. Which of the specific strategies for making your message more redundant would increase understanding of an audience whose primary language is different from yours?

Understanding Principles of Persuasive Speaking

14

> ... the power of speech, to stir
> men's blood.
>
> —William Shakespeare

George Caleb Bingham (1811–79), *Stump
Speaking* (1853–4), oil on canvas, Gift of
Bank of America, Saint Louis Art Museum,
Missouri. *Photo:* Library of Congress
[LC-DIG-cwpb-21538].

OBJECTIVES

After studying this chapter, you should be able to do the following:

14.1 Describe the goals of persuasive messages.

14.2 Explain classic and contemporary theories of how persuasion occurs.

14.3 Describe four ways to motivate listeners to respond to a persuasive message.

14.4 Prepare and present an audience-centered persuasive speech.

I
t happens to you hundreds of times each day. It appears as tweets, Internet pop-up ads, Facebook messages, commercials on TV, and requests from friends; as advertisements in magazines and on billboards; and as fund-raising messages from politicians and charities. It also occurs when you are asked to give money to a worthy cause or to donate blood. "It" is persuasion. Because persuasion is such an ever-present part of life, it is important to understand how it works. What are the principles of an activity that can shape your attitudes and behavior? What do crafters of Internet pop-up ads, salespeople, and politicians know about how to influence your thinking and behavior that you don't know?

In this chapter, we discuss how persuasion works. Such information can sharpen your persuasive skills and can also help you become a more informed receiver of persuasive messages. We will define persuasion and discuss the psychological principles underlying efforts to persuade others. We will also discuss tips for choosing a persuasive speech topic and developing arguments for your speeches. In Chapter 15, we will examine specific strategies for crafting a persuasive speech.

In Chapter 13, we discussed strategies for informative speaking—the oral presentation of new information to listeners so that they will understand and remember what is communicated. The purposes of informing and persuading are closely related. Why inform an audience? Why give new information to others? We often provide information to give listeners new insights that may affect their attitudes and behavior. Information alone has the potential to convince others, but when information is coupled with strategies to persuade, the chances of success increase.

The Goals of Persuasion

14.1 Describe the goals of persuasive messages.

Persuasion is the process of changing or reinforcing attitudes, beliefs, values, or behavior. In a persuasive speech, the speaker explicitly asks the audience to make a choice, rather than just informing them of the options. As a persuasive speaker, you will do more than teach; you will ask your listeners to respond to the information you share. Audience analysis is crucial to achieving your goal. To advocate a particular view or position successfully, you must understand your listeners' positions before you speak.

Note that when attempting to persuade someone, you may not necessarily try to change someone's point of view or behavior but, instead, aim to *reinforce* it. Your listeners may already like, believe, or value something, or *sometimes* do what you'd like them to do; you are trying to strengthen their current perspective. Suppose, for example, that your persuasive purpose is to encourage people to use their recycling bins. The audience may already think that recycling is a good thing and may even use their recycling bins at least some of the time. Your speaking goal is to reinforce their behavior so that they use the bins every time.

Because the goal of persuasion is to change or reinforce attitudes, beliefs, values, or behavior, it's important to clarify how these elements differ. Having a clear idea of precisely which of these elements you want to change or reinforce can help you develop your persuasive strategy.

Changing or Reinforcing Audience Attitudes

Our attitudes represent our likes and dislikes. Stated more precisely, an **attitude** is a learned predisposition to respond favorably or unfavorably toward something.[1] In a persuasive speech, you might try to persuade your listeners to favor or oppose a new shopping mall, to like bats because of their ability to eat insects, or to dislike an increase in the sales tax.

Changing or Reinforcing Audience Beliefs

A persuasive speech could also attempt to change or reinforce a belief. A **belief** is something you understand to be true or false. If you believe in something, you are convinced that it exists or is true. You have structured your sense of what is real and what is unreal to account for the existence of whatever you believe. If you believe in God, you have structured your sense of what is real and unreal to recognize the existence of God.

We hold some beliefs based on faith—we haven't directly experienced something, but we believe anyway. However, most beliefs are typically based on evidence, including past experiences. If you believe the sun will rise in the east again

persuasion
The process of changing or reinforcing a listener's attitudes, beliefs, values, or behavior

attitude
A learned predisposition to respond favorably or unfavorably toward something; likes and dislikes

belief
A way we structure reality to accept something as true or false

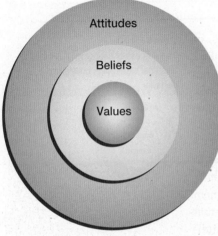

value
An enduring concept of good and bad, right and wrong

tomorrow, or that global climate change is occurring, you base these beliefs either on what you've directly experienced or on the experience of someone you find trustworthy. Beliefs are also changed by evidence. As a speaker, you might have a difficult time, for example, trying to change an audience's belief that the world is flat; you would need to show that existing evidence supports a different conclusion. Usually it takes a great deal of evidence to change a belief and alter the way your audience structures reality.

Changing or Reinforcing Audience Values

A persuasive speech could also seek to change or reinforce a value. A **value** is an enduring concept of right or wrong, good or bad. If you value something, you classify it as good or desirable, and you tend to think of its opposite or its absence as bad or wrong. If you do not value something, you are indifferent to it. Values form the basis of your life goals. They are also the motivating force behind your behavior. Most Americans value honesty, trustworthiness, freedom, loyalty, marriage, family, and money. Understanding what your listeners value can help you refine your analysis of them and adapt the content of your speech to those values.

Most of us acquired our values when we were very young and have held onto them into adulthood. Our values, therefore, are generally deeply ingrained. It is not impossible to change the values of your listeners, but it is much more difficult than trying to change a belief or an attitude. Political and religious points of view, which are usually based on long-held values, are especially difficult to modify.

As Figure 14.1 shows, values are the most deeply ingrained of the three predispositions; they change least frequently. That's why values are at the core of the model. Beliefs change, but not as much as attitudes. Trying to change an audience's attitudes (likes and dislikes) is easier than attempting to change their values. Today you may like the way your instructor is teaching your class (you have a favorable attitude of him or her). But after you receive a low grade on a test, you may dislike your instructor (you have an unfavorable attitude). You may still *believe* that the teacher is knowledgeable, and you still *value* the goals of education, but your *attitude* toward your teacher has changed because of the feedback you received.

We suggest that you think carefully about your purpose for making a persuasive speech. Know with certainty whether your objective is to change or to reinforce an attitude, a belief, or a value. Then decide what you have to do to achieve your objective.

Changing or Reinforcing Audience Behaviors

Persuasive messages often attempt to do more than change or reinforce attitudes, beliefs, or values; they may attempt to change or strengthen behaviors. Getting listeners to eat more fruits and vegetables and to exercise more are typical goals of the persuasive messages that we hear. It seems logical that knowing someone's attitudes, beliefs, and values will help us predict precisely how that person will behave. But we are complicated creatures, and human behavior is not always neatly predictable. Sometimes our attitudes, beliefs, and values may not appear to be consistent with how we act. For example, you may know that if you're on a low-carb diet, you should avoid a second helping of Dad's homemade chocolate cake, but you cut off a slice and gobble it up anyway.

RECAP
DEFINING PERSUASION

Persuasion attempts to change or reinforce the following:
- Attitudes: Likes and dislikes
- Beliefs: Perceptions of what is true or false
- Values: What you hold as right and wrong, good or bad
- Behavior: What we do or don't do

How Persuasion Works

14.2 Explain classic and contemporary theories of how persuasion occurs.

Now that you know what persuasion is and how attitudes, beliefs, and values influence your behavior, you may still have questions about how persuasion actually works. Knowing how and why listeners change their minds and their behavior can help you construct more effective persuasive messages.

Besides enabling you to persuade others, understanding how persuasion works can help you analyze why *you* are sometimes persuaded to think or behave in certain ways. Being conscious of why you respond to specific persuasive messages can help you be a better, more discriminating listener to persuasive pitches.

Many theories and considerable research describe how persuasion works. We'll discuss two approaches here: first, a classical approach identified by Aristotle, and second, a more contemporary theory that builds on the classical approach.

Aristotle's Traditional Approach: Using Ethos, Logos, and Pathos to Persuade

Aristotle, a Greek philosopher and rhetorician who lived and wrote in the fourth century BCE, is the source of many ideas about communication in general and persuasion in particular. As we noted in Chapter 4, he defined *rhetoric* as the process of discovering in any particular case the available means of persuasion. When the goal is to persuade, the communicator selects symbols (words and nonverbal messages, including images and music) to change attitudes, beliefs, values, or behavior. Aristotle identified three general methods (or, using his language, "available means") to persuade: ethos, logos, and pathos.[2]

ETHOS   To use **ethos** to persuade, an effective communicator must be credible. Aristotle believed that in order to be credible, a public speaker should be ethical, possess good character, have common sense, and be concerned for the well-being of the audience. The more credible and ethical a speaker is perceived to be, the greater the chances are that a listener will believe in, trust, and positively respond to the persuasive message of the speaker. So one of the means or methods of persuasion is for the communicator to present information that can be trusted and to be believable and trustworthy himself or herself. When a friend wants to convince you to let him borrow your car, he may say, "Trust me. I promise not to do anything wacky with your car. I'm a responsible guy." He's appealing to his credibility as an ethical, trusted friend. We'll discuss specific strategies to enhance your credibility and your persuasiveness in the next chapter.

LOGOS   Another means of persuading others is to use **logos**. The word *logos* literally means "the word." Aristotle used this term to refer to the rational, logical arguments a speaker uses to persuade someone. A skilled persuader not only reaches a logical conclusion but also supports the message with evidence and reasoning. The friend who wants to borrow your car may use a logical, rational argument supported with evidence to get your car keys. He may say, "I borrowed your car last week and I returned it without a scratch. I also borrowed it the week before that and there were no problems—and I filled the tank with gas. So if you loan me your

ethos
The term Aristotle used to refer to a speaker's credibility

logos
Literally, "the word"; the term Aristotle used to refer to logic—the formal system of using rules to reach a conclusion

Both Aristotle's traditional approach and the elaboration likelihood model suggest that appeals to emotion can help persuade listeners. Thus, a speaker might accompany a talk promoting the adoption of pets from a local animal shelter with photos of adorable animals to arouse listeners' emotions and propel them to bring home a puppy or kitten. *Photo:* MoustacheGirl/Fotolia.

car today, I'll return it just like I did in the past." Your friend is appealing to your rational side by using evidence to support his conclusion that your car will be returned in good shape. In Chapter 15 we'll provide strategies for developing logical, rational arguments and supporting those arguments with solid evidence.

pathos

The term used by Aristotle to refer to appeals to human emotion

PATHOS   Aristotle used the term **pathos** to refer to the use of appeals to emotion. We sometimes hold attitudes, beliefs, and values that are not logical but that simply make us feel positive. Likewise, we sometimes do things or buy things to make ourselves feel happy, powerful, or energized. The friend who wants to borrow your wheels may also use pathos—an emotional appeal—to get you to turn over your car keys. He may say, "Look, without transportation I can't get to my doctor's appointment. I'm feeling sick. I need your help. Friends help friends, and I could use a good friend right now." Your buddy is tugging on your emotional heartstrings to motivate you to loan him your car. He's hoping to convince you to behave in a way that makes you feel positive about yourself.

What are effective ways to appeal to listeners' emotions? Use emotion-arousing stories and concrete examples, as well as pictures and music. In the next chapter we'll identify more ethical strategies to appeal to emotions when persuading others.

motivation

The internal force that drives people to achieve their goals

All three traditional means of persuasion—ethos (ethical credibility), logos (logic), and pathos (emotion)—are ways of motivating a listener to think or behave in certain ways. **Motivation** is the underlying internal force that drives people to achieve their goals. Our motives explain why we do things.[3] Several factors motivate people to respond to persuasive messages: The need to restore balance to their lives and avoid stress, the need to avoid pain, and the desire to increase pleasure have been documented as motives that influence attitudes, beliefs, values, and behavior.

elaboration likelihood model (ELM) of persuasion

The theory that people can be persuaded by logic, evidence, and reasoning, or through a more peripheral route that may depend on the credibility of the speaker, the sheer number of arguments presented, or emotional appeals

elaborate

From the standpoint of the elaboration likelihood model (ELM) of persuasion, to think about information, ideas, and issues related to the content of a message

direct persuasion route

Persuasion that occurs when audience members critically examine evidence and arguments

indirect persuasion route

Persuasion that occurs as a result of factors peripheral to a speaker's logic and argument, such as the speaker's charisma or emotional appeals

ELM's Contemporary Approach: Using a Direct or Indirect Path to Persuade

A newer, research-based framework for understanding how persuasion works is called the **elaboration likelihood model (ELM) of persuasion**.[4] This theory with a long name is actually a simple idea that offers an explanation of how people are persuaded to do something or think about something. Rather than prescribe how to craft a persuasive message from the standpoint of the speaker, as Aristotle does, ELM theory describes how audience members *interpret* persuasive messages. It's an audience-centered theory of how people make sense of persuasive communication.

To **elaborate** means that you *think* about the information, ideas, and issues related to the content of the message you hear. When you elaborate on a message, you are critically evaluating what you hear by paying special attention to the arguments and the evidence the speaker is using. The likelihood of whether or not you elaborate (hence, the term *elaboration likelihood model*) on a message varies from person to person and depends on the topic of the message.

The theory suggests that there are two ways you can be persuaded: (1) the **direct persuasion route** that you follow when you elaborate, consciously think about, or critically evaluate a message, and (2) the **indirect persuasion route**, in which you don't elaborate and are instead influenced by the more peripheral factors of the message and the messenger—you are less aware of why you are persuaded to respond positively or negatively to a message.

THE DIRECT PERSUASION ROUTE   When you elaborate, you consider what Aristotle would call the underlying logos, or logic, of the message. You carefully and systematically think about the facts, reasoning, arguments, and evidence presented to you, and then you make a thoughtful decision as to whether to believe or do what the persuader wants. For example, you buy a good data package for your smartphone because you are convinced you will benefit from constant access to the Internet; you've read the literature and have made a logical, rational decision. There may be times, however, when you think you are making a decision based on logic, but instead you are being persuaded by less obvious strategies via an indirect path.

THE INDIRECT PERSUASION ROUTE   If you don't elaborate (that is, if you don't use critical thinking skills while listening), you simply develop an overall impression of what the speaker says and how the speaker says it. The indirect route is a more intuitive than rational process. You can be persuaded by such indirect factors as catchy music used in an advertisement or your positive reaction to the attractive and articulate salesperson who wants to sell you a product. It's not an evaluation of the logic or content of the advertisement or the salesperson's reasoning or evidence that persuades you; it's the overall feeling you have about the product or the salesperson that triggers your purchase. When hearing a speech, you may be persuaded by the appearance of the speaker (he looks nice; I trust him); by the sheer number of research studies in support of the speaker's proposal (there are so many reasons to accept this speaker's proposal; she's convinced me); or by the speaker's use of an emotionally charged story (I can't let that little girl starve; I'll donate 50 cents to save her).

Aristotle's theory and ELM theory both suggest that persuasion is a complex process. Not all of us are persuaded in the same way. Aristotle's theory emphasizes what the *speaker* should do to influence an audience. If the speaker discovers the proper application of a credible and ethical message (ethos), logic (logos), and emotion (pathos), then persuasion is likely to occur. ELM theory describes the different ways *listeners* process the messages they hear. Listeners can be persuaded when they directly elaborate (or actively think about what they hear) and logically ponder how evidence and reasoning make sense. Or, if they do not elaborate, listeners may be persuaded indirectly, based on peripheral factors that don't require as much thought to process, such as the speaker's personal appearance or delivery.

Both theories work together to explain how you can persuade others and how others persuade you. Because you may not know whether your listeners are directly or indirectly influenced by your message (whether they elaborate or not), you will want to use a balance of ethos, logos, and pathos as you think about how to persuade your listeners. However, it's your *audience,* not you, who will ultimately make sense out of what they hear. So, in addition to the carefully constructed logic and well-reasoned arguments you present, be attuned to the indirect factors that can influence your listeners, such as your delivery, your appearance, and a general impression of how prepared you seem to be.

These two theories also help explain how *you* are influenced by others. You are influenced by the ethical appeal, logical arguments, and emotions of a speaker. In addition, ELM theory suggests you may be directly affected by the logic and arguments of a speaker. You may also be influenced, even when you're not aware of it, by such peripheral or indirect elements of the message as the speaker's appearance and delivery. Remaining aware of how you are being persuaded can make you a more effective and critical listener to the multitude of persuasive messages that come your way each day.

> ## RECAP
>
> ## MODELS OF PERSUASION
>
> Aristotle's Classical Approach
> - Ethos: The credibility of the speaker
> - Logos: The logic used to reach a conclusion
> - Pathos: The appeal to emotion
>
> Elaboration Likelihood Model
> - Direct route—with elaboration; considering the facts, evidence, and logic of the message
> - Indirect route—without elaboration; relying on an intuitive feeling in response to peripheral aspects of the message

How to Motivate Listeners

14.3 Describe four ways to motivate listeners to respond to a persuasive message.

It's late at night and you're watching your favorite talk show. A commercial extolling the virtues of a well-known brand of ice cream interrupts the program. Suddenly you remember you have some of the advertised flavor, Royal Rocky Road. You apparently hadn't realized how hungry you were for ice cream until the ad reminded you of the lip-smacking goodness of the cold, creamy, smooth treat. Before you know it, you are at the freezer, helping yourself to a couple of scoops of ice cream.

If the makers of that commercial knew how persuasive it had been, they would be overjoyed. At the heart of the persuasion process is the audience-centered process of motivating listeners to respond to a message. The ad changed your behavior because the message was tailor-made for you.

Persuasion works when listeners are motivated to respond. What principles explain why you felt motivated to go to the freezer at midnight for a carton of ice cream? An audience is more likely to be persuaded when you help members solve their problems or meet their needs. They can also be motivated when you convince them that good things will happen if they follow your advice or bad things will occur if they don't. We next discuss several ways to motivate listeners; these approaches are summarized in Table 14.1.

Use Cognitive Dissonance

Dissonance theory is based on the principle that people strive to solve problems and manage stress and tension in a way that is consistent with their attitudes, beliefs, and values.[5] According to this theory, when you are presented with information inconsistent with your current attitudes, beliefs, values, or behavior, you become aware that you have a problem; you experience a kind of discomfort called **cognitive dissonance**. The word *cognitive* has to do with our thoughts. *Dissonance* means "lack of harmony or agreement." When you think of a dissonant chord in music, you probably think of a collection of unpleasant sounds not in tune with the melody or other chords. Most people seek to avoid problems or feelings of dissonance. Cognitive dissonance, then, means you are experiencing a way of thinking that is inconsistent and uncomfortable. If, for example, you smoke cigarettes and a speaker reminds you that smoking is unhealthy, this reminder creates dissonance. You can restore balance and solve the problem either by no longer smoking or by rejecting the message that smoking is harmful.

Creating dissonance with a persuasive speech can be an effective way to change attitudes and behavior. The first tactic in such a speech is to identify an existing problem or need. For example, Evie believes that we should only eat organic fruits and vegetables. If we don't eat organic foods, we increase the risk of getting cancer because we are consuming chemicals that have been linked to cancer. Evie seeks to create dissonance by suggesting we could more readily develop cancer unless we eat organic

cognitive dissonance

The sense of mental discomfort that prompts a person to change when new information conflicts with previously organized thought patterns

Table 14.1 How to Motivate Listeners to Respond to Your Persuasive Message

Method	Description	Example
Use Cognitive Dissonance	Telling listeners about existing problems or information that is inconsistent with their currently held beliefs or known information creates psychological discomfort.	Do you value your family's security? Then you're probably worried about supporting your family if you were injured and couldn't work. You can restore your peace of mind by buying our disability insurance policy.
Use Listeners' Needs	People are motivated by unmet needs. The most basic needs are physiological, followed by safety needs, social needs, self-esteem needs, and finally, self-actualization needs.	You could be the envy of people you know if you purchase this sleek new sports car. You will be perceived as a person of high status in your community.
Use Positive Motivation	People will be more likely to change their thinking or pursue a particular course of action if they are convinced that good things will happen to them if they support what the speaker advocates.	You should take a course in public speaking because it will increase your prospects of getting a good job. Effective communication skills are the most sought-after skills in today's workplace.
Use Negative Motivation	People seek to avoid pain and discomfort. They will be motivated to support what a speaker advocates if they are convinced bad things will happen to them unless they do.	If there is a hurricane, tornado, earthquake, or other natural disaster, the electrical power may go out and you may not be able to fill your car with gas. Without the basics of food and water, you could die. You need to be prepared for a worst-case scenario by having an emergency stockpile of water, food, and gas for your car.

farm products. The way to reduce our dissonance (and the threat of cancer) is to eat more healthful organic fruits and vegetables—precisely what Evie is advocating. Of course, a speaker can't just assert that something will create a problem. An ethical speaker needs to use evidence such as facts, statistics, or expert testimony to document any claims. With the strategy of creating dissonance by documenting the harm and then suggesting a way to minimize or eliminate the harm, the speaker seeks to change listener behavior.

In using dissonance theory to persuade, speakers have an ethical responsibility not to rely on false claims to create dissonance. Claiming that a problem exists when it does not or creating dissonance about a problem that is unlikely to happen is unethical. When listening to a persuasive message, pay particular attention to the evidence a speaker uses to convince you that a problem really does exist.

HOW LISTENERS COPE WITH DISSONANCE   Effective persuasion requires more than simply creating dissonance and then suggesting a solution. When your listeners confront dissonant information, various options are available to them besides following your suggestions. You need to be aware of the other ways your audience might react before you can reduce their cognitive dissonance.[6]

- **Listeners may discredit the source.**   Instead of believing everything you say, your listeners could choose to discredit you. Suppose you drive a Japanese-made car and you hear a speaker whose father owns a Chevrolet dealership advocate that all Americans should drive cars made in the United States. You could agree with him, or you could decide that the speaker is biased because of his father's occupation. Instead of selling your Japanese-made car and buying an American one, you could doubt the speaker's credibility and ignore his suggestion. As a persuasive speaker, you need to ensure that your audience will perceive you as competent and trustworthy so that they will accept your message.

- **Listeners may reinterpret the message.**   A second way your listeners might overcome cognitive dissonance and restore balance is to hear what they want to hear. They may choose to focus on the parts of your message that are consistent with what they already believe and ignore the unfamiliar or controversial parts. If you tell a customer looking to purchase new software that it takes ten steps to

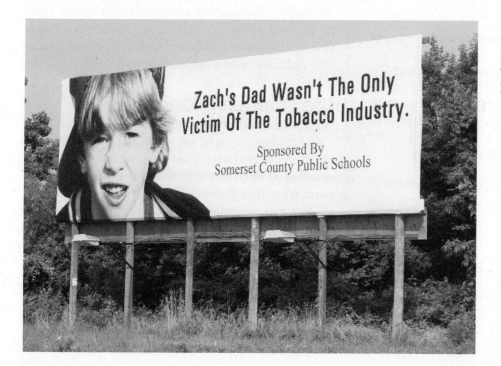

Effective public-service messages often use cognitive dissonance to change people's behaviors. This technique is also often effective for public speakers. *Photo:* Sonda Dawes/The Image Works.

install the program but that it is easy to use, the customer might focus on those first ten steps and decide it's too hard to use. Your job as an effective speaker is to make your message as clear as possible so your audience will not reinterpret it. In this case, your task is to emphasize that the software is easy to use. Choose your words carefully; use simple, vivid examples to keep listeners focused on what's most important.

- **Listeners may seek new information.** Another way that listeners cope with cognitive dissonance is to seek more information on the subject. Audience members may look for additional information to negate your position and to refute your well-created arguments. For example, as the owner of a minivan, you would experience dissonance if you heard a speaker describe a recent rash of safety problems with minivans. You might turn to a friend and whisper, "Is this true? Are minivans really dangerous? I've always thought they were safe." You would want new information to validate your ownership of a minivan.

- **Listeners may stop listening.** Some messages are so much at odds with listeners' attitudes, beliefs, and values that an audience may decide to stop listening. Most of us do not seek opportunities to hear or read messages that oppose our opinions. It is unlikely that a staunch Democrat would attend a fund-raiser for the state Republican party. The principle of selective exposure suggests that we tend to pay attention to messages that are consistent with our points of view and to avoid those that are not. When we do find ourselves trapped in a situation in which we must hear a message that doesn't support our beliefs, we tend to stop listening. Being aware of your audience's existing attitudes, beliefs, and values can help ensure that they won't tune you out.

- **Listeners may change their attitudes, beliefs, values, or behavior.** A fifth way an audience may respond to dissonant information is to do what the speaker wants them to do. As we have noted, if listeners change their attitudes, they will reduce the dissonance they experience. You listen to a life-insurance salesperson tell you that your family will have no financial support when you die. This creates dissonance; you prefer to think of your family as happy and secure. So you take out a $250,000 policy to protect your family. This action restores your sense of balance. The salesperson has persuaded you successfully. The goals of advertising copywriters, salespeople, and political candidates are similar: They want you to experience dissonance so that you will change your attitudes, beliefs, values, or behavior.

Use Listeners' Needs

Need is one of the best motivators. A person looking at a new car because he or she needs one is more likely to buy than a person who is just thinking about how nice it would be to drive the latest model. The more you understand what your listeners need, the greater the chances are that you can gain and hold their attention and ultimately get them to do what you want.

Abraham Maslow's classic theory, which you may have first learned about in psychology class, suggests that there is a hierarchy of needs that motivates everyone's behavior.[7] Figure 14.2 illustrates Maslow's five levels of needs with the most basic at the bottom. Maslow suggested that we need to meet basic physiological needs (food, water, and air) before we can be motivated to respond to higher-level needs. Although the hierarchical nature of Maslow's needs has not been consistently supported by research (we can be motivated by several needs at the same time), his theory provides

RECAP

COPING WITH COGNITIVE DISSONANCE

When your message gives listeners conflicting thoughts, they might:

- try to discredit you; you need to be competent and trustworthy.
- reinterpret your message; you need to be sure it's clear.
- seek other information; you need to make your information convincing.
- stop listening; you need to make your message interesting.
- be persuaded.

CONSIDER THE AUDIENCE

a useful checklist of potential listener motivations. When attempting to persuade an audience, a speaker should try to stimulate these needs in order to change or reinforce attitudes, beliefs, values, or behavior. Let's examine each of these needs.

PHYSIOLOGICAL NEEDS   The most basic needs for all humans are physiological: We all need air, water, and food. According to Maslow's theory, unless those needs are met, it will be difficult to motivate a listener to satisfy other needs. If your listeners are hot, tired, and thirsty, it will be more difficult to persuade them to vote for your candidate, buy your insurance policy, or sign your petition in support of local leash laws. Be sensitive to the basic physiological needs of your audience so that your appeals to higher-level needs will be heard.

SAFETY NEEDS   Listeners are concerned about their safety. We all have a need to feel safe, secure, and protected. We need to be able to predict that our needs for safety, as well as those of our loved ones, will be met. Many insurance sales efforts include photos of wrecked cars, anecdotes of people who were in ill health and could not pay their bills, or tales of the head of a household who passed away, leaving the basic needs of a family unmet. Appeals to use safety belts, stop smoking, start exercising, and use condoms all play to our need for safety and security.

SOCIAL NEEDS   We all need to feel loved and valued. We need contact with others and reassurance that they care about us. According to Maslow, these social needs translate into our need for a sense of belonging to a group (fraternity, religious organization, friendships). Powerful persuasive appeals are based on our need for social contact. We are encouraged to buy a product or support a particular issue because others are buying the product or supporting the issue. The message is that to be liked and respected by others, we must buy the same things they do or support the same causes they support.

SELF-ESTEEM NEEDS   The need for self-esteem reflects our desire to think well of ourselves. Civil rights activist Jesse Jackson is known for appealing to the self-worth of his listeners by inviting them to chant "I am somebody." This is a direct appeal to his listeners' need for self-esteem. Advertisers also appeal to that need when they encourage us to believe that we will be noticed by others or stand out in a crowd if we purchase their product. Commercials promoting luxury cars usually invite you to picture yourself in the driver's seat with a beautiful or handsome companion beside you while those you pass on the road look on with envy.

SELF-ACTUALIZATION NEEDS   At the top of Maslow's hierarchy is the need for **self-actualization**. This is the need to fully realize one's highest potential through seeking "peek experiences." For many years, the U.S. Army used the slogan "Be all that you can be" to tap into the need for self-actualization. Calls to be your best and brightest self are appeals to self-actualization. According to Maslow's hierarchy, needs at the other four levels must be satisfied before we can be motivated to satisfy the highest-level need.

Figure 14.2   According to Maslow, our needs are ordered in a hierarchy, so we must satisfy the needs at the base of the pyramid before we are motivated to address higher-level needs. For example, if listeners couldn't afford to meet their basic, physiological needs for food, it would be difficult to sell them a life insurance policy to address their safety needs.

SOURCE: Based on Maslow, Abraham (1954). *Motivation and Personality*. New York: HarperCollins.

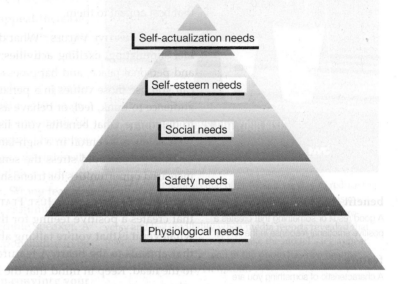

- Self-actualization needs
- Self-esteem needs
- Social needs
- Safety needs
- Physiological needs

self-actualization need
The need to achieve one's highest potential

Figure 14.4 According to social judgment theory, a realistic persuasive goal may be to nudge your audience along the continuum of acceptance, toward the latitude of noncommitment, rather than to propel them from one end to the other.

SOURCE: Copyrighted by Pearson Education, Hoboken, NJ.

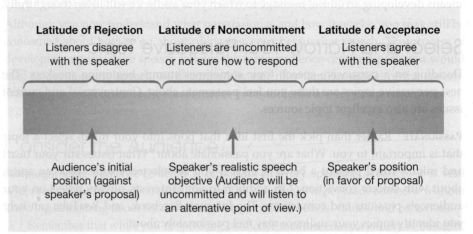

Develop Your Central Idea and Main Ideas

The overall structure of your speech flows from your central idea and the main ideas that support your central idea. Your central idea, as you recall, is a one-sentence summary of your speech. When persuading others, most speakers find it useful to state their central idea in the form of a proposition. A **proposition** is a statement with which you want your audience to agree. In the following list, note how each proposition is actually the central idea of the speech:

> All students should be required to take a foreign language.
>
> Organic gardening is better for the environment than gardening with chemicals.
>
> The United States should not provide economic aid to other countries.

There are three categories of propositions: propositions of fact, propositions of value, and propositions of policy. These three types of propositions are summarized in Table 14.2. Determining which category your persuasive proposition fits into not only can help you clarify your central idea, but can also give you an idea of how to select specific persuasive strategies that will help you achieve your specific purpose. Let's examine each type of proposition in more detail.

PROPOSITION OF FACT A **proposition of fact** focuses on whether something is true or false or on whether it did or did not happen. Some propositions of fact are undebatable: The number of people immigrating to the U.S. is increasing. The Denver Broncos won the 2016 Super Bowl. Texas is bigger than Poland. Each of these statements is a

proposition

A statement that summarizes the ideas a speaker wants an audience to agree with

proposition of fact

A proposition focusing on whether something is true or false or whether it did or did not happen

Table 14.2 Persuasive Propositions: Developing Your Central Idea

Type	Definition	Examples
Proposition of fact	A statement that focuses on whether something is true or false. Debatable propositions of fact can be good topics for persuasive speeches.	Undebatable: The state legislature has raised tuition 10 percent during the last three years.
		Debatable: There are more terrorist attacks in the world today than at any previous time in human history.
Proposition of value	A statement that either asserts that something is better than something else or presumes what is right and wrong or good and bad.	The electoral college is a better way to elect presidents than a direct popular vote would be.
		It is better to keep your financial records on a personal computer than to make calculations by hand.
Proposition of policy	A statement that advocates a change in policy or procedures.	Our community should adopt a curfew for all citizens under eighteen.
		All handguns should be abolished.

SOURCE: Copyrighted by Pearson Education, Hoboken, NJ.

proposition of fact that can be verified simply by consulting an appropriate source. For that reason, they do not make good topics for persuasive speeches.

Other propositions of fact will take time and skill—perhaps an entire persuasive speech—to prove. Here are examples of debatable propositions of fact that would make good topics:

When women joined the military, the quality of the military improved.

Adults who were abused as children by their parents are more likely to abuse their own children.

U.S. foreign policy has decreased the probability that the United States will experience more terrorist attacks.

Global climate change is not occurring in our atmosphere.

To prove each of these propositions, a speaker would need to offer specific supporting evidence. To persuade listeners to agree with a proposition of fact, the speaker must focus on changing or reinforcing their beliefs. Most persuasive speeches that focus on propositions of fact begin by identifying one or more reasons why the proposition is true.

The following persuasive speech outline on the topic of low-carb diets is based on a proposition of fact:

TOPIC:	Low-carbohydrate diets
GENERAL PURPOSE:	To persuade
PROPOSITION:	Low-carbohydrate diets are safe and effective.
SPECIFIC PURPOSE:	At the end of my speech, audience members will agree that low-carb diets are safe and effective.
MAIN IDEAS:	I. Carbohydrates are a significant part of our diets.

      A. Many people eat a significant amount of fast food that is laden with carbohydrates.

      B. Lunches provided by the cafeterias in elementary schools include significant amounts of carbohydrates.

      C. Many people eat a significant amount of highly processed, carb-rich foods.

  II. Carbohydrates are making people fat and unhealthy.

      A. A diet rich in carbohydrates leads to obesity.

      B. A diet rich in carbohydrates leads to Type II diabetes.

 III. Low-carb diets are a safe and effective way to lose weight and maintain your health.

      A. The safety of such low-carb diets as the South Beach diet or the Paleo Diet is documented by research.

      B. The effectiveness of such low-carb diets is documented by research.

PROPOSITION OF VALUE A **proposition of value** is a statement that calls for the listener to judge the worth or importance of something. Values, as you recall, are enduring concepts of good or bad, right or wrong. Value propositions are statements that something is either good or bad or that one thing or course of action is better than another. Consider these examples:

It is wrong to turn away immigrants who want to come to the United States.

Communication is a better major than history.

A private-school education is more valuable than a public-school education.

It is better for teachers to carry concealed weapons than to be defenseless against violent school intruders.

Each of these propositions either directly states or implies that something is better than something else. Value propositions often directly compare two things and suggest that one option is better than another.

proposition of value
A proposition calling for the listener to judge the worth or importance of something

Manny designed his speech to convince an audience that reggae music is better than rock music.

TOPIC:	Reggae music
GENERAL PURPOSE:	To persuade
PROPOSITION:	Reggae music is better than rock music for three reasons.
SPECIFIC PURPOSE:	After listening to my speech, the audience should listen to reggae music more often than they listen to rock music.
MAIN IDEAS:	I. Reggae music communicates a message of equality for all people. II. Reggae music and its rhythms evoke a positive, uplifting mood. III. Reggae music draws on a variety of cultural and ethnic traditions.

proposition of policy

A proposition advocating a change in a policy, procedure, or behavior

PROPOSITION OF POLICY   The third type of proposition, a **proposition of policy**, advocates a specific action—changing a policy, procedure, or behavior. Note how all the following propositions of policy include the word *should*; this is a tip-off that the speaker is advocating a change in policy or procedure.

The Gifted and Talented Program in our school district should have a full-time coordinator.

Our community should set aside one day each month as "Community Cleanup Day."

Wealthy senior citizens should pay for more of their medical costs than poor senior citizens.

In a speech based on a proposition of policy, Paul aimed to convince his audience that academic tenure for college professors should be abolished. He organized his speech topically, identifying reasons academic tenure is no longer a sound policy for most colleges and universities. To support his proposition of policy, he used several propositions of fact. Note, too, that Paul's specific purpose involved specific action on the part of his audience.

TOPIC:	Academic tenure
GENERAL PURPOSE:	To persuade
PROPOSITION:	Our college, along with other colleges and universities, should abolish academic tenure.
SPECIFIC PURPOSE:	After listening to my speech, audience members should sign a petition calling for the abolition of academic tenure.
MAIN IDEAS:	I. Academic tenure is outdated. II. Academic tenure is abused. III. Academic tenure contributes to ineffective education.

Gather Supporting Material

As you gather supporting material for your persuasive message, look for the available means of persuasion to support the main ideas you have developed to achieve your specific purpose. Recall from earlier in this chapter that Aristotle proposed three primary ways, or available means, of persuading listeners:

- Ethos: Being a credible and ethical speaker, which includes using credible and ethical supporting material.
- Logos: Using effective logic and reasoning to support your main ideas.
- Pathos: Using appropriate emotional support.

Because the supporting material you develop and use is vital to the effectiveness of achieving your persuasive goal, we devote a major portion of the next chapter to these three means of persuasion.

Organize Your Persuasive Speech

After identifying and gathering ethical, logical, and appropriate emotional support for your message, you'll make final decisions about how to organize your message. As with any speech, your introduction should grab the audience's attention, give them a reason to listen to your message, introduce the subject, establish your credibility, and preview your main ideas. The body of your speech should have clearly identified major points with appropriate transitions, signposts, and internal summaries to make sure your listeners understand your key ideas. And finally, you'll have a conclusion summarizing the essence of your message and providing closure to your speech. When your goal is to persuade, it is especially important to consider your audience and specific purpose as you consider how you will begin your message, organize your ideas, and conclude your talk. We'll discuss specific approaches and tips for organizing a persuasive speech in the next chapter.

Rehearse and Deliver Your Speech

To bring your ideas to life, the last two elements of the speechmaking process are to rehearse your message out loud and then, finally, to present your talk to your audience. When your goal is to persuade, you may want to make a special effort to rehearse your speech in front of another person or to run some of your ideas past others to check the overall clarity and structure of your message. You communicate your passion and enthusiasm for your ideas through your delivery, so it would be worthwhile to review the suggestions and prescriptions offered in Chapter 11 for how to ensure that your speech is well delivered.

Recall that the elaboration likelihood model predicts that your delivery can, in itself, be persuasive to some of your listeners. No matter how well-reasoned your message, at least some of your listeners are likely to fail to elaborate, or critically consider it. Instead, these listeners may be persuaded by an indirect route, one based on the emotional connection you make with them in the course of delivering your speech.

> ### RECAP
> ### AUDIENCE-CENTERED PERSUASIVE SPEAKING
>
> - Consider the audience's attitudes, beliefs, values, and behaviors.
> - Consider audience diversity.
> - Controversial and current issues make good persuasive topics.
> - Use social judgment theory to determine purpose.
> - State your central idea as a proposition of fact, value, or policy.
> - Find supporting materials that reinforce your credibility, logic, and emotional appeals.
> - Use a clear organizational pattern.
> - Get feedback as you rehearse.
> - Deliver your speech with appropriate emotion.

CONFIDENTLY CONNECTING WITH YOUR AUDIENCE
Breathe to Relax

When you feel your body start to tense, take a deep, relaxing breath to help quiet your fears. It's normal to experience a quickened heartbeat and a change in your breathing patterns as physiological responses to increased anxiety. To signal to your brain that *you* are in charge, consciously take several slow breaths. As you breathe, make your breaths unobtrusive; no one need know that you are using a deep-breathing technique to manage your fear. Whether you are at your seat in your classroom getting ready to be the next speaker or sitting on a platform in front of an audience, a few slow, calming breaths will help you relax and calm your spirit.

STUDY GUIDE: REVIEW, APPLY, AND ASSESS

The Goals of Persuasion

14.1 Describe the goals of persuasive messages.

REVIEW: Persuasion is the process of changing or reinforcing attitudes, beliefs, values, or behavior. Attitudes are learned predispositions to respond favorably or unfavorably toward something. A belief is a person's understanding of what is true and what is false. A value is an enduring conception of right and wrong.

Key Terms

persuasion	belief
attitude	value

APPLY: Zeta plans to give a persuasive speech to convince her classmates that term limits should be imposed for senators and members of Congress—even though she is personally against term limits. Is it ethical to develop a persuasive message supporting an attitude or belief with which you personally disagree?

ASSESS: As you listen to persuasive speeches in your speech class, determine whether a speaker attempts to change or reinforce an attitude, belief, value, or behavior or more than one of these outcomes.

How Persuasion Works

14.2 Explain classic and contemporary theories of how persuasion occurs.

REVIEW: Various theories explain how persuasion works. You can incorporate this theoretical knowledge into your speech preparation in order to deliver a persuasive message. Aristotle suggested using ethos, logos, and pathos as methods to persuade others. The elaboration likelihood model suggests that listeners either follow a direct route to persuasion, in which they elaborate (think about) the issues and evidence, or they can be persuaded via an indirect route when they don't elaborate.

Key Terms

ethos	elaborate
logos	direct persuasion route
pathos	indirect persuasion route
motivation	
elaboration likelihood model (ELM) of persuasion	

APPLY: If you were attempting to sell a new computer system to the administration of your school, what persuasive principles would you draw on to develop your message?

ASSESS: As you prepare your next persuasive speech, describe how both Aristotle's classic theory of persuasion and the more contemporary ELM theory of persuasion explain why your listeners would be persuaded by your message.

How to Motivate Listeners

14.3 Describe four ways to motivate listeners to respond to a persuasive message.

REVIEW: One way to motivate listeners is to cause cognitive dissonance, which evokes the human tendency to strive for balance or consistency in our thoughts. When a persuasive message invites us to change our attitudes, beliefs, values, or behavior, we respond by trying to maintain intellectual balance, or cognitive consistency. A second approach to motivation is to satisfy listeners' needs. Abraham Maslow identified a five-level hierarchy of needs, including physiological, safety, social, self-esteem, and self-actualization needs. Positive motivational appeal is a third approach that can help you develop a persuasive message by encouraging listeners to respond favorably to your message. A fourth approach to persuasion is the use of negative motivational appeals. Fear can motivate us to respond favorably to a persuasive suggestion. To avoid pain or discomfort, we may follow the recommendation of a persuasive speaker.

Key Terms

cognitive dissonance	feature
self-actualization need	fear appeal
benefit	

APPLY: Your local chamber of commerce has asked for your advice in developing a speakers' bureau that would address public-safety issues in your community. What suggestions would you offer to the speakers about how to motivate citizens to behave in ways that would protect them from gang violence, traffic, and severe weather?

ASSESS: Listen to famous historical speeches at history.com. As you listen, identify the strategies speakers use to motivate listeners to support a particular idea or conclusion.

How to Develop Your Audience-Centered Persuasive Speech

14.4 Prepare and present an audience-centered persuasive speech.

REVIEW: Speakers can prepare a persuasive speech by applying broad principles of persuasion to the same processes they use to prepare and present any other kind of speech. A key first concern is to consider the audience at each step of the process. The next concern is to choose an appropriate topic. When crafting your central idea for your persuasive speech, develop a proposition of fact, value, or policy that is reasonable based on your audience's background and expectations. Principles of persuasion can also guide you as you gather supporting materials, organize, rehearse, and deliver your speech.

Key Terms

social judgment theory   proposition of value
proposition   proposition of policy
proposition of fact

APPLY: Using the topic "immigration reform," develop an example of a proposition of fact, a proposition of value, and a proposition of policy for a persuasive speech on this subject.

ASSESS: Based on the discussion in this text, identify ways you have ethically attempted to adapt to your audience by keeping the diversity of your audience in mind.

Using Persuasive Strategies

Speech is power: speech is to persuade, to convert, to compel.

—Ralph Waldo Emerson

Felix Joseph Barrias (1822–1907), *Camille Desmoulins (1760–1794) Harangueing the Patriots in the Gardens of the Palais Royal*. Musée Municipal, Chalons-sur-Marne, France. *Photo:* Scala/White Images/Art Resource, NY.

OBJECTIVES

After studying this chapter, you should be able to do the following:

15.1 Identify and use strategies to improve your credibility.

15.2 Use principles of effective reasoning and evidence to develop a persuasive message.

15.3 Employ effective techniques of using emotional appeal in a persuasive speech.

15.4 Adapt your persuasive message to receptive, neutral, and unreceptive audiences.

15.5 Identify and use strategies for effectively organizing a persuasive speech.

"Persuasion," said rhetoric scholar Donald C. Bryant, "is the process of adjusting ideas to people and people to ideas."[1] To be an audience-centered persuasive speaker is to use ethical and effective strategies to adjust your message so that listeners will thoughtfully respond to your presentation. But precisely what strategies can enhance your credibility, help you develop logical arguments, and use emotional appeals to speak to the hearts of your listeners? In the last chapter, we noted that Aristotle defined rhetoric as the process of discovering the available means of persuasion. In this chapter, we provide more detailed strategies to help you prepare your persuasive speech. Specifically, we will suggest how to gain credibility, develop well-reasoned arguments, and move your audience with emotion. We will also discuss how to adapt your specific message to your audience, and we will end with suggestions for organizing your persuasive message.

Enhancing Your Credibility

15.1 Identify and use strategies to improve your credibility.

Credibility, as we discussed in Chapter 9, is the audience's perception of a speaker's competence, trustworthiness, and dynamism. As a public speaker, especially one who wishes to persuade an audience, you hope your listeners will have a favorable attitude toward you. There is a direct relationship between credibility and speech effectiveness: The more credible your audience perceives you to be, the more effective you will be as a persuasive communicator.

As we noted in Chapter 14, Aristotle used the term *ethos* to refer to a speaker's credibility. He thought that to be credible, a public speaker should be ethical, possess good character, have common sense, and be concerned for the well-being of the audience. Quintilian, a Roman teacher of public speaking, also believed that an effective public speaker should be a person of good character. Quintilian's advice was that a speaker should be "a good person speaking well." The importance to a speaker of a positive public image has been recognized for centuries. But don't get the idea that credibility is something a speaker inherently possesses or lacks. Credibility is based on the listeners' mind-set regarding the speaker. Your listeners, not you, determine whether you have credibility or lack it.

Understanding Credibility $\times$

Credibility is not just a single factor or single view of you on the part of your audience. Aristotle's speculations as to the factors that influence a speaker's credibility have been generally supported by modern experimental studies. To be credible, you should be perceived as competent, trustworthy, and dynamic.

COMPETENCE To be a **competent** speaker is to be considered informed, skilled, or knowledgeable about one's subject.

competent
Being informed, skilled, or knowledgeable about one's subject

When you give a speech, you will be more persuasive if you convince your listeners that you are knowledgeable about your topic. If, for example, you say it would be a good idea for everyone to have a medical checkup each year, your listeners might mentally ask, "Why? What are your qualifications to make such a proposal?" But if you support your conclusion with medical statistics showing how having a physical exam each year leads to a dramatically prolonged life, you enhance the credibility of your suggestion. Thus, one way to enhance your competence is to cite credible evidence to support your point.

TRUSTWORTHINESS A second major factor that influences your audience's response to you is **trustworthiness**. You trust people whom you believe to be honest; you can also predict what they will do or say in the future.

trustworthiness
An aspect of a speaker's credibility that reflects whether the speaker is perceived as being believable and honest

Earning an audience's trust is not something that you can do simply by saying "Trust me." You earn trust by demonstrating that you have had experience dealing with the issues you talk about. Your listeners would be more likely to trust your advice about how to tour Europe on $50 a day if you had visited or lived there than they would if you took your information from a travel guide. Your trustworthiness may be suspect if you advocate something that will result in a direct benefit to you. That's why salespersons and politicians are often stereotyped as being untrustworthy. If you do what they say, a salesperson will clearly benefit from a commission if you buy a product, or a politician will gain power and position if you give your vote.

DYNAMISM A third factor in credibility is the speaker's **dynamism**, or energy. Dynamism is often projected through delivery. **Charisma** is a form of dynamism. A charismatic person possesses charm, talent, magnetism, and other qualities that make the person attractive and energetic. Many people considered presidents Franklin Roosevelt and Ronald Reagan charismatic speakers.

dynamism
An aspect of a speaker's credibility that reflects whether the speaker is perceived as energetic

charisma
Characteristic of a talented, charming, attractive speaker

Your dynamism, or energy level, is one of the factors that contributes to your credibility as a persuasive speaker. *Photo:* Rawpixel.com/Shutterstock.

Your credibility evolves over time. Speakers typically establish their credibility in three phases: (1) initial credibility, (2) derived credibility, and (3) terminal credibility.

initial credibility

The impression of a speaker's credibility that listeners have before the speaker starts a speech

derived credibility

The perception of a speaker's credibility that is formed during a speech

terminal credibility

The final impression listeners have of a speaker's credibility after a speech concludes

- **Initial credibility** is the impression listeners have of your credibility before you speak. Even before you open your mouth, listeners have a perception of you based on your appearance, what they may have heard about you, and the previous times they have heard you speak.

- **Derived credibility** is the perception the audience develops about you after they meet you and as they see you present yourself and your message.

- **Terminal credibility** is the perception listeners have of your credibility when you finish your speech. The lasting impression you make on your audience is influenced by how you were first perceived (initial credibility) and what you did as you presented your message (derived credibility).

Improving Your Credibility

It's one thing to understand what credibility is and how it evolves, but quite another to develop it. To improve your credibility, we suggest you think about what you can do before, during, and after your speech to appear competent, trustworthy and dynamic. Consider the following suggestions for improving your credibility.

- *Make a good first impression.* Giving careful thought to your appearance and establishing eye contact before you begin your talk will enhance both your confidence and your credibility. Except, perhaps, for speeches you give in class, it is wise to prepare a brief description of your credentials and accomplishments so the person who introduces you can use it in his or her introductory remarks. Even if you are not asked for a statement beforehand, be prepared with one.

- *Establish common ground with your audience.* Establish common ground in your opening remarks by indicating that you share the values and concerns of your audience. A politician might speak of her own children if she's trying to persuade an audience that she understands why budget cuts upset parents.

- *Support your key arguments with evidence.* Having evidence to support your persuasive conclusions strengthens your credibility.[2]

- *Present a well-organized message.* A well-organized message also enhances your credibility as a competent and rational advocate.[3] Regardless of the organizational pattern you use, it is crucial to ensure that your message is logically structured and uses appropriate internal summaries, signposts, and enumeration of key ideas.

- *Deliver your message well.* For most North Americans, regular eye contact, varied vocal inflection, and appropriate attire positively influence your ability to persuade listeners to respond to your message.[4] Why does delivery affect how persuasive you are? Researchers suggest that when listeners expect you to be a good speaker and you aren't, they are less likely to do what you ask them to.[5] So don't violate their expectations by presenting a poorly delivered speech.

- *Use strategies to gain and maintain attention.* Effective delivery also helps you gain and maintain listener attention and affects whether listeners will like you.[6] If you can capture your listeners' attention, and if they like you, you'll be more persuasive. Do speakers who use humor enhance their credibility? There is some evidence that although using humor may contribute to making listeners like you, humor does not have a major impact on ultimately persuading listeners to support your message.[7]

- *End with a good impression.* Maintain eye contact with your audience as you deliver your conclusion. Also, don't start leaving the lectern or speaking area until you have finished your closing sentence. If the audience expects a question and answer period, be ready to listen and respond to their questions.

Using Reasoning and Evidence

15.2 Use principles of effective reasoning and evidence to develop a persuasive message.

"We need to cut taxes to improve the economy," claimed the politician on a Sunday-morning talk show. "The stock market has lost 300 points this month. People aren't buying things. A tax cut will put money in their pockets and give the economy a boost." In an effort to persuade reluctant members of her political party to support a tax cut, this politician used a logical argument supported with evidence that stock prices were dropping. As we noted in Chapter 4 when we discussed how to be a critical listener, *logic* is a formal system of rules for making inferences. *Reasoning* is the process of drawing a logical conclusion from evidence. Because wise audience members will be listening, persuasive speakers need to give careful attention to the way they use logic to reach a conclusion.

Aristotle said that any persuasive speech has two parts: First, you state your case; second, you prove your case. In essence, he was saying you must present a reasonable conclusion and use evidence to lead your listeners to support the conclusion you advocate. Proof consists of the evidence you offer, plus the conclusion you draw from it. **Evidence** is made up of the facts, examples, statistics, and expert opinions that you use to support the points you wish to make. Reasoning is the process you follow to reach a conclusion from the evidence. The Sunday-morning talk-show politician reached the conclusion that a tax cut was necessary from the evidence that stock prices had tumbled and people weren't buying things. Let's consider these two key elements of proof in greater detail. Specifically, we will look more closely at types of reasoning and ways of testing the quality of evidence.

evidence

The facts, examples, statistics, and expert opinions used to support a logical conclusion

Understanding Types of Reasoning

Developing well-reasoned arguments for persuasive messages has been important since antiquity. If your arguments are structured in a rational way, you will have a greater chance of persuading your listeners. There are three major ways to structure an argument to reach a logical conclusion: inductively (including reasoning by analogy and reasoning by sign), deductively, and causally. These three structures are summarized in Table 15.1. Let's examine each in detail.

Table 15.1   Comparing Types of Reasoning

	Inductive Reasoning	Deductive Reasoning	Causal Reasoning
Reasoning begins with...	Specific examples	A general statement	Something known
Reasoning ends with...	A general conclusion	A specific conclusion	A speculation about something unknown occurring, based on what is known
Conclusion of reasoning is that something is...	Probable or improbable	True or false	Likely or not likely
Goal of reasoning is...	To reach a general conclusion or discover something new	To reach a specific conclusion by applying what is known	To link something known with something unknown
Example	When tougher drug laws went into effect in Kansas City and St. Louis, drug traffic was reduced. Each city in the United States should therefore institute tougher drug laws because there will be a decrease in drug use.	Instituting tough drug laws in medium-sized communities results in diminished drug-related crime. San Marcos, Texas, is a medium-sized community. San Marcos should institute tougher drug laws to reduce drug-related crimes.	Since the 70-mile-per-hour speed limit was reinstated, traffic deaths have increased. The increased highway speed has caused an increase in highway deaths.

SOURCE: Copyrighted by Pearson Education, Hoboken, NJ.

inductive reasoning

Reasoning that uses specific instances or examples to reach a general, probable conclusion

INDUCTIVE REASONING   Reasoning that arrives at a general conclusion from specific instances or examples is known as **inductive reasoning**. Using this classical approach, you reach a general conclusion based on specific examples, facts, statistics, and opinions. You may not know for certain that the specific instances prove the conclusion is true, but you decide that, in all *probability*, the specific instances support the general conclusion. According to contemporary logicians, you reason inductively when you claim that an outcome is probably true because of specific evidence.

For example, if you were giving a speech attempting to convince your audience that foreign cars are unreliable, you might use inductive reasoning to make your point. You could announce that you recently bought a foreign car that gave you trouble. Your cousin also bought a foreign car that kept stalling on the freeway. Finally, your English professor told you her foreign car has broken down several times in the past few weeks. Based on these specific examples, you ask your audience to agree with your general conclusion: Foreign cars are unreliable.

TESTING THE VALIDITY OF INDUCTIVE REASONING   As a persuasive speaker, your job is to construct a sound argument. That means basing your generalization on evidence. When you listen to a persuasive message, notice how the speaker tries to support his or her conclusion. To judge the validity of a **generalization** arrived at inductively, ask the following questions.

generalization

An all-encompassing statement

- **Are there enough specific instances to support the conclusion?**   Are three examples of problems with foreign cars enough to prove your point that foreign cars are generally unreliable? Of the several million foreign cars manufactured, three cars, especially if they are of different makes, are not a large sample. If those examples were supported by additional statistical evidence that more than 50 percent of foreign-car owners complained of serious engine malfunctions, the evidence would be more convincing.

- **Are the specific instances typical?**   Are the three examples you cite representative of all foreign cars manufactured? How do you know? What are the data on the performance of foreign cars? Also, are you, your cousin, and your professor typical of most car owners? The three of you may be careless about routine maintenance of your autos.

- **Are the instances recent?**   If the foreign cars you are using as examples of poor reliability are more than three years old, you cannot reasonably conclude that today's foreign cars are unreliable products. Age alone may explain the poor performance of your sample.

The logic in this example of problematic foreign cars, therefore, is not particularly sound. The speaker would need considerably more evidence to prove his or her point.

REASONING BY ANALOGY Reasoning by analogy is a special type of inductive reasoning. An *analogy* is a comparison. This form of inductive reasoning compares one thing, person, or process with another to predict how something will perform and respond. In previous chapters we've suggested that using an analogy is an effective way to clarify ideas and enhance message interest. When you observe that two things have a number of characteristics in common and that a certain fact about one is likely to be true of the other, you have drawn an analogy, reasoning from one example to reach a conclusion about the other.

If you try to convince an audience that because laws against using a cell phone while driving in a school zone have cut down on injuries to children in Florida and Missouri, those laws should therefore should be instituted in Kansas, you are reasoning by analogy. You would also be reasoning by analogy if you claimed that because capital punishment reduced crime in Brazil, it should be used in the United States as well. But as with reasoning by generalization, there are questions that you should ask to check the validity of your conclusions.

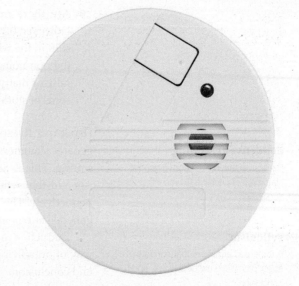

When a smoke alarm goes off, reasoning by sign suggests that something is on fire. What examples of reasoning by sign might you use in a speech? *Photo:* sasel77/Fotolia.

- **Do the ways in which the two things are alike outweigh the ways they are different?** Can you compare the crime statistics of Brazil to those of the United States and claim to make a valid comparison? Are the data collected in the same way in both countries? Could other factors besides the cell phone laws in Florida and Missouri account for the lower injury rate? Maybe differences in speed limits in school zones in those states can account for the difference.

- **Is the assertion true?** Is it really true that capital punishment has deterred crime in Brazil? You will need to give reasons why the comparison is valid and provide evidence proving your conclusion is true.

REASONING BY SIGN **Reasoning by sign**, another special type of inductive reasoning, occurs when two things are so closely related that the existence of one thing means that the other thing will happen. For example, white smoke billowing from the chimney of the Sistine Chapel in Rome's Vatican Square is a sign that there is a new pope. A clap of thunder and dark, swirling clouds are signs of rain. One specific sign, or the presence of multiple signs, leads you to a conclusion that something else has happened or will happen.

reasoning by sign
Using the existence of one or more events to reach a specific conclusion that another event has occurred or will occur

One student group observed many students on campus wearing T-shirts promoting other college and university sports teams rather than the teams on their home campus. They viewed the T-shirts of other teams as a sign of student apathy, deflated school spirit, and disinterest in campus sports. To fix the problem the group wanted to ban students from wearing shirts promoting teams from other schools.

When you use or hear reasoning by sign, consider these questions:

- **Is there a strong, predictive relationship between the sign and the asserted conclusion?** If white smoke always precedes the announcement of a new pope, then there is a strong relationship in which the sign (white smoke) predicts the conclusion (there is a new pope). Does the shirt someone wears (a sign) always predict a lack of school spirit?

- **Is there another explanation for the relationship between the sign and the asserted conclusion?** Simply because students wear shirts promoting another team, does that mean they really don't care about the home team? Perhaps the students just couldn't afford to buy new shirts.

- **Are there multiple signs?** Hearing only thunder may not mean it will rain. However, hearing thunder, seeing lightning and dark clouds, and feeling a sudden shift in the wind would increase the accuracy of your conclusion that it will rain. If the non-home-team-T-shirt-wearing students also didn't attend the pre-game pep rally or many didn't show up for campus sports events, those would be additional signs of student apathy.

deductive reasoning

Reasoning that moves from a general statement of principle to a specific, certain conclusion

DEDUCTIVE REASONING   According to a centuries-old perspective, reasoning from a general statement or principle to reach a specific conclusion is called **deductive reasoning**. This is just the opposite of inductive reasoning. Contemporary logic specialists add that when the conclusion is *certain* rather than probable, you are reasoning deductively. The certainty of your conclusion is based on the validity or truth in the general statement that forms the basis of your argument.

Deductive reasoning can be structured in the form of a syllogism. A **syllogism** is a way of organizing an argument into three elements: a major premise, minor premise, and conclusion.

syllogism

A three-part argument that consists of a major premise, a minor premise, and a conclusion

major premise

A general statement that is the first element of a syllogism

- Major Premise: To reach a conclusion deductively, you start with a general statement that serves as the **major premise**. In a speech attempting to convince your audience that the communication professor teaching your public-speaking class is a top-notch teacher, you might use a deductive reasoning process. Your major premise is "All communication professors have excellent teaching skills." The certainty of your conclusion hinges on the soundness of your major premise.

minor premise

A specific statement about an example that is linked to the major premise; the second element of a syllogism

- Minor Premise: The **minor premise** is a more specific statement about an example that is linked to the major premise. The minor premise you are advancing in your argument is "John Smith, our teacher, is a communication professor."

conclusion

The logical outcome of a deductive argument, which stems from the major premise and the minor premise

- Conclusion: The **conclusion** is based on the major premise and the more specific minor premise. The conclusion to our syllogism is "John Smith has excellent teaching skills."

In reasoning deductively, you need to ensure that both the major premise and the minor premise are true and can be supported with evidence. The persuasive power of deductive reasoning derives from the fact that the conclusion cannot be questioned *if* the major and minor premises are accepted as true.

Here's another example you might hear in a speech. Ann was trying to convince the city council to refuse a building permit to Mega-Low-Mart, a large chain discount store that wants to move into her town. She believes the new store would threaten her downtown clothing boutique. Here's the deductive structure of the argument she advanced:

Major premise:	Every time a large discount store moves into a small community, the merchants in the downtown area lose business and the town loses tax revenue from downtown merchants.
Minor premise:	Mega-Low-Mart is a large discount store that wants to build a store in our town.
Conclusion:	If Mega-Low-Mart is permitted to open a store in our town, the merchants in the downtown area will lose business and the city will lose tax revenue.

The strength of Ann's argument rests on the validity of her major premise. Her argument is sound if she can prove that the presence of large chain discount stores does, in fact, result in a loss of business and tax revenue for merchants in nearby towns. (Also note Ann's efforts to be audience-centered; addressing the city council, she argues that not only will she lose money, but the city will lose tax revenue as well.) In constructing arguments for your persuasive messages, assess the soundness of your major premise. Likewise, when listening to a persuasive pitch from someone using a deductive argument, critically evaluate the accuracy of his or her major premise.

To test the truth of an argument organized deductively, consider the following questions.

- **Is the major premise (general statement) true?**   In our example about communication professors, is it really true that *all* communication professors have excellent teaching skills? What evidence do you have to support this statement? The power of deductive reasoning hinges in part on whether your generalization is true.

- **Is the minor premise (the particular statement) also true?**   If your minor premise is false, your syllogism can collapse right there. In our example, it is easy enough to verify that John Smith is a communication professor. But not all minor premises can be verified as easily. For example, it would be difficult to prove the minor premise in this example:

    Major premise: All gods are immortal.

    Minor premise: Zeus is a god.

    Conclusion: Therefore, Zeus is immortal.

We can accept the major premise as true because immortality is part of the definition of *god*. But proving that Zeus is a god would be very difficult. In this case, the truth of the conclusion hinges on the truth of the minor premise.

Identifying whether you are using inductive or deductive reasoning can help you better analyze and assess your arguments. Although we have identified inductive and deductive reasoning as separate types of reasoning, they are related. For example, the general premise in a deductive argument is often reached by noting several examples supporting the general premise.[8]

CAUSAL REASONING   A third type of reasoning is called **causal reasoning**. When you reason by cause, you relate two or more events in such a way as to conclude that one or more of the events caused the others. For example, you might argue that having unprotected sex causes the spread of sexually transmitted diseases. When reasoning from sign, you suggest that two or more things are *related*. When reasoning from cause, you suggest that one thing actually *caused* the other thing to occur.

causal reasoning
Reasoning in which the relationship between two or more events leads you to conclude that one or more of the events caused the others

There are two ways to structure a causal argument. First, you can reason from cause to effect, moving from a known fact to a predicted result. You know, for example, that interest rates have increased in the past week. Therefore, you might argue that *because* the rates are increasing, the Dow Jones Industrial Average will decrease. In this case, you move from something known that has occurred (rising interest rates) to something unknown that has not yet occurred (decrease in the Dow). Meteorologists use the same method of reasoning when they predict the weather. They base a conclusion about tomorrow's weather on what they know about today's meteorological conditions.

A second way to frame a causal argument is to reason backward, from known effect to unknown cause. You know, for example, that a major earthquake has occurred (known effect). To explain this event, you propose that the cause of the earthquake was a shift in a fault line (unknown cause). You cannot be sure of the cause, but you are certain of the effect. A candidate for president of the United States may claim that the cause of current high unemployment (known effect) is mismanagement by the present administration (unknown cause). The candidate then constructs an argument to prove his assertion is accurate. To prove his case, he needs to have evidence that the present administration mismanaged the economy. The key to developing strong causal arguments is in the use of evidence to link something known with something unknown. An understanding of the appropriate use of evidence can enhance inductive, deductive, and causal reasoning.

ADAPTING REASONING FOR A CULTURALLY DIVERSE AUDIENCE   Effective strategies for achieving your persuasive objective will vary depending on the background and cultural expectations of your listeners. If a good portion of your audience has a cultural background different from your own, it's wise not to assume that they will share the same assumptions about what is logical and reasonable.

Most of the logical, rational methods of reasoning discussed in this chapter evolved from classical Greek and Roman traditions of argument. Rhetoricians from the United States typically use a straightforward, factual-inductive method of supporting ideas and reaching conclusions.[9] They identify facts and link them to support a specific proposition or conclusion. For example, in a speech to prove that the government spends more money than it receives, a speaker could cite year-by-year statistics on income and expenditures. North Americans also like debates involving a direct clash of ideas and opinions. Our low-context culture encourages people to be more direct and forthright in dealing with issues and disagreement than do high-context cultures.

Not all cultures assume a direct, linear, methodical approach to supporting ideas and proving a point.[10] People from high-context cultures, for example, may expect that participants will establish a personal relationship before debating issues. Some cultures use a deductive pattern of reasoning rather than an inductive pattern. They begin with a general premise and then link it to a specific situation when they attempt to persuade listeners. During several recent trips to Russia, your authors noticed that many Russians started their arguments about the ineffectiveness of communism with a general assumption: Communism didn't work. Then they used this assumption to explain specific, current problems in areas such as transportation and education.

Middle Eastern cultures usually do not use standard inductive or deductive structures. They are more likely to use narrative methods to persuade an audience. They tell stories that evoke feelings and emotions and use extended analogies, examples, and illustrations, allowing their listeners to draw their own conclusions by inductive association.[11]

Although this text stresses the kind of inductive reasoning that will be persuasive to most North Americans, you may need to use alternative strategies if your audience is from another cultural tradition.

Using Types of Evidence

You cannot persuade by simply stating a conclusion without proving it with evidence. Evidence consists of facts, examples, statistics, and expert opinions. When attempting to persuade listeners, it is essential to make sure that your evidence

The cultures of your audience members should influence the types of reasoning, evidence, message structure, and appeals to emotion that you include, as well as the way you deliver your persuasive message. *Photo:* Rob/Fotolia.

logically supports the inductive, deductive, or causal reasoning you are using to reach your conclusion.

FACTS   When using facts to support your conclusion, make sure each fact is really a fact. A **fact** is something that has been directly observed to be true or can be proved to be true. The shape of the earth, the number of women university presidents, and the winner of the 2016 World Series have all been directly observed or counted. Without direct observation or valid measurement, we can only make an inference. An **inference** is a conclusion based on available evidence or partial information. It's a fact that sales of foreign-made cars are increasing in the United States; it's an inference that foreign-made cars are the highest-quality cars.

EXAMPLES   **Examples** are illustrations that are used to dramatize or clarify a fact. For example, in an effort to document the increased violence in children's television programs, one speaker told her audience, "Last Saturday morning as I watched cartoons with my daughter, I was shocked by the countless times we saw examples of beatings and even the death of the cartoon characters in one half-hour program." The conclusion she wanted her audience to reach: Put an end to senseless violence in children's television programs.

Only valid, true examples can be used to help prove a point. A hypothetical example, one that is fabricated to illustrate a point, should not be used to reach a conclusion. It should be used only to clarify. David encouraged his listeners to join him in an effort to clean up the San Marcos River. He wanted to motivate his audience to help by asking them to "imagine bringing your children to the river ten years from now. You see the river bottom littered with cans and bottles." His example, while effective in helping the audience visualize what might happen in the future, does not prove that the river ecosystem will deteriorate. It only illustrates what might happen if action isn't taken.

OPINIONS   *Opinions* can serve as evidence if they are expressed by an expert, someone who can add credibility to your conclusion. The best opinions to use in support of a persuasive argument are those expressed by someone known to be unbiased, fair, and accurate. If the U.S. Surgeon General has expressed an opinion regarding drug testing, his or her opinion would be credible evidence. Even so, opinions are usually most persuasive when they are combined with other evidence, such as facts or statistics, that supports the expert's position.

STATISTICS   A *statistic* is a number used to summarize several facts or samples. In an award-winning speech, Jeffrey Jamison used statistics effectively to document the serious problem of alkali batteries polluting the environment. He cited evidence from the *New York Times* documenting that "each year we are adding 150 tons of mercury, 130 tons of lead, and 170 tons of cadmium to the environment."[12] Without these statistics, Jeffrey's claim that alkali batteries are detrimental to the environment would not have been as potent.

Does the type of evidence you use make a difference in whether your listeners will support your ideas? One research study found that examples and illustrations go a long way in helping to persuade listeners.[13] Additional research documents the clear power of statistical evidence to persuade.[14] And yet another research study concluded that using *both* statistics and specific examples is especially effective in persuading listeners.[15] Poignant examples may touch listeners' hearts, but statistical evidence appeals to their intellect.

Using Evidence Effectively

We've identified what evidence is and why it's important to use it to support your conclusions. But what are the strategies for using evidence effectively? Here are a few suggestions.[16]

fact
Something that has been directly observed to be true or can be proven to be true by verifiable evidence

inference
A conclusion based on available evidence or partial information

examples
Illustrations used to dramatize or clarify a fact

reluctant testimony

A statement by someone who has reversed his or her position on a given issue

USE CREDIBLE EVIDENCE   Your listeners are more likely to respond to your arguments when they believe the evidence you use is credible—from a trustworthy, knowledgeable, and unbiased source. Remember, it's the listener, not you, who determines whether evidence is credible.

One type of evidence that is especially powerful is reluctant testimony. **Reluctant testimony** is a statement by someone who has reversed his or her position on a given issue, or is a statement made that is not in the speaker's best interest. For example, at one point the owner of a large construction company, who wanted the contract to build a new dam, was in favor of building the new dam to create a water reservoir. But after further thought, he changed his mind and is now against building the dam. The reluctant testimony of that construction company owner would bolster your argument that the dam is a financial boondoggle. Reluctant testimony is especially effective when presented to a skeptical audience; it demonstrates how another person has changed his or her mind and implicitly suggests that listeners should do the same.[17]

USE NEW EVIDENCE   By "new" we don't just mean recent, although contemporary evidence to support your point is often perceived to be more credible than out-of-date evidence. But in addition to seeking up-to-date evidence, try to find evidence that the listener hasn't heard before—evidence that's new to the listener. You don't want your listener to think, "Oh, I've heard all of that before." Audience members are more likely to keep focusing on your message when they are learning something new.

USE SPECIFIC EVIDENCE   "Many people will be hurt if we don't do something now to stop global warming," Julia said. How many people will be hurt? What precisely will happen? Julia would make her point more effectively if she offered specific evidence that, for example, identified how many homes would be lost as a result of rising ocean levels rather than speaking of "many people" or "a lot of people."

USE EVIDENCE TO TELL A STORY   Facts, examples, statistics, and opinions may be credible, new, and specific; yet your evidence will be even more powerful if it fits together to tell a story to make your point. Besides listing the problems that will occur because of global warming, Julia could personalize the evidence by telling a story about how the rising ocean levels will hurt individual families. Using evidence to support a story adds emotional power to your message and makes your evidence seem less abstract.[18]

USE EVIDENCE APPROPRIATE TO A DIVERSE AUDIENCE   According to intercultural communication scholars Myron Lustig and Jolene Koester, "There are no universally accepted standards about what constitutes evidence."[19] They suggest that for some Muslim and Christian audiences, parables or stories are a dramatically effective way to make a point. A story is told and a principle is derived from the lesson of the story. For most North Americans and Europeans, a superior form of evidence is an observed fact. A study by two communication scholars reported that both African Americans and Hispanic Americans found statistical evidence more persuasive than stories alone.[20] Statistics, said the respondents, are more believable and verifiable; stories can more easily be modified. What may be convincing evidence to you may not be such an obvious piece of evidence for others. If you are uncertain whether your listeners will perceive your evidence as valid and reliable, test your evidence on a small group of people who will be in your audience before you address the entire group.

Avoiding Faulty Reasoning

We have emphasized the importance of developing sound, logical arguments supported with appropriate evidence. You have an ethical responsibility to construct arguments that are well supported with logical reasoning and sound evidence. Not all people who try to persuade you will use sound arguments to get you to vote for them, buy their product, or donate money

---

RECAP

EFFECTIVE EVIDENCE

You can use four types of evidence:

- Facts
- Examples
- Opinions from experts
- Statistics

The most effective evidence is:

- Credible
- New
- Specific
- Part of a story
- Appropriate to your audience

to their cause. Many persuaders use inappropriate techniques called fallacies. A **fallacy** is false reasoning that occurs when someone attempts to persuade without adequate evidence or with arguments that are irrelevant or inappropriate. You will be both a better and more ethical speaker and a better listener if you are aware of the following fallacies.

CAUSAL FALLACY   The Latin term for the causal fallacy is *post hoc, ergo propter hoc*, which translates as "after this, therefore, because of this." A **causal fallacy** is a statement that makes a faulty causal connection. Simply because one event follows another does not mean that the two are related. If you declared that your school's football team won this time because you sang your school song before the game, you would be guilty of a causal fallacy. There are undoubtedly other factors that explain why your team won—perhaps they were better prepared than the weaker opponent. For something to be a cause, it has to have the power to bring about a result. "That howling storm last night knocked down the tree in our backyard" is a logical causal explanation.

Here are two examples of causal fallacies:

The increased earthquake and hurricane activity is caused by the increase in violence and war in our society.

As long as you wear this lucky rabbit's foot, you will never have an automobile accident.

In each instance, there is not enough evidence to support the cause-and-effect conclusion.

BANDWAGON FALLACY   Someone who argues that "everybody thinks it's a good idea, so you should too" is using the **bandwagon fallacy**. Simply because "everyone" is "jumping on the bandwagon," or supporting a particular point of view, does not make the point of view correct. Sometimes speakers use the bandwagon fallacy in subtler ways in their efforts to persuade:

Everybody knows that talk radio is our primary link to a free and democratic society.

Most people agree that we spend too much time worrying about the future of Medicare.

Beware of sweeping statements that include you and others without offering any evidence that the speaker has solicited opinions.

EITHER–OR FALLACY   Someone who argues that there are only two approaches to a problem is trying to oversimplify the issue by using the **either–or fallacy**. "It's either vote for higher property taxes or close the library," Daryl asserts at a public hearing on tax increases. Such a statement ignores all other possible solutions to a complex problem. When you hear someone simplifying the available options by saying it's either this or that, you should be on guard for the either–or fallacy. Rarely is any issue as simple as a choice between only two alternatives. The following are examples of inappropriate either–or reasoning:

Either television violence is reduced, or we will have an increase in child and spouse abuse.

Either more people start volunteering their time to work for their community, or your taxes will increase.

HASTY GENERALIZATION   A person who reaches a conclusion from too little evidence or nonexistent evidence is making a **hasty generalization**. For example, just because one person became ill after eating the meat loaf in the cafeteria does not mean that everyone eating in the cafeteria will develop food poisoning. Here are additional hasty generalizations:

It's clear our schools can't educate children well; my niece went to school for six years and she still can't read at her grade level.

The city does a terrible job of taking care of the elderly; my grandmother lives in a city-owned nursing home, and the floors there are always filthy.

fallacy
False reasoning that occurs when someone attempts to persuade without adequate evidence or with arguments that are irrelevant or inappropriate

causal fallacy
A faulty cause-and-effect connection between two things or events

bandwagon fallacy
Reasoning that suggests that because everyone else believes something or is doing something, then it must be valid or correct

either–or fallacy
The oversimplification of an issue into a choice between only two outcomes or possibilities

hasty generalization
A conclusion reached without adequate evidence

ad hominem
An attack on irrelevant personal characteristics of the person who is proposing an idea, rather than on the idea itself

AD HOMINEM   Also known as attacking the person, an **ad hominem** (Latin for "to the man") approach involves attacking characteristics of the person who is proposing an idea rather than attacking the idea itself. A statement such as "We know Janice's idea won't work because she has never had a good idea" does not really deal with the idea, which may be valid. Don't dismiss an idea solely because you have been turned against the person who presented it. Here are examples of ad hominem attacks:

> She was born in a foreign country and could not possibly have good ideas for improving education in our community.

> Tony is an awful musician and is not sensitive enough to chair the parking committee.

red herring
Irrelevant facts or information used to distract someone from the issue under discussion

RED HERRING   The **red herring** fallacy is used when someone attacks an issue by using irrelevant facts or arguments as distractions. This fallacy gets its name from an old trick of dragging a red herring across a trail to divert the dogs that may be following. Speakers use a red herring when they want to distract an audience from the real issues. For example, a politician who has been accused of taking bribes calls a press conference. During the press conference, he talks about the evils of child pornography rather than addressing the charge against him. He is using the red herring technique to divert attention from the real issue—did he or did he not take the bribe? Consider another red herring argument from a speech against gun control: The real problem is not eliminating handguns; the real problem is that pawnshops that sell guns are controlled by the Mafia.

appeal to misplaced authority
Use of the testimony of an expert in a given field to endorse an idea or product for which the expert does not have the appropriate credentials or expertise

non sequitur
Latin for "it does not follow"; an idea or conclusion that does not logically relate to or follow from the previous idea or conclusion

APPEAL TO MISPLACED AUTHORITY   When ads use baseball catchers to sell automobiles and TV heroes endorse political candidates, an airline, or a hotel, we are faced with the fallacious **appeal to misplaced authority**. Although we have great respect for these people in their own fields, they are no more expert than we are in the areas they are promoting. As both a public speaker and a listener, you must recognize what is valid expert testimony and what is not. For example, a physicist who speaks on the laws of nature or the structure of matter could reasonably be accepted as an expert. But when the physicist speaks on politics, his or her opinion is not that of an expert and may be no more significant than your own. The following examples are appeals to misplaced authority:

> Former Congressman Smith endorses the new art museum, so every business should get behind it, too.

> *Today Show* host Savannah Guthrie thinks this cookie recipe is the best, so you will like it too.

RECAP

AVOID THESE FALLACIES

- Causal: Assuming a faulty cause-and-effect relationship
- Bandwagon: Assuming that because others approve then the conclusion must be valid
- Either–or: Oversimplifying options to either one thing or the other
- Hasty Generalization: Reaching a conclusion without adequate evidence
- Ad Hominem: Critiquing the person rather than the merit of the idea presented
- Red Herring: Using irrelevant information to distract from the real issue
- Appeal to Misplaced Authority: Using the nonexpert testimony of someone who does not have appropriate credentials
- Non Sequitur: Using a conclusion that does not logically follow the information presented

NON SEQUITUR   When you argue that a new parking garage should not be built on campus because the grass has not been mowed on the football field for three weeks, you are guilty of a **non sequitur** (Latin for "it does not follow"). Grass growing on the football field has nothing to do with the parking problem. Your conclusion simply does not follow from your statement. The following are examples of non sequitur conclusions:

> We should not give students condoms because social media has such a pervasive influence on our youth today.

> You should endorse me for Congress because I have three children.

> We need more parking on campus because we are the national football champions.

Using Emotional Appeals

15.3 Employ effective techniques of using emotional appeal in a persuasive speech.

Effective speakers know how to use emotion to make their point. Note these three emotionally evocative moments in classic speeches:[21]

- In his inaugural address, delivered with perfect timing, President John F. Kennedy inspiringly intoned, "And so, my fellow Americans, ask not what your country can do for you—ask what you can do for your country. My fellow citizens of the world, ask not what America will do for you, but what together we can do for the freedom of man."

- After being dismissed from his command duties by President Harry Truman, a still-popular General Douglas MacArthur ended his poignant farewell speech to Congress by saying, "Old soldiers never die; they just fade away. And like the old soldier of that ballad, I now close my military career and just fade away."

- When encouraging the British people to be valiant during World War II, Prime Minister Winston Churchill resolutely declared, "We shall go on to the end, we shall fight in France, we shall fight on the seas and oceans, we shall fight with growing confidence and growing strength in the air, we shall defend our island, whatever the cost may be, we shall fight on the beaches, we shall fight on the landing grounds, we shall fight in the fields and the streets, we shall fight on the hills; we shall never surrender."

Great moments in memorable speeches occur when both the minds and hearts are engaged.

As a public speaker trying to sway your listeners to your viewpoint, your job is to ethically use emotional appeals to achieve your goal. If you wanted to persuade your listeners that capital punishment should be banned, you would try to arouse feelings of displeasure and turn them against capital punishment. Advertisers selling soft drinks typically strive to arouse feelings of pleasure in those who think of their product. Smiling people, upbeat music, and good times are usually part of the formula for selling soda.

Tips for Using Emotion to Persuade

As a public speaker your key concern is "How can I ethically use emotional appeals to achieve my persuasive purpose?" Let's consider several methods.

Arousing your listeners' emotions is often helpful in persuading them to agree with your message.
Photo: Anton Gvozdikov/Fotolia.

USE CONCRETE EXAMPLES THAT HELP YOUR LISTENERS VISUALIZE WHAT YOU DESCRIBE   This speaker used a vivid description of the devastation caused by a tornado in Saragosa, Texas, to evoke strong emotions and persuade listeners to take proper precautions when a storm warning is sounded.

> The town is no more. No homes in the western Texas town remain standing. The church where twenty-one people perished looks like a heap of twisted metal and mortar. A child's doll can be seen in the street. The owner, four-year-old Maria, will no longer play with her favorite toy; she was killed along with five of her playmates when the twister roared through the elementary school.

USE EMOTION-AROUSING WORDS   Words and phrases can trigger emotional responses in your listeners. *Mother, flag, freedom*, and *slavery* are among a large number of emotionally loaded words. Patriotic slogans such as "Remember Pearl Harbor" and "Remember 9/11" can also produce strong emotional responses. [22]

TELL STORIES WITH AN EMOTIONAL MESSAGE   Besides just using emotion-arousing examples and words, telling a story with an emotional message that pulls at the heartstrings can be a powerful persuasive strategy.[23] For example, telling an inspiring story about a teenage Olympic athlete with a learning disability who worked for years to perfect her figure skating form and then win a gold medal can encourage and motivate others to endure a struggle to achieve the results they seek. A well-told true story that packs an emotional punch can be a useful persuasive method.

USE NONVERBAL BEHAVIOR TO COMMUNICATE YOUR EMOTIONAL RESPONSE   The great Roman orator Cicero believed that if you want your listeners to experience a certain emotion, you should first model that emotion for them. If you want an audience to feel anger at a particular law or event, you must display anger and indignation in your voice, movement, and gesture. As we have noted, delivery plays a key role in communicating your emotional responses. When you want your audience to become excited about and interested in your message, you must communicate that excitement and interest through your delivery.

Keep in mind that listeners' cultures influence how receptive they are to a message and to a speaker's presentation style. Some Latin American listeners, for example, expect speakers to express more emotion and passion when speaking than U.S. listeners are accustomed to. The best way to assess the preferred speaking style of an unfamiliar audience is to observe other successful speakers addressing the same listeners you will face. Or talk with audience members before you speak to identify expectations and communication-style preferences.

USE VISUAL IMAGES TO EVOKE EMOTIONS   In addition to nonverbal expressions, pictures or images of emotion-arousing scenes can amplify your speech. An image of a lonely homeowner looking out over his waterlogged house following a ravaging flood in Sea Isle City, New Jersey, can communicate his sense of despair. A picture of children in war-torn Syria can communicate the devastating effects of violence with greater impact than mere words alone. In contrast, a photo of a refugee mother and child reunited after an enforced separation can communicate the true meaning of joy. Remember, however, that when you use visual images, you have the same ethical responsibilities as you have when using verbal forms of support: Make sure your image is from a credible source and that it has not been altered or taken out of context.

USE APPROPRIATE METAPHORS AND SIMILES   A metaphor is an implied comparison between two things. The person who says, "Our lives are quilts upon which we stitch the patterns of our character. If you don't pay attention to the ethical dimension of the decisions you make, you will be more likely to make a hideous pattern in your life quilt," is using a metaphor. A simile makes a direct comparison between two things using the word *like* or *as*. Here's an example: "Not visiting your academic counselor regularly is like being a gambler in a high-stakes poker game; you're taking a big chance that you're taking the right courses." Several research studies have found that speakers who use appropriate and interesting metaphors and similes are more persuasive than those who don't use such stylistic devices.[24] Using metaphors and similes can create a fresh, emotional perspective on a persuasive point.[25]

USE APPROPRIATE FEAR APPEALS   The threat that harm will come to your listeners unless they follow your advice is an appeal to fear. As discussed in Chapter 14, listeners can be motivated to change their behavior if appeals to fear are used appropriately. Research suggests that high fear arousal ("You will be killed in an auto accident unless you wear a safety belt") is more effective than moderate or low appeals, if you are a highly credible speaker.[26]

CONSIDER USING APPEALS TO SEVERAL EMOTIONS   Appealing to the fears and anxieties of your listeners is one of the most common types of emotional appeals used to persuade, but you could also elicit other emotions to help achieve your persuasive goal.

- **Hope.**   Listeners could be motivated to respond to the prospect of a brighter tomorrow. When Franklin Roosevelt said, "The only thing we have to fear is fear itself," he was invoking hope for the future.

- **Pride.**   When a politician says, "It's time to restore our nation's legacy as a beacon of freedom for all people," she is appealing to national pride. To appeal to pride is to invoke feelings of pleasure and satisfaction based on accomplishing something important.

- **Courage.**   Patrick Henry's famous "Give me liberty, or give me death!" speech encouraged his audience to take a courageous stand on the issues before them. Referring to courageous men and women as role models can help motivate your listeners to take similar actions.

- **Reverence.**   The appeal to the sacred and the revered can be an effective way to motivate. The late Mother Teresa, holy writings, and the school your listeners attended are examples of people, things, and institutions that your listeners may perceive as sacred. As an audience-centered speaker, however, you need to remember that what may be sacred to one individual or audience may not be sacred to another.

TAP AUDIENCE MEMBERS' BELIEFS IN SHARED MYTHS   Often people talk about a myth as something that is factually untrue. The Easter Bunny, the Tooth Fairy, and Santa Claus are often labeled myths. But in a rhetorical sense, a **myth** is a belief held in common by a group of people and based on their values, cultural heritage, and faith. A myth may be factual—or it may be based on a partial truth that a group of people believes to be true.

Myths are the "big" stories that give meaning and coherence to a group of people or a culture. The myth of the Old West is that the pioneers of yesteryear were strong, adventurous people who sacrificed their lives in search of a better tomorrow. Similarly, our grandparents and great-grandparents belonged to "the greatest generation" because they overcame a devastating economic depression and were triumphant in two world wars. Religious myths are beliefs shared by a group of faithful disciples. So a myth is not necessarily false; it is a belief that a group of people share, one that provides emotional support for the way they view the world.

As a public speaker, referring to a shared myth is a way to identify with your listeners and help them see how your ideas support their ideas; it can help you develop a common bond with audience members. In trying to convince his listeners to vote, Jason argued, "We can't let down those who fought for our freedom. We must vote to honor those who died for the privilege of voting that we enjoy today." He was drawing on the powerful myth that people have died for our freedoms. Again we emphasize that *myth* does not mean "false" or "made up." People *did* die for our freedom; a myth is powerful because the audience knows that those events occurred. Myth is the

myth
A shared belief based on the underlying values, cultural heritage, and faith of a group of people

RELATE YOUR TOPIC NOT ONLY TO YOUR LISTENERS BUT ALSO TO THEIR FAMILIES, FRIENDS, AND LOVED ONES   You can capture the interest of your listeners by appealing to the needs of people they care about. Parents will be interested in ideas and policies that affect their children. People are generally interested in matters that may affect their friends, neighbors, and others with whom they identify, such as members of their own religion or economic or social class.

BE REALISTIC ABOUT WHAT YOU CAN ACCOMPLISH   Don't overestimate the response you may receive from a neutral audience. People who start with an attitude of indifference are probably not going to become as enthusiastic as you are after hearing just one speech. Persuasion does not occur all at once or on a first hearing of arguments.

Persuading the Unreceptive Audience

One of the biggest challenges in public speaking is to persuade audience members who are against you or your message. If they are hostile toward you personally, your job is to seek ways to enhance your credibility and persuade them to listen to you. If they are unreceptive to your point of view, there are several approaches you can use to encourage them to listen.

DON'T ANNOUNCE IMMEDIATELY THAT YOU PLAN TO CHANGE THEIR MINDS   Paul wondered why his opening sales pitch ("Good morning. I plan to convince you to purchase this fine set of knives at a cost to you of only $250") was not greeted enthusiastically. If you immediately and bluntly tell your listeners that you plan to change their opinions, it can make them defensive. It is usually better to take a subtler approach when announcing your persuasive intent.[30]

BEGIN YOUR SPEECH BY NOTING AREAS OF AGREEMENT BEFORE YOU DISCUSS AREAS OF DISAGREEMENT   In addressing the school board, one community member began his persuasive effort to convince board members they should not raise taxes by stating, "I think each of us here can agree with one common goal: We want the best education for our children." Once you help your audience understand that there are issues you agree on (even if only that the topic you will discuss is controversial), your listeners may be more attentive when you explain your position.

DON'T EXPECT A MAJOR SHIFT IN ATTITUDE FROM A HOSTILE AUDIENCE   Set a realistic limit on what you can achieve. Remember our discussion of social judgment theory in Chapter 14, which suggested that listeners fall into three latitudes of reaction to persuasive messages: acceptance, noncommitment, or rejection. You may not be able to move hostile listeners out of the latitude of rejection of your message. A more realistic goal might be to have your listeners hear you out and at least consider some of your points.

CONFIDENTLY CONNECTING WITH YOUR AUDIENCE

Enhance Your Initial Credibility

Initial credibility is the impression your listeners have of you before you deliver your speech. Strategies for enhancing your initial credibility are likely to enhance your confidence as well.

For example, prepare a brief written statement of your credentials and accomplishments so that the person who introduces you can give accurate and relevant information about you to the audience. Give careful thought to your appearance, and establish eye contact with your listeners before you begin to talk. You will feel more confident when you know that your audience believes you to be credible before you even begin to speak.

ACKNOWLEDGE THE OPPOSING POINTS OF VIEW THAT MEMBERS OF YOUR AUDIENCE MAY HOLD   Summarize the reasons individuals may oppose your point of view. Your listeners will be more likely to listen to you if they know you understand their viewpoint. [31] Of course, after you acknowledge the opposing point of view, you will need to cite evidence and use arguments to refute the opposition and support your conclusion. Early in his speech to a neighborhood group about the possibility of building a new airport near their homes, City Manager Anderson acknowledged, "I am aware that a new airport brings unwanted changes to a neighborhood. Noise and increased traffic are not the type of challenges you want near your homes." He went on to identify the actions the city would take to minimize the problems a new airport would cause.

ESTABLISH YOUR CREDIBILITY   Being thought credible is always an important goal of a public speaker, and it is especially important when talking to an unreceptive audience. Let your audience know about the experience, interest, knowledge, and skill that give you special insight into the issues at hand.

CONSIDER MAKING UNDERSTANDING RATHER THAN ADVOCACY YOUR GOAL   Sometimes your audience disagrees with you because its members just don't understand the point you're trying to make. Or they may harbor a misconception about you and your message. For example, if your listeners think that AIDS is transmitted through kissing or other casual contact rather than through unprotected sexual contact, you'll first have to acknowledge their beliefs and then construct a sound argument to show how inaccurate their assumptions are. To change such a misconception and enhance accurate understanding, experienced speakers use a four-part strategy. [32]

1. **Summarize the common misconceptions about the issue or idea you are discussing.** "Many people think that AIDS can be transmitted through casual contact such as kissing or that it can be easily transmitted by your dentist or physician."

2. **State why these misconceptions may seem reasonable.**   Tell your listeners why it is logical for them to hold that view, or identify "facts" they may have heard that would lead them to their current conclusion. "Since AIDS is such a highly contagious disease, it may seem reasonable to think it can be transmitted through such casual contact."

3. **Dismiss the misconceptions and provide evidence to support your point.**   Here you need sound and credible data to be persuasive. "In fact, countless medical studies have shown that it is virtually impossible to be infected with the AIDS virus unless you have unprotected sexual contact or use unsterilized hypodermic needles that have also been used by someone who has AIDS." In this instance, you would probably cite specific results from two or three studies to lend credibility to your claim.

4. **State the accurate information that you want your audience to remember.** Reinforce the conclusion you want your listeners to draw from the information you presented with a clear summary statement, such as "According to recent research, the most common factor contributing to the spread of AIDS is unprotected sex. This is true for individuals of both sexes and all sexual orientations."

Strategies for Organizing Persuasive Messages

15.5 Identify and use strategies for effectively organizing a persuasive speech.

Is there one best way to organize a persuasive speech? The answer is no. Specific approaches to organizing speeches depend on the audience, message, and desired objective. But how you organize your speech does have a major effect on your listeners' response to your message.

Research suggests some general principles to keep in mind when preparing your persuasive message.[33]

- **If you feel that your audience may be hostile to your point of view, advance your strongest arguments first.** If you save your best argument for last, your audience may have already stopped listening.

- **Do not bury key arguments and evidence in the middle of your message.** Your listeners are more likely to remember information presented first and last.[34] In speaking to his fraternity about the dangers of drunk driving, Frank wisely began his speech with his most powerful evidence: The leading cause of death among college-age males is alcohol-related automobile accidents. He got their attention with his sobering fact.

- **If you want your listeners to take some action, it is best to tell them what you want them to do at the end of your speech.** Don't call for action in the middle of your speech. It will be more powerful if you wait until your conclusion.

- **When you think your listeners are well informed and familiar with the disadvantages of your proposal, it is usually better to present both sides of an issue, rather than just the advantages of the position you advocate.** If you don't acknowledge arguments your listeners have heard, they will probably think about them anyway.

- **Make reference to the counterarguments and then refute them with evidence and logic.** It may be wise to compare your proposal with an alternative proposal, perhaps one offered by someone else. By comparing and contrasting your solution with another recommendation, you can show how your proposal is better.[35]

- **Adapt organization to the culture of your audience.** Most U.S. audiences tend to like a well-organized message with a clear, explicit link between the evidence used and the conclusion drawn. U.S listeners are also comfortable with a structure that focuses on a problem and then offers a solution or a message in which causes are identified and the effects are specified. As we mentioned previously in this chapter, audiences in the Middle East, however, would expect less formal structure and greater use of a narrative style of message development. Depending on your audience, being indirect or implicit may sometimes be the best persuasive strategy.

We discussed ways of organizing speeches in Chapter 8, but there are special ways to organize persuasive speeches. In Table 15.2 we summarize four organizational patterns: problem–solution, refutation, cause and effect, and motivated sequence.

Table 15.2 Organizational Patterns for Persuasive Messages

Pattern	Definition	Example
Problem–solution	Present the problem; then present the solution.	I. The national debt is too high. II. We need to raise taxes to lower the debt.
Refutation	Anticipate your listeners' key objections to your proposal and then address them.	I. Even though you may think we pay too much in taxes, we are really undertaxed. II. Even though you may think the national debt will not go down, tax revenue will lower the deficit.
Cause and effect	First present the cause of the problem; then note how the problem affects the listeners. Or identify a known effect; then document what causes the effect.	I. The high national debt is caused by too little tax revenue and too much government spending. II. The high national debt will increase both inflation and unemployment.
Motivated sequence	A five-step pattern of organizing a speech; its steps are attention, need, satisfaction, visualization, and action.	I. *Attention:* Imagine a pile of $1,000 bills 67 miles high. That's our national debt. II. *Need:* The increasing national debt will cause hardships for our children and grandchildren. III. *Satisfaction:* We need higher taxes to reduce our debt. IV. *Visualization:* Imagine our country in the year 2050; it could have low inflation and full employment or be stuck with ten times the debt we have today. V. *Action:* If you want to lower the debt by increasing tax revenue, sign this petition that I will send to our representatives.

Problem–Solution

The most basic organizational pattern for a persuasive speech is to make the audience aware of a problem and then present a solution that clearly solves it. Almost any problem can be phrased in terms of something you want more of or less of. The problem–solution pattern works best when a clearly evident problem can be documented and a solution can be proposed to deal with the well-documented problem.

When you are speaking to an apathetic audience or when listeners are not aware that a problem exists, a problem–solution pattern works nicely. Your challenge will be to provide ample evidence to document that your perception of the problem is accurate. The Sample Persuasive Speech in this chapter shows how Texas State University student Colter Ray met this challenge. You'll also need to convince your listeners that the solution you advocate is the most appropriate one to resolve the problem.

Many political candidates use a problem–solution approach. *Problem:* The government wastes your tax dollars. *Solution:* Vote for me and I'll see to it that government waste is eliminated. *Problem:* We need more and better jobs. *Solution:* Vote for me and I'll institute a program to put people back to work.

Note in the following outline of Jason's speech, "The Dangers of Electromagnetic Fields," how he plans to first document a clear problem and then recommend strategies for managing the problem.

PROBLEM: Power lines and power stations around the country emit radiation and are now being shown to increase the risk of cancer.

I. Childhood leukemia rates are higher in children who live near large power lines.
II. The International Cancer Research Institute in Lyon, France, published a report linking electromagnetic fields and childhood cancer.

SOLUTION: Steps can be taken to minimize our risk of health hazards caused by electromagnetic energy.

I. The federal government should establish enforceable safety standards for exposure to electromagnetic energy.
II. Contact your local power company to make sure its lines are operated safely.
III. Stop using electric blankets.
IV. Use protective screens for computer-display terminals.

The problem–solution arrangement of ideas applies what you learned about cognitive dissonance in Chapter 14. Identify and document a concern that calls for change, and then suggest specific behaviors that can restore cognitive balance.

Refutation

Another way to persuade an audience to support your point of view is to prove that the arguments against your position are false—that is, to refute them. To use refutation as a strategy for persuasion, you first identify objections to your position that your listeners might raise and then refute or overcome those objections with arguments and evidence.

Suppose, for example, you plan to speak to a group of real-estate developers to advocate for a new zoning ordinance that would reduce the number of building permits granted in your community. Your listeners will undoubtedly have concerns about how the ordinance will affect their ability to build homes and make money. You could organize your presentation using those two obvious concerns as major issues to refute. Your major points could be as follows:

I. The new zoning ordinance will not cause an overall decrease in the number of new homes built in our community.
II. The new zoning ordinance will have a positive effect on the profits of local real-estate developers.

To document the significance of the problem of children being used as soldiers and the need to do something to address the problem, Heather provided specific evidence:

> …at any one time, 300,000 children under the age of 18 are forced to fight in military conflicts. As Peter Warren Singer, director of the 21st Century Defense Initiative at the Brookings Institute, states, child warfare is not only a human rights travesty, but also a great threat to global and national security.

She personalized the problem for her audience this way:

> Clearly, this crisis is having an enormous impact on the children themselves, on their nation states, and finally on our own country.

3. Satisfaction.   After you present the problem or need for concern, briefly identify how your plan will satisfy the need. What is your solution to the problem? At this point in the speech, you need not go into great detail. Present enough information so that your listeners have a general understanding of how the problem may be solved.

Heather suggested that a solution to the problem of children serving as soldiers included using the United Nations to take legal action to enforce existing treaties and to bring this issue to the attention of government leaders throughout the world. At this point in her speech, she kept her solution—to involve government leaders—general. She waited until the end of her speech to provide specific action that audience members could take to implement her solution. Heather also reinforced the urgency of the need for the audience to act by stating,

> Clearly, the time has come to take a stand against the atrocities that child soldiers face.

4. Visualization.   Now you need to give your audience a sense of what it would be like if your solution were or were not adopted. You could take a *positive-visualization* approach: Paint a picture with words to communicate how wonderful the future will be if your solution is adopted. You could take a *negative-visualization* approach: Tell your listeners how awful things will be if your solution is not adopted. If they think things are bad now, just wait: Things will get worse.

Heather wanted her listeners to visualize the significant negative results likely to occur if the problem of child soldiers went unsolved. She began with a general statement of what would happen to children if no action were taken.

> The first consequence of child warfare is that these children are left with serious emotional and psychological scarring due to the violence and abuse they must endure.

She further painted her negative picture by using a specific emotional example in which she described additional consequences.

> Ten-year-old Jacques from the Congo described how the Mayi-Mayi militia would often starve him and beat him severely. He says, "I would see others die in front of me. I was hungry very often and I was scared."

Heather also pointed out that if the problem is not addressed soon, it will grow, and more children will be negatively affected.

Heather used only a negative-visualization approach. She could, however, have made her visualization step even stronger by combining negative and positive visualization. A combined positive and a negative visualization tells how the problem will be solved if your solution is adopted and describes how the world will be a much worse place if your solution is not adopted. Heather might, for example, have added a description that helped her listeners visualize the virtues of taking action, by describing poignant scenes of children being reunited with their families. Using both a positive and a negative visualization approach demonstrates how the solution you present in the satisfaction step directly addresses the problem you described in the need step of your motivated sequence.

Martin Luther King Jr. drew on visualization as a rhetorical strategy in his moving "Dream" speech (Appendix B). In this speech, note how King powerfully and poetically painted a picture with words that continue to provide hope and inspiration today.

5. Action.   This last step forms the basis of your conclusion. You tell your audience the specific action they can take to implement your solution. Identify exactly what you want your listeners to do. Give them simple, clear, easy-to-follow steps to achieve your goal. For example, you could give them a phone number to call for more information, provide an address so that they can write a letter of support, hand them a petition to sign at the end of your speech, or tell them for whom to vote.

Heather offered specific actions her listeners could take to address the problem of children serving as soldiers: "The first step we can take is to petition the members of the United Nations to enforce the treaties they have signed, and we can do this by joining the Red Hand Campaign." She made her action step simple and easy when she further explained to her audience:

> You can join this campaign by simply signing your name to a pre-written letter and tracing your hand on a red piece of construction paper after this [speech]. I will then cut and paste your handprint to your letter and forward them on to the UN.

The best action step spells out precisely the action your audience should take. Here, Heather tells her listeners what to do and what will happen next.

You can modify the motivated sequence to suit the needs of your topic and your audience. If, for example, you are speaking to a receptive audience, you do not have to spend a great deal of time on the need step. They already agree that the need is serious. They may, however, want to learn about specific actions they can take to implement a solution to the problem. Therefore, you would be wise to emphasize the satisfaction and action steps.

Conversely, if you are speaking to a hostile audience, you should spend considerable time on the need step. Convince your audience that the problem is significant and that they should be concerned about the problem. You would probably not propose a lengthy, detailed action.

If your audience is neutral or indifferent, spend time getting their attention and inviting their interest in the problem. The attention and need steps should be emphasized.

The motivated sequence is a guide, not an absolute formula. Use it and the other suggestions about speech organization to help achieve your specific objective. Be audience-centered; adapt your message to your listeners.

STUDY GUIDE: REVIEW, APPLY, AND ASSESS

Enhancing Your Credibility

15.1 Identify and use strategies to improve your credibility.

REVIEW: Credibility is a listener's view of a speaker. Three factors contributing to credibility are competence, trustworthiness, and dynamism. Initial credibility is your listeners' impression of your credibility before you start speaking. Derived credibility is the perception they form while you speak. Terminal credibility is the perception that remains after you've finished speaking. Specific strategies can enhance all three types of credibility.

Key Terms

competent	initial credibility
trustworthiness	derived credibility
dynamism	terminal credibility
charisma	

APPLY: Catherine's father has been an editor for a popular Web site. Consequently, she knows a lot about Internet journalism. Is it ethical for Catherine to be introduced as an expert Internet journalist even though she has never been formally trained as a journalist and has held no professional positions as a journalist?

ASSESS: Imagine you are delivering your final speech of the semester in your public-speaking class. What specific strategies can you implement to enhance your initial, derived, and final credibility as a public speaker in the minds of your classmates?

Using Reasoning and Evidence

15.2 Use principles of effective reasoning and evidence to develop a persuasive message.

REVIEW: The effectiveness of logical arguments hinges on the proof you employ. Proof consists of evidence plus the reasoning you use to draw conclusions from the evidence. Three types of reasoning are inductive reasoning, which moves from specific instances or examples to reach a general, probable conclusion; deductive reasoning, which moves from a general statement to reach a specific, more certain conclusion; and causal reasoning, which relates two or more events so as to be able to conclude that one or more of the events caused the others. Two popular types of inductive reasoning include reasoning by analogy and reasoning by sign. You can use four types of evidence: facts, examples, opinions, and statistics. Avoid using fallacious arguments.

Key Terms

evidence	generalization
inductive reasoning	reasoning by sign
deductive reasoning	fallacy
syllogism	causal fallacy
major premise	bandwagon fallacy
minor premise	either–or fallacy
conclusion	hasty generalization
causal reasoning	ad hominem
fact	red herring
inference	appeal to misplaced
examples	authority
reluctant testimony	non sequitur

APPLY: Josh is speaking to his neighborhood homeowners' association, attempting to persuade his neighbors that a crime-watch program should be organized. What logical arguments and evidence would help him ethically achieve his persuasive objective?

ASSESS: The following Web sites expand our discussion of reasoning fallacies and can help you better assess the arguments in persuasive messages you encounter. Consult these sites to assess your mastery of reasoning fallacies:

- www.nizkor.org/features/fallacies
- www.fallacyfiles.org

Using Emotional Appeals

15.3 Employ effective techniques of using emotional appeal in a persuasive speech.

REVIEW: Specific suggestions for appealing to audience emotions include using examples; emotion-arousing words; nonverbal behavior; selected appeals to fear; and appeals to such emotions as hope, pride, and courage. An appeal to the sacred and the revered can also be an effective way to motivate.

Key Terms

myth
demagogue

APPLY: Karl believes strongly that the tragedy of the Holocaust could occur again. He plans to show exceptionally graphic photographs of Holocaust victims during his speech to his public-speaking class. Is it ethical to show graphic, emotion-arousing photos to a captive audience?

ASSESS: You plan to convince your audience that they should donate to a drought-relief organization to help farmers cope with the effects climate change has had on agriculture in your state. What emotional appeals would be both ethical and effective to support your position?

Strategies for Adapting Ideas to People and People to Ideas

15.4 Adapt your persuasive message to receptive, neutral, and unreceptive audiences.

REVIEW: Consider the following strategies to adapt ideas to people and people to ideas:

- *To persuade the receptive audience.* Identify with the audience. State your speaking objective. Tell the audience members what you want them to do. Ask for an immediate show of support. Use emotional appeals effectively. Make it easy for your listeners to act.

- *To persuade the neutral audience.* Capture your listeners' attention early in your speech by referring to beliefs that many listeners share. Relate your topic not only to your listeners but also to their families, friends, and loved ones. Be realistic in what you expect to accomplish.

- *For an unreceptive audience.* Don't immediately announce that you plan to change your listeners' minds. Begin your speech by noting areas of agreement before you discuss areas of disagreement. Establish your credibility early in your message. Acknowledge the opposing points of view that members of your audience may hold. Consider making understanding rather than advocacy your goal. Advance your strongest argument first. Don't expect a major shift in attitude from a hostile audience.

APPLY: Martika wants to convince her classmates, a captive audience, that they should join her in a twenty-four-hour sit-in at the university president's office to protest the recent increase in tuition and fees. The president has made it clear that any attempt to occupy his office after normal office hours will result in arrests. Is it appropriate for Martika to use a classroom speech to encourage her classmates to participate in the sit-in?

ASSESS: You are speaking to your public-speaking class to seek their help to clean up the beautiful San Marvelous River that runs through your community. Because most of the students in your class do not live in your community, they are not particularly interested in this topic, although some of your listeners are interested in environmental issues. What kind of audience are you facing, and what persuasive speaking strategies would be helpful in achieving your speaking goal?

Strategies for Organizing Persuasive Messages

15.5 Identify and use strategies for effectively organizing a persuasive speech.

REVIEW: Four patterns for organizing a persuasive speech are problem–solution, refutation, cause and effect, and the motivated sequence. The five steps of the motivated sequence are attention, need, satisfaction, visualization, and action. Adapt the motivated sequence to your specific audience and persuasive objective.

APPLY: Janice is pondering options for organizing her persuasive speech, which has the following purpose: "The audience should support the establishment of a wellness program for our company." Using this purpose, draft the main ideas for a speech organized according to each of the following organizational patterns: problem–solution, refutation, cause and effect, and motivated sequence.

ASSESS: Analyze the "Dream" speech by Martin Luther King that appears in Appendix B to identify Dr. King's strategies for establishing credibility and his use of logic and emotion to achieve his persuasive goals. What elements of the motivated sequence do you see in the speech?

Speaking for Special Occasions and Purposes

It's like singing "The Star-Spangled Banner" at the World Series. Nobody came to hear you. But it's not an official event unless you do it.

—Barney Frank

Ruskin Spear (1911-90), *Portrait of Sir Winston Churchill*. Oil on canvas.
Photo: Private Collection/Bridgeman Images.

OBJECTIVES

After studying this chapter, you should be able to do the following:

16.1 Identify and explain the requirements for two types of speaking situations likely to arise in the workplace.

16.2 List and describe nine types of ceremonial speeches.

16.3 List and explain strategies for creating humor in a speech.

There is money in public speaking. Many of the politicians, athletes, and celebrities who speak professionally earn six- or even seven-figure fees for a single talk.

- Former president George W. Bush has charged about $150,000 per speech since leaving the presidency.[1]
- Former vice president and Nobel Peace Prize winner Al Gore has made as much as $156,000 for a speech on global climate change.[2]
- Former British prime minister Tony Blair made almost $616,000—more than $10,000 a minute—for two 30-minute speeches.[3]
- And former president Bill Clinton made nearly $40 million in speaking fees in the first years after he left the White House.[4]
- But the record speaking fee may still be the $2 million for two 20-minute speeches given by former president Ronald Reagan to a Japanese company in 1989.[5]

Although most of us will never be rewarded so lavishly for our public-speaking efforts, it is likely that at some time we will be asked to make a business or professional presentation or to speak on some occasion that calls for celebration, commemoration, inspiration, or entertainment. Special occasions are important enough and frequent enough to merit study, regardless of the likelihood of their resulting in wealth or fame for the speaker.

In this chapter, we discuss the various types of speeches that may be called for on special occasions, and we examine the specific and unique audience expectations for each one. First, we will discuss two speaking situations that are likely to occur in the workplace. Then we will turn our attention to several types of ceremonial speeches and the humorous after-dinner speech.

Public Speaking in the Workplace

16.1 Identify and explain the requirements for two types of speaking situations likely to arise in the workplace.

In many careers and professions, public speaking is a daily part of the job. Workplace audiences may range from a group of three managers to a huge auditorium filled with company employees. Presentations may take the form of routine meeting management, reports to company executives, training seminars within the company, or public-relations speeches to people outside the company. The occasions and opportunities are many, and chances are good that you will be asked or expected to do some on-the-job public speaking in the course of your career.

Group Presentations

After a group has reached a decision, solved a problem, or uncovered new information, group members often present their findings to others. The audience-centered principles of preparing an effective speech apply to group members who are designing a group oral presentation just as they do to individual speakers.

As our familiar model in Figure 16.1 suggests, the central and most important step is to analyze the audience who will listen to the presentation. Who are these listeners? What are their interests and backgrounds? And what do they need to know? One business consultant suggests,

> Tune your audience in to radio station WIIFM— What's In It For Me. Tell your listeners where the benefits are for them, and they'll listen to everything you have to say.[6]

As you do when developing an individual speech, make sure you have a clear purpose and a central idea divided into logical main ideas. This is a group effort, so you need to make sure *each* group member can articulate the purpose, central idea, main ideas, key supporting material, and overall outline for the presentation.

SELECTING A PRESENTATION FORMAT Unless a format for your group presentation has been specified, your group will need to determine how to deliver the presentation. Three primary formats for sharing reports and recommendations with an audience are the

Figure 16.1 Use the audience-centered model of public speaking to plan a group presentation.

SOURCE: Copyrighted by Pearson Education, Hoboken, NJ.

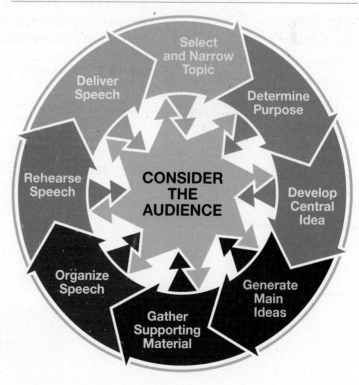

Table 16.1 Formats and Recommendations for Sharing Group Reports with an Audience

Format	Definition	Role of Group Members	Role of Audience Members
Symposium	A public discussion in which several short speeches are presented to an audience. The moderator and group members are seated in front of audience.	Along with your fellow group members, be prepared to give a distinct report. Know what the other members plan to say to avoid covering the same ground twice. The moderator may summarize key points at the end of the members' speeches.	May participate in a question-and-answer session or a forum presentation.
Forum	A question-and-answer session that usually follows a public discussion or symposium.	Know the issues and be prepared to respond. Respond to audience questions with short impromptu speeches.	Direct questions and comments to group members.
Panel Discussion	A group discourse designed to inform an audience about issues or problems, or to make recommendations.	Be prepared with notes on key facts or statistics. Do not present formal speeches. The appointed chairperson or moderator summarizes key points and serves as a gatekeeper.	May participate in question-and-answer session or forum.

symposium

A public discussion in which a series of short speeches is presented to an audience

forum

A question-and-answer session that usually follows a public discussion or symposium

panel discussion

Group discourse designed to inform an audience about issues or a problem, or to make recommendations

symposium, **forum**, and **panel discussion**. These three primary formats are defined and described in Table 16.1.

PLANNING A GROUP PRESENTATION Working in groups requires a coordinated team effort. If you are used to developing reports and speeches on your own, it may be a challenge to work with others on a group assignment. Figure 16.2 offers seven suggestions for enhancing teamwork.

MAKING A GROUP PRESENTATION By now it should be clear that the skills needed to give a group presentation mirror those we've presented throughout the book. But because a group presentation creates the additional challenge of coordinating your communication efforts with other group or team members, keep the following tips in mind as you offer your conclusions or recommendations.

- **Clarify your purpose.** Just as with an individual speech, it is important for listeners to know what your group's speaking goal is and to understand why you are presenting the information to them. It is also important for each group member to be reminded of the overarching goal of the presentation. It would be useful

Figure 16.2 Suggestions for Enhancing Teamwork

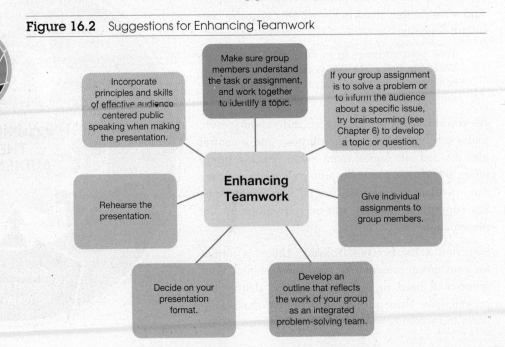

The skills you learn in public-speaking class can help you when you are part of a panel discussion. *Photo:* epa european pressphoto agency b.v./ Alamy Stock Photo.

if the first speaker could ensure that the audience has a good understanding of the group's purpose. If your group is responding to a specific discussion question, it may be useful to write the question or purpose of the presentation on a chalkboard, whiteboard, flipchart, or PowerPoint™ slide.

- **Use presentation aids effectively.** You can use presentation aids not only to clarify your purpose, but also to summarize key findings and recommendations. Visual aids can serve the important function of unifying your group presentation. If your group is using PowerPoint visuals, consider having each group member use the same template and font style to add to the coordinated look and feel of your presentation.

- **Choose someone to serve as coordinator or moderator.** Groups need a balance between structure and interaction. Without adequate structure, conversation can bounce from person to person and the presentation will lack a clear focus. A moderator can help provide needed structure to a group presentation by introducing both the topic and the group members. A moderator can also help keep track of time and ensure that no one either dominates the discussion or speaks too little.

- **Be ready to answer questions.** Communication, as we've emphasized, is more than just giving people information; it also includes responding to feedback and questions from listeners. Group presentations often include a question-and-answer session (forum) following the presentation. Besides being informed about your topic, it's a wise idea to have thoroughly read any written report the group has distributed.

In Chapter 11, we presented strategies for responding to questions, including tips for responding to hostile questions. If someone asks a question that has just been asked and answered, or asks an irrelevant or poorly worded question, don't criticize the questioner. Be polite, tactful, and gracious. Rather than self-righteously saying, "That's a dumb question" or "Someone just asked that," calmly provide an answer and move on. If you

RECAP

TIPS FOR SUCCESSFUL GROUP PRESENTATIONS

Work as a group to
- Understand the task.
- Brainstorm problem solutions.
- Choose a presentation format.
- Outline and rehearse the presentation.
- Make the presentation and answer questions.

Work as an individual to
- Complete your assignment.
- Contribute to meetings and rehearsals.
- Participate in the presentation.

don't understand a question, ask for more clarification. Also, don't let a questioner start making a speech. If it looks as if a questioner is using the question-and-answer period to give an oration, gently ask, "And what is your question?" or "How can we help you?" This approach should elicit a question that you can then address and return the communication process back to the control of the group.

Public-Relations Speeches

People who work for professional associations, blood banks, utility companies, government agencies, universities, churches, or charitable institutions, as well as those employed by commercial enterprises, are often called on to speak to an audience about what their organization does or about a special project the organization has taken on. These speeches are **public-relations speeches**. They are designed to inform the public and improve relations with them—either in general, or because a particular program or situation has raised questions.

A public-relations speaker begins by discussing the need or problem that has prompted the speech. Then he or she goes on to explain how the company or organization is working to meet the need or solve the problem—or why it believes there is no problem.

It is important in public-relations speaking to anticipate criticism. The speaker may acknowledge and counter potential problems or objections, especially when past presenters have encountered opposition to the policy or program. The speaker should emphasize the positive aspects of the policy or program and take care not to become defensive. He or she wants to leave the impression that the company or organization has carefully worked through the potential pitfalls and drawbacks. It should be noted that not all public-relations speeches make policy recommendations. Many simply summarize information for those who need to know.

For example, local developer Jack Brooks is well aware that many of those present at the city council meeting are opposed to his developing an area of land within the popular Smythson Creek greenbelt. Rather than ignore their objections, he deliberately and carefully addresses them:

> Many of you here tonight played in the Smythson Creek greenbelt as children. It was there that you learned to swim and that you hiked with your friends. I, too, share memories of those experiences.
>
> I want to assure you that my proposed development will actually help to preserve the greenbelt. We will dedicate in perpetuity an acre of unspoiled greenbelt for each acre we develop. Further, we will actively seek to preserve that unspoiled land by hiring an environmental specialist to oversee its protection.
>
> As things stand now, we risk losing the entire greenbelt to pollution and unmanaged use. I can promise a desirable residential development, plus the preservation of at least half the natural environment.

Mediated Workplace Presentations

More and more frequently, speakers use video chat applications such as Skype and FaceTime for workplace presentations. Although these technologies offer a cost-effective, time-saving way to reach large audiences in multiple locations, they also call for some specialized presentation skills. In addition to the recommendations that appear in Chapter 11, public-speaking coaches suggest the following:[7]

- Raise your computer so you can look directly into your camera. You will appear to have eye contact with your audience.
- Place your speaking notes and the audience's image at the top of your screen so you do not have to look down to see them during your speech.
- Because audience members tend to be less focused on a remote speaker than a face-to-face speaker, use plenty of variation in your volume, speech rate, and supporting material, as well as other content and delivery factors over which you have control.

- Actively engage your audience. Encourage audience members to respond to your questions by a show of hands or with a verbal response.

Of course, video chat applications are not limited to the workplace. You may be taking an online public-speaking class for which you deliver your assigned speeches on Skype. Speakers may make ceremonial speeches, like those discussed later in this chapter, via video chat. Learning to use this technology will serve you well in a variety of contemporary public-speaking contexts.

Ceremonial Speaking

16.2 List and describe nine types of ceremonial speeches.

Kairos is the Greek term rhetoricians use to describe the circumstances surrounding, or the occasion for, a speech. If the occasion is one that brings people together to celebrate, thank, or praise someone, or to mourn, a speech given on that occasion is known as a **ceremonial,** or **epideictic, speech**. We will explore nine types of ceremonial speeches: introductions, toasts, award presentations, nominations, acceptances, keynote addresses, commencement addresses, commemorative addresses and tributes, and eulogies.

kairos
The circumstances surrounding the speech or the occasion for a speech

ceremonial (epideictic) speech
A speech delivered on a special occasion for celebration, thanksgiving, praise, or mourning

Introductions

Most of us have heard poor introductions. A nervous speaker making a **speech of introduction** stands up and mispronounces the main speaker's name. Or the introducer speaks for five or ten minutes before yielding to the main speaker.

speech of introduction
A speech that provides information about another speaker

An introductory speech is much like an informative speech. The speaker delivers the introduction to provide information to the audience about the main speaker.

The ultimate purpose of an introduction, however, is to arouse interest in the speaker and his or her topic. In fact, when you are asked to introduce a featured speaker or an honored guest, your purposes are similar to those of a good speech introduction: You need to capture the audience's attention, build the speaker's credibility, and introduce the speaker's general subject. You also need to make the speaker feel welcome, while revealing some of the speaker's personal qualities so the audience can feel they know him or her more intimately. There are two cardinal rules for giving introductory speeches:

BE BRIEF   The audience has come to hear the main speaker or honor the guest, not to listen to you.

BE ACCURATE   Nothing so disturbs a speaker as having to begin by correcting the introducer. If you are going to introduce someone at a meeting or dinner, ask that person to supply you with biographical data beforehand. If someone else provides you with the speaker's background, make sure the information is accurate. Be certain that you know how to pronounce the speaker's name and any other names or terms you will need to use.

The following short speech of introduction adheres to the two criteria: It's brief, and it's accurate.

CONFIDENTLY CONNECTING WITH YOUR AUDIENCE

Seek a Variety of Speaking Opportunities

The more positive experiences you have when speaking publicly, the more likely you are to grow more confident when you speak.[8] Look at new speaking situations as opportunities to increase your confidence so that communication apprehension becomes less of an obstacle when you speak to others.

This evening, friends, we have the opportunity to hear one of the most innovative mayors in the history of our community. Mary Norris's experience in running her own real-estate business gave her an opportunity to pilot a new approach to attracting new businesses to our community, even before she was elected mayor in last year's landslide victory. She was recently recognized as the most successful mayor in our state by the Good Government League. Not only is she a skilled manager and spokesperson for our city, but she is also a warm and caring person. I am pleased to introduce my friend Mary Norris.

Finally, keep the needs of your audience in mind at all times. If the person you are introducing truly needs no introduction to the group, do not give one! Just welcome the speaker and step aside. (Note that the president of the United States is always introduced simply: "Ladies and gentlemen, the president of the United States.")

Toasts

toast

A brief salute to a momentous occasion

Most people are asked at one time or another to provide a **toast** for some momentous occasion—a wedding, a celebration of the birth of a baby, a reunion of friends, a successful business venture. A toast is a brief salute to such an occasion, usually accompanied by a round of drinks and immediately followed by the raising or clinking together of glasses or goblets. The custom is said to have taken its name from the old custom of tossing a bit of bread or a crouton into a beverage for flavoring.[9] "Drinking the toast" was somewhat like enjoying a dunked doughnut.

The modern toast is usually quite short—only a few sentences at most. Some toasts are personal, as, for example, one given by a wedding guest who is a close friend of both the bride and the groom:

> I would like to say a few words about this couple. You see, I knew Rachel and Ben before they were a couple—when they were friends. I first met Rachel when we were freshmen in high school. Her sarcastic sense of humor has kept me laughing ever since.[10]

In contrast, a toast made by someone who does not know the primary celebrants so well may be more generic. Here is an example of such a generic wedding toast:

> When the roaring flames of your love have burned down to embers, may you find that you've married your best friend.[11]

If you are asked to make an impromptu toast, let your audience and the occasion dictate what you say. Sincerity is more important than wit. At a dinner your authors attended in Moscow a few years ago, all the guests were asked to stand at some point during the meal and offer a toast. Although this Russian custom took us by surprise, one of our friends gave a heartfelt and well-received toast that went something like this:

> We have spent the past week enjoying both the natural beauty and the man-made marvels of your country. We have visited the exquisite palaces of the czars and stood in amazement before some of the world's great art treasures. But we have also discovered that the most important national resource of Russia is the warmth of her people. Here's to new and lasting friendships.

award presentation

A speech that accompanies the conferring of an award

Our Russian hosts were most appreciative. The rest of us were impressed. Mary's toast was a resounding success because she spoke sincerely about her audience and the occasion.

Award Presentations

Presenting an award is somewhat like introducing a speaker or a guest: Remember that the audience did not come to hear you, but to see and hear the award winner. Nevertheless, making an **award presentation**, a speech accompanying the conferring of an award, is an important responsibility. An award presentation has several distinct components.

REFER TO THE OCCASION OF THE PRESENTATION   First, when presenting an award, you should refer to the occasion of the presentation. Awards are often given to mark the anniversary of a special event, the completion of a long-range task, the accomplishments of a lifetime, or high achievement in some field.

EXPLAIN THE HISTORY AND SIGNIFICANCE OF THE AWARD   Next, you should talk about the history and significance of the award. This section of the speech may be fairly long if the audience knows little about the award; it will be brief if the audience is already familiar with the history and purpose of the award. Whatever the award, a discussion of its significance will add to its meaning for the person who receives it.

NAME THE AWARD RECIPIENT   Finally, you will name the person to whom the award has been given. The longest part of this segment of the speech is a glowing description of the achievements that elicited the award. If the name of the person receiving the award has already been made public, you may refer to him or her by name throughout your description. If you are going to announce the individual's name for the first time, you will probably want to recite the achievements first and leave the person's name for last. Even though some members of the audience may recognize the recipient from your description, you should still save the drama of the actual announcement until the last moment.

Both award presenters and speakers accepting awards should speak about the award and what it means to the audience as well as to the winner. *Photo:* ispstock/Fotolia.

Nominations

A **nomination speech** is similar to an award presentation. It too involves noting the occasion and describing the purpose and significance of, in this case, the office to be filled. The person making the nomination speech should explain clearly why the nominee's skills, talents, and past achievements serve as qualifications for the position. And the actual nomination should come at the end of the speech.

nomination speech
A speech that officially names someone as a candidate for an office or a position

When Senate minority leader Everett Dirksen nominated Barry Goldwater as the Republican presidential candidate in 1964, he emphasized those personal qualities that he thought would appeal to the audience:

> Whether in commerce or finance, in business or industry, in private or public service, there is such a thing as competence.... Barry Goldwater has demonstrated it over and over in his every activity. As Chief of Staff of his state National Guard, he brought about its desegregation shortly after World War II and long before Civil Rights became a burning issue. He brought integration to his own retail enterprises. For his own employees he established the five-day week and a health and life insurance plan. All this was done without fanfare or the marching of bands.[12]

And Dirksen ended his speech with the nomination itself:

> I nominate my friend and colleague Barry Goldwater of Arizona to be the Republican candidate for President of the United States.

Acceptances

Anyone who receives an award or a nomination usually responds with a brief **acceptance speech**. Acceptance speeches may have something of a bad name because of the lengthy, emotional, rambling, and generally boring speeches delivered annually on prime-time TV by the winners of the film industry's Oscars. In contrast, brief acceptance speeches can be quite insightful, even inspiring, and they can leave the audience feeling no doubt that the right person won the award.

acceptance speech
A speech of thanks for an award, nomination, or other honor

Speaking at Pointe du Hoc, France, during ceremonies in June 1994 to commemorate the fifty-year anniversary of D-Day, President Bill Clinton paid tribute to the assembled veterans:

> We are the children of your sacrifice. We are the sons and daughters you saved from tyranny's reach. We grew up behind the shield of the strong alliances you forged in blood upon these beaches, on the shores of the Pacific, and in the skies above us. We flourished in the nation you came home to build. The most difficult days of your lives bought us fifty years of freedom.[23]

His tribute completed, Clinton added this challenge:

> Let us carry on the work you began here. You completed your mission here, but the mission of freedom goes on; the battle continues.

Eulogies

eulogy

A speech of tribute delivered when someone has died

A **eulogy**—a speech of tribute delivered when someone has died—can be one of the most significant and memorable and also one of the most challenging forms of commemorative address. As the editor of a recent collection of eulogies notes,

> A good eulogy can be…a bridge between the living and the dead, between us and them, memory and eternity. The more specific and real the remembrances spoken, the stronger the bridge.[24]

When you deliver a eulogy, you should mention—indeed, linger on—the unique achievements of the person to whom you are paying tribute and, of course, express a sense of loss. The mother of a child killed in the 2012 Newtown, Connecticut, school shooting, opened her eulogy for her little boy on this heart-wrenching note of grief:

> The sky is crying, and the flags are at half-mast. It is a sad, sad day.[25]

But it is also proper in a eulogy to include personal and even humorous recollections of the person who has died. In his eulogy for his beloved Aunt Betty, John T. Masterson, Jr., related this humorous story:

> Whereas other relatives sent books, clothing, or sensible toys for Christmas and birthdays, Aunt Betty tended toward the offbeat…. There was the year she (or the mail order house) got the order number wrong and sent me reflective driveway markers for Christmas. The thing about Aunt Betty was that if you received a gift like that, you didn't recognize it as a mistake; instead, my family and I sat around the Christmas tree trying to figure out the joke![26]

Finally, turn to the living, and encourage them to transcend their sorrow and sense of loss and feel instead gratitude that the dead person was once alive among them.

RECAP

TYPES OF CEREMONIAL SPEECHES

- Introductions
- Toasts
- Award presentations
- Nominations
- Acceptances
- Keynote addresses
- Commencement addresses
- Commemorative addresses and tributes
- Eulogies

After-Dinner Speaking: Using Humor Effectively

16.3 List and explain strategies for creating humor in a speech.

If you are a human being or even a reasonably alert shrub, chances are that sooner or later a club or organization will ask you to give a speech. The United States is infested with clubs and organizations, constantly engaging in a variety of worthwhile group activities such as (1) eating lunch; (2) eating dinner; (3) eating breakfast; and of course (4) holding banquets. The result is that there is a constant demand for post-meal speakers, because otherwise all you'd hear would be the sounds of digestion.[27]

With typically irreverent wit, columnist Dave Barry thus begins his observations of the activity known as after-dinner speaking. Certainly he is right about one thing: the popularity of mealtime meetings and banquets with business and professional organizations and service clubs. And such a meeting inevitably requires a humorous **after-dinner speech**.

Interestingly, not only is the after-dinner speech not always after *dinner* (as Barry points out, the meal is just as likely to be breakfast or lunch), but it is also not always *after* anything. The after-dinner speech may be delivered before the meal or even between courses.

Former First Lady Barbara Bush preferred to schedule speeches first and dinner later during state dinners. In another variation, Librarian of Congress James Billington, at a dinner in honor of philosopher Alexis de Tocqueville, served up one speech between each course, "so that one had to earn the next course by listening to the speech preceding it."[28] Regardless of the variation, the after-dinner speech is something of an institution, one with which a public speaker should be prepared to cope.

After-dinner speeches may present information or persuade, but their primary purpose is to entertain—arguably the most inherently audience-centered of the three general purposes for speaking discussed in Chapter 6. We summarize several strategies for entertaining audiences with humor in Table 16.2 and discuss them in detail next.

after-dinner speech
A humorous presentation, usually delivered in conjunction with a mealtime meeting or banquet

Humorous Topics

Because humor is listener-centered, the central question for the after-dinner speaker seeking a topic must be this: What do audiences find funny?

The Comedy Gym in Austin, Texas, a school for aspiring stand-up comedians, advocates that speakers start with "themselves, their lives, what makes them laugh."[29] Audiences almost always enjoy hearing a speaker poke fun at himself or herself. Comedy writer John Macks points out that self-deprecating humor is "an instant way to establish a rapport with an audience."[30]

Even serious subjects can lend themselves to humorous presentations. One speech-writer notes that humor can help a speaker achieve rapport with the audience and can also help the audience remember the speaker's message:

> If you can find a way to make a point with humor, you've improved the odds of making your message stick. For example, say you're expecting a tax increase, and you want to let your audience know. You might say, "Well, Congress has finally decided how to divide up the pie; trouble is, *we're* the pie."[31]

Increased taxes, not an inherently humorous topic, can still be treated humorously. So can other serious topics. Previously in this chapter we discussed the use of humor in eulogies. Gun control, the U.S. healthcare industry, and the economy—subjects tackled by Michael Moore in the documentary films *Bowling for Columbine*, *Sicko*, and *Where to*

Table 16.2 Strategies for Achieving Humor in After-Dinner Speeches

Humorous Topics	Inherently funny subjects or humorous treatments of more serious subjects
Humorous Stories	Funny anecdotes
Humorous Verbal Strategies	
Play on words	An intentional error such as puns, spoonerisms, and malapropisms
Hyperbole	Exaggeration
Understatement	Downplaying a fact or event
Verbal irony	Saying just the opposite of what one means
Wit	An unexpected turn at the end of a fact or incident
Humorous Nonverbal Strategies	Physical or vocal elements such as posture, gesture, pauses, and intonation

The purpose of most after-dinner speeches is to entertain the audience. What humorous strategies can this speaker use? *Photo:* Halfpoint/Fotolia.

Invade Next—are serious topics made more palatable to listeners by the use of humor. For example, in *Sicko*,

> a scrolling text of the pre-existing medical conditions that insurance companies use to reject prospective applicants is set to the *Star Wars* theme against an outer-space backdrop.[32]

Although Moore's medium is film rather than speech, the same principle applies: Many serious subjects can be treated with humor.

Are any subjects *in*appropriate for an after-dinner speech? Keep in mind that it is the audience that "gives attempts at humor their success or failure."[33] Therefore, topics that might create a great deal of emotional noise (such as grief or anger) for particular groups would not be good topics for humorous speeches to those audiences. For example, a humorous treatment of childhood cancer would most likely only distress an audience of parents who had lost children to that disease.

Humorous Stories

Humorous stories should be simple. Complicated stories and jokes are rarely perceived by audiences as funny. Jay Leno claims that

> Jokes work best when they're easy to understand."[34]

Co-writers Michael Blastland and David Spiegelhalter agree, adding,

> If nothing happens in a story, it is not usually a story, it's a joke.[35]

Successful after-dinner speakers also need a broad repertoire of jokes, humorous anecdotes, and one-liners. One speaker says that she gathers approximately twenty-five to thirty in preparation for writing a speech.[36] She explains,

> This will be reduced to the best and most appropriate 6 or 7, but one needs as much material as possible to begin with.

Finally, it is important to know your anecdotes very well. Nothing deflates a humorous story more than getting halfway through one and saying, "Oh, and I forgot to tell you…." Rehearse your jokes. Only if you know the material can you hope to deliver it with the intonation and timing that will make it funny.

Humorous Verbal Strategies

A funny story or a one-liner may rely on any of the following verbal strategies for humorous effect.

pun
The use of double meanings to create humor

PUN Most of us are familiar with the **pun**, which relies on double meanings to create humor. For example, an old joke in which an exasperated speaker tries to explain the meaning of "hide" by shouting, "Hide! Hide! A cow's outside!" provokes the response, "I'm not afraid of cows." The joke relies on two meanings of the word *hide:* to conceal oneself and the skin (*outside*) of an animal.

spoonerism
A phrase in which the initial sounds of words are switched

SPOONERISM Another play on words is the **spoonerism**, named for William Spooner, a professor at Oxford University in the 1930s who frequently used it (inadvertently, in his case). A spoonerism occurs when someone switches the initial sounds of words in a single phrase: "sublic peaking" instead of "public speaking," for example. In one joke that relies on a spoonerism, the Chatanooga Choo-choo becomes the "cat who chewed the new shoes." Many parodies and satires employ spoonerisms to avoid charges of libel or copyright infringement; a spoonerism might be employed to name a boy wizard "Perry Hotter."

MALAPROPISM   Named for the unfortunate character Mrs. Malaprop in Richard Brinsley Sheridan's eighteenth-century play *The School for Scandal*, a **malapropism** is the mistaken use of a word that sounds much like the intended word: "destruction" for "instruction," for example.

HYPERBOLE   Exaggeration, or **hyperbole**, is often funny. In an after-dinner speech on "The Alphabet and Simplified Spelling," Mark Twain claimed,

> Simplified spelling brought about sun-spots, the San Francisco earthquake, and the recent business depression, which we would never have had if spelling had been left all alone.[37]

Of course, spelling could not have caused such catastrophes, so by using hyperbole, Twain makes his point in a humorous way.

UNDERSTATEMENT   The opposite of hyperbole, **understatement** involves downplaying a fact or event. Microsoft founder and Harvard dropout Bill Gates downplayed his meteoric success by telling a graduating class at one Ivy League university,

> I did the best of everyone who failed.[38]

VERBAL IRONY   A speaker who employs **verbal irony** says just the opposite of what he or she really means. Student Chris O'Keefe opens his speech on reading Shakespeare with this statement:

> At a certain point in my life, I came to the realization that I wanted to spend my life's effort to become a great playwright.[39]

Chris reveals the verbal irony of the statement when he continues,

> It has been about an hour and a half now and the feeling is still going strong.

WIT   One of the most frequently used verbal strategies for achieving humor is the use of **wit**: relating an incident that takes an unexpected turn at the end. Research suggests that witty humor may enhance a speaker's credibility.[40] Accepting the 2007 Oscar for Best Actress, Helen Mirren paid tribute to the monarch she had portrayed on screen in *The Queen*,

> For 50 years and more, Elizabeth Windsor has maintained her dignity, her sense of duty, and her hairstyle.[41]

The wit occurs in the final phrase "her hairstyle," which catches the audience off-guard because they anticipate another majestic attribute.

Humorous Nonverbal Strategies

After-dinner speakers often create humor through such nonverbal cues as posture, gesture, and voice. Well-timed pauses are especially crucial delivery cues for after-dinner speakers to master. One experienced after-dinner speaker advocates

> a slight pause before the punch line, then pause while the audience is laughing.[42]

It is true that some people seem to be "naturally" funny. If you are not one of them—if, for example, you struggle to get a laugh from even the funniest joke—you may still be able to use these strategies to prepare and deliver an after-dinner speech that is lighthearted and clever, if not uproariously funny. Such a speech can still be a success.

---

malapropism
The mistaken use of a word that sounds much like the intended word

hyperbole
Exaggeration

understatement
Downplaying a fact or event

verbal irony
Saying the opposite of what one means

wit
Relating an incident that takes an unexpected turn at the end

STUDY GUIDE: REVIEW, APPLY, AND ASSESS

Public Speaking in the Workplace

16.1 Identify and explain the requirements for two types of speaking situations likely to arise in the workplace.

REVIEW: Public-speaking skills are used frequently in the workplace when making group presentations or representing your company or profession before the public. Group presentation formats include symposium, forum, and panel discussion events. Group members should work individually and with the group to plan and make group presentations. Public-relations speeches inform the public and improve an organization's relationships with its public.

Key Terms

symposium	panel discussion
forum	public-relations speeches

ASSESS: A friend asks your advice about how to prepare for her first presentation to her colleagues in a new job. Explain how she can apply some of the principles and skills you have learned in this book to her workplace presentation.

Ceremonial Speaking

16.2 List and describe nine types of ceremonial speeches.

REVIEW: Chances are that at some time you will be called on to speak at an occasion that calls for celebration, commemoration, inspiration, or entertainment. These special-occasion speeches require you to apply your speaking skills to unique situations. This chapter offers advice for making these ceremonial speeches, including introductions, toasts, award presentations, nominations, acceptances, keynote addresses, commencement addresses, commemorative addresses and tributes, and eulogies.

Key Terms

kairos	nomination speech
ceremonial (epideictic) speech	acceptance speech
	keynote address
speech of introduction	commencement address
toast	commemorative address
award presentation	eulogy

APPLY: Several Web sites offer eulogy writing services or prewritten generic eulogies, such as a eulogy "for a grandmother," for around $30 to $40. If you were asked to deliver a eulogy, would it be ethical to buy such a speech?

ASSESS: You have been asked to introduce a Pulitzer Prize–winning poet who will be reading from her work at your school. What will you do to ensure that you follow the two cardinal rules of introductory speeches?

After-Dinner Speaking: Using Humor Effectively

16.3 List and explain strategies for creating humor in a speech.

REVIEW: After-dinner speaking is an established institution in which speakers entertain through the use of humorous topics and stories, as well as humorous verbal and nonverbal strategies.

Key Terms

after-dinner speech	hyperbole
pun	understatement
spoonerism	verbal irony
malapropism	wit

APPLY: You have been asked to give an after-dinner speech at a fund-raiser for an animal shelter where you volunteer. What kinds of humor might be appropriate for the occasion? What would be inappropriate?

Speaking in Small Groups

OBJECTIVES

After studying this appendix, you should be able to do the following:

A.1 Identify and describe the five steps for solving problems in groups and teams.

A.2 Explain how to make your small group an effective problem-solving team.

A.3 Identify appropriate leadership roles and styles for small groups.

roups are an integral part of our lives. Work groups, family groups, therapy groups, committees, and class-project groups are just a few of the groups in which we may participate at one time or another. Chances are that you have had considerable experience in communicating in small groups.

Why learn about group communication in a public-speaking class? Aristotle identified the link between public speaking and group discussion more than two thousand years ago when he wrote "Rhetoric is the counterpart of dialectic." He meant that our efforts to persuade are closely linked to our group efforts to search for truth.

In Aristotle's time, people gathered to discuss and decide public issues in a democratic manner. Today we still turn to a committee, jury, or task force to get facts and make recommendations. We still "search for truth" in groups. And, as in ancient Athens, once we believe we have found the truth, we present the message to others in speeches and lectures.

In this appendix, you will learn essential communication principles and skills to help you work as a productive member of a small group. Specifically, you will discover what small group communication is, learn ways to improve group problem solving, enhance your leadership skills, and become an effective group participant or group leader.[1]

What is **small group communication**? It is interaction among three to a dozen people who share a common purpose, feel a sense of belonging to the group, and influence one another.[2] Communication in groups larger than 12 people usually resembles public speaking more than small group communication.

A **team** is a special kind of group. It is a coordinated small group of people organized to work together with clearly defined roles and responsibilities, explicitly stated rules for operation, and well-defined goals.[3] All teams are groups, but not all groups are teams. A team, as our definition suggests, coordinates its efforts through a clearly defined structure of who does what. Think of a sports team in which members play by rules, have assigned roles, and work toward a clear objective—to win the game. Work teams also have well-defined procedures for accomplishing tasks. Teams are formed for a variety of reasons, such as to sell products, elect a political candidate, or build an international space station.

Working in groups and teams has several advantages compared to working on projects alone. Groups typically make better-quality decisions than do individuals for several reasons:[4]

- Groups usually have more information available.
- Groups are often more creative; the very presence of others can spark innovation.

small group communication
Interaction among three to twelve people who share a common purpose, feel a sense of belonging to the group, and influence one another

team
A coordinated small group of people organized to work together with clearly defined roles and responsibilities, explicit rules, and well-defined goals

- When you work in groups, you're more likely to remember what you discussed because you were actively involved in processing information.
- Group participation usually results in members being more satisfied with their results than if someone had just told them what to do.

Although we've characterized working in groups as a positive experience, working in groups can also be challenging, mainly for these reasons:[5]

- Group members may use excessive pressure to get others to conform to their point of view.
- One person may dominate the discussion.
- Some group members may rely too much on others and may not do their part.
- Group work is more time-consuming (many people consider this the biggest disadvantage).

The goal of this appendix is to help decrease the disadvantages and increase the advantages of working with others.

Solving Problems in Groups and Teams

A.1 Identify and describe the five steps for solving problems in groups and teams.

A central purpose of many groups and teams is to solve problems. Problem solving is a process of finding ways of overcoming obstacles to achieve a desired goal: How can we raise money for the new library? What should be done to improve the local economy? How can we make higher education affordable for everyone in our state? Each of these questions implies that there is an obstacle (lack of money) blocking the achievement of a desired goal (new library, stronger local economy, affordable education).

Imagine you have been asked to suggest ways to make a college education more affordable. The problem: The high cost of higher education keeps many people from attending college. How would you begin to organize a group to solve this problem? In 1910, John Dewey, philosopher and educator, identified a method of problem solving that he called **reflective thinking**.[6] Many groups have adapted his multistep method as a way to organize the process of solving problems. Here are the steps Dewey recommended:

1. Identify and define the problem.
2. Analyze the problem.
3. Generate possible solutions.
4. Select the best solution.
5. Test and implement the solution.

Although not every problem-solving discussion has to follow these steps, reflective thinking does provide a helpful blueprint that can relieve some of the uncertainty that exists when groups try to solve problems.

1. **Identify and Define the Problem** Groups work best when they define their problem clearly and early in their problem-solving process. To reach a clear definition, the group should consider the following questions:

   - What is the specific problem that concerns us?
   - What terms, concepts, or ideas do we need to understand in order to solve the problem?

reflective thinking

A method of structuring a problem-solving discussion that involves (1) identifying and defining the problem, (2) analyzing the problem, (3) generating possible solutions, (4) selecting the best solution, and (5) testing and implementing the solution

- Who is harmed by the problem?
- When do the harmful effects occur?

Policy questions can help define a problem and also identify the course of action that should be taken to solve it. A policy question usually begins with a phrase such as "What should be done about" or "What could be done to improve." Here are examples:

- What should be done to improve security at U.S. airports?
- What should be done to increase employment in our state?
- What steps could be taken to improve the U.S. trade balance with other countries?

If your group were investigating the high cost of pursuing a college education, for example, after defining such key terms as *higher education* and *college* and gathering statistics about the magnitude of the problem, you could phrase your policy question this way: "What could be done to reduce the high cost of attending college?"

2. **Analyze the Problem**   Ray Kroc, founder of McDonald's, said, "Nothing is particularly hard if you divide it into small jobs." Once the group understands the problem and has a well-worded question, the next step is to analyze the problem. **Analysis** is a process of examining the causes, effects, symptoms, history, and other background information that will help a group reach a solution. Analysis breaks a large problem into smaller parts. When analyzing a problem, a group should consider the following questions:

analysis
Examination of the causes, effects, and history of a problem in order to understand it better

- What is the history of the problem?
- How extensive is the problem?
- What are the causes, effects, and symptoms of the problem?
- Can the problem be subdivided for further definition and analysis?
- What methods do we already have for solving the problem, and what are their limitations?
- What obstacles might keep us from reaching a solution?

To analyze the problem of the high cost of attending college, your discussion group will have to conduct research into the history of the problem and existing methods of solving it (see Chapter 7).

Included in the process of analyzing the problem is identifying criteria. **Criteria** are standards for identifying an acceptable solution. They help you recognize a good solution when you discover one; criteria also help the group stay focused on its goal. Typical criteria for an acceptable solution specify that the solution should be implemented on schedule, should be agreed to by all group members, should be achieved within a given budget, and should remove the obstacles causing the problem.

criteria
Standards for identifying an acceptable solution to a problem

3. **Generate Possible Solutions**   When your discussion group has identified, defined, and analyzed the problem, you will be ready to generate possible solutions using group brainstorming. Guidelines for effective group brainstorming are similar to those presented in Chapter 6 for brainstorming speech topics.

- **Set aside judgment and criticism.**   Criticism and faultfinding stifle creativity. If group members find withholding judgment difficult, you can have the individual members write suggestions on paper first and then share the ideas with the group or use an electronic brainstorming app that allows participants to share ideas anonymously.
- **Think of as many possible solutions to the problem as you can.**   All ideas are acceptable, even wild and crazy ones. Piggyback off one another's ideas. All members must come up with at least one idea.

- **Have a member of the group record all the ideas that are mentioned.** Use a flipchart or chalkboard for in-person brainstorming, or an app or collaboration tool for electronic brainstorming, so that all group members can see and respond to the ideas.

- **After a set time has elapsed, evaluate the ideas, using criteria the group has established.** Approach the solutions positively. Do not be quick to dismiss an idea, but do voice any concerns or questions you might have. The group can brainstorm again later if it needs more creative ideas.

As we've noted, some groups find it useful to use technology to help them generate options and solutions.[7] In addition to apps and collaborative tools, a simple method is for group members to brainstorm solutions to a problem individually and then e-mail their list of ideas to each other. Or the group's leader could collect all of the ideas, eliminate duplicate suggestions, and then share them with the group. Research suggests that groups can generate more ideas if members first generate ideas individually before sharing them with the entire group.[8]

4. **Select the Best Solution** Next, the group needs to select the solution that best meets the criteria and solves the problem. At this point, the group may need to modify its criteria or even its definition of the problem.

Research suggests that after narrowing the list of possible solutions, the most effective groups carefully consider the pros and the cons of each proposed solution.[9] Groups that don't do this often make poor decisions because they haven't carefully evaluated the implications of their solution; they haven't looked before they leaped.

To help in evaluating the solution, consider the following questions:

- Which of the suggested solutions deals best with the obstacles?
- Does the suggestion solve the problem in both the short and the long term?
- What are the advantages and disadvantages of the suggested solution?
- Does the solution meet the established criteria?
- Should the group revise its criteria?
- What is required to implement the solution?
- When can the group implement the solution?
- What result will indicate success?

If the group is to reach agreement on a solution, some group members will need to abandon their attachment to their individual ideas for the overall good of the group. Experts who have studied how to achieve **consensus**—support for the final decision by all members—suggest that summarizing the group's progress frequently and keeping the group oriented toward its goal are helpful. Emphasizing where group members agree, clarifying misunderstandings, writing down known facts for all members to see, and keeping the discussion focused on issues rather than on emotions are also strategies that facilitate group consensus.[10]

consensus

The support and commitment of all group members to the decision of the group

5. **Test and Implement the Solution** The group's work is not finished when it has identified a solution. The important questions "How can we put the solution into practice?" and "How can we evaluate the quality of the solution?" have yet to be addressed. The group may want to develop a step-by-step plan that describes the process for implementing the solution, a time frame for implementation, and a list of individuals who will be responsible for carrying out specific tasks.

RECAP

STEPS IN PROBLEM SOLVING

1. Identify and clearly define the problem.
2. Analyze the problem and identify criteria.
3. Generate possible solutions.
4. Select the best solution.
5. Test and implement the solution.

Participating in Small Groups

A.2   Explain how to make your small group an effective problem-solving team.

To be an effective group participant, you have to understand how to manage the problem-solving process. But knowing the steps is not enough; you also need to prepare for meetings, evaluate evidence, effectively summarize the group's progress, listen courteously, and be sensitive to conflict.

Come Prepared for Group Discussions

To contribute to group meetings, you need to be informed about the issues. Prepare for group discussions by researching the issues. If the issue before your group is removing old asbestos from school buildings, for example, research the most recent scientific findings about various methods of removal. Chapter 7 described how to gather information for your speeches using the Internet and library resources. Use those same research techniques to prepare for group deliberations as well. Bring your research notes to the group; don't just rely on your memory or your personal opinion to carry you through the discussion. Without research, you will not be able to analyze the problem adequately.

Do Not Suggest Solutions before Analyzing the Problem

Research suggests that you should analyze a problem thoroughly before trying to zero in on a solution.[11] Resist the temptation to settle quickly on one solution until your group has systematically examined the causes, effects, history, and symptoms of a problem.

Evaluate Evidence

One study found that a key difference between groups that make successful decisions and those that don't is group members' ability to examine and evaluate evidence.[12] Ineffective groups are more likely to reach decisions quickly without considering the validity of evidence (or sometimes without any evidence at all). Such groups usually reach flawed conclusions.

Help Summarize the Group's Progress

Because it is easy for groups to get off the subject, group members frequently need to summarize what has been achieved and point the group toward the goal or task at hand. One research study suggests that periodic overviews of the discussion's progress can help the group stay on target.[13] Ask questions about the discussion process rather than about the topic under consideration: "Where are we now?" "Could someone summarize what we have accomplished?" and "Aren't we getting off the subject?"

Listen and Respond Courteously to Others

Chapter 4's suggestions for improving listening skills are useful when you work in groups, but understanding what others say is not enough. You also need to respect their points of view. Even when you disagree with someone's ideas, keep your emotions in check and respond courteously. Being closed-minded and defensive usually breeds group conflict.

Help Manage Conflict

In the course of exchanging ideas and opinions about controversial issues, disagreements are bound to occur.[14] You can help prevent conflicts from derailing the problem-solving process by doing the following:

- Keep the discussion focused on issues, not on personalities.
- Rely on facts rather than on personal opinions for evidence.
- Seek ways to compromise; don't assume that there must be a winner and a loser.
- Try to clarify misunderstandings in meaning.
- Be descriptive rather than evaluative and judgmental.
- Keep emotions in check.

If you can apply these basic principles, you can help make your group an effective problem-solving team.

Leading Small Groups

A.3 Identify appropriate leadership roles and styles for small groups.

Rudyard Kipling wrote, "For the strength of the pack is the wolf, and the strength of the wolf is the pack." Group members typically need a leader to help the group collaborate effectively and efficiently, and a leader needs followers in order to lead. In essence, **leadership** is the process of influencing others through communication. Some see a leader as one individual empowered to delegate work and direct the group. In reality, however, group leadership is often shared.

leadership
The process of influencing others through communication

Leadership Responsibilities

Leaders are needed to help accomplish tasks and to maintain a healthy social climate for the group. Table A.1 lists specific roles for both *task* leaders and *maintenance* leaders. Rarely does one person perform all these leadership responsibilities, even if a leader is

Table A.1 Leadership Roles in Groups and Teams

	Leadership Role	Description
Task Leaders Help get tasks accomplished	Agenda setter	Helps establish the group's agenda
	Secretary	Takes notes during meetings and distributes handouts before and during the meeting
	Initiator	Proposes new ideas or approaches to group problem solving
	Information seeker	Asks for facts or other information that helps the group deal with the issues and may also ask for clarification of ideas or obscure facts
	Opinion seeker	Asks for clarification of the values and opinions expressed by group members
	Information giver	Provides facts, examples, statistics, and other evidence that helps the group achieve its task
	Opinion giver	Offers opinions about the ideas under discussion
	Elaborator	Provides examples to show how ideas or suggestions would work
	Evaluator	Makes an effort to judge the evidence and the conclusion the group reaches
	Energizer	Tries to spur the group to further action and productivity
Group Maintenance Leaders Help maintain a healthy social climate	Encourager	Offers praise, understanding, and acceptance of others' ideas
	Harmonizer	Mediates disagreements that occur between group members
	Compromiser	Attempts to resolve conflicts by trying to find an acceptable middle ground between disagreeing group members
	Gatekeeper	Encourages the participation of less talkative group members and tries to limit lengthy contributions of other group members

SOURCE: Based on Kenneth D. Benne and Paul Sheats, "Functional Roles of Group Members," *Journal of Social Issues* 4 (Spring 1948), pp. 41–49.

formally appointed or elected. Most often a number of individual group members will each assume some specific leadership task, based on their personalities, skills, sensitivity, and the group's needs. If you determine that the group needs a clearer focus on the task or that maintenance roles are needed, be ready to influence the group appropriately to help get the job done in a positive, productive way. Leaders of large or formal groups may use parliamentary procedure to bring structure to meetings, for example. If you find yourself in such a leadership situation, Web sites such as Robert's Rules of Order (www.robertsrules.com) can help you implement parliamentary procedure.

Leadership Styles

Leaders can be described by the types of behavior, or leadership styles, they exhibit as they influence the group to help achieve its goal. When you are called on to lead, do you give orders and expect others to follow you? Or do you ask the group to vote on the course of action to follow? Or maybe you don't try to influence the group at all; perhaps you prefer to hang back and let the group work out its own problems.

These strategies describe three general leadership styles: *authoritarian, democratic,* and *laissez-faire*.[15] Authoritarian leaders assume positions of superiority, giving orders and assuming control of the group's activity. Although authoritarian leaders can usually organize group activities with a high degree of efficiency and virtually eliminate uncertainty about who should do what, most problem-solving groups prefer democratic leaders.

Having more faith in their groups than do authoritarian leaders, democratic leaders involve group members in the decision-making process rather than dictate what should be done. Democratic leaders focus more on guiding discussion than on issuing commands.

Laissez-faire leaders allow group members complete freedom in all aspects of the decision-making process. They do little to help the group achieve its goal. This style of leadership (or nonleadership) often leaves a group frustrated because the group then lacks guidance and has to struggle with organizing the work. Table A.2 compares the three styles.

What is the most effective leadership style? Research suggests that no single style is effective in every group situation. Sometimes a group needs a strong authoritarian leader to make decisions quickly so the group can achieve its goal. Although most groups prefer a democratic leadership style, leaders sometimes need to assert their authority to get the job done. The best leadership style depends on the nature of the group task, the power of the leader, and the relationship between the leader and his or her followers.

Table A.2 Leadership Style

	Authoritarian leaders	Democratic leaders	Laissez-faire leaders
Group Policy Formation	All policies are determined by the leader.	All policies are a matter of group discussion and decision; leader assigns and encourages group discussion and decision making.	Complete non-participation by leader in policy decisions.
Group Activity Development	Leader dictates group techniques and activities one at a time; future steps are largely unknown to group members.	Discussion yields broad perspectives and general steps to the group goal; when technical advice is needed, leader suggests alternative procedures.	Leader supplies needed materials, making it clear that he or she can supply information when asked, but takes no other part in the discussion.
Source of Work Assignments	Leader dictates specific work tasks and teams; leader tends to remain aloof from active group participation except when directing activities.	Members are free to work with anyone; group decides on division of tasks.	Complete freedom for individuals or group to choose assignments; minimal leader participation.
Praise/Criticism	Leader tends to be personal in praise or criticism of each member.	Leader is objective and fact-oriented in praise and criticism, trying to be a regular group member in spirit without doing too much of the work.	Leader offers infrequent spontaneous comments on member activities and makes no attempt to appraise or control the course of events.

transformational leadership

The process of influencing others by building a shared vision of the future, inspiring others to achieve, developing high-quality individual relationships with others, and helping people see how what they do is related to a larger framework or system

One contemporary approach to leadership is transformational leadership. Transformational leadership is not so much a particular style of leadership as it is a quality or characteristic of relating to others.[16] **Transformational leadership** is the process of influencing others by building a shared vision of the future, inspiring others to achieve, developing high-quality individual relationships with others, and helping people see how what they do is related to a larger framework or system. To be a transformational leader is not just to perform specific tasks or skills but also to have a philosophy of helping others see the big picture and inspiring them to make the vision of the future a reality.[17] Transformational leaders are good communicators who support and encourage rather than demean or demand.

RECAP

LEADERS OF SMALL GROUPS

1. Contribute to tasks and maintenance.
2. Adapt their leadership style to group needs.
3. Work toward transformational leadership.

Speeches for Analysis and Discussion

I Have a Dream

by Martin Luther King Jr., August 28, 1963

On August 28, 1963, civil rights leader and human rights activist Dr. Martin Luther King Jr. delivered one of the greatest historical speeches as the keynote of the civil rights march on Washington, D.C. To watch a recording of this speech, please access the REVEL course to accompany this book. If you do not have access to REVEL, we encourage you to search for the transcript of this speech online.

Photo: The LIFE Picture Collection/ Getty.

Inaugural Address[1]

by John F. Kennedy, January 20, 1961

Vice President Johnson, Mr. Speaker, Mr. Chief Justice, President Eisenhower, Vice President Nixon, President Truman, Reverend Clergy, fellow citizens:

We observe today not a victory of party but a celebration of freedom—symbolizing an end as well as a beginning—signifying renewal as well as change. For I have sworn before you and Almighty God the same solemn oath our forbears prescribed nearly a century and three-quarters ago.

The world is very different now. For man holds in his mortal hands the power to abolish all forms of human poverty and all forms of human life. And yet the same revolutionary beliefs for which our forebears fought are still at issue around the globe—the belief that the rights of man come not from the generosity of the state but from the hand of God.

We dare not forget today that we are the heirs of that first revolution. Let the word go forth from this time and place, to friend and foe alike, that the torch has been passed to a new generation of Americans—born in this century, tempered by war, disciplined by a hard and bitter peace, proud of our ancient heritage—and unwilling to witness or permit the slow undoing of those human rights to which this nation has always been committed, and to which we are committed today at home and around the world.

Let every nation know, whether it wishes us well or ill, that we shall pay any price, bear any burden, meet any hardship, support any friend, oppose any foe to assure the survival and the success of liberty.

This much we pledge—and more.

To those old allies whose cultural and spiritual origins we share, we pledge the loyalty of faithful friends. United there is little we cannot do in a host of cooperative ventures. Divided there is little we can do—for we dare not meet a powerful challenge at odds and split asunder.

To those new states whom we welcome to the ranks of the free, we pledge our word that one form of colonial control shall not have passed away merely to be replaced by a far more iron tyranny. We shall not always expect to find them supporting our view. But we shall always hope to find them strongly supporting their own freedom—and to remember that, in the past, those who foolishly sought power by riding the back of the tiger ended up inside.

To those people in the huts and villages of half the globe struggling to break the bonds of mass misery, we pledge our best efforts to help them help themselves, for whatever period is required—not because the communists may be doing it, not because we seek their votes, but because it is right. If a free society cannot help the many who are poor, it cannot save the few who are rich.

To our sister republics south of our border, we offer a special pledge—to convert our good words into good deeds—in a new alliance for progress—to assist free men and free governments in casting off the chains of poverty. But this peaceful revolution of hope cannot become the prey of hostile powers. Let all our neighbors know that we shall join with them to oppose aggression or subversion anywhere in the Americas. And let every other power know that this Hemisphere intends to remain the master of its own house.

To that world assembly of sovereign states, the United Nations, our last best hope in an age where the instruments of war have far outpaced the instruments of peace, we renew our pledge of support—to prevent it from becoming merely a forum for invective—to strengthen its shield of the new and the weak—and to enlarge the area in which its writ may run.

Finally, to those nations who would make themselves our adversary, we offer not a pledge but a request: that both sides begin anew the quest for peace, before the dark powers of destruction unleashed by science engulf all humanity in planned or accidental self-destruction.

We dare not tempt them with weakness. For only when our arms are sufficient beyond doubt can we be certain beyond doubt that they will never be employed.

But neither can two great and powerful groups of nations take comfort from our present course—both sides overburdened by the cost of modern weapons, both rightly alarmed by the steady spread of the deadly atom, yet both racing to alter that uncertain balance of terror that stays the hand of mankind's final war.

So let us begin anew—remembering on both sides that civility is not a sign of weakness, and sincerity is always subject to proof. Let us never negotiate out of fear. But let us never fear to negotiate.

Let both sides explore what problems unite us instead of belaboring those problems which divide us.

Let both sides, for the first time, formulate serious and precise proposals for the inspection and control of arms—and bring the absolute power to destroy other nations under the absolute control of all nations.

Let both sides seek to invoke the wonders of science instead of its terrors. Together let us explore the stars, conquer the deserts, eradicate disease, tap the ocean depths and encourage the arts and commerce.

Let both sides unite to heed in all corners of the earth the command of Isaiah—to "undo the heavy burdens . . . (and) let the oppressed go free."

And if a beachhead of cooperation may push back the jungle of suspicion, let both sides join in creating a new endeavor, not a new balance of power, but a new world of law, where the strong are just and the weak secure and the peace preserved.

All this will not be finished in the first one hundred days. Nor will it be finished in the first one thousand days, nor in the life of this Administration, nor even perhaps in our lifetime on this planet. But let us begin.

In your hands, my fellow citizens, more than mine, will rest the final success or failure of our course. Since this country was founded, each generation of Americans has been summoned to give testimony to its national loyalty. The graves of young Americans who answered the call to service surround the globe.

Now the trumpet summons us again—not as a call to bear arms, though arms we need—not as a call to battle, though embattled we are— but a call to bear the burden of a long twilight struggle, year in and year out, "rejoicing in hope, patient in tribulation"—a struggle against the common enemies of man: tyranny, poverty, disease and war itself.

Can we forge against these enemies a grand and global alliance, North and South, East and West, that can assure a more fruitful life for all mankind? Will you join in that historic effort?

In the long history of the world, only a few generations have been granted the role of defending freedom in its hour of maximum danger. I do not shrink from this responsibility—I welcome it. I do not believe that any of us would exchange places with any other people or any other generation. The energy, the faith, the devotion which we bring to this endeavor will light our country and all who serve it—and the glow from that fire can truly light the world.

And so, my fellow Americans: ask not what your country can do for you—ask what you can do for your country.

My fellow citizens of the world: ask not what America will do for you, but what together we can do for the freedom of man.

Finally, whether you are citizens of America or citizens of the world, ask of us here the same high standards of strength and sacrifice which we ask of you. With a good conscience our only sure reward, with history the final judge of our deeds, let us go forth to lead the land we love, asking His blessing and His help, but knowing that here on earth God's work must truly be our own.

Second Inaugural Address[2]
by Barack Obama, January 21, 2013

Vice President Biden, Mr. Chief Justice, Members of the United States Congress, distinguished guests, and fellow citizens:

Each time we gather to inaugurate a President we bear witness to the enduring strength of our Constitution. We affirm the promise of our democracy. We recall that what binds this Nation together is not the colors of our skin or the tenets of our faith or the origins of our names. What makes us exceptional—what makes us American—is our allegiance to an idea articulated in a declaration made more than two centuries ago:

> We hold these truths to be self-evident, that all men are created equal; that they are endowed by their Creator with certain unalienable rights; that among these are life, liberty, and the pursuit of happiness.

Today we continue a never-ending journey to bridge the meaning of those words with the realities of our time. For history tells us that while these truths may be self-evident, they've never been self-executing; that while freedom is a gift from God, it must be secured by His people here on Earth. The patriots of 1776 did not fight to replace the tyranny of a king with the privileges of a few or the rule of a mob. They gave to us a republic, a government of and by and for the people, entrusting each generation to keep safe our founding creed.

And for more than 200 years, we have.

Through blood drawn by lash and blood drawn by sword, we learned that no union founded on the principles of liberty and equality could survive half-slave and half-free. We made ourselves anew, and vowed to move forward together.

Together, we determined that a modern economy requires railroads and highways to speed travel and commerce, schools and colleges to train our workers.

Together, we discovered that a free market only thrives when there are rules to ensure competition and fair play.

Together, we resolved that a great nation must care for the vulnerable and protect its people from life's worst hazards and misfortune.

Through it all, we have never relinquished our skepticism of central authority nor have we succumbed to the fiction that all society's ills can be cured through government alone. Our celebration of initiative and enterprise, our insistence on hard work and personal responsibility, these are constants in our character.

But we have always understood that when times change, so must we; that fidelity to our founding principles requires new responses to new challenges; that preserving our individual freedoms ultimately requires collective action. For the American people can no more meet the demands of today's world by acting alone than American soldiers could have met the forces of fascism or communism with muskets and militias. No single person can train all the math and science teachers we'll need to equip our children for the future, or build the roads and networks and research labs that will bring new jobs and businesses to our shores. Now more than ever, we must do these things together, as one nation and one people.

This generation of Americans has been tested by crises that steeled our resolve and proved our resilience. A decade of war is now ending. An economic recovery has begun. America's possibilities are limitless, for we possess all the qualities that this world without boundaries demands: youth and drive; diversity and openness; an endless capacity for risk and a gift for reinvention. My fellow Americans, we are made for this moment and we will seize it—so long as we seize it together.

For we, the people, understand that our country cannot succeed when a shrinking few do very well and a growing many barely make it. We believe that America's prosperity must rest upon the broad shoulders of a rising middle class. We know that America thrives when every person can find independence and pride in their work; when the wages of honest labor liberate families from the brink of hardship. We are true to our creed when a little girl born into the bleakest poverty knows that she has the same chance to succeed as anybody else, because she is an American; she is free and she is equal, not just in the eyes of God, but also in our own.

We understand that outworn programs are inadequate to the needs of our time. So we must harness new ideas and technology to remake our government, revamp our tax code, reform our schools, and empower our citizens with the skills they need to work harder, learn more, reach higher. But while the means will change, our purpose endures: a nation that rewards the effort and determination of every single American. That is what this moment requires. That is what will give real meaning to our creed.

We, the people, still believe that every citizen deserves a basic measure of security and dignity. We must make the hard choices to reduce the cost of health care and the size of our deficit. But we reject the belief that America must choose between caring for the generation that built this country and investing in the generation that will build its future. For we remember the lessons of our past, when twilight years were spent in poverty and parents of a child with a disability had nowhere to turn.

We do not believe that in this country freedom is reserved for the lucky, or happiness for the few. We recognize that no matter how responsibly we live our lives, any one of us at any time may face a job loss or a sudden illness or a home swept away in a terrible storm. The commitments we make to each other through Medicare and Medicaid and Social Security, these things do not sap our initiative, they strengthen us. They do not make us a nation of takers; they free us to take the risks that make this country great.

We, the people, still believe that our obligations as Americans are not just to ourselves, but to all posterity. We will respond to the threat of climate change, knowing that the failure to do so would betray our children and future generations. Some may still deny the overwhelming judgment of science, but none can avoid the devastating impact of raging fires and crippling drought and more powerful storms.

The path towards sustainable energy sources will be long and sometimes difficult. But America cannot resist this transition, we must lead it. We cannot cede to other nations the technology that will power new jobs and new industries, we must claim its promise. That's how we will maintain our economic vitality and our national treasure—our forests and waterways, our croplands and snow-capped peaks. That is how we will preserve our planet, commanded to our care by God. That's what will lend meaning to the creed our fathers once declared.

We, the people, still believe that enduring security and lasting peace do not require perpetual war. Our brave men and women in uniform, tempered by the flames of battle, are unmatched in skill and courage. Our citizens, seared by the memory of those we have lost, know too well the price that is paid for liberty. The knowledge of their sacrifice will keep us forever vigilant against those who would do us harm. But we are also heirs to those who won the peace and not just the war; who turned sworn enemies into the surest of friends—and we must carry those lessons into this time as well.

We will defend our people and uphold our values through strength of arms and rule of law. We will show the courage to try and resolve our differences with other nations peacefully—not because we are naive about the dangers we face, but because engagement can more durably lift suspicion and fear.

America will remain the anchor of strong alliances in every corner of the globe. And we will renew those institutions that extend our capacity to manage crisis abroad, for no one has a greater stake in a peaceful world than its most powerful nation. We will support democracy from Asia to Africa, from the Americas to the Middle East, because our interests and our conscience compel us to act on behalf of those who long for freedom. And we must be a source of hope to the poor, the sick, the marginalized, the victims of prejudice—not out of mere charity, but because peace in our time requires the constant advance of those principles that our common creed describes: tolerance and opportunity, human dignity and justice.

We, the people, declare today that the most evident of truths—that all of us are created equal—is the star that guides us still; just as it guided our forebears through Seneca Falls and Selma and Stonewall; just as it guided all those men and women, sung and unsung, who left footprints along this great Mall, to hear a preacher say that we cannot walk alone; to hear a King proclaim that our individual freedom is inextricably bound to the freedom of every soul on Earth.

It is now our generation's task to carry on what those pioneers began. For our journey is not complete until our wives, our mothers and daughters can earn a living equal to their efforts. Our journey is not complete until our gay brothers and sisters are treated like anyone else under the law—for if we are truly created equal, then surely the love we commit to one another must be equal as well. Our journey is not complete until no citizen is forced to wait for hours to exercise the right to vote. Our journey is not complete until we find a better way to welcome the striving, hopeful immigrants who still see America as a land of opportunity—until bright young students and engineers are enlisted in our workforce rather than expelled from our country. Our journey is not complete until all our children, from the streets of Detroit to the hills of Appalachia, to the quiet lanes of Newtown, know that they are cared for and cherished and always safe from harm.

That is our generation's task—to make these words, these rights, these values of life and liberty and the pursuit of happiness real for every American. Being true to our founding documents does not require us to agree on every contour of life. It does not mean we all define liberty in exactly the same way or follow the same precise path to happiness. Progress does not compel us to settle centuries-long debates about the role of government for all time, but it does require us to act in our time.

For now decisions are upon us and we cannot afford delay. We cannot mistake absolutism for principle or substitute spectacle for politics or treat name-calling as reasoned debate. We must act, knowing that our work will be imperfect. We must act, we must act knowing that today's victories will be only partial and that it will be up to those who stand here in 4 years and 40 years and 400 years hence to advance the timeless spirit once conferred to us in a spare Philadelphia hall.

My fellow Americans, the oath I have sworn before you today, like the one recited by others who serve in this Capitol, was an oath to God and country, not party or faction. And we must faithfully execute that pledge during the duration of our service. But the words I spoke today are not so different from the oath that is taken each time a soldier signs up for duty or an immigrant realizes her dream. My oath is not so different from the pledge we all make to the flag that waves above and that fills our hearts with pride.

They are the words of citizens and they represent our greatest hope. You and I, as citizens, have the power to set this country's course. You and I, as citizens, have the obligation to shape the debates of our time—not only with the votes we cast, but with the voices we lift in defense of our most ancient values and enduring ideals.

Let us, each of us, now embrace with solemn duty and awesome joy what is our lasting birthright. With common effort and common purpose, with passion and dedication, let us answer the call of history and carry into an uncertain future that precious light of freedom.

Thank you. God bless you, and may He forever bless these United States of America.

Remarks to the U.S. Congress[3]
by Pope Francis, September 24, 2015

I am most grateful for your invitation to address this joint session of Congress in "the land of the free and the home of the brave." I would like to think that the reason for this is that I, too, am a son of this great continent, from which we have all received so much and toward which we share a common responsibility.

Each son or daughter of a given country has a mission, a personal and social responsibility. Your own responsibility as members of Congress is to enable this country, by your legislative activity, to grow as a nation. You are the face of its people, their representatives. You are called to defend and preserve the dignity of your fellow citizens in the tireless and demanding pursuit of the common good, for this is the chief aim of all politics. A political society endures when it seeks, as a vocation, to satisfy common needs by stimulating the growth of all its members, especially those in situations of greater vulnerability or risk. Legislative activity is always based on care for the people. To this you have been invited, called, and convened by those who elected you.

Yours is a work which makes me reflect in two ways on the figure of Moses. On the one hand, the patriarch and lawgiver of the people of Israel symbolizes the need of peoples to keep alive their sense of unity by means of just legislation. On the other, the figure of Moses leads us directly to God and thus to the transcendent dignity of the human being. Moses provides us with a good synthesis of your work: you are asked to protect, by means of the law, the image and likeness fashioned by God on every human face.

Today, I would like not only to address you, but through you the entire people of the United States. Here, together with their representatives, I would like to take this opportunity to dialogue with the many thousands of men and women who strive each day to do an honest day's work, to bring home their daily bread, to save money and—one step at a time—to build a better life for their families. These are men and women who are not concerned simply with paying their taxes, but in their own quiet way sustain the life of society. They generate solidarity by their actions, and they create organizations which offer a helping hand to those most in need.

I would also like to enter into dialogue with the many elderly persons who are a storehouse of wisdom forged by experience, and who seek in many ways, especially through volunteer work, to share their stories and their insights. I know that many of them are retired, but still active; they keep working to build up this land. I also want to dialogue with all those young people who are working to realize their great and noble aspirations, who are not led astray by facile proposals, and who face difficult situations, often as a result of immaturity on the part of many adults. I wish to dialogue with all of you, and I would like to do so through the historical memory of your people.

My visit takes place at a time when men and women of good will are marking the anniversaries of several great Americans. The complexities of history and the reality of human weakness notwithstanding, these men and women, for all their many differences and limitations, were able by hard work and self-sacrifice—some at the cost of their lives—to build a better future. They shaped fundamental values which will endure forever in the spirit of the American people. A people with this spirit can live through many crises, tensions and conflicts, while always finding the resources to move forward, and to do so with dignity. These men and women offer us a way of seeing and interpreting reality. In honoring their memory, we are inspired, even amid conflicts, and in the here and now of each day, to draw upon our deepest cultural reserves.

I would like to mention four of these Americans: Abraham Lincoln, Martin Luther King, Dorothy Day and Thomas Merton.

This year marks the 150th anniversary of the assassination of President Abraham Lincoln, the guardian of liberty, who labored tirelessly that "this nation, under God, [might] have a new birth of freedom." Building a future of freedom requires love of the common good and cooperation in a spirit of subsidiarity and solidarity.

All of us are quite aware of, and deeply worried by, the disturbing social and political situation of the world today. Our world is increasingly a place of violent conflict, hatred and brutal atrocities, committed even in the name of God and of religion. We know that no religion is immune from forms of individual delusion or ideological extremism. This means that we must be especially attentive to every type of fundamentalism, whether religious or of any other kind. A delicate balance is required to combat violence perpetrated in the name of a religion, an ideology or an economic system, while also safeguarding religious freedom, intellectual freedom and individual freedoms. But there is another temptation which we must especially guard against: the simplistic reductionism which sees only good or evil; or, if you will, the righteous and sinners. The contemporary world, with its open wounds which affect so many of our brothers and sisters, demands that we confront every form of polarization which would divide it into these two camps. We know that in the attempt to be freed of the enemy without, we can be tempted to feed the enemy within. To imitate the hatred and violence of tyrants and murderers is the best way to take their place. That is something which you, as a people, reject.

Our response must instead be one of hope and healing, of peace and justice. We are asked to summon the courage and the intelligence to resolve today's many geopolitical and economic crises. Even in the developed world, the effects of unjust structures and actions are all too apparent. Our efforts must aim at restoring hope, righting wrongs, maintaining commitments, and thus promoting the well-being of individuals and of peoples. We must move forward together, as one, in a renewed spirit of fraternity and solidarity, cooperating generously for the common good.

The challenges facing us today call for a renewal of that spirit of cooperation, which has accomplished so much good throughout the history of the United States. The complexity, the gravity and the urgency of these challenges demand that we pool our resources and talents, and resolve to support one another, with respect for our differences and our convictions of conscience.

In this land, the various religious denominations have greatly contributed to building and strengthening society. It is important that today, as in the past, the voice of faith continues to be heard, for it is a voice of fraternity and love, which tries to bring out the best in each person and in each society. Such cooperation is a powerful resource in the battle to eliminate new global forms of slavery, born of grave injustices which can be overcome only through new policies and new forms of social consensus.

Politics is, instead, an expression of our compelling need to live as one, in order to build as one the greatest common good: that of a community which sacrifices particular interests in order to share, in justice and peace, its goods, its interests, its social life. I do not underestimate the difficulty that this involves, but I encourage you in this effort.

Here, too, I think of the march which Martin Luther King led from Selma to Montgomery 50 years ago as part of the campaign to fulfill his "dream" of full civil and political rights for African Americans. That dream continues to inspire us all. I am happy that America continues to be, for many, a land of "dreams." Dreams which lead to action, to participation, to commitment. Dreams which awaken what is deepest and truest in the life of a people.

In recent centuries, millions of people came to this land to pursue their dream of building a future in freedom. We, the people of this continent, are not fearful of foreigners, because most of us were once foreigners. I say this to you as the son of immigrants, knowing that so many of you are also descended from immigrants. Tragically, the rights of those who were here long before us were not always respected. For those peoples and their nations, from the heart of American democracy, I wish to reaffirm my highest esteem and appreciation. Those first contacts were often turbulent and violent, but it is difficult to judge the past by the criteria of the present. Nonetheless, when the stranger in our midst appeals to us, we must not repeat the sins and the errors of the past. We must resolve now to live as nobly and as justly as possible, as we educate new generations not to turn their back on our "neighbors" and everything around us. Building a nation calls us to recognize that we must constantly relate to others, rejecting a mindset of hostility in order to adopt one of reciprocal subsidiarity, in a constant effort to do our best. I am confident that we can do this.

Our world is facing a refugee crisis of a magnitude not seen since the Second World War. This presents us with great challenges and many hard decisions. On this continent, too, thousands of persons are led to travel north in search of a better life for themselves and for their loved ones, in search of greater opportunities. Is this not what we want for our own children? We must not be taken aback by their numbers, but rather view them as persons, seeing their faces and listening to their stories, trying to respond as best we can to their situation. To respond in a way which is always humane, just and fraternal. We need to avoid a common temptation nowadays: to discard whatever proves troublesome. Let us remember the Golden Rule: "Do unto others as you would have them do unto you" (Mt 7:12).

This rule points us in a clear direction. Let us treat others with the same passion and compassion with which we want to be treated. Let us seek for others the same possibilities which we seek for ourselves. Let us help others to grow, as we would like to be helped ourselves. In a word, if we want security, let us give security; if we want life, let us give life; if we want opportunities, let us provide opportunities. The yardstick we use for others will be the yardstick which time will use for us. The Golden Rule also reminds us of our responsibility to protect and defend human life at every stage of its development.

This conviction has led me, from the beginning of my ministry, to advocate at different levels for the global abolition of the death penalty. I am convinced that this way is the best, since every life is sacred, every human person is endowed with an inalienable dignity, and society can only benefit from the rehabilitation of those convicted of crimes. Recently, my brother bishops here in the United States renewed their call for the abolition of the death penalty. Not only do I support them, but I also offer encouragement to all those who are convinced that a just and necessary punishment must never exclude the dimension of hope and the goal of rehabilitation.

In these times when social concerns are so important, I cannot fail to mention the servant of God Dorothy Day, who founded the Catholic Worker Movement. Her social activism, her passion for justice and for the cause of the oppressed, were inspired by the Gospel, her faith and the example of the saints.

How much progress has been made in this area in so many parts of the world! How much has been done in these first years of the third millennium to raise people out of extreme poverty! I know that you share my conviction that much more still needs to be done, and that in times of crisis and economic hardship a spirit of global solidarity must not be lost. At the same time I would encourage you to keep in mind all those people around us who are trapped in a cycle of poverty. They too need to be given hope. The fight against poverty and hunger must be fought constantly and on many fronts, especially in its causes. I know that many Americans today, as in the past, are working to deal with this problem.

It goes without saying that part of this great effort is the creation and distribution of wealth. The right use of natural resources, the proper application of technology and the harnessing of the spirit of enterprise are essential elements of an economy which seeks to be modern, inclusive and sustainable. "Business is a noble vocation, directed to producing wealth and improving the world. It can be a fruitful source of prosperity for the area in which it operates, especially if it sees the creation of jobs as an essential part of its service to the common good" (Laudato Si', 129). This common good also includes the Earth, a central theme of the encyclical which I recently wrote in order to "enter into dialogue with all people about our common home" (ibid., 3). "We need a conversation which includes everyone, since the environmental challenge we are undergoing, and its human roots, concern and affect us all" (ibid., 14).

In Laudato Si', I call for a courageous and responsible effort to "redirect our steps" (ibid., 61), and to avert the most serious effects of the environmental deterioration caused by human activity. I am convinced that we can make a difference and I have no doubt that the United States—and this Congress—have an important role to play. Now is the time for courageous actions and strategies, aimed at implementing a "culture of care" (ibid., 231) and "an integrated approach to combating poverty, restoring dignity to the excluded, and at the same time protecting nature" (ibid., 139). "We have the freedom needed to limit and direct technology" (ibid., 112); "to devise intelligent ways of…developing and limiting our power" (ibid., 78); and to put technology "at the service of another type of progress, one which is healthier, more human, more social, more integral" (ibid., 112). In this regard, I am confident that America's outstanding academic and research institutions can make a vital contribution in the years ahead.

A century ago, at the beginning of the Great War, which Pope Benedict XV termed a "pointless slaughter," another notable American was born: the Cistercian monk Thomas Merton. He remains a source of spiritual inspiration and a guide for many people. In his autobiography, he wrote: "I came into the world. Free by nature, in the image of God, I was nevertheless the prisoner of my own violence and my own selfishness, in the image of the world into which I was born. That world was the picture of Hell, full of men like myself, loving God, and yet hating him; born to love him, living instead in fear of hopeless self-contradictory hungers." Merton was above all a man of prayer, a thinker who challenged the certitudes of his time and opened new horizons for souls and for the Church. He was also a man of dialogue, a promoter of peace between peoples and religions.

From this perspective of dialogue, I would like to recognize the efforts made in recent months to help overcome historic differences linked to painful episodes of the past. It is my duty to build bridges and to help all men and women, in any way possible, to do the same. When countries which have been at odds resume the path of dialogue—a dialogue which may have been interrupted for the most legitimate of reasons—new opportunities open up for all. This has required, and requires, courage and daring, which is not the same as irresponsibility. A good political leader is one who, with the interests of all in mind, seizes the moment in a spirit of openness and pragmatism. A good political leader always opts to initiate processes rather than possessing spaces (cf. Evangelii Gaudium, 222–223).

Being at the service of dialogue and peace also means being truly determined to minimize and, in the long term, to end the many armed conflicts throughout our world. Here we have to ask ourselves: Why are deadly weapons being sold to those who plan to inflict untold suffering on individuals and society? Sadly, the answer, as we all know, is simply for money: money that is drenched in blood, often innocent blood. In the face of this shameful and culpable silence, it is our duty to confront the problem and to stop the arms trade.

Three sons and a daughter of this land, four individuals and four dreams: Lincoln, liberty; Martin Luther King, liberty in plurality and non-exclusion; Dorothy Day, social justice and the rights of persons; and Thomas Merton, the capacity for dialogue and openness to God.

I will end my visit to your country in Philadelphia, where I will take part in the World Meeting of Families. It is my wish that throughout my visit the family should be a recurrent theme. How essential the family has been to the building of this country! And how worthy it remains of our support and encouragement! Yet I cannot hide my concern for the family, which is threatened, perhaps as never before, from within and without. Fundamental relationships are being called into question, as is the very basis of marriage and the family. I can only reiterate the importance and, above all, the richness and the beauty of family life.

In particular, I would like to call attention to those family members who are the most vulnerable, the young. For many of them, a future filled with countless possibilities beckons, yet so many others seem disoriented and aimless, trapped in a hopeless maze of violence, abuse and despair. Their problems are our problems. We cannot avoid them. We need to face them together, to talk about them and to seek effective solutions rather than getting bogged down in discussions. At the risk of oversimplifying, we might say that we live in a culture which pressures young people not to start a family, because they lack possibilities for the future. Yet this same culture presents others with so many options that they too are dissuaded from starting a family.

A nation can be considered great when it defends liberty as Lincoln did, when it fosters a culture which enables people to "dream" of full rights for all their brothers and sisters, as Martin Luther King sought to do; when it strives for justice and the cause of the oppressed, as Dorothy Day did by her tireless work, the fruit of a faith which becomes dialogue and sows peace in the contemplative style of Thomas Merton.

In these remarks, I have sought to present some of the richness of your cultural heritage, of the spirit of the American people. It is my desire that this spirit continue to develop and grow, so that as many young people as possible can inherit and dwell in a land which has inspired so many people to dream.

God bless America!

The Need for Minority Bone Marrow Donors[4]

by Julio Gonzalez, The University of Texas, 2016

In the summer of 2015, Gustavo Moreno packed his uniform, his combat boots, and kissed his wife and daughter goodbye. As a soon-to-be member of the U.S. army, he was aware of the dangers he would face overseas; he had no idea his biggest enemy would be lurking inside his own body. At 20 years old, Gustavo was diagnosed with T-cell acute lymphoma, a rare form of cancer that deteriorated his body until it killed him. On July 21st, 2015, the Brooke Army Medical Center revealed Gustavo could have very well been saved with a bone marrow transplant, but it was impossible for him to get one—because he's a Latino. The April 8th, 2015, Institute for Justice explains while white patients have a 93 percent chance of finding a donor, only 33 percent of Latinos, 33 percent of Asians, and 25 percent of African-Americans seeking a donor will never find a match. It's hard to match with a donor in general, but it's basically impossible to find a donor if you're a minority. The National Marrow Donor Program on September 27th, 2015, points out [that] since tissue types are inherited, patients can only match with someone of their own race and ethnicity. Yet this year alone, 20,000 people will be diagnosed with a disease that requires a bone marrow transplant, and among those we will lose at least 1,000 lives of people of color simply because we do not have enough people on a list. This problem exists because of an inherently racist medical industry but persists because all of us, minority or not, are not active. We have the power to change that. So let's look at three reasons for our lack of minority bone marrow donors, and figure out how to solve each one because disease doesn't discriminate but our response to disease does.

Sophia Trujillo loved practicing ballet until she was diagnosed with aplastic anemia and the six-year-old Filipina watched her body shut down. The September 13th, 2015, Chicago Tribune reports a bone marrow transplant could keep her alive and in time, back in ballet, but there are no donors for her. To understand why, let's look to the first cause: complete lack of information, and then provide a solution.

Minority donors are dangerously low in number simply because of a complete lack of information across the board. We don't know about the lack of donors unless it directly affects us; we don't know why minorities are affected so greatly; and we don't know how registering could help. An April 25th, 2015, Atlantic article calls this information gap out for what it is—White privilege. Because poverty plagues communities of color, minorities are less likely to have access to healthcare, which means they have a limited access to understanding how serious issues like these are. It's really hard to think about being a bone marrow donor, when you don't even know it's a problem, especially not over things you do know are problems, like being able to feed your kids.

The origin of this issue is systematic, but individual action is the best way of bringing information to minorities directly. I've taken the first step by designing a model for how to raise awareness in my community. In this folder, I've compiled all the necessary information, from statistics, to the registration process, to the donation process and everything in between. On this handout I've included a link to an electronic version of this folder. Please download it, and pass it along to areas in your community where minorities have guaranteed access—Planned Parenthood, Boys and Girls Club, low-income school districts. When a system fails to educate minorities on a deadly issue like this, it's up to us to take the initiative to help bridge this inequality.

It's been two years since Dorothy's diagnosis, and still chances of finding a donor seem impossible. On October 2nd, 2015, Diane Thompson, professor of physical medicine at Columbia University explained that while patients in need are racially diverse, target donors aren't. For women of African descent like Dorothy, this is a matter of life and death. Let's understand our next cause—ineffective organizational strategy, and then eradicate the problem.

Organizations like Be the Match and the Love Hope Strength Foundation are trying to increase outreach but their strategies are ineffective. LHS prides itself on hosting drives at concerts and music festivals, where audiences are comprised of affluent, mostly white crowds. Be the Match primarily targets college students, which makes sense because they're the ideal age for donating, but it neglects what the May 26th, 2015, Pew Research Center reveals: colleges are still overwhelmingly white. Ultimately we're reminded these spaces weren't built for us, so even if we are well informed about the issue, large populations of minorities don't have access to register.

In order to make the registration process more accessible, we have to modify the way we do outreach. I've become an ambassador for the Love Hope Strength Foundation, which allows me to advocate in school presentations, speech tournaments, anywhere I go. Most importantly, it allows me to host bone marrow drives where minorities are. When I called the organization they offered to host a bone marrow drive in a location of my choosing, including supplies and volunteers free of charge. You can do the same by following the information I've included on these handouts. We need to bring the registration process closer to home in cheaper, more accessible places. Diane Thompson argues if you truly believe Black Lives like Dorothy Brown's matter, this is the way to show it.

As a mother of three suffering from Leukemia, Adriana Vidals desperately needs a bone marrow donor. She told Fox News on September 27th, 2015, "I can deal with the chemotherapy. I can't deal with being without my children." To understand how Adriana's condition goes ignored, let's explore our final cause: we're terrified of donation, and figure out how to overcome our fears.

First, no matter how accessible the registration process is, or what information is provided, there are too many people who will walk by a bone marrow drive without giving it a second thought because we're scared. In a personal interview on December 2nd, 2015, Oncologist Katie Poppert notes as a general public, we're hesitant to register because we don't want to get matched. We fear the process will be painful. This hesitance is then magnified when minorities are the subject because once we learn minority donors are scarce, we realize our chances of being a match, and having to donate are that much higher. It's easier to prioritize ourselves and our fears over people we don't even know—like Gustavo, Sophia, Dorothy, Adriana, and the thousands of people who lie awake at night praying that someone like you will help keep them alive.

We need to get learn how to prioritize someone else's life over our inconvenience. In a personal interview on January 14, 2015, Love Hope Strength Coordinator Alvaro Iragorri clarifies [that] thanks to recent advancements, donating marrow is a simple 10 minute procedure no more complicated than donating blood, and no more painful than a being sore after a workout. All medical expenses are covered by the organization and in some instances you may receive compensation. I've become certified to register donors myself. Here are some swabs. Let me register you right here, right now, or at any point this week. In these handouts are information on how to become certified yourself, so you can absolutely help even if you are not a minority yourself. There is a real life person with a name and a face who needs you and only you. Will it hurt? Maybe a little. But you'll survive. They won't.

Even after his passing, Gustavo's family continues to host bone marrow drives in their community because they know how crucial one single match can be. Today we've explored three individual causes to the lack of minority bone marrow donors but at the end of the day this is an issue you can help solve in a simple and practical way. It literally takes two seconds to swab your cheeks. It's a lot harder to say no when you realize what you're really saying no to is the chance for that one person to live.

Endnotes

Chapter 1

1. "Speaking about the TED Effect," CBS News. 7 February 2016.
2. Judy C. Pearson, Jeffrey T. Child, and David H. Kahl, Jr., "Preparation Meeting Opportunity: How Do College Students Prepare for Public Speeches?" *Communication Quarterly* 54, no. 3 (Aug. 2006), p. 351.
3. Pearson, Child, and Kahl, "Preparation Meeting Opportunity," p. 355.
4. "Speaking about the TED Effect."
5. Kimo A. Yuh, Cassie Constantini, and Sarah Billingsley, "The Effect of Taking a Public Speaking Class on One's Writing Abilities." *Communication Research Reports* 29, no. 4 (2012), pp. 285–291.
6. James C. Humes, *The Sir Winston Method: Five Secrets of Speaking the Language of Leadership* (New York: Morrow, 1991), pp. 13–14.
7. Charles Schwab, as quoted in Brent Filson, *Executive Speeches: Tips on How to Write and Deliver Speeches from 51 CEOs* (New York: Wiley, 1994), p. 45.
8. Value investors portal. "Warren Buffet on Communication Skills." *YouTube.* 6 December 2010. http://www.youtube.com/watch?v=tpgcEYpLzP0 Accessed May 14, 2013.
9. Sherwyn P. Morreale and Judy C. Pearson, "Why Communication Education Is Important: The Centrality of the Discipline in the 21st Century." *Communication Education* 57, no. 2 (2008, April), pp. 224–240; also see: Sherwyn P. Morreale, Michael M. Osborn, and Judy C. Pearson. "Why Communication Is Important: A Rationale for the Centrality of the Study of Communication." *Journal of the Association for Communication Administration* 29 (2000), pp. 1–25; also see: Blake J. Neff, "Preachers, Politicians and People of Character: A Rationale for the Centrality of a Public-Speaking Course in the core Curriculum." *Journal of the Association for Communication Administration* 32 (2013), pp. 46–53.
10. Dee-Ann Durbin, "Study: Plenty of Jobs for Graduates in 2000," *Austin American-Statesman*, Dec. 5, 1999), p. A28.
11. Iain Hay, "Justifying and Applying Oral Presentations in Geographical Education." *Journal of Geography in Higher Education* 18 no. 1 (1994), pp. 44–45; also see: Morreale and Pearson, "Why Communication Education Is Important."
12. L. M. Boyd, syndicated column, *Austin American-Statesman* (8 Aug. 2000), p. E3.
13. Herman Cohen, *The History of Speech Communication: The Emergence of a Discipline: 1914–1945* (Annandale, VA: Speech Communication Association, 1994), p. 2; for a discussion of the history of public speaking see, J. Michael Sproule, "Inventing Public Speaking: Rhetoric and the Speech Book, 1730–1930," *Rhetoric & Public Affairs* 15 (2012), pp. 563–608; W. Keith and C. Lundberg, "Creating A History for Public Speaking Instruction," *Rhetoric and Public Affairs* 17 (2014), pp. 139–146.
14. Barack Obama, "Remarks by the President at Sandy Hook Interfaith Prayer Vigil," *The White House Briefing Room*, Dec 16, 2012. www.whitehouse.gov/the-press-office/2012/12/16/remarks-president-sandy-hook-interfaith-prayer-vigil.
15. Survey conducted by R. H. Bruskin and Associates, *Spectra* 9 (Dec. 1973), p. 4; D. Wallechinsky, Irving Wallace, and Amy Wallace, *The People's Almanac Presents the Book of Lists* (New York: Morrow, 1977).
16. Karen K. Dwyer and Marlin M. Davidson, "Is Public Speaking Really More Feared Than Death?" *Communication Research Reports* 29, no. 2 (April–June 2012), pp. 99–107.
17. Steven Booth Butterfield, "Instructional Interventions for Reducing Situational Anxiety and Avoidance," *Communication Education* 37 (1988), pp. 214–223; also see Michael Motley, *Overcoming Your Fear of Public Speaking: A Proven Method* (New York: McGraw-Hill, 1995).
18. Joe Ayres and Theodore S. Hopf, "The Long-Term Effect of Visualization in the Classroom: A Brief Research Report." *Communication Education* 39 (1990), pp. 75–78.
19. John Burk, "Communication Apprehension among Masters of Business Administration Students: Investigating a Gap in Communication Education." *Communication Education* 50 (Jan. 2001), pp. 51–58; Lynne Kelly and James A. Keaten, "Treating Communication Anxiety: Implications of the Communibiological Paradigm." *Communication Education* 49 (Jan. 2000), pp. 45–57; Amber N. Finn, Chris R. Sawyer, and Ralph R. Behnke, "Audience-Perceived Anxiety Patterns of Public Speakers." *Communication Education* 51 (Fall 2003), pp. 470–481.
20. Judy C. Pearson, Lori DeWitt, Jeffery T. Child, David H. Kahl, and Vijay Dandamudi, "Facing the Fear: An Analysis of Speech-Anxiety Content in Public-Speaking Textbooks." *Communication Research Reports* 24 (2007), pp. 159–168; G. D. Bodie, "A Racing Heart, Rattling Knees, and Ruminative Thoughts: Defining and Explaining Public Speaking Anxiety."

Communication Education 59 (2010), pp. 70–105; also see, Kaitlin H. White, Matt C. Howard, Bu Zhong, José A. Soto, Christopher R. Perez, Elizabeth A. Lee, Nana A. Dawson-Andoh and Mark R. Minnick, "The Communication Anxiety Regulation Scale: Development and Initial Validation." *Communication Quarterly* 63 (2015), pp. 23–43.

21. Kay B. Harris, Chris R. Sawyer, and Ralph R. Behnke, "Predicting Speech State Anxiety from Trait Anxiety, Reactivity, and Situational Influences." *Communication Quarterly* 54 (2006), pp. 213–226; Michael J. Beatty, Alan D. Heisel, Robert J. Lewis, Michelle E. Pence, Amber Reinhart, and Yan Tian, "Communication Apprehension and Resting Alpha Range Asymmetry in the Anterior Cortex." *Communication Education* 60, no. 4 (2011), pp. 441–460.

22. Amy M. Bippus and John A. Daly, "What Do People Think Causes Stage Fright? Naïve Attributions About the Reasons for Public-Speaking Anxiety." *Communication Education* 48 (1999), pp. 63–72.

23. Yang Lin and Andrew S. Rancer, "Sex Differences in Intercultural Communication Apprehension, Ethnocentrism, and Intercultural Willingness to Communicate." *Psychological Reports* 92 (2003), pp. 195–200.

24. S. Shimotsu and T. P. Mottet, "The Relationships Among Perfectionism, Communication Apprehension, and Temperament," *Communication Research Reports* 26, no. 3 (2009), pp. 188–197.

25. Bodie, "A Racing Heart, Rattling Knees, and Ruminative Thoughts: Defining, Explaining, and Treating Public Speaking Anxiety."

26. Amber N. Finn, Chris R. Sawyer, and Paul Schrodt, "Examining the Effect of Exposure Therapy on Public Speaking State Anxiety." *Communication Education* 58 (2009), pp. 92–109.

27. Michael J. Beatty, James C. McCroskey, and Alan D. Heisel, "Communication Apprehension as Temperamental Expression: A Communibiological Paradigm." *Communication Monographs* 65 (1998), pp. 197–219; Michael J. Beatty and Kristin Marie Valencic, "Context-Based Apprehension Versus Planning Demands: A Communibiological Analysis of Anticipatory Public Speaking Anxiety." *Communication Education* 49 (Jan. 2000), pp. 58–71; Valerie A. MacIntyre, Peter D. MacIntyre, and Gefoff Carre, "Heart Rate as a Predictor of Speaking Anxiety." *Communication Research Reports*, 27, no. 4 (2010), pp. 286–297; Michael J. Beatty, Alan D. Heisel, Robert J. Lewis, Michelle E. Pence, Amber Reinhart, and Yan Tian, "Communication Apprehension and Resting Alpha Range Asymmetry in the Anterior Cortex." *Communication Education* 60, no. 4 (2011), pp. 441–460.

28. Kay B. Harris, Chris R. Sawyer, and Ralph R. Behnke, "Predicting Speech State Anxiety from Trait Anxiety, Reactivity, and Situational Influences," *Communication Quarterly* 54 (May 2006), pp. 213–226.

29. Kelly and Keaten, "Treating Communication Anxiety."

30. Maili Porhola, "Orientation Styles in a Public-Speaking Context." Paper presented at the National Communication Association convention, Seattle, Washington, Nov. 2000; Ralph R. Behnke and Michael J. Beatty, "A Cognitive-Physiological Model of Speech Anxiety," *Communication Monographs* 48 (1981), pp. 158–163.

31. Shannon C. McCullough, Shelly G. Russell, Ralph R. Behnke, Chris R. Sawyer, and Paul L. Witt, "Anticipatory Public Speaking State Anxiety as a Function of Body Sensations and State of Mind." *Communication Quarterly* 54 (2006), pp. 101–109.

32. Ralph R. Behnke and Chris R. Sawyer, "Public Speaking Anxiety as a Function of Sensitization and Habituation Processes." *Communication Research Reports* 53 (Apr. 2004), pp. 164–173.

33. Paul L. Witt and Ralph R. Behnke, "Anticipatory Speech Anxiety as a Function of Public Speaking Assignment Type," *Communication Education* 55 (2006), pp. 167–177.

34. Beatty, et al., "Communication Apprehension and Resting Alpha Range Asymmetry in the Anterior Cortex."

35. Leon Fletcher, *How to Design and Deliver Speeches* (New York: Longman, 2001), p. 3.

36. Research suggests that because public-speaking anxiety is complex (both a trait and a state), with multiple and idiosyncratic causes, using a combination of intervention strategies may be best in attempting to manage communication apprehension. See Bodie, "A Racing Heart, Rattling Knees, and Ruminative Thoughts."

37. Desiree C. Duff, Timothy R. Levine, Michael J. Beatty, Jessica Woolbright, and Hee Sun Park, "Testing Public Anxiety Treatments Against a Credible Placebo Control." *Communication Education* 56 (2007), pp. 72–88.

38. Peter D. MacIntyre and J. Renee MacDonald, "Public-Speaking Anxiety: Perceived Competence and Audience Congeniality." *Communication Education* 47 (Oct. 1998), pp. 359–365.

39. Ralph R. Behnke and Chris R. Sawyer, "Public-Speaking Procrastination as a Correlate of Public-Speaking Communication Apprehension and Self-Perceived Public-Speaking Competence." *Communication Research Reports* 16 (1999), pp. 40–47.

40. Quoted by Petula Dovrak, "Channeling the Grief," *Austin American-Statesman* (14 Oct., 2009), p. A9.

41. Dovrak, "Channeling the Grief."

42. Joe Ayres, Terry Schliesman, and Debbie Ayres Sonandre, "Practice Makes Perfect but Does It Help Reduce Communication Apprehension?" *Communication Research Reports* 15 (Spring 1998), pp. 170–179.

43. Melanie Booth-Butterfield, "Stifle or Stimulate? The Effects of Communication Task Structure on Apprehensive and Non-Apprehensive Students." *Communication Education* 35 (1986), pp. 337–348; Charles R. Berger, "Speechlessness: Causal Attributions, Emotional Features, and Social Consequences." *Journal of Language & Social Psychology* 23 (June 2004), pp. 147–179.

44. Joe Ayres, Tim Hopf, and Elizabeth Peterson, "A Test of Communication-Orientation Motivation (COM) Therapy." *Communication Reports* 13 (Winter 2000), pp. 35–44; Joe Ayres and Tanichya K. Wongprasert, "Measuring the Impact of Visualization on Mental Imagery: Comparing Prepared Versus Original Drawings." *Communication Research Reports* 20 (Winter 2003), pp. 45–53.

45. Joe Ayers and Theodore S. Hopf, "Visualization: A Means of Reducing Speech Anxiety." *Communication Education* 34 (1985), pp. 318–323. Although researchers have found evidence that visualization is helpful, some question whether visualization techniques work better than just gaining experience in public speaking. Critics of systematic desensitization argue that there may be a placebo effect: Just thinking that a treatment will reduce apprehension may contribute to reduced apprehension. See Duff, Levine, Beatty, Woolbright, and Park, "Testing Public Anxiety Treatments Against a Credible Placebo Control."

46. Ayres and Wongprasert, "Measuring the Impact of Visualization on Mental Imagery."

47. Ayres and Wongprasert, "Measuring the Impact of Visualization on Mental Imagery."

48. Joe Ayres and Debbie M. Ayres Sonandre, "Performance Visualization: Does the Nature of the Speech Model Matter?" *Communication Research Reports* 20 (Summer 2003), pp. 260–268.

49. Duff, Levine, Beatty, Woolbright, and Park, "Testing Public Anxiety Treatments Against a Credible Placebo Control."

50. Joe Ayres and Brian L. Heuett, "An Examination of the Impact of Performance Visualization." *Communication Research Reports* 16 (1999), pp. 29–39.

51. Stephen R. Covey, *The 7 Habits of Highly Successful People* (New York: Simon and Schuster, 1989).

52. Penny Addison, Ele Clay, Shuang Xie, Chris R. Sawyer, and Ralph R. Behnke, "Worry as a Function of Public Speaking State Anxiety Type." *Communication Reports* 16 (Summer 2003), pp. 125–131.

53. Chad Edwards and Suzanne Walker, "Using Public Speaking Learning Communities to Reduce Communication Apprehension." *Texas Speech Communication Journal* 32 (2007), pp. 65–71; also see Chia-Fang (Sandy) Hsu, "The Relationship of Trait Anxiety, Audience Nonverbal Feedback, and Attributions to Public Speaking State Anxiety." *Communication Research Reports* 26, no. 3 (August 2009), pp. 237–246.

54. Diane Honour, "Speech Performance Anxiety for Non-Native Speakers." *The Florida Communication Journal* 36 (2007), pp. 57–66.

55. Finn, Sawyer, and Schrodt, "Examining the Effect of Exposure Therapy on Public Speaking State Anxiety."

56. Lisa M. Schroeder, "The Effects of Skills Training on Communication Satisfaction and Communication Anxiety in the Basic Speech Course." *Communication Research Reports* 19 (2002), pp. 380–388; Alain Morin, "History of Exposure to Audiences as a Developmental Antecedent of Public Self-Consciousness." *Current Research in Social Psychology* 5 (Mar. 2000), pp. 33–46.

57. Karla M. Hunter, Joshua N. Westwick, and Laurie L. Haleta, "Assessing Success: The Impacts of a Fundamentals of Speech Course on Decreasing Public Speaking Anxiety." *Communication Education* 63, no. 2 (2014), pp. 124–135; MacIntyre and MacDonald, "Public-Speaking Anxiety"; Peter D. MacIntyre and K. A. Thivierge, "The Effects of Audience Pleasantness, Audience Familiarity, and Speaking Contexts on Public-Speaking Anxiety and Willingness to Speak." *Communication Quarterly* 43 (1995), pp. 456–466; Peter D. MacIntyre, K. A. Thivierge, and J. Renee MacDonald, "The Effects of Audience Interest, Responsiveness, and Evaluation on Public-Speaking Anxiety and Related Variables." *Communication Research Reports* 14 (1997), pp. 157–168.

58. MacIntyre and MacDonald, "Public-Speaking Anxiety"; Rebecca B. Rubin, Alan M. Rubin, and Felecia F. Jordan, "Effects of Instruction on Communication Apprehension and Communication Competence." *Communication Education* 46 (1997), pp. 104–114.

59. Georgeta M. Hodis, Nilanjana R. Bardhan, and Flavia A. Hodis, "Patterns of Change in Willingness to Communicate in Public Speaking Contexts: A Latent Growth Modeling Analysis." *Journal of Applied Communication Research* 38, no. 3 (2010), pp. 248–267.

Chapter 2

1. The late Waldo Braden, long-time professor of speech communication at Louisiana State University, presented a memorable speech at the 1982 meeting of the Florida Speech Communication Association in which he emphasized "The audience writes the speech" to indicate the importance and centrality of being an audience-centered speaker.

2. Judy C. Pearson, Jeffrey T. Child, and David H. Kahl, Jr., "Preparation Meeting Opportunity: How Do

College Students Prepare for Public Speeches?" *Communication Quarterly*, 54, no. 3 (Aug. 2006), pp. 351–366.

3. Clifford Stoll, as cited in Kevin A. Miller, "Capture: The Essential Survival Skill for Leaders Buckling Under Information Overload," *Leadership* (Spring 1992), p. 85.

4. Don Hewitt, interview broadcast on *60 Minutes*, 24 Jan. 2010.

5. Greg Winter, "The Chips Are Down: Frito-Lay Cuts Costs with Smaller Servings," *Austin American-Statesman* 2 Jan. 2001, p. A6.

6. These statistics are from an Allstate Insurance advertisement, *The New York Times* 17 Feb. 2010, p. A24.

7. We thank Barbara Patton of Texas State University for sharing her speech outline with us.

8. Pearson, Child, and Kahl, "Preparation Meeting Opportunity."

9. Grace Hildenbrand, "Cinderella," Texas State University student speech, 2013.

Chapter 3

1. Mark Schierbecker, "Clash Between Media and ConcernedStudent1950," video in article by Austin Huguelet and Daniel Victor, "'I Need Some Muscle': Missouri Activists Block Journalists," nytimes.com 10 Nov. 2015.

2. National Communication Association, "NCA Credo for Communication Ethics," 1999. 27 June 2001.

3. "Obama Counter-Terrorism Speech Interrupted by Heckler," UPI.com. 23 May 2013.

4. Samuel Walker, *Hate Speech* (Lincoln: U of Nebraska P, 1994), p. 162.

5. "Libel and Slander," *The Ethical Spectacle*. 1 June 1997.

6. Donald Downs, John Sharpless, and Mary Anderson, "University of Wisconsin Directive Devalues Free Speech on Campus," *WiscNews.com*. 30 Nov. 2015.

7. James S. Tyre, "Legal Definition of Obscenity, Pornography." 1 June 1997.

8. "Supreme Court Rules: Cyberspace Will Be Free! ACLU Hails Victory in Internet Censorship Challenge." *American Civil Liberties Union Freedom Network*. 26 June 1997.

9. Sue Anne Pressley, "Oprah Winfrey Wins Case Filed by Cattlemen," *Washington Post* 27 Feb. 1998.

10. Brian Schweitzer, "Proclamation of Clemency for Montanans Convicted under the Montana Sedition Act in 1918–1919." 3 May 2006. (Thanks to George Moss, Vaughn College, Flushing, NY, for providing the authors with a copy of this document.)

11. "Facebook 'Like' Button Is Free Speech Right: US Court." *Yahoo News*. 19 Sept. 2013.

12. Bill Carter and Felicity Barringer, "Patriotic Time, Dissent Muted," *The New York Times* 28 Sept. 2001, p. A1.

13. Ian McEwan, "Freedom of Expression Sustains All the Other Freedoms We Enjoy." *Vital Speeches of the Day* (Aug. 2015), p. 247.

14. Dorreen Carvajal and Alan Cowell, "French Rein in Speech Backing Acts of Terror," *The New York Times* 16 January 2005, p. A12.

15. Walker, *Hate Speech*, p. 2.

16. Daniel Downs and Gloria Cowan, "Predicting the Importance of Freedom of Speech and the Perceived Harm of Hate Speech." *Journal of Applied Social Psychology* 42, no. 6 (June 2012), p. 1372.

17. Edwin R. Bayley, *Joe McCarthy and the Press* (Madison: Wisconsin UP, 1981), p. 29.

18. Chidsey Dickson, "Re: question." Online posting. 27 Oct. 2005. WPA Listserv.

19. "Spurlock Sorry for Speech." *Austin American-Statesman* (29 Mar. 2006), p. A2.

20. Kathy Fitzpatrick, "U.S. Public Diplomacy." *Vital Speeches of the Day* (April 2004), pp. 412–417.

21. *Publication Manual of the American Psychological Association*, 6th ed. (Washington, DC: American Psychological Association, 2010), p. 16.

22. Scott Jaschik, "Graduation Shame." *Insidehighered.com*. 22 Apr. 2010.

23. Michele Eodice, "Plagiarism, Pedagogy, and Controversy: A Conversation with Rebecca Moore Howard." *Issues in Writing* 13, no. 1 (Fall/Winter 2002).

24. "75 to 98 Percent of College Students Have Cheated," *Education-portal.com*. 29 June 2011.

25. www.non-plagiarized-termpapers.com.

26. Todd Holm, "Public Speaking Students' Perceptions of Cheating." *Communication Research Reports* (Winter 2002), p. 70.

27. "FAQ: Legal Punishments," plagiarism.org. 2014.

28. Jeff Langan, "Student Slapped with Plagiarism Fine." *nbcconnecticut.com*. 11 March 2010.

29. Jonathan Martin, "Plagiarism Costs Degree for Senator John Walsh." *nytimes.com*. 10 Oct. 2014.

30. Waldo W. Braden, *Abraham Lincoln, Public Speaker* (Baton Rouge: Louisiana State UP, 1988), p. 90.

Chapter 4

1. Study conducted by Paul Cameron, as cited in Ronald B. Adler and Neil Town, *Looking Out/Looking In: Interpersonal Communications* (New York: Holt, Rinehart and Winston, 1981), p. 218.

2. G. D. Bodie, K. St. Cyr, M. Pence, M. Rold, and J. Honeycutt, "Listening Competence in Initial Interactions I: Distinguishing Between What Listening Is and What Listeners Do," *The Intl. Journal of Listening* 26 (2012), pp. 1–28.

3. B. R. Brunner, "Listening, Communication & Trust: Practitioners' Perspectives of Business/Organizational Relationships," *The International Journal of Listening* 22 (2008), pp. 123–132; S. A. Welch and W. T. Mickelson, "A Listening Competence Comparison of

Working Professionals," *International Journal of Listening* 27, no. 2 (2013), pp. 85–99; M. W. Purdy and L. M. Manning, "Listening in the Multicultural Workplace: A Dialogue of Theory and Practice," *International Journal of Listening* 29 (2015), pp. 1–11; D. W. Srader, "Performative Listening," *International Journal of Listening* 29, no. 2 (2015), pp. 95–102

4. See: L. A. Janusik, "Listening Pedagogy: Where Do We go From Here?" in A. Wolvin (ed.), *Listening and Human Communication in the 21st Century.* (West Sussex: Blackwell, 2010), p. 193; A. N. Kluger and K. Zaidel, "Are Listeners Perceived as Leaders?," *International Journal of Listening* 27, no. 2 (2013), pp. 73–84

5. Paul Rankin, "Listening Ability: Its Importance, Measurement and Development," *Chicago Schools Journal* 12 (Jan. 1930), pp. 177–179.

6. R. Emmanuel, J. Adams, K. Baker, E. K. Daufin, C. Ellington, F. Fits, J. Himsel, L. Holladay, and David Okeowo, "How College Students Spend Their Time Communicating," *International Journal of Listening* 22 (2008), pp. 13–28.

7. L. Boyd, Syndicated column, *Austin American-Statesman* 7 Dec. 1995, p. E7.

8. John T. Masterson, Steven A. Beebe, and Norman H. Watson, *Invitation to Effective Speech Communication* (Glenview, IL: Scott, Foresman, 1989), p. 4.

9. Laura Ann Janusik, "Building Listening Theory: The Validation of the Conversational Listening Span," *Communication Studies* 58, no. 2 (2007), pp. 139–156.

10. Frank E. X. Dance, *Speaking Your Mind: Private Thinking and Public Speaking* (Dubuque, IA: Kendall/Hunt, 1994).

11. A. K. Przybylski and N. Weinstein, "Can you connect with me now? How the presence of mobile communication technology influences face-to-face conversation quality," *Journal of Social and Personal Relationships* 30, no. 3 (2012), pp. 237–246.

12. Ralph G. Nichols and Leonard A. Stevens, "Six Bad Listening Habits," in *Are You Listening?* (New York: McGraw-Hill, 1957).

13. Albert Mehrabian, *Nonverbal Communication* (Hawthorne, NY: Aldine, 1972); also see: M. Imhof, "Listening to Voices and Judging People," *The Intl. Journal of Listening* 24 (2010), pp. 19–33.

14. Paul Ekman and Wallace Friesen, "Head and Body Cues in the Judgement of Emotion: A Reformulation," *Perceptual and Motor Skills* 25 (1967), pp. 711–724.

15. K. K. Halone and L. L. Pecchioni, "Relational Listening: A Grounded Theoretical Model," *Communication Reports* 14 (2001), pp. 59–71.

16. Halone and Pecchioni, "Relational Listening."

17. Nichols and Stevens, "Six Bad Listening Habits."

18. Kitty W. Watson, Larry L. Barker, and James B. Weaver, *The Listener Style Inventory* (New Orleans: LA SPECTRA, 1995).

19. G. D. Bodie, D. L. Worthington, and C. C. Gearhart, "The Listening Styles Profile-Revised (LSP-R): A Scale Revision and Evidence for Validity," *Communication Quarterly* 16 (2013), pp. 72–90; S. L. Sargent and James B. Weaver, "Correlates Between Communication Apprehension and Listening Style Preferences," *Communication Research Reports* 14 (1997), pp. 74–78.

20. See Larry L. Barker and Kitty W. Watson, *Listen Up* (New York: St. Martin's Press, 2000); also see M. Imhof, "Who Are We as We Listen? Individual Listening Profiles in Varying Contexts," *International Journal of Listening* 18 (2004), pp. 36–45.

21. G. D. Bodie, J. P. Denham, and C. C. Gearhart, "Listening as a Goal-Directed Activity," *Western Journal of Communication* 78, no. 5 (2014), pp. 668–684.

22. Sargent and Weaver, "Correlates Between Communication Apprehension and Listening Style Preference."

23. D. L. Worthington, "Exploring the Relationship Between Listening Style Preferences and Personality," *International Journal of Listening* 17 (2003), pp. 68–87.

24. M. D. Kirtley and J. M. Honeycutt, "Listening Styles and Their Correspondence with Second Guessing," *Communication Research Reports* 13 (1996), pp. 174–182.

25. Bodie, Denham and Gearhart, "Listening as a Goal-Directed Activity."

26. For research about the effectiveness of active listening see: H. Weger Jr., G. C. Bell, E. M. Minel, and M. C. Robinson, "The Relative Effectiveness of Active Listening in Initial Interactions," *International Journal of Listening* 28, no. 1 (2014), pp. 13–31.

27. Harold Barrett, *Rhetoric and Civility: Human Development, Narcissism, and the Good Audience* (Albany: SUNY, 1991), p. 154.

28. Chad Edwards and Suzanne Walker, "Using Public Speaking Learning Communities to Reduce Communication Apprehension," *Texas Speech Communication Journal* 32 (2007), pp. 65–71.

29. Cited in Marie Hochmuth, ed., *A History and Criticism of American Public Address*, Vol. 3 (New York: Longmans, Green, 1955), 4; and in James R. Andrews, *The Practice of Rhetorical Criticism* (New York: Macmillan, 1983), pp. 3–4.

30. Mike Allen, Sandra Berkowitz, Steve Hunt, and Allan Louden, "A Meta-Analysis of the Impact of Forensics and Communication Education on Critical Thinking," *Communication Education* 48 (Jan. 1999), pp. 18–30.

31. For a comprehensive list of definitions of rhetoric, see Patricia Bizzell and Bruce Herzberg, eds., *The Rhetorical Tradition: Readings from Classical Times to the Present* (Boston: Bedford, 1990).

32. Aristotle, *On Rhetoric.* Translated by George A. Kennedy (New York: Oxford University Press, 1991), p. 14.

33. Kenneth Burke, *A Rhetoric of Motives* (Berkeley: University of California Press, 1950). Also see Barry Brummett, *Reading Rhetorical Theory* (Fort Worth, TX: Harcourt College Publishers, 2000), p. 741.

34. Andrews, *The Practice of Rhetorical Criticism*; for a discussion of a review of assessing public speaking competence see: L. M. Schreiber, G. D. Paul, and L. R. Shibley, "The Development and Test of the Public Speaking Competence Rubric," *Communication Education* 61, no. 3 (2012), pp. 205–233.

35. Robert Rowland, *Analyzing Rhetoric: A Handbook for the Informed Citizen in a New Millennium* (Dubuque, IA: Kendall/Hunt, 2002), pp. 17–28.

36. For research about the importance of assessing public speaking competence see: L. M. Schreiber, et al., "The Development and Test of the Public Speaking Competence Rubric."

37. L. LeFebvre, L. LeFebvre, K. Blackburn, and R. Boyd, "Student Estimates of Public Speaking Competency: The Meaning Extraction Helper and Video Self-evaluation," *Communication Education* 64, no. 3 (2015), pp. 261–279.

Chapter 5

1. Robert H. Farrell, ed., *Off the Record: The Private Papers of Harry S Truman* (New York: Harper & Row, 1980), p. 310.

2. For background information about this quotation see http://answers.google.com/answers/threadview?id=398104.

3. N. Howe and W. Strauss, *Millennials Rising: The Next Great Generation* (New York: Vintage, 2000). Also see Hank Karp, Connie Fuller, and Danilo Sirias, *Bridging the Boomer–Xer Gap: Creating Authentic Teams for High Performance at Work* (Palo Alto, CA: Davies-Black, 2002); J. Anderson and L. Rainie, "Millennials will benefit and suffer due to their hyperconnected lives," *The Pew Research Center's Internet and American Life Project* (2012), pp. 1–36; B. Horovits, "After Gen X, Millennials, what shuld next generation be? *USA Today*, May 4, 2012, p. 1; A. Williams, "Move Over, Millennnials, Here Comes Generation Z, *The New York Times*, December 16, 2015, p. 1; G. Leopold, "Traveling Beyond Millennials: Get Ready for Generation Z," *Engage: Teens* www.mediapost.com/publications/article/262451 accessed February 5, 2016.

4. For an excellent review of gender and persuasibility research see Daniel J. O'Keefe, *Persuasion: Theory and Research* (Newbury Park, CA: Sage, 1990), pp. 176–177. Also see James B. Stiff, *Persuasive Communication* (New York: Guilford Press, 1994), pp. 133–136.

5. O'Keefe, *Persuasion*.

6. Gregory Herek, "Study Offers 'Snapshot' of Sacramento-Area Lesbian, Gay, and Bisexual Community." 23 July 2001 <psc.dss.ucdavis.edu/rainbow/html/sacramento_study.html>. For an excellent literature review about sexual orientation and communication, see T. P. Mottet, "The Role of Sexual Orientation in Predicting Outcome Value and Anticipated Communication Behaviors," *Communication Quarterly* 48 (2000), pp. 233–239.

7. *Random House Webster's Unabridged Dictionary* (New York: Random House, 1998), p. 1590.

8. See R. Lewontin, "The Apportionment of Human Diversity," *Evolutionary Biology* 6 (1973), pp. 381–397; H. A. Yee, H. H. Fairchild, F. Weizmann, and E. G. Wyatt, "Addressing Psychology's Problems with Race," *American Psychologist* 48 (1994), pp. 1132–1140; D. Matsumoto and L. Juang, *Culture and Psychology* (Belmont, CA: Wadsworth/Thompson, 2004), p. 16.

9. Intercultural communication apprehension is reduced when communicators are focused on the listener or audience. L. T. Fall, S. Kelly, P. MacDonald, C. Primm, and W. Holmes, "Intercultural Communication Apprehension and Emotional Intelligence in Higher Education: Preparing Business Students for Career Services," *Business Communication Quarterly* 76, no. 4 (2013), pp. 412–426.

10. The research summarized here is based on pioneering work by Geert Hofstede, *Culture's Consequences: International Differences in Work-Related Values* (Beverly Hills, CA: Sage, 1984). Also see Edward T. Hall, *Beyond Culture* (New York: Doubleday, 1976); G. Hofstede, "Dimensionalizing Cultures: The Hofstede Model in Context," *Online Readings in Psychology and Culture* 2 (2011), pp. 3–40; The Hofsteade Center, "What About the U.S.A.?" geert-hofstede.com/united-states.html (accessed February 6, 2016).

11. The Hofsteade Center, "What About the U.S.A.?"

12. The Hofsteade Center, "What About the U.S.A.?"

13. The Hofsteade Center, "What About the U.S.A.?"

14. Richard Perez-Pena, "U.S. Bachelor Degree Rate Passes Milestone," *The New York Times*, 23 February 12 <www.nytimes.com/2012/02/24/education/census-finds-bachelors-degrees-at-record-level.html?_r=0>.

15. United States Census Bureau, <www.census.gov/hewsroom/releases/archives/population/cb12-243.html>.

16. David W. Kale, "Ethics in Intercultural Communication," *Intercultural Communication: A Reader,* 6th ed., eds. Larry A. Samovar and Richard E. Porter (Belmont, CA: Cengage, 2012), p. 423; also see discussion in M. Lustig and J. Koester, *Intercultural Competence.* (Belmont, CA: Cengage, 2012).

17. Larry A. Samovar and Richard E. Porter, *Communication Between Cultures.* (Stamford, CT: Cengage, 2012), p. 29.

18. Matthew Fagan, "Public-Speaking Anxiety," Texas State University, 2015.

19. Joseph P. Mazer and Scott Titsworth, "Passion and Preparation in the Basic Course: The Influence of Students' Ego-Involvement with Speech Topics and Preparation Time on Public Speaking Grades," *Communication Teacher* 26, no. 4 (October 2012), pp. 236–251.

20. Sweets, "Mark Twain in India," *The Fence Painter: Bulletin of the Mark Twain Boyhood Home Associates* 26 (Winter 1996), p. 1.
21. For an excellent discussion of how to adapt to specific audience situations, see Jo Sprague and Douglas Stuart, *The Speaker's Handbook* (Belmont, CA: Cengage, 2015), p. 330.
22. Devorah Lieberman, *Public Speaking in the Multicultural Environment* (Boston: Allyn & Bacon, 2000). Also see Edward T. Hall, *Silent Language* (Greenwich, CT: Fawcett, 1959); and Edward T. Hall, The *Hidden Dimension* (Garden City, NY: Doubleday, 1966).

Chapter 6

1. Bruce Gronbeck, from his presidential address delivered at the annual conference of the Speech Communication Association, Nov. 1994.
2. Carmichael.
3. Henry H. Sweets III, "Mark Twain's Lecturing Career Continuation—Part II," *The Fence Painter* (Winter 2000–2001).
4. Alex F. Osborn, *Applied Imagination* (New York: Scribner's, 1962).
5. Nick Pasternak, "Accountability and the Supplement Industry," *Winning Orations 2015* (Mankato, MN: Interstate Oratorical Association, 2015), p. 93.
6. Adapted from Alex Amos, "Broadband Internet Access Should Be a Human Right," *Winning Orations 2015* (Mankato, MN: Interstate Oratorical Association, 2015), pp. 88–90.
7. Judith Humphrey, "Taking the Stage: How Women Can Achieve a Leadership Presence," *Vital Speeches of the Day* (May 2001), p. 437.
8. Adapted from Erin Gallagher, "Upholstered Furniture Fires: Sitting in the Uneasy Chair," *Winning Orations 2000* (Mankato, MN: Interstate Oratorical Association, 2000), pp. 99–101.
9. "Shuttle Missions." *Space Shuttle.* Nasa.gov, 29 August 2011.
10. Adapted from Nicole Tremel, "The New Wasteland: Computers," *Winning Orations 2000* (Mankato, MN: Interstate Oratorical Association, 2000), pp. 37–40.
11. Patrick Martin, "The Energy Cure that Kills: Hydraulic Fracturing for Natural Gas," *Winning Orations 2011* (Mankato, MN: Interstate Oratorical Association, 2011), p. 147.

Chapter 7

1. "Types of Web Sites," Xavier University Library, 2010.
2. Elizabeth Kirk, "Practical Steps in Evaluating Internet Resources." 7 May 2001.
3. Ralph R. Behnke and Chris R. Sawyer, "Public-Speaking Procrastination as a Correlate of Public-Speaking Communication Apprehension and Self-Perceived Public-Speaking Competence,"

Communication Research Reports 16 (1999), pp. 40–47; J. C. Pearson, J. T. Child, and D. H. Kahl, Jr., "Preparation Meeting Opportunity: How Do College Students Prepare for Public Speeches?" *Communication Quarterly* 54, no. 3 (Aug. 2006), pp. 351–366.
4. Michael Cunningham, quoted in Dinitia Smith, "In the Age of the Overamplified, a Resurgence for the Humble Lecture," *New York Times* 17 Mar. 2006, pp. B1, B5.
5. Sandra Zimmer, quoted in Vickie K. Sullivan, "Public Speaking: The Secret Weapon in Career Development," *USA Today* 24–25 May 2005, p. 133.
6. Steven Stack, "The Other Side of America's Healthcare Story," *Vital Speeches of the Day* (September 2015), p. 272.
7. Haisam Hassanein, "A Year of Countless Surprises," *Vital Speeches of the Day* (November 2015), p. 359.
8. Rebecca Brown, "Mental Illness Is Not a Learning Disability," *Winning Orations 2015*.
9. Olli-Pekka Kallasvuo, "Connecting the Next Billion: The New Frontier of Upward Mobility," *Vital Speeches of the Day* (March 2010), pp. 130–133.
10. Andrew B. Wilson, "How to Craft a Winning Speech," *Vital Speeches of the Day* (September 2005), pp. 685–689.
11. David Cameron, "I'm for a Referendum on British Membership in the EU," *Vital Speeches of the Day* (February 2013), pp. 34–35.
12. Alexandria Wisner, "Lithium Cell Batteries: The Power to Kill," *Winning Orations 2011* (Mankato, MN: Interstate Oratorical Association, 2011), p. 30.
13. Karin Nordin, "911's Deadly Flaw," *Winning Orations 2015* (Mankato, MN: Interstate Oratorical Association, 2015), p. 57.
14. Patrick Martin, "The Energy Cure that Kills: Hydraulic Fracturing for Natural Gas," *Winning Orations 2012* (Mankato, MN: Interstate Oratorical Association, 2012), p. 147.
15. Nicole Platzar, "Rated 'D' for Deficiency: The Sunshine Vitamin," *Winning Orations 2012* (Mankato, MN: Interstate Oratorical Association, 2012), p. 71.
16. James Stanfill, "Entomophagy: The Other Other White Meat," *Winning Orations 2009* (Mankato, MN: Interstate Oratorical Association, 2009), p. 24.
17. Charles Bodlen, "We're Moving Beyond the Limits of Our Imagination," *Vital Speeches of the Day* (August 2015), p. 241.
18. Ivan Seidenberg, "How the Government Can Promote a Healthy, Competitive Communications Industry," *Vital Speeches of the Day* (1 Dec. 2009), pp. 540–543.
19. "Sorry, You've Got the Wrong Number," *New York Times* 26 May 2001, p. A17.
20. Michael Blastland and David Spiegelhalter, *The Norm Chronicles: Stories and Numbers about Danger* (London: Profile Books, 2013), p. 47.
21. Pierre Ferrari, "Think Outside the Coffee Cup," *Vital Speeches of the Day* (July 2015), p. 205.

22. A. Barry Rand, "Rebuilding the Middle Class: A Blueprint for the Future," *Vital Speeches of the Day* (March 2013), pp. 72–76.
23. Associated Press, "This Supernova Can Outshine the Milky Way," *Austin American-Statesman* 15 Jan. 2016, p. A2.
24. Dena Craig, "Clearing the Air about Cigars," *Winning Orations 1998* (Mankato, MN: Interstate Oratorical Association, 1998), p. 13.
25. Sergio Marchionne, "Navigating the New Automotive Epoch," *Vital Speeches of the Day* (1 Mar. 2010), pp. 134–137.

Chapter 8

1. Joel Ayres, "The Impact of Time, Complexity, and Organization on Self-Reports of Speech Anxiety," *Communication Research Reports* 5, no. 1 (June 1988), pp. 58–63.
2. Information in this example comes from National Institutes of Health, "Stem Cell Information," 5 March 2015.
3. Adapted from Brooke Cardwell, "Being a Resident Assistant," Texas State University, 2015.
4. Adapted from John Kuehn, untitled speech, *Winning Orations 1994* (Mankato, MN: Interstate Oratorical Association, 1994), pp. 83–85.
5. "Statistics," YouTube Press, 2016; Sarah Perez, "YouTube Reaches 4 Billion Views Per Day," techcrunch.com 23 January 2012; Glenn Chapman, "YouTube Serving Up Two Billion Videos Daily," *Google News* 16 May 2010.
6. Beth Survant, "Let There Be Light," *Winning Orations 2011* (Mankato, MN: Interstate Oratorical Association, 2011), p. 53.
7. "Architecture and Landscape," National Museum of the American Indian Website, 2016.
8. Adapted from Vonda Ramey, "Can You Read This?" *Winning Orations 1985* (Mankato, MN: Interstate Oratorical Association, 1985), pp. 32–35.
9. Adapted from Kelsey Koberg, "Re-evaluating Charities," *Winning Orations 2015* (Mankato, MN: Interstate Oratorical Association, 2015), pp. 29–31.
10. Cynthia Starks, "How to Write a Speech," *Vital Speeches of the Day* (April 2010).
11. The following information is adapted from Deborah A. Lieberman, *Public Speaking in the Multicultural Environment* (Englewood Cliffs, NJ: Prentice Hall, 1994).
12. Martin Medhurst, "The Text(ure) of the World in Presidential Rhetoric," *Vital Speeches of the Day* (June 2012).
13. John Seffrin, "The Worst Pandemic in the History of the World," *Vital Speeches of the Day* (April 2004).
14. Anastasia Danilyuk, "Alternatives to Imprisonment," *Winning Orations 2011* (Mankato, MN: Interstate Oratorical Association, 2011), p. 97.
15. Nichole Olson, "Flying the Safer Skies," *Winning Orations 2000* (Mankato, MN: Interstate Oratorical Association, 2000), p. 122.
16. Thomas Muscha, "Combating Disability Discrimination in the Workplace," *Winning Orations 2015* (Mankato, MN: Interstate Oratorical Association, 2015), p. 79.
17. Robert Gore, untitled speech, *Winning Orations 2012* (Mankato, MN: Interstate Oratorical Association, 2012), p. 87.
18. Molly A. Lovell, "Hotel Security: The Hidden Crisis," *Winning Orations 1994* (Mankato, MN: Interstate Oratorical Association, 1994), p. 18.
19. Neela Latey, "U.S. Customs Procedures: Danger to Americans' Health and Society," *Winning Orations 1986* (Mankato, MN: Interstate Oratorical Association, 1986), p. 22.
20. Susan Stevens, "Teacher Shortage," *Winning Orations 1986* (Mankato, MN: Interstate Oratorical Association, 1986), p. 27.
21. Nicole Platzar, "Rated 'D' for Deficiency: The Sunshine Vitamin," *Winning Orations 2012* (Mankato, MN: Interstate Oratorical Association, 2012), p. 73.
22. Ben Crosby, "The New College Disease," *Winning Orations 2000* (Mankato, MN: Interstate Oratorical Association, 2000), p. 133.
23. Lori Van Overbeke, "NutraSweet," *Winning Orations 1986* (Mankato, MN: Interstate Oratorical Association, 1986), p. 58.
24. John O'Brien, quoted in Brent Filson, *Executive Speeches* (New York: Wiley, 1994), pp. 144–145.
25. Charles Parnell, "Speechwriting: The Profession and the Practice," *Vital Speeches of the Day* (15 Jan. 1990), p. 56.
26. The sample outline in this chapter is adapted from Matthew Fagan, "Public-Speaking Anxiety." Texas State University, 2015.
27. Clive Thompson, "PowerPoint Makes You Dumb," *New York Times Magazine* 14 December 2003, p. 88.

Chapter 9

1. K. Phillip Taylor, "Speech Teachers' Pet Peeves: Student Behaviors That Public Instructors Find Annoying, Irritating, and Unwanted in Student Speeches," *Florida Communication Journal* 33, no. 2 (2005), p. 56.
2. Lauren Holstein, "Slavery in the Sunshine State," *Winning Orations 2012* (Mankato, MN: Interstate Oratorical Association, 2012), p. 34.
3. Charles W. Chesnutt, *Frederick Douglass*. Electronic edition published by Academic Affairs Library, University of North Carolina at Chapel Hill, 2001.
4. Cadie Thompson, "Twitter CEO Dick Costolo Gives New Grads Advice to Be 'Bold,'" *CNBC* 6 May 2013.
5. Jennifer Sweeney, "Racial Profiling," *Winning Orations 2000* (Mankato, MN: Interstate Oratorical Association, 2000), p. 1.

6. Jacob Miller, "Migrant Child Workers Deserve Better Protection," *Winning Orations 2015* (Mankato, MN: Interstate Oratorical Association, 2015), p. 38.

7. Statistics from "Which Law School Graduates Have the Most Debt?" *U.S. News and World Report Best Law Schools*, 2013.

8. Terrika Scott, "Curing Crisis with Community," *Winning Orations 1995* (Mankato, MN: Interstate Oratorical Association, 1995), p. 11.

9. Theresa Clinkenbeard, "The Loss of Childhood," *Winning Orations 1984* (Mankato, MN: Interstate Oratorical Association, 1984), p. 4.

10. Thad Noyes, "Dishonest Death Care," *Winning Orations 1999* (Mankato, MN: Interstate Oratorical Association, 1999), p. 73.

11. Michael Ward, "Of Hills and Dales," *Vital Speeches of the Day* (August 2015), p. 256.

12. Douglas MacArthur, "Farewell to the Cadets," address delivered at West Point, 12 May 1962. Reprinted in Richard L. Johannesen, R. R. Allen, and W. A. Linkugel, eds., *Contemporary American Speeches*, 7th ed. (Dubuque, IA: Kendall/Hunt, 1992), p. 393.

13. Muhtar Kent, "Are We Ready for Tomorrow, Today?" *Vital Speeches of the Day* (March 2010), pp. 117–121.

14. Richard Propes, "Alone in the Dark," *Winning Orations 1985* (Mankato, MN: Interstate Oratorical Association, 1985), p. 22.

15. Luis Proenza, "Relevance, Connectivity and Productivity." *Vital Speeches of the Day* (February 2010), pp. 89–92.

16. Cynthia Starks, "How to Write a Speech," *Vital Speeches of the Day* (April 2010), pp. 153–156.

17. Adam Winegarden, "The After-Dinner Speech," in Tasha Van Horn, Lori Charron, and Michael Charron, eds., *Allyn & Bacon Video II User's Guide*, 2002.

18. William G. Durden, "Just Do Science," *Vital Speeches of the Day* (March 2013), pp. 67–71.

19. Chris Miller, "Remember Both the Art and the Business Involved in Collision Repair," *Vital Speeches of the Day* (May 2010), pp. 203–213.

20. Jeffrey Immelt, "Volatility Is the New Norm," *Vital Speeches of the Day* (August 2015), p. 251.

21. Student speech, University of Miami, 1981.

22. Lou Gehrig, "Farewell Speech," *Lou Gehrig: The Official Web Site* 23 June 2007.

23. Robert Lehrman, "Victory Speeches," *The New York Times* 7 November 2012.

24. John Ryan, "Emissions Tampering: Get the Lead Out," *Winning Orations 1985* (Mankato, MN: Interstate Oratorical Association, 1985), p. 63.

25. Tiffany Hornback, "Demanding Rape Law Reform," *Winning Orations 2015* (Mankato, MN: Interstate Oratorical Association, 2015), p. 9.

26. Bono, "Because We Can, We Must." University of Pennsylvania, *Almanac Between Issues* 19 May 2004.

27. Miller, "Migrant Child Workers Deserve Better Protection," p. 40.

28. James W. Robinson, "Create a Fireworks Finale," *Executive Speeches* (April 1989), pp. 41–44.

29. Kailash Satyarthi, Let Us Globalize Compassion, and Set Our Children Free, *Vital Speeches of the Day* (February 2015), p. 36.

Chapter 10

1. "10 Hilarious Protest Signs," *Blognoscor* 16 October 2010.

2. David Crystal, "Speaking of Writing and Writing of Speaking," *Longman Dictionaries: Express Yourself with Confidence!* (Pearson Education, 2005).

3. S. I. Hayakawa and A. R. Hayakawa, *Language in Thought and Action* (New York: Harcourt, Brace, Jovanovich, 1990); Alfred Korzybski, *Science and Sanity* (Lancaster, PA: Science Press, 1941).

4. Nemanja Savic, "Hope—in the Voices of Africa," speech delivered at Wake Forest University, 14 May 2006. *Window on Wake Forest.* 15 May 2006.

5. Max Woodfin, "Three among Many Lives Jordan Touched," *Austin American-Statesman* 20 January 1996, p. A13.

6. Paul Roberts, "How to Say Nothing in Five Hundred Words," in William H. Roberts and Gregoire Turgeson, eds., *About Language* (Boston: Houghton Mifflin, 1986), p. 28.

7. George Orwell, "Politics and the English Language," in William H. Roberts and Gregoire Turgeson, eds., *About Language* (Boston: Houghton Mifflin, 1986), p. 282.

8. Erma Bombeck, "Missing Grammar Genes Is, Like, the Problem," *Austin American-Statesman* 3 March 1992.

9. Sik Ng and James J. Bradac, *Power in Language: Verbal Communication and Social Influence. Language and Language Behaviors,* Vol. 3. (1993). psycnet.apa.org/psycinfo/1993-98279-000

10. John Lister, quoted in "At the End of the Day, It Annoys," Associated Press. 24 March 2004.

11. Shelley Matheson, "The Most Annoying Clichés Ever," *The Scottish Sun* 8 January 2010.

12. Jon Reed, How Social Media Is Changing Language," blog.oxforddictionaries.com June 2014.

13. William Safire, "Words at War," *New York Times Magazine* 30 September 2001.

14. John S. Seiter, Jarrod Larsen, and Jacey Skinner, "'Handicapped' or 'Handicapable?': The Effects of Language about Persons with Disabilities on Perceptions of Source Credibility and Persuasiveness," *Communication Reports* 11:1 (1998), pp. 21–31.

15. Peggy Noonan, *What I Saw at the Revolution* (New York: Random House, 1990), p. 71.

16. Michael M. Klepper, *I'd Rather Die Than Give a Speech* (New York: Carol Publishing Group, 1994), p. 45.

17. Erik Stolhanske, "Advice from a Kid with a Wooden Leg," *Vital Speeches of the Day* (July 2012), pp. 211–216.

18. Scott Davis, "Class Begins Today," *Vital Speeches of the Day* (August 2011), pp. 279–280.

19. Franklin Roosevelt, inaugural address of 1933 (Washington, DC: National Archives and Records Administration, 1988), p. 22.

20. We acknowledge the following source for several examples used in our discussion of language style: William Jordan, "Rhetorical Style," *Oral Communication Handbook* (Warrensburg, MO: Central Missouri State U, 1971–1972), pp. 32–34.

21. Samuel Hazo, "Poetry and Public Speech," *Vital Speeches of the Day* (April 2007), pp. 685–689.

22. Michiko Kakutani, "Struggling to Find Words for a Horror Beyond Words," *New York Times* 13 September 2001, p. E1.

23. George F. Will, "'Let Us …'? No, Give It a Rest," *Newsweek* 22 January 2001, p. 64.

24. John F. Kennedy, inaugural address, 20 Jan. 1961, in Bower Aly and Lucille F. Aly, eds., *Speeches in English* (New York: Random House, 1968), p. 272.

25. Barack Obama, "Can We Honestly Say We're Doing Enough?" *Vital Speeches of the Day* (February 2013), pp. 34–35.

26. Garrison Keillor, *The Writer's Almanac.* 20 August 2012.

27. Adapted from Jordan, *Oral Communication Handbook,* p. 34.

28. Kennedy, inaugural address.

29. John Kerry, "This Is Not a Clash of Civilizations," *Vital Speeches of the Day* (Jan. 2016), p. 2.

30. Barack Obama, "Look at the World Through Their Eyes," *Vital Speeches of the Day* (May 2013), pp. 138–142.

31. William Faulkner, speech in acceptance of the Nobel Prize for Literature, delivered 10 Dec. 1950, in Houston Peterson, ed., *A Treasury of the World's Great Speeches* (New York: Simon & Schuster, 1965), pp. 814–815.

32. David Brooks, baccalaureate address at Sewanee: The University of the South. *Sewanee Today* 11 May 2013.

33. Barack Obama, inaugural address of 2013. washingtonpost.com 21 January 2013.

34. Rona Fairhead, "A Necessary Debate about the Future, Size and Shape of the BBC," *Vital Speeches of the Day* (April 2015), p. 124.

35. "Reference to Rape Edited from Graduation Speech," *Kansas City Star* 5 June 1995, p. B3.

36. "Dear Abby," *San Marcos Daily Record* 5 January 1993, p. 7.

37. Activity developed by Loren Reid, *Speaking Well* (New York: McGraw-Hill, 1982), p. 96.

Chapter 11

1. For an excellent discussion of the importance of speaker delivery according to both classical and contemporary rhetoricians, see Fredal, J. "The Language of Delivery and the Presentation of Character: Rhetorical Action in Demosthenes' 'Against Meidias.'" *Rhetoric Review*, vol. 20, 2001, pp. 251–267.

2. Wagner, T. R. "The Effects of Speaker Eye Contact and Gender on Receiver's Assessments of the Speaker and Speech." *Ohio Communication Journal*, vol. 51, 2013, pp. 217–236; R. B. Adams and R. E. Cleck. "Effects of Direct and Averted Gaze on the Perception of Facially Communicated Emotion." *Emotion*, vol. 5, 2005, pp. 3–11; Sally Planalp. "Varieties of Emotional Cues in Everyday Life." In L. K. Guerrero and M. L. Hect, editors. *The Nonverbal Communication Reader: Classical and Contemporary Readings.* Long Grove, IL. Waveland, 2008, pp. 397–401.

3. Birdwhistle, Ray. *Kinesics and Context.* Philadelphia: University of Pennsylvania, 1970.

4. Burgoon, Judee K. and Beth A. Le Poire. "Nonverbal Cues and Interpersonal Judgments: Participant and Observer Perceptions of Intimacy, Dominance, Composure, and Formality." *Communication Monographs*, vol. 66, 1999, pp. 105–124; Beth A. Le Poire and Stephen M. Yoshimura. "The Effects of Expectancies and Actual Communication on Nonverbal Adaptation and Communication Outcomes: A Test of Interaction Adaptation Theory." *Communication Monographs*, vol. 66, 1999, pp. 1–30.

5. Mehrabian, Albert. *Nonverbal Communication.* Hawthorne, NY: Aldine, 1972. Wagner, "The Effects of Speaker Eye Contact." Adams and Cleck, "Effects of Direct and Averted Gaze."

6. Beebe, Steven A. and Thompson Biggers. "The Effect of Speaker Delivery upon Listener Emotional Response." Paper presented at the International Communication Association meeting, May 1989.

7. Hatfield, Elaine, J. T. Cacioppo, and R. L. Rapson. *Emotional Contagion,* New York: Cambridge University Press, 1994. Also see John T. Cacioppo, Gary G. Berntson, Jeff T. Larsen, Kirsten M. Poehlmann, and Tiffany A. Ito. "The Psychophysiology of Emotion." In Michael Lewis and Jeannette M. Haviland-Jones, editors, *Handbook of Emotions,* 2nd ed., New York: Guilford Press, 2004, pp. 173–191.

8. Ekman, Paul, Wallace V. Friesen, and K. R. Schere. "Body Movement and Voice Pitch in Deception Interaction." *Semiotica*, vol. 16, 1976, pp. 23–27. Mark Knapp, R. P. Hart, and H. S. Dennis. "An Exploration of Deception as a Communication Construct." *Human Communication Research*, vol. 1, 1974, pp. 15–29.

9. Brody, Marjorie, "Capture an Audience's Attention: Points on Posture, Eye Contact, and More." 1999. www.presentation-pointers.com; Gellis Communications. "Top Tips for Preparing and Delivering a Manuscript Speech." 4 Nov. 2011. www.gellis.com/blog/top-tips-preparing-and-deliveringmanuscript-speech; Stephen Boyd, "The Manuscript Presentation: When and How." Feb. 2013. sboyd.com; David W. Richardson, "Delivering a Manuscript Speech."

2013. www.richspeaking.com/articles/manuscript_speech.html.

10. *Austin-American Statesman*, 15 Jan. 2007, p. A11.

11. Sundquist, Eric J. *King's Dream*, New Haven: Yale University Press, 2009, p. 14.

12. Sundquist. *King's Dream*, p. 2.

13. Cicero, *De Oratore*, vol. 4, translated by E. W. Sutton, Cambridge: Harvard University Press, 1988.

14. Beebe, Steven A. "Eye Contact: A Nonverbal Determinant of Speaker Credibility." *Speech Teacher*, vol. 23, Jan. 1974, pp. 21–25; Steven A. Beebe. "Effects of Eye Contact, Posture and Vocal Inflection upon Credibility and Comprehension." *Australian Scan Journal of Nonverbal Communication*, pp. 7–8, 1979–1980, pp. 57–70; Martin Cobin. "Response to Eye Contact." *Quarterly Journal of Speech*, vol. 48, 1963, pp. 415–419; Wagner. "The Effects of Speaker Eye Contact."

15. Beebe. "Eye Contact." pp. 21–25.

16. Khera Communications. "Doing Business in India: Business Tips for India." *More Business*, 8 July 1999. www.morebusiness.com/running_your_business/management/d930585271.brc

17. Filson, Brent. *Executive Speeches: Tips on How to Write and Deliver Speeches from 51 CEOs*, New York: Wiley, 1994.

18. Mehrabian, Albert. *Silent Messages*, Belmont, CA: Wadsworth, 1971.

19. For a comprehensive review of immediacy in an instructional context, see Richmond, Virginia P., Derek R. Lange, and James C. McCroskey. "Teacher Immediacy and the Teacher-Student Relationship." In Timothy P. Mottet, Virginia P. Richmond, and James C. McCroskey. *Handbook of Instructional Communication: Rhetorical and Relational Perspectives*, Boston: Allyn & Bacon, 2006, pp. 167–193.

20. See Richmond, Virginia P., Joan Gorham, and James C. McCroskey. "The Relationship Between Selected Immediacy Behaviors and Cognitive Learning." In M. McLaughlin, editor. *Communication Yearbook*, vol. 10, Beverly Hills, CA: Sage, 1987, pp. 574–590; Joan Gorham. "The Relationship Between Verbal Teacher Immediacy Behaviors and Student Learning." *Communication Education*, vol. 37, 1988, pp. 40–53; Diane M. Christophel. "The Relationship Among Teacher Immediacy Behaviors, Student Motivation, and Learning." *Communication Education*, vol. 39, 1990, pp. 323–340; James C. McCroskey, Virginia P. Richmond, Aino Sallinen, Joan M. Fayer, and Robert A. Barraclough. "A Cross-Cultural and Multi-Behavioral Analysis of the Relationship Between Nonverbal Immediacy and Teacher Evaluation." *Communication Education*, vol. 44, 1995, pp. 281–290; Timothy P. Mottet and Steven A. Beebe. "Relationships Between Teacher Nonverbal Immediacy, Student Emotional Response, and Perceived Student Learning." *Communication Research Reports*, vol. 19, Jan. 2002.

21. For an excellent review of the effects of immediacy in the classroom, see Mehrabian. *Silent Messages*; also see James C. McCroskey, Aino Sallinen, Joan M. Fayer, Virginia P. Richmond, and Robert A. Barraclough. "Nonverbal Immediacy and Cognitive Learning: A Cross-Cultural Investigation." *Communication Education*, vol. 45, 1996, pp. 200–211.

22. Michael J. Beatty. "Some Effects of Posture on Speaker Credibility." Library paper, University of Central Missouri, 1973.

23. Mehrabian, Albert and M. Williams. "Nonverbal Concomitants of Perceived and Intended Persuasiveness." *Journal of Personality and Social Psychology*, vol. 13, 1969, pp. 37–58.

24. Ekman, Paul, Wallace V. Friesen, and S. S. Tomkins. "Facial Affect Scoring Technique: A First Validity Study." *Semiotica*, vol. 3, 1971.

25. Ekman, Paul and Wallace Friesen. *Unmasking the Face*, Englewood Cliffs, NJ: Prentice Hall, 1975; D. Keltner and P. Ekman. "Facial Expression of Emotion." In M. Lewis and J. M. Haviland-Jones, editors. *Handbook of Emotions*, New York: Gilford, 2000, pp. 236–249; D. Keltner, P. Ekman, G. S. Gonzaga, and J. Beer. "Facial Expression of Emotion." In R. J. Davidson, K. R. Scherer, and H. H. Goldsmith, editors. *Handbook of Affective Sciences*, New York: Oxford University Press, 2003, pp. 415–432.

26. Adapted from Schilling, Lester. *Voice and Diction for the Speech Arts*, San Marcos: Southwest Texas State University, 1979.

27. Gill, Mary M. "Accent and Stereotypes: Their Effect on Perceptions of Teachers and Lecture Comprehension." *Journal of Applied Communication*, vol. 22, 1994, pp. 348–361.

28. Sereno, Kenneth K. and G. J. Hawkins. "The Effects of Variations in Speakers' Nonfluency upon Audience Ratings of Attitude Toward the Speech Topic and Speakers' Credibility." *Speech Monographs*, vol. 34, 1967, pp. 58–74; Gerald R. Miller and M. A. Hewgill. "The Effect of Variations in Nonfluency on Audience Ratings of Source Credibility." *Quarterly Journal of Speech*, vol. 50, 1964, pp. 36–44; Mehrabian and Williams. "Nonverbal Concomitants of Perceived and Intended Persuasiveness."

29. These suggestions were made by Sprague, Jo and Douglas Stuart. *The Speaker's Handbook*. Fort Worth, TX, Harcourt Brace Jovanovich, 1992, p. 331, and were based on research by Patricia A. Porter, Margaret Grant, and Mary Draper. *Communicating Effectively in English: Oral Communication for Non-Native Speakers*. Belmont, CA: Wadsworth, 1985.

30. Stephen Lucas. *The Art of Public Speaking*. New York: Random House, 1986, p. 231.

31. Research cited by Fletcher, Leo. *How to Design and Deliver Speeches*. New York: Addison Wesley Longman, 2001, p. 73.

32. "Comment." *The New Yorker*, 1 Mar. 1993.

33. Nash, Jackie. "Unforgettably Awkward Presidential Moments." Biography online newsletter, 26 Sept. 2012. www.biography.com/news/unforgettably-awkward-presidential-moments-20965079. Accessed January 4, 2016.

34. Swanger, Nancy. "Visible Body Modification (VBM): Evidence from Human Resource Managers and Recruiters and the Effects on Employment." *Journal of Hospitality Management*, vol. 25, 2006, pp. 154–158; John S. Seiter and Andrea Sandry. "Pierced for Success? The Effects of Ear and Nose Piercing on Perceptions of Job Candidates' Credibility, Attractiveness, and Hirability." *Communication Research Reports*, vol. 20.4, 2003, pp. 287–298.

35. Menzel, Kent E. and Lori J. Carrell. "The Relationship Between Preparation and Performance in Public Speaking." *Communication Education*, vol. 43, 1994, pp. 17–26; Tony E. Smith and Ann Bainbridge Frymier. "Get 'Real': Does Practicing Speeches Before an Audience Improve Performance?" *Communication Quarterly*, vol. 54.1, Feb. 2006, pp. 111–125; Judy C. Pearson, Jeffrey T. Child, and David H. Kahl, Jr. "Preparation Meeting Opportunity: How Do College Students Prepare for Public Speeches?" *Communication Quarterly*, vol. 54.3, Aug. 2006, pp. 351–366.

36. Behnke, Ralph R. and Chris R. Sawyer. "Public-Speaking Procrastination as a Correlate of Public-Speaking Communication Apprehension and Self-Perceived Public-Speaking Competence." *Communication Research Reports*, vol. 16, 1999, pp. 40–47.

37. Daly and Redlick, "Handling Questions and Objections."

38. Filson. *Executive Speeches.*

39. Filson. *Executive Speeches.*

Chapter 12

1. Dale Cyphert, "The Problem of PowerPoint: Visual Aid or Visual Rhetoric?" *Business Communication Quarterly* (Mar. 2004), pp. 80–84.

2. Melinda Knight, The Ubiquitousness of PowerPoint," *Business and Professional Communication Quarterly* 78, no. 3 (2015) pp. 271–272.

3. J. S. Wilentz, *The Senses of Man* (New York: Crowell, 1968).

4. Emil Bohn and David Jabusch, "The Effect of Four Methods of Instruction on the Use of Visual Aids in Speeches," *Western Journal of Speech Communication* 46 (Summer 1982), pp. 253–265; Michael E. Patterson, Donald F. Dansereau, and Dianna Newbern, "Effects of Communication Aids and Strategies on Cooperative Teaching," *Journal of Educational Psychology* 84 (1992), pp. 453–461; Richard E. Mayer and Valerie K. Sims, "For Whom Is a Picture Worth a Thousand Words? Extensions of a Dual-Coding Theory of Multimedia Learning," *Journal of Educational Psychology* 86 (1994), pp. 389–401.

5. Roxanne Parrott, Kami Sikl, Kelly Dorgan, Celeste Condit, and Tina Harris, "Risk Comprehension and Judgments of Statistical Evidentiary Appeals: When a Picture Is Not Worth a Thousand Words," *Human Communication Research* 31 (July 2005), pp. 423–452.

6. For a good discussion of how to develop and use PowerPoint visuals, see Jerry Weissman, *Presenting to Win: The Art of Telling Your Story* (Upper Saddle River, NJ: Financial Times/Prentice Hall, 2003).

7. We thank Stan Crowley, a student at Texas State University, for his permission to use his speech outline.

8. Andrew Wilson, "In Defense of Rhetoric," *Toastmaster* 70.2 (Feb. 2004), pp. 8–11.

9. A. Buchko, K. Buchko, and J. Meyer, "Perceived Efficacy and the Actual Effectiveness of PowerPoint on the Retention and Recall of Religious Messages in the Weekly Sermon: An Empirical Field Study," *Journal of Communication & Religion* 36, no. 3 (2013), pp. 149–165.

10. S. Kernbach, S. Bresciani, and M. J. Eppler, "Slip-Sliding-Away: A Review of the Literature on the Constraining Qualities of PowerPoint," *Business and Professional Communication Quarterly* 78, no. 3 (2015), pp. 292–313.

11. Rebecca B. Worley and Marilyn A. Dyrud, "Presentations and the PowerPoint Problem," *Business Communication Quarterly* 67 (Mar. 2004), pp. 78–80.

12. M. T. Thielsch and I. Perabo, "Use and Evaluation of Presentation Software," *Technical Communication* 59, no. 2 (2012), pp. 112–123.

13. H. J. Bucher and P. Niemann, "Visualizing science: the reception of powerpoint presentations," *Visual Communication* 11, no. 3 (2015), pp. 283–306.

14. Filson, *Executive Speeches.*

15. We acknowledge Dan Cavanaugh's excellent supplement *Preparing Visual Aids for Presentation* (Boston: Allyn & Bacon/Longman, 2001) as a source for many of our tips and suggestions.

Chapter 13

1. John R. Johnson and Nancy Szczupakiewicz, "The Public Speaking Course: Is It Preparing Students with Work-Related Public Speaking Skills?" *Communication Education* 36 (Apr. 1987), pp. 131–137.

2. Steven A. Beebe, Timothy P. Mottet, and K. David Roach, *Training and Development: Communicating for Success* (Boston: Pearson, 2013).

3. Pamela J. Hinds, "The Curse of Expertise: The Effects of Expertise and Debiasing Methods on Predicting Novice Performance," *Journal of Experimental Psychology: Applied* 5 (1999), pp. 205–221. Research summarized in Chip Heath and Dan Heath, *Made to Stick: Why Some Ideas Survive and Others Die* (New York: Random House, 2007), pp. 19–21.

4. Joseph L. Chesebro, "Effects of Teacher Clarity and Nonverbal Immediacy on Student Learning, Receiver Apprehension, and Affect," *Communication Education* 52 (Apr. 2003), pp. 135–147; Scott Titsworth, Joseph P. Mazer, Alan K. Goodboy, San Bolkan and

Scott A. Myers, "Two Meta-analysis Exploring the Relationship between Teacher Clarity and Student Learning," *Communication Education*, 64, no. 4 (2015), pp. 385–418.

5. Malcolm Knowles, Elwood F. Holton III, and Richard Sanson, *The Adult Learner: The Definitive Classic in Adult Education and Human Resource Development*, 12th ed. (London: Routledge: Taylor & Francis, 2012).

6. Beebe, Mottet, and Roach, *Training and Development*.

7. Katherine E. Rowan, "A New Pedagogy for Explanatory Public Speaking: Why Arrangement Should Not Substitute for Invention," *Communication Education* 44 (1995), pp. 236–250.

8. Philip Yancy, *Prayer: Does It Make Any Difference?* (Grand Rapids, MI: Zondervan, 2006), p. 20.

9. Michael A. Boerger and Tracy B. Henley, "The Use of Analogy in Giving Instructions," *Psychological Record* 49 (1999), pp. 193–209.

10. Heath and Heath, *Made to Stick*, pp. 63–64.

11. Marcie Groover, "Learning to Communicate: The Importance of Speech Education in Public Schools," *Winning Orations 1984* (Mankato, MN: Interstate Oratorical Association, 1984), p. 7.

12. As cited by Eleanor Doan, *The New Speaker's Sourcebook* (Grand Rapids, MI: Zondervan, 1968).

13. C. S. Lewis, "On Stories," *Essays Presented to Charles Williams*, C. S. Lewis, ed. (Oxford: Oxford University Press, 1947); also see Walter R. Fisher, *Communication as Narration: Toward a Philosophy of Reason, Value, and Action* (Columbia: University of South Carolina Press, 1987).

14. Christopher Booker, *The Seven Basic Plots: Why We Tell Stories* (London: Continuum, 2004). The theory that all stories are about "finding home" is from Steven A. Beebe, *C. S. Lewis: Chronicles of a Master Communicator* (San Marcos, TX: Texas State University, 2013).

15. Heath and Heath, *Made to Stick*.

16. Roger Fringer, "Choosing a Speech Topic," *Student Speeches Video* (Boston: Allyn & Bacon, 2003).

17. See Bruce W. A. Whittlesea and Lisa D. Williams, "The Discrepancy-Attribution Hypothesis II: Expectation, Uncertainty, Surprise, and Feelings of Familiarity," *Journal of Experimental Psychology: Learning, Memory, and Cognition* 2 (2001), pp. 14–33; also see Suzanne Hidi, "Interest and Its Contribution as a Mental Resource for Learning," *Review of Educational Research* 60 (1990), pp. 549–571; Mark Sadoski, Ernest T. Goetz, and Maximo Rodriguez, "Engaging Texts: Effects of Concreteness of Comprehensibility, Interest, and Recall in Four Text Types," *Journal of Educational Psychology* 92 (2000), pp. 85–95.

18. Heath and Heath, *Made to Stick*, pp. 51–52.

19. George Miller, "The Magical Number Seven, Plus or Minus Two," *Psychological Review* 63 (1956), pp. 81–97.

20. D. K. Cruickshank and J. J. Kennedy, "Teacher Clarity," *Teaching & Teacher Education* 2 (1986), pp. 43–67.

Chapter 14

1. Martin Fishbein and I. Ajzen, *Belief, Attitude, Intention, and Behavior: An Introduction to Theory and Research* (Reading, MA: Addison-Wesley, 1975); also see Richard E. Petty and John T. Cacioppo, *Attitudes and Persuasion: Classic and Contemporary Approaches* (New York: Westview Press, 1996).

2. Aristotle, *On Rhetoric*, translated by George A. Kennedy (New York: Oxford University Press, 1991), p. 14.

3. For a discussion of motivation in social settings, see Douglas T. Kenrick, Steven L. Neuberg, and Robert B. Cialdini, *Social Psychology: Unraveling the Mystery* (Boston: Allyn & Bacon, 2002).

4. For a discussion of the elaboration likelihood model, see R. Petty and D. Wegener, "The Elaboration Likelihood Model: Current Status and Controversies," in S. Chaiken and Y. Trope, eds., *Dual Process Theories in Social Psychology* (New York: Guilford, 1999), pp. 41–72; also see R. Petty and J. T. Cacioppo, *Communication and Persuasion: Central and Peripheral Routes to Attitude Change* (New York: Springer-Verlag, 1986).

5. Leon Festinger, *A Theory of Cognitive Dissonance* (Evanston, IL: Row, Peterson, 1957).

6. For additional discussion, see Wayne C. Minnick, *The Art of Persuasion* (Boston: Houghton Mifflin, 1967).

7. Abraham H. Maslow, "A Theory of Human Motivation," in *Motivation and Personality* (New York: Harper & Row, 1954), chapter 5. Although Maslow updated his model (A. H. Maslow, *Motivation and Personality* [New York: Haper & Row, 1970]), and the model has been critiqued by several researchers (M. A. Wahba and L. G. Bridwell, "Maslow Reconsidered: A Review of Research on the Need Hierarchy Theory," *Organizational Behavior and Human Performance* 15, no. 2 [April 1976], pp. 212–240), the basic assumptions of Need Hierarch Theory remain applicable to explaining human motivation.

8. C. Yan, J. P. Dillard, and F. Shen, "Emotion, Motivation, and the Persuasive Effects of Message Framing," *Journal of Communication* 62 (2012), pp. 682–700.

9. For a discussion of fear appeal research, see Irving L. Janis and Seymour Feshbach, "Effects of Fear-Arousing Communications," *Journal of Abnormal and Social Psychology* 48 (January 1953), pp. 78–92; Frederick A. Powell and Gerald R. Miller, "Social Approval and Disapproval Cues in Anxiety-Arousing Situations," *Speech Monographs* 34 (June 1967), pp. 152–159; Kenneth L. Higbee, "Fifteen Years of Fear Arousal: Research on Threat Appeals,

1953–68," *Psychological Bulletin* 72 (December 1969), pp. 426–444; Kim Wittee and Mike Allen, "A Meta-Analysis of Fear Appeals: Implications for Effective Public Health Campaigns," *Health Education & Behavior* 27 (2000), pp. 591–615.

10. Paul A. Mongeau, "Another Look at Fear-Arousing Persuasive Appeals," in Mike Allen and Raymond W. Preiss, eds., *Persuasion: Advances Through Meta-Analysis* (Cresskill, NJ: Hampton Press, 1998), p. 65.

11. K. Witte, "Putting the Fear Back into Fear Appeals: The Extended Parallel Process Model," *Communication Monographs* 59 (1992), pp. 329–347.

12. Patrick McGeehan, "Blame Photoshop, Not Diabetes, for This Amputation," *New York Times*, January 24, 2012 www.nytimes.com/2012/01/25/nyregion/in-health-dept-ad-photoshop-not-diabetes-took-leg.html

13. See discussions in Myron W. Lustig and Jolene Koester, *Intercultural Competence: Interpersonal Communication Across Cultures* (Boston: Allyn & Bacon, 2015), p. 340; Larry A. Samovar and Richard E. Porter, *Communication Between Cultures* (Stamford, CT: Wadsworth and Thomson Learning, 2015), p. 30.

14. Joseph P. Mazer and Scott Titsworth, "Passion and Preparation in the Basic Course: The Influence of Students' Ego-Involvement with Speech Topics and Preparation Time on Public Speaking Grades," *Communication Teacher* 26, 4 (October 2012), pp. 236–251.

15. C. W. Sherif, M. Sherif, and R. E. Nebergall, *Attitudes and Attitude Change: The Social Judgment-Involvement Approach* (Philadelphia: Saunders, 1965).

Chapter 15

1. Donald C. Bryant, "Rhetoric: Its Functions and Its Scope," *Quarterly Journal of Speech* 39 (December 1953), p. 26.

2. J. C. Reinard, "The Empirical Study of the Persuasive Effects of Evidence: The Status after Fifty Years of Research," *Human Communication Research* 15 (1988), pp. 3–59.

3. James C. McCroskey and R. S. Rehrley, "The Effects of Disorganization and Nonfluency on Attitude Change and Source Credibility," *Speech Monographs* 36 (1969), pp. 13–21.

4. John F. Kennedy, "Inaugural Address (January 20, 1961)," in Bower Aly and Lucille F. Aly, eds., *Speeches in English* (New York: Random House, 1968), p. 272.

5. Judee K. Burgoon, T. Birk, and M. Pfau, "Nonverbal Behaviors, Persuasion, and Credibility," *Human Communication Research* 17 (1990), pp. 140–169.

6. Segrin, "The Effects of Nonverbal Behavior on Outcomes of Compliance Gaining Attempts." Also see: Steven A. Beebe, "Eye Contact: A Nonverbal Determinant of Speaker Credibility," *Speech Teacher* 23 (Jan. 1974), pp. 21–25; Steven A. Beebe, "Effects of Eye Contact, Posture and Vocal Inflection upon

Credibility and Comprehension," *Australian Scan Journal of Nonverbal Communication* 7–8 (1979–1980), pp. 57–70; John A. Daly and Madeleine H. Redlick, "Handling Questions and Objections Affects Audience Judgments of Speakers," *Communication Education* 65 (April 2016), pp. 164–181.

7. Robin L. Nabi, Emily Moyer-Guse, and Sahara Byrne, "All Joking Aside: A Serious Investigation into the Persuasive Effect of Funny Social Issue Messages," *Communication Monographs* 74 (March 2007), pp. 29–54.

8. For a discussion of the perceived link between inductive and deductive reasoning, see Evan Heit and Caren M. Rotello, "Relations Between Inductive Reasoning and Deductive Reasoning," *Journal of Experimental Psychology* 36 (2010), pp. 805–812.

9. For an excellent discussion of the influence of culture on public speaking, see Devorah A. Lieberman, *Public Speaking in the Multicultural Environment* (Englewood Cliffs, NJ: Prentice Hall, 1994), p. 10.

10. Devorah Lieberman and G. Fisher, "International Negotiation," in Larry A. Samovar and Richard E. Porter, eds., *Intercultural Communication: A Reader* (Belmont, CA: Wadsworth, 1991), pp. 193–200.

11. Lieberman and Fisher, "International Negotiation."

12. Jeffrey E. Jamison, "Alkali Batteries: Powering Electronics and Polluting the Environment," *Winning Orations 1991* (Mankato, MN: Interstate Oratorical Association, 1991), p. 43.

13. H. B. Brosius and A. Bathelt, "The Utility of Exemplars in Persuasive Communications," *Communication Research* 21 (1994), pp. 48–78.

14. Lisa L. Massi-Lindsey and Kimo Ah Yun, "Examining the Persuasive Effect of Statistical Messages: A Test of Mediating Relationships," *Communication Studies* 54 (Fall 2003), pp. 306–321; D. C. Kazoleas, "A Comparison of the Persuasive Effectiveness of Qualitative versus Quantitative Evidence: A Test of Explanatory Hypotheses," *Communication Quarterly* 41 (1993), pp. 40–50; also see M. Allen and R. W. Preiss, "Comparing the Persuasiveness of Narrative and Statistical Evidence Using Meta-Analysis," *Communication Research Reports* (1997), pp. 125–131.

15. Franklin J. Boster, Kenzie A. Cameron, Shelly Campo, Wen-Ying Liu, Janet K. Lillie, Esther M. Baker, and Kimo Ah Yun, "The Persuasive Effects of Statistical Evidence in the Presence of Exemplars," *Communication Studies* 51 (Fall 2000), pp. 296–306; also see E. J. Baesler and Judee K. Burgoon, "The Temporal Effects of Story and Statistical Evidence on Belief Change," *Communication Research* 21 (1994), pp. 582–602.

16. Reinard, "The Empirical Study of the Persuasive Effects of Evidence," pp. 37–38.

17. William L. Benoit and I. A. Kennedy, "On Reluctant Testimony," *Communication Quarterly* 47 (1999), pp. 376–387. Although this study raises questions about whether reluctant testimony is persuasive, reluctant

(New York: Currency Doubleday, 1995); D. D. Chrislip and C. E. Larson, *Collaborative Leadership* (San Francisco, CA: Jossey-Bass, 1994); C. Klein, D. DiazGranados, E. Salas, H. Le, C. S. Burke, R. Lyons, and G. F. Goodwin, "Does Team Building Work?" *Small Group Research* 40, no. 2 (2009), pp. 181–222; A. N. Pieterse, D. van Knippenberg, and W. P. van Ginkel, "Diversity in Goal Orientation, Team Reflexivity, and Team Performance," *Organizational Behavior and Human Decision Processes* 114 (2011), pp. 153–164.

4. For discussions of the advantages and disadvantages of working in small groups, see Norman R. F. Maier, "Assets and Liabilities in Group Problem Solving: The Need for an Integrative Function," *Psychological Review* 74 (1967), pp. 239–249; Michael Argyle, *Cooperation: The Basis of Sociability* (London: Routledge, 1991); J. Surowiecki, *The Wisdom of Crowds* (New York: Anchor, 2005); P. R. Laughlin, E. C. Hatch, J. Silver, and L. Boh, "Groups Perform Better Than the Best Individuals on Letters-to-Numbers Problems: Effects on Group Size," *Journal of Personality and Social Psychology* 90 (2006), pp. 644–651. J. S. Mueller, "Why Individuals in Larger Teams Perform Worse," *Organizational Behavior and Human Decision Processes* 117 (2012), pp. 111–124; B. R. Staats, K. L. Milkman, and C. R. Fox, "The Team Scaling Fallacy: Underestimating the Declining Efficiency of Larger Teams," *Organizational Behavior and Human Decision Processes* 118 (2012), pp. 132–142; B. M. Waller, L. Hope, N. Burrowes, and E. R. Morrison, "Twelve (Not So) Angry Men: Managing Conversational Group Size Increases Perceived Contribution by Decision Makers," *Group Processes & Intergroup Relations* 14, no. 6 (2011), pp. 835–843.

5. Maier, "Assets and Liabilities in Group Problem Solving"; Argyle, *Cooperation.*

6. John Dewey, *How We Think* (Boston: Heath, 1910).

7. P. L. McLeod, "Effects of Anonymity and Social Comparison of Rewards on Computer-Mediated Group Brainstorming," *Small Group Research* 42, no. 2 (2011), pp. 475–503; H. Barki, "Small Group Brainstorming and Idea Quality: Is Electronic Brainstorming the Most Effective Approach?" *Small Group Research* 32 (2001), pp. 158–205; B. A. Nijstad, W. Stroebe, and H. F. M. Lodewijkx, "Cognitive Stimulation and Interference in Groups: Exposure Effects in an Idea Generation Task," *Journal of Experimental Social Psychology* 38 (2002), pp. 535–544; E. F. Rietzschel, B. A. Nijstad, and W. Stroebe, "Productivity Is Not Enough: A Comparison of Interactive and Nominal Brainstorming Groups on Idea Generation and Selection," *Journal of Experimental Social Psychology* 42 (2006), pp. 244–251; also see P. B. Paulus, M. T. Dzindolet, H. Coskun, and V. K. Putman, "Social and Cognitive Influences in Group Brainstorming: Predicting Production Gains and Losses," *European Review of Social Psychology* 12 (2002), pp. 299–326; P. B. Paulus, D. S. Levine, V. Brown, A. A. Minai, and S. Doboli, "Modeling Ideational Creativity in Groups: Connecting Cognitive, Neural, and Computational Approaches," *Small Group Research* 41, no. 6 (2010), pp. 688–724; T. M. Hess, T. L. Queen and T. R. Paterson, "To Deliberate or Not to Deliberate: Interactions Between Age, Task Characteristics, and Cognitive Activity on Decision Making." *Journal of Behavioral Decision Making* 25 (2012), pp. 29–40.

8. K. L. Dugosh, P. B. Paulus, E. J. Roand, and H. C. Yang, "Cognitive Stimulation in Brainstorming," *Journal of Personality and Social Psychology* 79 (2000), pp. 722–735.

9. R. Y. Hirokawa and A. J. Salazar, "Task-Group Communication and Decision-Making Performance," in L. Frey, ed., *The Handbook of Group Communication Theory and Research* (Thousand Oaks, CA: Sage, 1999), pp. 167–191; D. Gouran and R. Y. Hirokawa, "Functional Theory and Communication in Decision-Making and Problem-Solving Groups: An Expanded View," in R. Y. Hirokawa and M. S. Poole, eds., *Communication and Group Decision Making* (Thousand Oaks, CA: Sage, 1996), pp. 55–80.

10. C. A. VanLear and E. A. Mabry, "Testing Contrasting Interaction Models for Discriminating Between Consensual and Dissentient Decision-Making Groups," *Small Group Research* 30 (1999), pp. 29–58; also see T. J. Saine and D. G. Bock, "A Comparison of the Distributional and Sequential Structures of Interaction in High and Low Consensus Groups," *Central States Speech Journal* 24 (1973), pp. 125–139.

11. Randy Y. Hirokawa and Roger Pace, "A Descriptive Investigation of the Possible Communication-Based Reasons for Effective and Ineffective Group Decision Making," *Communication Monographs* 50 (Dec. 1983), pp. 363–379.

12. Randy Y. Hirokawa, "Group Communication and Problem-Solving Effectiveness: An Investigation of Group Phases," *Human Communication Research* 9 (Summer 1983), pp. 291–305.

13. Dennis S. Gouran, "Variables Related to Consensus in Group Discussion of Question of Policy," *Speech Monographs* 36 (Aug. 1969), pp. 385–391.

14. For a summary of research about conflict management in small groups, see S. M. Farmer and J. Roth, "Conflict-Handling Behavior in Work Groups: Effects of Group Structure, Decision Processes, and Time," *Small Group Research* 29 (1998), pp. 669–713; also see Beebe and Masterson, *Communicating in Small Groups*; J. Sell, M. J. Lovaglia, E. A. Mannix, C. D. Samuelson, and R. K. Wilson, "Investigating Conflict, Power, and Status Within and Among Groups," *Small Group Research* 30 (1999), pp. 44–72; K. J. Behfar, E. A. Mannix, Randall S. Peterson, and W. M. Trochim, "Conflict in Small Groups: The Meaning and Consequences of Process Conflict," *Small Group Research* 42, no. 2 (2011), pp. 127–176; L. L. Greer, H. M. Caruso, and K. A. Jehn,

"The Bigger They Are, the Harder They Fall: Linking Team Power, Team Conflict, and Performance," *Organizational Behavior and Human Decision Process* 116 (2011), pp. 116–128.

15. Ralph White and Ronald Lippitt, "Leader Behavior and Member Reaction in Three 'Social Climates,'" in Darwin Cartwright and Alvin Zander, eds., *Group Dynamics*, 3rd ed. (New York: Harper & Row, 1968), p. 319.

16. Peter M. Senge, "Leading Learning Organizations," in Richard Beckhard et al., eds., *The Leader of the Future* (San Francisco: Jossey-Bass, 1996); Bernard M. Bass and M. J. Avolio, "Transformational Leadership and Organizational Culture," *International Journal of Public Administration* 17 (1994), pp. 541–554; Lynn Little, "Transformational Leadership," *Academic Leadership* 15 (Nov. 1999), pp. 4–5.

17. Francis Y. Yammarino and Alan J. Dubinsky, "Transformational Leadership Theory: Using Levels of Analysis to Determine Boundary Conditions,"

Personnel Psychology 47 (1994), pp. 787–809; L. Little, "Transformational Leadership," *Academic Leadership* 15 (Nov. 1999), pp. 4–9.

Appendix B

1. John F. Kennedy: "Inaugural Address," January 20, 1961, as appeared in https://www.jfklibrary.org/Research/Research-Aids/Ready-Reference/JFK-Quotations/Inaugural-Address.aspx, October 30, 2016.

2. Barack Obama, "Inaugural Address," as appeared in *Daily Compilation of Presidential Documents*. January 21, 2013.

3. Pope Francis, "Remarks to the U.S. Congress," as appeared in www.popefrancisvisit.com/schedule/address-to-joint-meeting-of-congress, September 24, 2015.

4. Julio Gonzalez, "The Need for Minority Blood Marrow Donors," The University of Texas student speech, 2016.

Glossary

acceptance speech A speech of thanks for an award, nomination, or other honor

accommodation Sensitivity to the feelings, needs, interests, and backgrounds of other people

ad hominem An attack on irrelevant personal characteristics of the person who is proposing an idea, rather than on the idea itself

after-dinner speech A humorous presentation, usually delivered in conjunction with a mealtime meeting or banquet

alliteration The repetition of a consonant sound (usually the first consonant) several times in a phrase, clause, or sentence

analogy A comparison

analysis Examination of the causes, effects, and history of a problem in order to understand it better

analytical listener Someone who prefers messages that are supported with facts and details

andragogy The art and science of teaching adults

anecdote An illustration or story

antithesis Opposition, such as that used in parallel two-part sentences in which the second part contrasts in meaning with the first

appeal to misplaced authority Use of the testimony of an expert in a given field to endorse an idea or product for which the expert does not have the appropriate credentials or expertise

articulation The production of clear and distinct speech sounds

attend To focus on incoming information for further processing

attitude A learned predisposition to respond favorably or unfavorably toward something; likes and dislikes

audience adaptation The process of ethically using information about an audience to adapt one's message so that it is clear and achieves the speaking objective

audience analysis The process of examining information about those who are expected to listen to a speech

award presentation A speech that accompanies the conferring of an award

bandwagon fallacy Reasoning that suggests that because everyone else believes something or is doing something, then it must be valid or correct

bar graph A graph in which bars of various lengths represent information

belief An individual's perception of what is true or false

benefit A good result or something that creates a positive emotional response in the listener

blueprint The central idea of a speech plus a preview of the main ideas

boom microphone A microphone suspended from a bar and moved to follow the speaker; often used in movies and TV

brainstorming A creative problem-solving technique used to generate many ideas

brief illustration An unelaborated example, often only a sentence or two long

cadence The rhythm of language

causal fallacy A faulty cause-and-effect connection between two things or events

causal reasoning Reasoning in which the relationship between two or more events leads you to conclude that one or more of the events caused the others

cause-and-effect organization Organization that focuses on a situation and its causes or a situation and its effects

central idea A one-sentence statement of what a speech is about

ceremonial (epideictic) speech A speech delivered on a special occasion for celebration, thanks giving, praise, or mourning

channels The visual and auditory means by which a message is transmitted from sender to receiver

charisma Characteristic of a talented, charming, attractive speaker

chart A display that summarizes information by using words, numbers, or images

chronological organization Organization by time or sequence

citation manager Web-based software package for collecting, organizing, and formatting citation information

cliché An overused expression

clip art Images or pictures stored in a computer file or in printed form that can be used in a presentation aid

closed-ended questions Questions that offer alternatives from which to choose, such as true/false, agree/disagree, or multiple-choice questions

closure The quality of a conclusion that makes a speech "sound finished"

clustering A concept mapping strategy that illustrates connections between ideas

code A verbal or nonverbal symbol for an idea or image

cognitive dissonance The sense of mental discomfort that prompts a person to change when new information conflicts with previously organized thought patterns

commemorative address A speech delivered during ceremonies held in memory of some past event and/or the person or persons involved

commencement address A speech delivered at a graduation or commencement ceremony

common ground Similarities between a speaker and audience members in attitudes, values, beliefs, or behaviors

competent Being informed, skilled, or knowledgeable about one's subject

complexity Arrangement of ideas from the simple to the more complex

concise Succinct or to the point

conclusion The logical outcome of a deductive argument, which stems from the major premise and the minor premise

connotation The meaning listeners associate with a word, based on their experience

consensus The support and commitment of all group members to the decision of the group

context The environment or situation in which a speech occurs

credibility An audience's perception of a speaker as competent, knowledgeable, dynamic, and trustworthy

crisis rhetoric Language used by speakers during momentous or overwhelming times

criteria Standards for identifying an acceptable solution to a problem

critical listener Someone who prefers to evaluate messages

critical listening Evaluating the quality of information, ideas, and arguments presented by a speaker

critical thinking Analyzing information to judge its accuracy and relevance

culture A learned system of knowledge, behavior, attitudes, beliefs, values, and norms shared by a group of people

declamation The delivery of an already famous speech

declarative sentence A grammatically complete sentence, rather than a clause, phrase, or question

decode To translate verbal or nonverbal symbols into ideas and images

deductive reasoning Reasoning that moves from a general statement of principle to a specific, certain conclusion

definition A statement about what a term means or how it is applied in a specific instance

definition by classification A "dictionary definition," constructed by both placing a term in the general class to which it belongs and differentiating it from all other members of that class

demagogue A speaker who gains control over others by using unethical emotional pleas and appeals to listeners' prejudices

demographic audience analysis Examining demographic information about an audience so as to develop a clear and effective message

demographics Statistical information about the age, race, gender, sexual orientation, educational level, and religious views of an audience

denotation The literal meaning of a word

derived credibility The perception of a speaker's credibility that is formed during a speech

description A word picture of something

dialect A consistent style of pronouncing words common to an ethnic group or geographic region

direct persuasion route Persuasion that occurs when audience members critically examine evidence and arguments

disposition The organization and arrangement of ideas and illustrations

domain Category in which a Web site is located on the Internet, indicated by the last three letters of the site's URL

dynamism An aspect of a speaker's credibility that reflects whether the speaker is perceived as energetic

either–or fallacy The over simplification of an issue into a choice between only two outcomes or possibilities

elaborate From the standpoint of the elaboration likelihood model (ELM) of persuasion, to think about information, ideas, and issues related to the content of a message

elaboration likelihood model (ELM) of persuasion The theory that people can be persuaded by logic, evidence, and reasoning, or through a more peripheral route that may depend on the credibility of the speaker, the sheer number of arguments presented, or emotional appeals

elocution The expression of emotion through posture, movement, gesture, facial expression, and voice

emotional contagion theory A theory suggesting that people tend to "catch" the emotions of others

empowerment Having resources, information, and attitudes that lead to action to achieve a desired goal

encode To translate ideas and images into verbal or nonverbal symbols

ethical speech Speech that is responsible, honest, and tolerant

ethics The beliefs, values, and moral principles by which people determine what is right or wrong

ethnicity The portion of a person's cultural background that includes such factors as nationality, religion, language, and ancestral heritage, which are shared by a group of people who also share a common geographic origin

ethnic vernacular A variety of English that includes words and phrases used by a specific ethnic group

ethnocentrism The assumption that one's own cultural perspectives and methods are superior to those of other cultures

ethos The term Aristotle used to refer to a speaker's credibility

eulogy A speech of tribute delivered when someone has died

evidence The facts, examples, statistics and expert opinions used to support a logical conclusion

examples Illustrations used to dramatize or clarify a fact

expert testimony An opinion offered by someone who is an authority on a subject

explanation A statement that clarifies how something is done or why it exists in its present form or existed in its past form

extemporaneous speaking Speaking from a written or memorized speech outline without having memorized the exact wording of the speech

extended illustration A detailed example

external noise Physical sounds that interfere with communication

fact Something that has been directly observed to be true or can be proven to be true by verifiable evidence

fallacy False reasoning that occurs when someone attempts to persuade without adequate evidence or with arguments that are irrelevant or inappropriate

fear appeal Seeking to motivate or persuade by threatening harm or danger unless action is taken to reduce the harm or danger

feature A characteristic of something you are describing

feedback Verbal and nonverbal responses provided by an audience to a speaker

figurative analogy A comparison between two essentially dissimilar things that share some common feature on which the comparison depends

figurative language Words that deviate from their ordinary, expected meaning to make a description or comparison unique, vivid, and memorable

final summary A restatement of the main ideas of a speech, occurring near the end of the speech

First Amendment The amendment to the U.S. Constitution guaranteeing free speech; the first of the ten amendments to the U.S. Constitution known collectively as the Bill of Rights

fonts Particular styles of typefaces

forum A question-and-answer session that usually follows a public discussion or symposium

free speech The open exchange of information and ideas

gender The culturally constructed and psychologically based perception of one's self as feminine or masculine

generalization An all-encompassing statement

general purpose The overarching goal of a speech—to inform, persuade, or entertain

graph A pictorial representation of statistical data

hard evidence Factual examples and statistics

hasty generalization A conclusion reached without adequate evidence

hyperbole Exaggeration

hypothetical illustration An example that might happen but that has not actually occurred

illustration A story or anecdote that provides an example of an idea, issue, or problem a speaker is discussing

immediacy The degree of perceived physical or psychological closeness between people

immediacy behaviors Behaviors such as making eye contact, making appropriate gestures, and adjusting physical distance that enhance the quality of the relationship between speaker and listeners

impromptu speaking Delivering a speech without advance preparation

indirect persuasion route Persuasion that occurs as a result of factors peripheral to a speaker's logic and argument, such as the speaker's charisma or emotional appeals

inductive reasoning   Reasoning that uses specific instances or examples to reach a general, probable conclusion

inference   A conclusion based on partial information or an evaluation that has not been directly observed

inflection   The variation in the pitch of the voice

initial credibility   The impression of a speaker's credibility that listeners have before the speaker starts a speech

initial preview   A statement in the introduction of a speech about what the main ideas of the speech will be

internal noise   Physiological or psychological interference with communication

internal preview   A statement in the body of a speech that introduces and outlines ideas that will be developed as the speech progresses

internal summary   A restatement in the body of a speech of the ideas that have been developed so far

invention   The development or discovery of ideas and insights

inversion   Reversal of the normal word order of a phrase or sentence

jargon   The specialized language of a profession or interest group

kairos   The circumstances surrounding the speech or the occasion for a speech

keynote address   A speech that sets the theme and tone for a meeting or conference

ladder of abstraction   Continuum model of abstract and concrete words for a concept, idea, or thing

lavaliere microphone   A microphone that can be clipped to an article of clothing or worn on a cord around your neck

lay testimony   An opinion or description offered by a nonexpert who has firsthand experience

leadership   The process of influencing others through communication

line graph   A graph that uses lines or curves to show relationships between two or more variables

listening   The process by which receivers select, attend to, understand, remember, and respond to senders' messages

listening styles   Preferred ways of making sense out of spoken messages

literal analogy   A comparison between two similar things

literary quotation   An opinion or description by a writer who speaks in a memorable and often poetic way

logos   Literally, "the word"; the term Aristotle used to refer to logic—the formal system of using rules to reach a conclusion

main ideas   The key points of a speech

major premise   A general statement that is the first element of a syllogism

malapropism   The mistaken use of a word that sounds much like the intended word

manuscript speaking   Reading a speech from a written text

memorized speaking   Delivering a speech word for word from memory without using notes

message   The content of a speech and the mode of its delivery

metaphor   An implied comparison between two things or concepts

minor premise   A specific statement about an example that is linked to the major premise; the second element of a syllogism

model   A small object that represents a larger object

motivated sequence   A five-step adaptation of the problem-solution pattern; used to organize persuasive speeches

motivation   The internal force that drives people to achieve their goals

myth   A shared belief based on the underlying values, cultural heritage, and faith of a group of people

nomination speech   A speech that officially names someone as a candidate for an office or a position

non sequitur   Latin for "it does not follow"; an idea or conclusion that does not logically relate to or follow from the previous idea or conclusion

nonverbal communication   Communication other than written or spoken language that creates meaning

nonverbal expectancy theory   A communication theory that suggests that if listeners' expectations about how communication should be expressed are violated, listeners will feel less favorable toward the communicator of the message

nonverbal transition   A facial expression, vocal cue, or physical movement indicating that a speaker is moving from one idea to the next

omission   Leaving out a word or phrase that the listener expects to hear

online databases   Subscription-based electronic resources that may offer access to abstracts or the full texts of entries, as well as bibliographic data

onomatopoeia When a word is pronounced like its meaning

open-ended questions Questions that allow for unrestricted answers by not limiting answers to choices or alternatives

operational definition A statement that shows how something works or what it does

opinions Statements expressing an individual's attitudes, beliefs, or values

oral citation The spoken presentation of source information, including the author, title, and year of publication

panel discussion Group discourse designed to inform an audience about issues or a problem, or to make recommendations

parallelism Use of the same grammatical pattern for two or more phrases, clauses, or sentences

patchwriting Failing to give credit for phrases taken from another source

pathos The term used by Aristotle to refer to appeals to human emotion

pedagogy The art and science of teaching children

personal illustration An anecdote drawn from the speaker's experience

personification The attribution of human qualities to inanimate things or ideas

persuasion The process of changing or reinforcing a listener's attitudes, beliefs, values, or behavior

picture graph A graph that uses images or pictures to symbolize data

pie graph A circular graph divided into wedges that show each part's percentage of the whole

pitch How high or low the voice sounds

plagiarizing Presenting someone else's words or ideas as though they were one's own

prejudice Preconceived opinions, attitudes, and beliefs about a person, place, thing, or message

preliminary bibliography A list of potential resources to be used in the preparation of a speech

preparation outline A detailed outline of a speech that includes the central idea, main ideas, and supporting material; and that may also include the specific purpose, introduction, conclusion, and references

presentation aid Any image, object, or sound that reinforces your point visually or aurally so that your audience can better understand it

preview A statement of what is to come

primacy Arrangement of ideas from the most to the least important

problem-solution organization Organization focused on a problem and its various solutions or on a solution and the problems it would solve

pronunciation The use of sounds to form words clearly and accurately

proposition A statement that summarizes the ideas a speaker wants an audience to agree with

proposition of fact A proposition focusing on whether something is true or false or whether it did or did not happen

proposition of policy A proposition advocating a change in a policy, procedure, or behavior

proposition of value A proposition calling for the listener to judge the worth or importance of something

psychological audience analysis Examining the attitudes, beliefs, values, and other psychological information about an audience to develop a clear and effective message

public-relations speeches Speeches designed to inform the public, to strengthen alliances with them, and in some cases to recommend policy

public speaking The process of presenting a spoken message to an audience

pun The use of double meanings to create humor

race A group of people with a common cultural history, nationality, or geographical location, as well as genetically transmitted physical attributes

reasoning by sign Using the existence of one or more events to reach a specific conclusion that another event has occurred or will occur

receiver A listener or an audience member

recency Arrangement of ideas from the least to the most important

red herring Irrelevant facts or information used to distract someone from the issue under discussion

reflective thinking A method of structuring a problem-solving discussion that involves (1) identifying and defining the problem, (2) analyzing the problem, (3) generating possible solutions, (4) selecting the best solution, and (5) testing and implementing the solution

regionalisms Words or phrases used uniquely by speakers in one part of a country

relational-oriented listener Someone who is comfortable listening to others express feelings and emotions

relationship An ongoing connection you have with another person

reluctant testimony A statement by someone who has reversed his or her position on a given issue

remembering Recalling ideas and information

repetition Use of a key word or phrase more than once for emphasis

responding Reacting with a change in behavior to a speaker's message

rhetoric The strategic use of words and symbols to achieve a goal

rhetorical criticism The process of using a method or standards to evaluate the effectiveness and appropriateness of messages

rhetorical question A question intended to provoke thought rather than elicit an answer

select To single out a message from several competing messages

self-actualization need The need to achieve one's highest potential

sex A person's biological status as male or female, as reflected in his or her anatomy and reproductive system

signposts Cues about the relationships between a speaker's ideas

simile A comparison between two things that uses the word *like* or *as*

situational audience analysis Examination of the time and place of a speech, the audience size, and the speaking occasion to develop a clear and effective message

small group communication Interaction among three to twelve people who share a common purpose, feel a sense of belonging to the group, and influence one another

social judgment theory A theory that categorizes listener responses to a persuasive message according to the latitude of acceptance, the latitude of rejection, or the latitude of noncommitment

socioeconomic status A person's perceived importance and influence based on income, occupation, and education level

soft evidence Supporting material based mainly on opinion or inference; includes hypothetical illustrations, descriptions, explanations, definitions, and analogies

source The public speaker

spatial organization Organization based on location or direction

speaking notes A brief outline used when a speech is delivered

specific purpose A concise statement of the desired audience response, indicating what you want your listeners to remember, feel, or do when you finish speaking

speech act A behavior, such as flag burning, that is viewed by law as nonverbal communication and is subject to the same protections and limitations as verbal speech

speech of introduction A speech that provides information about another speaker

speech to inform A speech that teaches others new information, ideas, concepts, principles, or processes to enhance their knowledge or understanding about something

speech topic The key focus of the content of a speech

spoonerism A phrase in which the initial sounds of words are switched

stacks The collection of books in a library

Standard American English (SAE) The English taught by schools and used in the media, business, and government in the United States

standard outline form Numbered and lettered headings and subheadings arranged hierarchically to indicate the relationships among parts of a speech

stationary microphone A microphone attached to a lectern, sitting on a desk, or standing on the floor

statistics Numerical data that summarize facts or samples

summary A recap of what has been said

suspension Withholding a key word or phrase until the end of a sentence

syllogism A three-part argument that consists of a major premise, a minor premise, and a conclusion

symbols Words, images, and behaviors that create meaning

symposium A public discussion in which a series of short speeches is presented to an audience

target audience A specific segment of an audience that you most want to influence

task-oriented listener Someone who prefers information that is well organized, brief, and precise

team A coordinated small group of people organized to work together with clearly defined roles and responsibilities, explicit rules, and well-defined goals

terminal credibility The final impression listeners have of a speaker's credibility after a speech concludes

toast A brief salute to a momentous occasion

topical organization Arrangement of the natural divisions in a central idea according to recency, primacy, complexity, or the speaker's discretion

transformational leadership The process of influencing others by building a shared vision of the future, inspiring others to achieve, developing high-quality individual relationships with others, and helping people see how what they do is related to a larger framework or system

transition A verbal or nonverbal signal indicating that a speaker has finished discussing one idea and is moving to another

trustworthiness An aspect of a speaker's credibility that reflects whether the speaker is perceived as being believable and honest

understand To assign meaning to the information to which you attend

understatement Downplaying a fact or event

value An enduring concept of good and bad, right and wrong

verbal irony Saying the opposite of what one means

verbal transition A word or phrase that indicates the relationship between two ideas

vertical search engine A Web site that indexes World Wide Web information in a specific field

visual rhetoric The use of images as an integrated element in the total communication effort a speaker makes to achieve a speaking goal

volume The softness or loudness of a speaker's voice

wit Relating an incident that takes an unexpected turn at the end

word picture A vivid description that appeals to the senses

working memory theory of listening A theory that suggests that listeners find it difficult to concentrate and remember when their short-term working memories are full

written citation The print presentation of source information including the author, title, and year of publication, usually formatted according to a conventional style guide

Credits

Chapter 1

p. 1: Mark Twain/The Mark Twain House and Museum; p. 2: TED curator Chris Anderson/TED Conferences, LLC; p. 3: Charles Schwab, as quoted in Brent Filson, *Executive Speeches: Tips on How to Write and Deliver Speeches from 51 CEOs* (New York: Wiley, 1994), p. 45; p. 3: James C. Humes, *The Sir Winston Method: Five Secrets of Speaking the Language of Leadership* (New York: Morrow, 1991) pp. 13–14; p. 4: Iain Hay, "Justifying and Applying Oral Presentations in Geographical Education," *Journal of Geography in Higher Education* 18 no. 1 (1994), p. 44–45; also see: Morreale and Pearson, "Why Communication Education is Important,"; p. 4: Dee-Ann Durbin, "Study: Plenty of Jobs for Graduates in 2000," *Austin American-Statesman* 5 (December 1999), p. A28; p. 4: Valueinvestorsportal. "Warren Buffet on Communication Skills." YouTube. 6 December, 2010. Web. www.youtube.com/watch?v=tpgcEYpLzP0 Accessed May 14, 2013; p. 5: Roosevelt/Franklin D. Roosevelt Library; p. 5: Public Domain; p. 5: Reagan, Ronald/Public Domain; p. 5: Elie Wiesel, The Perils of Indifference, April 12, 1999; p. 5: L. M. Boyd, syndicated column, *Austin American-Statesman* 8 Aug. 2000, p. E3; p. 6: Obama, Barack. "Remarks by the President at Sandy Hook Interfaith Prayer Vigil" The White House Briefing Room. 16 Dec 2012. Web. 05 July 2013 www.whitehouse.gov/the-press-office/2012/12/16/remarks-president-sandy-hook-interfaith-prayer-vigil; p. 9: George Jessel/Sheboygan Press; p. 9: Jerry Seinfeld/Shapiro/West & Associates; p. 13: Quoted by Petula Dovrak, "Channeling the Grief," *Austin American-Statesman*. 14 October, 2009, p. A9; p. 15: Stephen R. Covey, *The 7 Habits of Highly Successful People* (New York: Simon and Schuster, 1989).

Chapter 2

p. 19: Daniel Webster, U.S. Secretary of State, 1850–1852; p. 25: H.V. Prochnow. *700 Illustrations and Ideas for Speakers*. Baker Publishing Group, Reprint Edition, December 1994. p. 21; p. 27: Source Don Hewitt/Estate of Don Hewitt; p. 27: Clifford Stoll, as cited in Kevin A. Miller, "Capture: The Essential Survival Skill for Leaders Buckling Under Information Overload," *Leadership* (Spring 1992), p. 85; p. 27: Woodrow Wilson/Public Domain; p. 31: Source: Jonathan Swift/Public Domain; p. 31: Franklin D. Roosevelt/Public Domain; pp. 33–34: Grace Hildenbrand.

Chapter 3

p. 47: Waldo W. Braden, *Abraham Lincoln, Public Speaker* (Baton Rouge: Louisiana State University Press, 1988), p. 90; p. 36: Mark Schierbecker, "Clash Between Media and ConcernedStudent1950," video in article by Austin Huguelet and Daniel Victor, "'I Need Some Muscle': Missouri Activists Block Journalists," nytimes.com (10 November 2015); p. 37: National Communication Association Credo for Communication Ethics, 1999. 27 June 2001; p. 37: "Obama Counter-Terrorism Speech Interrupted by Heckler," UPI.com. 23 May 2013; p. 38: "Libel and Slander," *The Ethical Spectacle*. 1 June 1997; p. 38: Samuel Walker, Hate Speech (Lincoln: University of Nebraska Press, 1994), p. 162; p. 39: "Supreme Court Rules: Cyberspace Will Be Free! ACLU Hails Victory in Internet Censorship Challenge." *American Civil Liberties Union Freedom Network*. 26 June 1997; p. 39: Donald Downs, John Sharpless, and Mary Anderson, "University of Wisconsin Directive Devalues Free Speech on Campus," WiscNews.com. 30 November 2015; p. 39: James S. Tyre, "Legal Definition of Obscenity, Pornography." 1 June 1997/Public Domain; p. 39: Sue Anne Pressley, "Oprah Winfrey Wins Case Filed by Cattlemen," *The Washington Post* 27 Feb. 1998; p. 40: Source Ian McEwen/Rogers, Coleridge & White Ltd.; p. 40: Brian Schweitzer, "Proclamation of Clemency for Montanans Convicted under the Montana Sedition Act in 1918–1919." 3 May 2006. (Thanks to George Moss, Vaughn College, Flushing, NY, for providing the authors with a copy of this document.); p. 40: www.freespeechdebate.com; p. 41: Daniel Downs and Gloria Cowan, "Predicting the Importance of Freedom of Speech and the Perceived Harm of Hate Speech," *Journal of Applied Social Psychology* 42.6 (June 2012), p. 1372; p. 41: Edwin R. Bayley, Joe McCarthy and the Press (Madison: University of Wisconsin Press, 1981), p. 29; p. 38: "Libel and Slander," The Ethical Spectacle. 1 June 1997; p. 38: Samuel Walker, Hate Speech (Lincoln: University of Nebraska Press, 1994), p. 162; p. 39: "Supreme Court Rules: Cyberspace Will Be Free! ACLU Hails Victory in Internet Censorship Challenge." American Civil Liberties Union Freedom Network. 26 June 1997; p. 40: www.freespeechdebate.com; p. 41: From "French Rein in Speech Backing Acts of Terror," by Dorreen Carvajal and Alan Cowell, *The New York Times*, January 16, 2005, p. A12; p. 41: Source Mathieu Davy/University of Nebraska Press; p. 42: Kathy Fitzpatrick; p. 42: "Spurlock Sorry for Speech," *Austin American-Statesman* 29 Mar. 2006, p. A2; p. 43: The Publication Manual of the American Psychological Association 6th ed. (Washington, DC: American Psychological Association, 2010), p. 16; p. 43: President Bill Clinton/The White House; p. 43: Scott Jaschik, "Graduation Shame." Insidehighered.com. 22 Apr. 2010; p. 44: Michele Eodice, "Plagiarism, Pedagogy, and Controversy: A Conversation with Rebecca Moore Howard," Issues in Writing 13.1 (Fall/Winter 2002); pp. 45–46: "Bed Bugs." Centers for Disease Control and Prevention, Web. June 9, 2013 www.cdc.gov/parasites/bedbugs; p. 47: Waldo W. Braden,

Abraham Lincoln, Public Speaker (Baton Rouge: Louisiana State University Press, 1988), p. 90.

Chapter 4

p. 48: Plutarch/Public Domain; p. 58: Aristotle/Public Domain; p. 58 Harold Barrett, *Rhetoric and Civility: Human Development, Narcissism, and the Good Audience* (Albany: State University of New York Press, 1991), p. 154; p. 59: John Dewey/Macmillan; p. 60: Kenneth Burke, *A Rhetoric of Motives* (Berkeley: University of California Press, 1950). Also see Barry Brummett, *Reading Rhetorical Theory* (Fort Worth, TX: Harcourt College Publishers, 2000), p. 741.

Chapter 5

p. 67: Aristotle/Public Domain; p. 74: PQ - Truman - "I wonder how … poll in Egypt"? (15 wds)/Harper & Row; p. 75: Socrates/Public Domain; p. 77: The research summarized here is based on pioneering work by Geert Hofstede, *Culture's Consequences: International Differences in Work-Related Values* (Beverly Hills, CA: Sage, 1984). Also see Edward T. Hall, Beyond Culture (New York: Doubleday, 1976).

Chapter 6

p. 95: Cicero/Public Domain; p. 96: Bruce Gronbeck, from his presidential address delivered at the annual conference of the Speech Communication Association, Nov. 1994; p. 103: Nick Pasternak, "Accountability and the Supplement Industry," *Winning Orations 2015* (Mankato, MN: Interstate Oratorical Association, 2015), p. 93; p. 106: Judith Humphrey, "Taking the Stage: How Women Can Achieve a Leadership Presence," *Vital Speeches of the Day* (May 2001), p. 437; p. 110: "Shuttle Missions." Space Shuttle. Nasa.gov, 29 August 2011; p. 111: Adapted from Nicole Tremel, "The New Wasteland: Computers," *Winning Orations 2000* (Mankato, MN: Interstate Oratorical Association, 2000), p. 37–40; p. 111: Patrick Martin, "The Energy Cure that Kills: Hydraulic Fracturing for Natural Gas," *Winning Orations 2011* (Mankato, MN: Interstate Oratorical Association, 2011), p. 147.

Chapter 7

p. 115: Ivan Petrovich Pavlov, Bequest to the Academic Youth of Soviet Russia (1936); p. 128: "Sorry, You've Got the Wrong Number," *The New York Times* 26 May 2001, p. A17; p. 128: Michael Blastland and David Spiegelhalter, *The Norm Chronicles: Stories and Numbers about Danger* (London: Profile Books, 2013), p. 42; p. 119: Courtesy of Albert B. Alkek Library, Texas State University, San Marcos/Texas State University- University News Service; p. 123: Haisam Hassanein, "A Year of Countless Surprises," *Vital Speeches of the Day* (November 2015), pp. 358–359; p. 123: Michael Cunningham, quoted in Dinitia Smith, "In the Age of the Overamplified, a Resurgence for the Humble Lecture," *The New York Times* 17 Mar. 20 pp. B1, B5; p. 123: Sandra Zimmer, quoted in Vickie K. Sullivan, "Public Speaking: The Secret Weapon in Career Development," *USA Today* 24–25 May 2005, p. 133; p. 123: Steven Stack, "The Other Side of America's Healthcare Story," *Vital Speeches of the Day* (September 2015), p. 272; p. 124: Olli-Pekka Kallasvuo, "Connecting the Next Billion: The New Frontier of Upward Mobility," *Vital Speeches of the Day* (March 2010), pp. 130–33; p. 124: Rebecca Brown, "Mental Illness Is Not a Learning Disability," *Winning Orations 2015*; p. 125: Alexandria Wisner, "Lithium Cell Batteries: The Power to Kill," *Winning Orations 2011* (Mankato, MN: Interstate Oratorical Association, 2011), p. 30; p. 125: Andrew B. Wilson, "How to Craft a Winning Speech," *Vital Speeches of the Day* (September 2005), pp. 685–689; p. 125: David Cameron, "I'm for a Referendum on British Membership in the EU," *Vital Speeches of the Day* (February 2013), pp. 34–35; p. 126: Nicole Platzar, "Rated 'D' for Deficiency: The Sunshine Vitamin," *Winning Orations 2012* (Mankato, MN: Interstate Oratorical Association, 2012), p. 71; p. 127: Charles Bodlen, "We're Moving Beyond the Limits of Our Imagination," *Vital Speeches of the Day* (August 2015), p. 241; p. 127: Ivan Seidenberg, "How the Government Can Promote a Healthy, Competitive Communications Industry," *Vital Speeches of the Day* (1 Dec. 2009), pp. 540–543; p. 127: James Stanfill, "Entomophagy: The Other Other White Meat," *Winning Orations 2009* (Mankato, MN: Interstate Oratorical Association, 2009), p. 24; p. 128: Pierre Ferrari, "Think Outside the Coffee Cup," *Vital Speeches of the Day*. July 2015, Vol. 81 Issue 7, p. 205, 3 p. Published 2015; p. 128: A. Barry Rand, "Rebuilding the Middle Class: A Blueprint for the Future," *Vital Speeches of the Day* (March 2013), pp. 72–76; p. 128: Michael Blastland and David Spiegelhalter, The Norm Chronicles: Stories and Numbers about Danger (London: Profile Books, 2013), p. 47; p. 128: Marcia Dunn, "Scientists spot brightest supernova yet, outshines Milky Way," January 14, 2016. Copyright © 2016 Associated Press; p. 129: Dena Craig, "Clearing the Air about Cigars," *Winning Orations 1998* (Mankato, MN: Interstate Oratorical Association, 1998), p. 13; p. 129: Sergio Marchionne, "Navigating the New Automotive Epoch," *Vital Speeches of the Day* (1 Mar. 2010), p. 134–37.

Chapter 8

p. 133: Alfred North Whitehead; p. 137: Adapted from John Kuehn, Untitled Speech, *Winning Orations 1994* (Mankato, MN: Interstate Oratorical Association, 1994), p. 83–85; p. 137: Sarah Perez, "YouTube Reaches 4 Billion Views Per Day," techcrunch.com 23 January 2012; Glenn Chapman, "YouTube Serving Up Two Billion Videos Daily," Google News 16 May 2010; p. 139: Adapted from Vonda Ramey, "Can You Read This?" *Winning Orations 1985* (Mankato, MN: Interstate Oratorical Association, 1985), p. 32–35; p. 140: Cynthia Starks, "How to Write a Speech," *Vital Speeches of the Day* (April 2010); p. 141: Deborah A. Lieberman, Public Speaking in the Multicultural Environment, "Organizational patterns by culture" © 1997. Reproduced by permission of Pearson Education, Inc.; p. 142: Martin Medhurst, "The Text(ure) of the World in Presidential Rhetoric," *Vital Speeches of the Day* (June 2012); p. 142: John Seffrin, "The Worst Pandemic in the History of the World," *Vital Speeches of the Day* (April 2004); p. 143: Nichole Olson, "Flying the Safer Skies," *Winning Orations 2000* (Mankato, MN: Interstate Oratorical Association, 2000), p. 122; p. 144: Robert Gore, Untitled Speech, *Winning Orations 2012* (Mankato, MN: Interstate Oratorical Association, 2012), p. 87; p. 145: Molly A. Lovell, "Hotel Security: The Hidden Crisis," *Winning Orations 1994* (Mankato, MN: Interstate Oratorical Association, 1994), p. 18; p. 146–147: Neela Latey, "U.S. Customs Procedures: Danger to Americans' Health and Society," Winning Orations 1986 (Mankato, MN: Interstate Oratorical Association, 1986), p. 22; p. 147: Ben Crosby, "The New College Disease," *Winning Orations 2000* (Mankato, MN: Interstate Oratorical Association, 2000), p. 133; p. 147: John O'Brien, quoted in Brent Filson, Executive Speeches (New York: Wiley, 1994), pp. 144–45; p. 147: Lori Van Overbeke, "NutraSweet," *Winning Orations 1986* (Mankato, MN: Interstate Oratorical Association, 1986), p. 58; p. 147: Nicole Platzar, "Rated 'D' for Deficiency: The Sunshine Vitamin," *Winning Orations 2012* (Mankato, MN: Interstate Oratorical Association, 2012), p. 73; p. 147: Susan Stevens, "Teacher Shortage," *Winning Orations 1986* (Mankato, MN: Interstate Oratorical Association, 1986), p. 27; p. 148: Charles Parnell, "Speechwriting: The Profession and the Practice," *Vital Speeches of the Day* (15 Jan. 1990), p. 56; p. 152: Ghandi/Public Domain; p. 153: Clive Thompson, "PowerPoint Makes You Dumb," *The New York Times Magazine* 14 December 20, p. 88.

Chapter 9

p. 163: Thad Noyes, "Dishonest Death Care," *Winning Orations 1999* (Mankato, MN: Interstate Oratorical Association, 1999), p. 73; p. 157: Anonymous/Public Domain; p. 159: Lauren Holstein, "Slavery in the Sunshine State," *Winning Orations 2012* (Mankato, MN: Interstate Oratorical Association, 2012), p. 34; p. 160: Cadie Thompson, "Twitter CEO Dick Costolo Gives New Grads Advice to Be 'Bold,'" CNBC 6 May 2013; p. 160: Charles W. Chesnutt, *Frederick Douglass*. Electronic edition published by Academic Affairs Library, University of North Carolina at Chapel Hill, 2001; p. 161: Jacob Miller, "Migrant Child Workers Deserve Better Protection," *Winning Orations 2015*. Interstate Oratorical Assoc. Mankato, MN. Editor Larry Schnoor; p. 161: Jennifer Sweeney, "Racial Profiling," *Winning Orations 2000* (Mankato, MN: Interstate Oratorical Association, 2000), p. 1; p. 162: Terrika Scott, "Curing Crisis with Community," *Winning Orations 1995* (Mankato, MN: Interstate Oratorical Association, 1995), p. 11; p. 162: Theresa Clinkenbeard, "The Loss of Childhood," *Winning Orations 1984* (Mankato, MN: Interstate Oratorical Association, 1984), p. 4; p. 162: *U.S. News and World Report Best Law Schools, 2013;* p. 163: Michael Ward, "Of Hills and Dales," *Vital Speeches of the Day* (August 2015), p. 256; p. 163: Douglas MacArthur, "Farewell to the Cadets," address delivered at West Point, 12 May 1962. Reprinted in Richard L. Johannesen, R. R. Allen, and Wil A. Linkugel, eds., Contemporary American Speeches, 7th ed. (Dubuque, IA: Kendall/Hunt, 1992), p. 393; p. 164: President Abraham Lincoln/Public Domain; p. 164: Luis Proenza, "Relevance, Connectivity and Productivity." *Vital Speeches of the Day* (February 2010), pp. 89–92; p. 164: Muhtar Kent, "Are We Ready for Tomorrow, Today?" *Vital Speeches of the Day* (March 2010), pp. 117–21; p. 164: Richard Propes, "Alone in the Dark," *Winning Orations 1985* (Mankato, MN: Interstate Oratorical Association, 1985), p. 22; p. 165: Jeffrey Immelt, "Volatility Is the New Norm," *Vital Speeches of the Day* (August 2015), p. 251; p. 165: Adam Winegarden, "The After-Dinner Speech," in Tasha Van Horn, Lori Charron, and Michael Charron, eds., Allyn & Bacon Video II User's Guide, 2002; p. 165: Chris Miller, "Remember Both the Art and the Business Involved in Collision Repair," *Vital Speeches of the Day* (May 2010), pp. 203–13; p. 165: Cynthia Starks, "How to Write a Speech," *Vital Speeches of the Day* (April 2010), pp. 153–56; p. 165: William G. Durden, "Just Do Science," *Vital Speeches of the Day* (March 2013), pp. 67–71; p. 166: Lou Gehrig, "Farewell Speech," Lou Gehrig: The Official Web Site 23 June 2007/CMG Worldwide; p. 166: Student speech, University of Miami, 1981; p. 167: John Ryan, "Emissions Tampering: Get the Lead Out," *Winning Orations 1985* (Mankato, MN: Interstate Oratorical Association, 1985), p. 63; p. 167: Robert Lehrman, "Victory Speeches," *The New York Times* 7 November 2012; p. 168: Jacob Miller, "Migrant Child Workers Deserve Better Protection," *Winning Orations 2015* (Mankato, MN: Interstate Oratorical Association, 2015), p. 40; p. 168: Bono, "Because We Can, We Must." University of Pennsylvania, Almanac Between Issues 19 May 2004; p. 168: Tiffany Hornback, "Demanding Rape Law Reform," *Winning Orations 2015*. Interstate Oratorical Assoc. Mankato, MN. Editor Larry Schnoor; p. 169: "Kailash Satyarthi-Nobel Lecture: Let Us March!" Nobelprize.org. Nobel Media AB 2014. Web. 22 Aug 2016; p. 169: James W. Robinson, "Create a Fireworks Finale," *Executive Speeches* (April 1989), pp. 41–44.

Chapter 10

p. 171: Peggy Noonan. *What I Saw at the Revolution: A Political Life in the Reagan Era*. Random House, 2003; p. 173: Nemanja Savic, "Hope in the Voices of Africa," speech delivered at Wake Forest University, 14 May 2006. Window on Wake Forest. 15 May 2006; p. 174: Paul Roberts, "How to Say Nothing in Five Hundred Words," in William H. Roberts and Gregoire Turgeson, eds., *About Language* (Boston: Houghton Mifflin, 1986) p. 28; p. 174: Erma Bombeck, "Missing Grammar

Genes Is, Like, the Problem," *Austin American-Statesman* 3 March 1992; p. 174: George Orwell, "Politics and the English Language," in William H. Roberts and Gregoire Turgeson, eds., *About Language* (Boston: Houghton Mifflin, 1986), p. 282; p. 174: Rep. Barbara Jordan, 1992 Democratic National Convention Keynote Address; p. 175: John Lister, quoted in "At the End of the Day, It Annoys." *Associated Press*. 24 March 2004; p. 175: Shelley Matheson, "The Most Annoying Clichés Ever," *The Scottish Sun* 8 January 2010; p. 177: William Safire, "Words at War," *The New York Times Magazine* 30 September 2001; p. 178: Michael M. Klepper, *I'd Rather Die Than Give a Speech* (New York: Carol Publishing Group, 1994), p. 45; p. 178: Peggy Noonan, *What I Saw at the Revolution* (New York: Random House, 1990), p. 71; p. 179: Michiko Kakutani, "Struggling to Find Words for a Horror Beyond Words," *The New York Times* 13 September 2001, p. E1; p. 179: Samuel Hazo, "Poetry and Public Speech," *Vital Speeches of the Day* (April 2007), pp. 685–689; p. 179: Eric Stolhanske, "Advice from a Kid with a Wooden Leg," *Vital Speeches of the Day* (July 2012), pp. 211-216; p. 179: Franklin Roosevelt, Inaugural Address of 1933 (Washington, DC: National Archives and Records Administration, 1988), p. 22; p. 179: Scott Davis, "Class Begins Today," *Vital Speeches of the Day* (August 2011), pp. 279-280; p. 179: We acknowledge the following source for several examples used in our discussion of language style: William Jordan, "Rhetorical Style," *Oral Communication Handbook* (Warrensburg, MO: Central Missouri State U, 1971–1972), pp. 32–34; p. 180: Barack Obama, "Look at the World Through Their Eyes," *Vital Speeches of the Day* (May 2013), pp. 138–142; p. 180: Barack Obama, Inaugural Address of 2013. washingtonpost.com 21 January 2013; p. 180: Coca Cola; p. 180: John Kerry, "This Is Not a Clash of Civilizations," *Vital Speeches of the Day* (Jan. 2016), p. 2; p. 180: Rona Fairhead, "A Necessary Debate about the Future, Size and Shape of the BBC," *Vital Speeches of the Day* (April 2015), p. 124; p. 180: Barack Obama, "Can We Honestly Say We're Doing Enough?" *Vital Speeches of the Day* (February 2013), pp. 34-35; p. 180: Caesar; p. 180: David Brooks, Baccalaureate Address at Sewanee: The University of the South. *Sewanee Today* 11 May 2013; p. 180: George F. Will, "'Let Us . . .'? No, Give It a Rest," *Newsweek* 22 January 2001, p. 64; p. 180: John F. Kennedy, Inaugural Address, 20 Jan. 1961, in Bower Aly and Lucille F. Aly, eds., *Speeches in English* (New York: Random House, 1968), p. 272; p. 180: Kennedy, Inaugural Address; p. 180: William Faulkner, Speech in Acceptance of the Nobel Prize for Literature, delivered 10 Dec. 1950, in Houston Peterson, ed., *A Treasury of the World's Great Speeches* (New York: Simon & Schuster, 1965), pp. 814–815; p. 183: Activity developed by Loren Reid, Speaking Well (New York: McGraw-Hill, 1982), p. 96.

Chapter 11

p. 184: William Shakespeare, *Hamlet*, (3.2.1-36), Act 3, Scene 2; p. 188: Mark Twain; p. 190: Cicero, *De Oratore*, vol. 4, translated by E. W. Sutton (Cambridge: Harvard University Press, 1988) p. 193: Albert Mehrabian, Silent Messages (Belmont, CA: Wadsworth, 1971); p. 193: Brent Filson, *Executive Speeches: Tips on How to Write and Deliver Speeches from 51 CEOs* (New York: Wiley, 1994); p. 199: Comment, *The New Yorker* 1 Mar. 1993; p. 200: Bio online newsletter. www.biography.com/news/ronald-reagan-bombing-in-5-minutes-joke Accessed January 4, 2016.

Chapter 12

p. 209: Aristotle. *On the Soul* (350 BCE); p. 213: Data from Netmarketshare www.netmarketshare.com/search-enginemarketshare.aspx?qprid=4&qpcustomd=0; p. 213: United States Bureau of Labor Statistics http://data .bls.gov/pdq/SurveyOutputServlet?request_action= wh&graph_name=LN_cpsbref3; p. 213: Statista, Number of smartphone users (past and projected) in the United States from 2010 to 2019 (in millions), www.statista.com/ statistics/201182/forecast-of-smartphone-users-in-the-us; p. 214: Data from U.S. Census Bureau, "Facts for Features: Irish-American Heritage Month and St. Patrick's Day,"; p. 216: Courtesy of Stan Crowley; p. 218: Andrew Wilson, "In Defense of Rhetoric," Toastmaster 70.2 (Feb. 2004), pp. 8–11; p. 220: Filson, Brent. 1991. *Executive Speeches*. Williamstown Pub Co.

Chapter 13

p. 228: Cicero. *De Legibus*, II, p. 19; p. 235: *Made to Stick: Why Some Ideas Survive and Others Die* (New York: Random House, 2007), pp. 19–21; p. 236: As cited by Eleanor Doan, *The New Speaker's Sourcebook* (Grand Rapids, MI: Zondervan, 1968); p. 236: Marcie Groover, "Learning to Communicate: The Importance of Speech Education in Public Schools," *Winning Orations 1984* (Mankato, MN: Interstate Oratorical Association, 1984), p. 7.

Chapter 14

p. 245: Shakespeare; p. 253: Based on Maslow, Abraham (1954). *Motivation and Personality*. New York: Harper-Collins.

Chapter 15

p. 264: Donald C. Bryant, "Rhetoric: Its Functions and Its Scope," *Quarterly Journal of Speech* 39 (Dec. 1953), p. 26; p. 264: Ralph Waldo Emerson; p. 273: Jeffrey E. Jamison, "Alkali Batteries: Powering Electronics and Polluting the Environment," *Winning Orations 1991* (Mankato, MN: Interstate Oratorical Association, 1991), p. 43; p. 277: Jamie Frater, "Top 10 Great Historic Speeches," http:// listverse.com/2008/06/01/top-10-great-historic-speeches/ accessed June 14, 2013; p. 279: "Franklin Delano Roosevelt: The Great Depression." 6 June 2004; p. 280: Donald C. Bryant, "Rhetoric: Its Functions and Its Scope," Quarterly Journal of Speech 39 (Dec. 1953), p. 26;

pp. 286–287: Colter Ray, "You Are What You Eat: Why You Should Eat Grass Fed Organic Beef," Original speech presented at Texas State University, 2013. Used by permission; pp. 286–287: Tasha Carlson, "License to Save." From *Winning Orations 2009*, Mankato, MN: Interstate Oratorical Association, 2009. Reprinted with permission; pp. 289–291: Heather Zupanic, "End the Use Child Soldiers." Speech excerpts on pages 289 through 291 from *Winning Orations 2009*, Mankato, MN: Interstate Oratorical Association, 2009. Reprinted with permission.

Chapter 16

p. 294: Barney Frank, Graduation Speech. Barney Frank addressed the graduating seniors of Harvard College on May 23, 2012; p. 300: Jeff Brooks, *Wedding Toasts*. March 1998. http://zinnia.umfacad.maine.edu/~donaghue/toasts07.html; p. 300: Sarah Husberg, "A Wedding Toast," in Tasha Van Horn, Lori Charron, and Michael Charron, eds. *Allyn & Bacon Video II User's Guide*, 2002; p. 301: Everett M. Dirksen, "Nominating Speech for Barry Goldwater" (15 July 1964), in James R. Andrews and David Zarefsky, eds., *Contemporary American Voices* (New York: Simon & Schuster, 1965), p. 815; p. 302: Malala Yousafzai, Nobel Lecture, 10 Dec. 2014, Nobelprize.org; p. 302: Barbara Jordan, "Change: From What to What?" *Vital Speeches of the Day* (15 August 1992), p. 651; p. 302: Cindy Pearlman, "Oscar Speeches: Statues in Their Hands, Feet in Their Mouths," *Austin American-Statesman* 24 March 1997, p. E8; p. 302: William Faulkner, acceptance of the Nobel Prize for literature (December 10, 1950), in Houston Peterson, ed., *A Treasury of the World's Great Speeches* (New York: Simon & Schuster, 1965), p. 815; p. 303: David Abel, "Commencement Addresses Leave Audiences Lost," *The Boston Globe* 5 June 2000, p. B4; p. 304: Bill Clinton, speech at Pointe du Hoc, France (June 1994), as quoted in David Shribman, "President, a Child of World War II, Thanks a Generation," The Boston Globe 7 June 1994, p. 1; p. 304: Cyrus Copeland, "Death, Be Not Ponderous," *The New York Times* 31 October 2004; p. 304: Dave Barry, "Speak! Speak!" *Austin American-Statesman* 2 June 1991, p. C4; p. 304: John T. Masterson, Jr., Eulogy for Betty Stalvey,

New Braunfels, TX, 26 March 2005; 304: Veronique Pozner, "Momma Loves you, Little Man," *Vital Speeches of the Day* (February 2013), p. 36; p. 305: Debi Martin, "Laugh Lines," *Austin American-Statesman* 20 May 1988, p. D1; p. 305: Jon Macks, *How to Be Funny* (New York: Simon & Schuster, 2003); p. 305: Matt Hughes, "Tricks of the Speechwriter's Trade," *Management Review* 79 (November 1990), pp. 56–58; p. 305: Sarah Booth Conroy, "State Dinners Offer Speech as First Course," *Austin American-Statesman* 10 November 1989; p. 306: Alison White, "Writing a Humorous Speech," bizinternet.com June 2004; p. 306: Joe Queenan, "How to Tell a Joke," *Reader's Digest* September 2003, p. 73; p. 306: John C. Meyer, "Humor as a Double-Edged Sword: Four Functions of Humor in Communication," *Communication Theory* 10 (August 2000), p. 311; p. 306: Michael Blastland and David Spiegelhalter, *The Norm Chronicles: Stories and Numbers about Danger* (London: Profile Books, 2013), p. 42; p. 306: Michael Koresky, "Prognosis: Dire, Michael Moore's 'Sicko'," *indieWIRE* 22 June 2007; p. 307: "Mirren 'Too Busy' to Meet Queen," *BBC News* 10 May 2007; p. 307: Bill Gates, 2007 Harvard commencement address, *Harvard University Gazette Online* 7 June 2007; p. 307: Chris O'Keefe, Untitled Speech, in John K. Boaz and James Brey, eds., *1987 Championship Debates and Speeches* (Speech Communication Association and American Forensic Association, 1987), p. 99; p. 307: Mark Twain, "The Alphabet and Simplified Spelling," Address at the Dedication of the New York Engineers' Club, 9 December 1907. *Mark Twain's Speeches; with an Introduction by William Dean Howells* (University of Virginia Library: Electronic Text Center); p. 307: Susan Wallace, "Seriously, How Do I Write a Humorous Speech?" as reported by Mike Dicerbo, *Leadership in Action* 1 November 2000.

Appendix

p. 318: John F. Kennedy, *Inaugural Address*, 20 January 1961. John F. Kennedy Presidential Library and Museum; p. 320: Obama, Barack. 2012. *Second Inaugural Address*; p. 323: Pope Francis, "Remarks to the U.S. Congress,"; p. 328: Courtesy of Julio Gonzalez.

Index

A

AARP, 128

AAVE (African American Vernacular English), 176

ABI/INFORM Global, 119

Abstraction, ladder of, 173, 174

Academic Search Complete, 119

Acceptance speeches, 301–302

Accommodation, 42

Accomplishments, focus on, 16

Accountability of Internet resources, 118

Accuracy
  of Internet resources, 118
  of interpretation of nonverbal communication, 53–54
  of quotations, 130

Action
  communication as, 6–7
  desired, making clear and easy, 281
  motivated sequence and, 291
  motivating audience to, 167–168

Active listening, 57

Ad hominem, 276

Adult learning principles and techniques, 234

African American Vernacular English (AAVE), 176

After-dinner speeches, 304–307
  nonverbal strategies for, 307
  stories for, 306
  topics for, 305–306
  verbal strategies for, 306–307

Age in audience analysis, 75–76

Alliteration, 180

Amanpour, Christiane, 3

American Cancer Society, 142

American Civil Liberties Union (ACLU), 38

American Psychological Association (APA), 45–46, 151

Analogies, 126–127
  effective use of, 127
  to enhance understanding, 235
  figurative, 126, 127
  literal, 126–127
  reasoning by analogy, 269

Analysis. See Audience analysis; Rhetorical criticism

Analytical listeners, 56

Andragogy, 234

Anecdotes, in introduction, 161–162

Animals as presentation aids, 224–225

Ansari, Aziz, 198

Antithesis, 180

Anxiety. *See also* Nervousness
  as trait and state, 10

APA (American Psychological Association), 45–46, 151

Appeal to misplaced authority, 276

Appeals
  emotional, 277–280
  fear, 279
  inspirational, in conclusion, 169
  to several emotions, 279

Appearance during delivery, 200–201

Apple, 200

Apprehension. *See also* Nervousness
  follows a predictable pattern, 10–11

Aristotle, 4, 46, 58, 60, 67, 76, 209, 247–249, 260, 264, 265, 267

Arrangement, 4

The Art of Rhetoric (Aristotle), 4

Articles of Faith (Luther), 5

Articulation, 196

Attending as part of listening, 49

Attention
  getting with introduction, 281
  handouts and, 225
  listening and, 54–55
  for motivated sequence, 289
  presentation aids and, 211, 225–226

Attention getting with introduction, 159

Attitudes
  in audience analysis, 84, 85–86
  persuasive speeches to change or reinforce, 245
  toward speaker, analyzing, 85–86

Audience. *See also* Motivating the audience
  captive vs. voluntary, 85
  central idea and, 108
  connecting with, 15, 31, 43, 64, 77, 100, 120, 135, 158, 179, 188, 221, 261, 282, 299
  cultural diversity of, 22 (*see also* Cultures; Diversity)
  customizing message to, 90–91
  getting attention of, 159, 281
  identifying with, 280–281
  informative speeches and, 241–242
  interested vs. uninterested, 84
  neutral, persuading, 281–282
  passing objects among, 224
  persuasive speeches and, 256–257
  receptive, persuading, 280–281
  size of, 86
  strategies to enhance recall by, 239–241
  topic selection and narrowing and, 22–24, 96–97
  unreceptive, persuading, 282–283

Audience adaptation, 73–74
  during speech, 87–91

Audience analysis, 20–21, 67–92
  adaptation and, 73–74, 87–91
  after speaking, 91–92
  behavioral responses in, 92
  common ground and, 72–73
  confidence building and, 12–13
  defined, 72
  demographic, 74–83
  differences in, 72
  information gathering for, 69–71